Finding the Law

Legal Research for Librarians and Paralegals

Bryan M. Carson

D0169024

THE SCARECROW PRESS, INC.
Lanham • Toronto • Plymouth, UK
2011

Published by Scarecrow Press, Inc.
A wholly owned subsidiary of The Rowman & Littlefield Publishing Group, Inc.
4501 Forbes Boulevard, Suite 200, Lanham, Maryland 20706
http://www.scarecrowpress.com

Estover Road, Plymouth PL6 7PY, United Kingdom

British Library Cataloguing in Publication Information Available

Library of Congress Cataloging-in-Publication Data
Carson, Bryan M., 1965–
 Finding the law : legal research for librarians and paralegals / Bryan M. Carson.
  p. cm.
 Includes bibliographical references and index.
 ISBN 978-0-8108-8105-1 (hardcover : alk. paper)
 1. Legal research—United States. I. Title.
 KF240.C37 2011
 340.072'073—dc22   2011009655

Printed in the United States of America

To my parents,
Ada Lou Carson and Herbert L. Carson,
who taught me how to write.
Mom, I miss your help with my writing.
Dad, I look forward to future collaborations.

and

to my wife, Gayle Novick.
Gayle, I never cease to be amazed at your artistic talent.

Contents

Expanded Contents

Acknowledgments

Books don't just write themselves, and this one is no exception. Every author stands on the back of many people. I would like to thank some of the people that helped to make this book possible.

Dr. Michael Binder, Dean of the Western Kentucky University Libraries, and Dr. Brian Coutts, Head of the Department of Library Public Services. Dr. Binder and Dr. Coutts both encouraged me to pursue this project. They also provided the time I needed to write this manuscript.

The Interlibrary Loan office at Western Kentucky University helped facilitate my research by finding materials the university didn't own. Without the assistance of Dan Forrest, Terri Baker, Debra Day, Ken Foushee, Selina Langford, and Jan Gao, my work would have been much more difficult. My colleague Haiwang Yuan provided emotional support and advice, and helped me find sources for some quotes.

It was my colleague Jack Montgomery who first suggested that I apply my law background to an analysis of legal issues in libraries. Jack introduced me to Katina Strauch, the editor of *Against the Grain*. Some of the material in this book began life as columns in that publication.

The chapter on the Constitution was initially written for a leadership studies class at Vanderbilt University's Peabody College of Education. Thanks to the flexibility of Dr. Michael McLendon, I was able to write a term paper that fit into the framework of this book.

Several librarians contributed material for this book. Laurel E. Davis, law librarian for the Massachusetts Office of the Attorney General, wrote the section on Massachusetts legal research. I am particularly grateful to Laurel, as the nuances of legal research can vary greatly between states.

Several people suggested websites for inclusion in this book, many as part of the 2008 Core Reference Tools created by Diane Kovacs of Kovacs Consulting, which have been reused with her permission. Other results came from a question I posted on Lawlib-L. The following people provided suggestions and gave permission (in alphabetical order): Betty Agin, Carol Bredemeyer, Rick Buckingham, Paul Bush, Beverly Butula, Robb Farmer, Ronald Huttner, Sid Kaskey, Damien MacRae, Sybil Marshall, LaVern Pritchard, Brian Raphael, Mary Rice, Dave Rodgers, Brad Small, Maria Sosnowski, and Mary Lou Wilker. Brad Small contributed a sidebar on research strategies for non-legal librarians. Stewart Dean gave me permission to include a blog post he wrote on his family's experience with "Shufflin' Sam" Thompson.

A conference presentation on the Freedom of Information Act by Jo Staggs-Neel provided the inspiration (with Jo's permission) for a "Legally Speaking" column in *Against the Grain*. That article provided the basis for part of the chapter on the Freedom of Information Act (FOIA).

I appreciate the assistance I got from Katie Algeo, an associate professor of geography and geology at Western Kentucky University. She spent several hours drawing the map of the National Reporter System in figure 9.1. This was a somewhat difficult task because there were seven regions (some non-contiguous) and the map had to be grayscale. I also received assistance with images from photographer Alan Davis and from my colleagues Charles Smith and Amanda Hardin.

I would be remiss if I didn't thank my staff for all the assistance and understanding that they have given me during the time I was writing this book. They have helped me in ways too numerous to mention. I really could not have completed this work without the assistance of (in alphabetical order) Rob Harbison, Amanda Hardin, Katherine King, Maria Lewis, Alan Logsdon, Robin McGinnis, Alesha McPeak, Lisa Miller, Lee Pedigo, Nancy Richey, Ayush Vats, and Nikole Wolfe.

Production editor Jayme Bartles Reed and the proofreader at Scarecrow worked hard to help eliminate errors. Colleen Dunham, my indexer, worked very hard to ensure that readers will be able to find information in the book. If you find any errors in the text, it is my fault, not theirs.

I need to thank my editor, Martin Dillon, for providing assistance, answering my questions, and generally guiding me towards a better book. Martin, I couldn't have done this without you. Thank you for everything!

Last but not least, I need to thank my parents, Ada Lou Carson and Herbert L. Carson, and my wife, Gayle Novick. Before we lost my mother, she gave me permission to use Major Royall Tyler's military dispatches as excerpted in her doctoral dissertation. My father and my wife still provide inspiration and encourage me to work harder and smarter.

Introduction

Legal research has traditionally been taught as an afterthought. Law students, librarians, and paralegals are generally taught in three very different ways—despite the fact that all three groups need to know the same information. In many law schools, the first-year legal research and writing class emphasizes legal reasoning. Most legal research and writing classes for paralegals emphasize legal procedure and writing while minimizing research. Library science courses on law librarianship are generally built around annotations and lists of legal sources, with little or no discussion of writing.

There are certainly reasons why these differing approaches have developed. Law students need to understand the substance of the law and must have the ability to reason, to "think like a lawyer." Both law students and paralegals need to learn how to write. It is necessary for paralegal students to become innately familiar with the workings of motions and briefs and with legal procedure. The role of the librarian usually ends once the research has been assembled, at which point the paralegal or lawyer will take over. So there is probably little reason to teach librarians how to write briefs.

However, these three philosophies of teaching legal research mask the fact that all three fields can benefit from the other approaches. Law students have an entire curriculum that teaches them to "think like a lawyer," yet all too often the research process is given short shrift. Paralegals must perform complex research before beginning to write. And the biggest problem that librarians face when performing legal research is not understanding legal procedure.

This book is intended to bring together the three philosophies under one cover. My goal is to bring legal reasoning and "thinking like a lawyer" to paralegals and librarians, while simultaneously teaching procedure for librarians and research sources for paralegals.

Although I do not discuss legal writing in this book, it is not to be minimized. My belief is that combining legal research and legal writing in a single book does the students a disservice. While the research and writing processes should be taught together, writing is so important that it must have its own book. While writing and oral advocacy are sometimes taught together, the books are generally separate. It takes a specialized work to deal with all the issues that legal writers face. Legal writing is every bit as important as knowledge of the law and understanding how to conduct research.

Similarly, the research process cannot be covered adequately in one or two chapters of a book on writing. The move to online resources has not reduced the complexity of legal research. In fact, discovery has become more complicated over time. Although many tools are easier to use online, the proliferation of sources and tools has resulted in *more* uncertainty (not to mention bad information), along with an even greater possibility of missing necessary information. Just as I would not combine a book on torts with a book on commercial paper, so too should legal writing and legal research have their own works.

Books on Legal Writing

I have listed a number of current books on legal writing, ranging from specialty works such as *Legal Opinion Letters Formbook* by Holderness and Wunnicke, Print on Demand books such as *Plain Language Legal Writing* by Stephens, and general works such as *Legal Writing: Getting It Right and Getting It Written* by Ray and Ramsfield. I recommend using my book in combination with one or more of these writing manuals.

◆ Bahrych, Lynn B., & Rombauer, Marjorie Dick. (2009). *Legal Writing in a Nutshell.* 4th edition. St. Paul, MN: West. ISBN: 0-314-90691-6; ISBN 13: 978-0-314-90691-5.

◆ Bouchoux, Deborah E. (2000). *Cite Checker: A Hands-on Guide to Learning Citation Form.* Albany, NY: West/Thomson Learning. ISBN: 0-7668-1893-4; ISBN 13: 978-0-7668-1893-4.

◆ Bowlan, Russell T. (2009). *Legal Writing for Real Lawyers: A Legal Research & Writing Book.* Pittsburgh, PA: RoseDog Books. ISBN: 1-4349-9796-0; ISBN 13: 978-1-4349-9796-8.

◆ Calleros, Charles R. (2006). *Legal Method and Writing.* 5th edition. New York: Aspen. ISBN 13: 978-0-7355-5375-0.

◆ Clary, Bradley G., & Lysaght, Pamela. (2010). *Successful Legal Analysis and Writing: The Fundamentals.* 3rd edition. St. Paul, MN: West. ISBN: 0-314-90804-8; ISBN 13: 978-0-314-90804-9.

◆ Dernbach, John C., et al. (2010). *A Practical Guide to Legal Writing and Legal Method.* New York: Aspen. ISBN: 0-7355-9189-X; ISBN 13: 978-0-7355-9189-9.

◆ Drennan, William. (2009). *Lay Words for Lawyers: Analogies and Key Words to Advance Your Case and Communicate with Clients.* Chicago: American Bar Association. ISBN: 1-60442-096-0; ISBN 13: 978-1-60442-096-8.

◆ Edwards, Linda H. (2010). *Legal Writing: Process, Analysis, and Organization.* 5th edition. New York: Aspen. ISBN-13: 9780-735-58514-0.

♦ Edwards, Linda H. (2011). *Legal Writing and Analysis*. 3rd edition. New York: Aspen. ISBN: 0-7355-9850-9; ISBN 13: 978-0-7355-9850-8.

♦ Fajans, Elizabeth, Falk, Mary R., & Shapo, Helene S. (2010). *Writing for Law Practice: Advanced Legal Writing*. 2nd edition. St. Paul, MN: West. ISBN: 1-59941-630-1; ISBN 13: 978-1-59941-630-4.

♦ Garfinkel, Marvin. (2009). *Real World Document Drafting: A Dispute-Avoidance Approach*. 2nd edition. Philadelphia, PA: American Law Institute. ISBN: 0-8318-9980-8; ISBN 13: 978-0-8318-9980-6.

♦ Garner, Bryan A. (2003). *Legal Writing in Plain English: A Text with Exercises*. Chicago: University of Chicago Press. ISBN: 0-226-28418-2; ISBN 13: 978-0-226-28418-7.

♦ Garner, Bryan A. (2004). *The Winning Brief: 100 Tips for Persuasive Briefing in Trial and Appellate Courts*. New York: Oxford University Press. ISBN: 019517075X; ISBN-13: 978-019-517075-7.

♦ Gilmore, Harley C. (2009). *The Art of Writing Legal Descriptions*. Charleston, SC: CreateSpace (Print on Demand). ISBN: 1-4499-0657-5; ISBN 13: 978-1-4499-0657-3.

♦ Haggard, Thomas R., and Kuney, George W. (2007). *Legal Drafting*. St. Paul, MN: West. ISBN-13: 978-0-314-18418-4.

♦ Haigh, Rupert. (2009). *Legal English*. New York: Routledge-Cavendish. ISBN: 0-415-48715-3; ISBN 13: 978-0-415-48715-3.

♦ Holderness, A. Sidney, & Wunnicke, Brooke. (2010). *Legal Opinion Letters Formbook*. 3rd edition. New York: Aspen. ISBN: 0-7355-9328-0; ISBN-13: 978-073-559328-2.

♦ Kuney, George W., & Looper, Donna C. (2009). *Mastering Legal Analysis and Drafting*. Durham, NC: Carolina Academic Press. ISBN: 1-59460-628-5; ISBN 13: 978-1-59460-628-1.

♦ Murray, Michael D., & DeSanctis, Christy H. (2009). *Advanced Legal Writing and Oral Advocacy: Trials, Appeals, and Moot Court*. St. Paul, MN: West. ISBN: 1-59941-397-3; ISBN 13: 978-1-59941-397-6.

♦ Murray, Michael D., & DeSanctis, Christy H. (2009). *Legal Research and Writing Across the Curriculum: Problems and Exercises*. St. Paul, MN: West. ISBN: 1-59941-398-1; ISBN 13: 978-1-59941-398-3.

♦ Murray, Michael D., & DeSanctis, Christy H. (2009). *Murray and DeSanctis' Legal Writing and Analysis*. St. Paul, MN: West. ISBN-13: 978-1-59941-395-2.

◆ Oates, Laurel Currie, & Enquist, Anne. (2010). *The Legal Writing Handbook: Analysis, Research, & Writing.* 5th edition. New York: Aspen. ISBN: 0-7355-8518-0; ISBN 13: 978-0-7355-8516-4.

◆ Putman, William H. (2009). *Legal Analysis and Writing for Paralegals.* Clifton Park, NY: Delmar Cengage. ISBN: 1418080926; ISBN-13: 978-1-41808-092-1.

◆ Ray, Mary Barnard, & Ramsfield, Jill J. (2010). *Legal Writing: Getting It Right and Getting It Written.* 5th edition. St. Paul, MN: West. ISBN: 0-314-26277-6; ISBN 13: 978-0-314-26277-6.

◆ Samborn, Hope Viner, & Yelin, Andrea B. (2009). *Basic Legal Writing for Paralegals.* 3rd edition. New York: Aspen. ISBN: 0-7355-7858-3; ISBN 13: 978-0-7355-7858-6.

◆ Schiess, Wayne. (2009). *The Legal Memo: A Basic Guide.* Dubuque, IA: Kendall/Hunt Publishing. ISBN: 0-7575-5210-2; ISBN 13: 978-0-7575-5210-6.

◆ Schultz, Nancy, & Sirico, Louis. (2010). *Legal Writing and Other Lawyering Skills.* New York: Aspen. ISBN: 0-7355-9402-3; ISBN 13: 978-0-7355-9402-9.

◆ Stephens, Cheryl. (2009). *Plain Language Legal Writing.* Raleigh, NC: Lulu Enterprises Inc. (Print on Demand). ISBN: 0-557-01450-6; ISBN 13: 978-0-557-01450-7.

◆ Stevens, Anne M. (2002). *Finding, Reading and Using the Law.* St. Paul, MN: West. ISBN: 0-314-12578-7; ISBN 13: 978-0-314-12578-1.

◆ Stinson, Judith M. (2009). *The Tao of Legal Writing.* Durham, NC: Carolina Academic Press. ISBN: 1-59460-633-1; ISBN 13: 978-1-59460-633-5.

◆ Teply, Larry L. (2008). *Teply's Legal Writing Citation in a Nutshell.* St. Paul, MN: West. ISBN-13: 978-0-314-16938-9.

◆ Tepper, Pamela R. (2006). *Basic Legal Writing for Paralegals.* New York: McGraw-Hill/Irwin. ISBN: 0-07-340303-2; ISBN 13: 978-0-07-340303-8.

◆ Thompson, Stephanie J. (2010). *Thompson's Legal Writing Exercises: A Case File and Formula-Based Approach to Legal Reasoning.* St. Paul, MN: West. ISBN: 0-314-26395-0; ISBN 13: 978-0-314-26395-7.

◆ Tjaden, Ted. (2010). *Legal Research and Writing.* Toronto, ON: Irwin Law, Inc. ISBN: 1-4593-3978-9; ISBN 13: 978-1-4593-3978-1.

♦   Webley, Lisa. (2009). *Legal Writing*. New York: Routledge-Cavendish. ISBN: 0-203-87688-1; ISBN 13: 978-0-203-87688-6.

♦   Weresh, Melissa H. (2009). *Legal Writing: Ethical and Professional Considerations*. Newark, NJ: LexisNexis Matthew Bender. ISBN: 1-4224-7305-8; ISBN 13: 978-1-4224-7305-4.

♦   Williams, Pamela. (2010). *Legal Writing*. San Diego, CA: University Readers. ISBN: 1-60927-967-0; ISBN 13: 978-1-60927-967-7.

A Note for Instructors

The material in this book lays the foundation for legal research. However, since a good class requires more material, I have created a legal research Website for instructors. The site contains sample exercises, a bibliography of books and articles on teaching legal research classes, and tips for designing classes. The site also allows individual teachers to create a community for sharing exercises and teaching tips. The Internet has given us the ability to easily share experiences and to avoid having to reinvent the wheel.

The instructor Website also contains supplemental material on teaching Boolean searching. Many library students will have already learned this skill by the time they take a law librarianship class. Similarly, some paralegal students will already be familiar with "AND/OR" searching. However, since some students may take this course prior to learning the fundamentals of online searching, I have included basic materials and exercises to complement the book.

I will also use the instructor's site to obtain feedback and suggestions for the next edition. Teachers sharing their experiences will improve every book, and this one is no exception. I want to hear from you. To access the instructor's Website, go to the Scarecrow Press bibliographic record for this book at http://www.scarecrowpress.com.

A Note on Citation Formats

Citations are one of the most important parts of any publication. They promote clarity, transparency, and accountability. The purpose of style manuals is to help standardize citations and provide a fast and easy way for readers to find referenced materials. However, citation styles also sometimes create a trade-off for the author.

In writing this book, I struggled with the desire to provide easy citations that my readers can understand, while still adhering to the legal citation format used in the law. Certainly cases, statutes, and other primary legal materials should be referenced using standard legal citation formats. However, I was less sure about books and journal articles. The 19th edition of *The Bluebook: A*

*Uniform System of Citation,** the bible of legal style, treats these references different from other style manuals. After much internal struggle, I eventually decided that the *Bluebook* format for books and journal articles was not as clear as I would like for those outside the law.

After analyzing the citation formats, I opted to use different styles for annotations discussed in the body of the text and items referenced in the endnotes and bibliography. Citations from books, articles, and websites listed in the body of the text are based on the 6th edition of the *Publication Manual of the American Psychological Association* ("APA"), which is familiar to many readers in the social and behavioral sciences, as well as in the humanities and in librarianship. The APA format provides additional information beyond that found in the *Bluebook*, including both starting and ending page numbers (often necessary when ordering from interlibrary loan).

I had a similar quandary with the bibliography at the back of the book. Since much of the text of this book *is* a bibliography, the "bibliography" at the back only includes materials that are cited in endnotes. These items are cited in APA format. The sources that are discussed within the main text are listed in the index, while statutes and cases are listed in the Table of Authorities.

Please note that there are a few modifications from the pure APA format. For example, you will find the full names of authors, instead of their first and middle initials. Also, I used the *"available at"* signal for web addresses as required by the APA 5th edition instead of the 6th edition. Since this is the same signal used by the 19th edition of the *Bluebook*, the parallel use provides consistency and harmony between the two citation styles.

Remember, however, that the *Bluebook* is the place to go for legal materials. The APA guide, the *MLA Style Manual* from the Modern Language Association, and the *Chicago Manual of Style*, all recommend using *Bluebook* format for legal materials and government documents. Readers will note that I have used *Bluebook* style for this type of material. Luckily for the reader, most cases, statutes, regulations, and other legal documents are cited in the endnotes and Table of Authorities rather than in the body of the text.

Bibliography styles are meant to be clear and consistent. I certainly hope that this decision will help to provide clarity to the reader. That is the intention of both the APA and the *Bluebook*, and that is my intention as well.

---

* *The Bluebook: A Uniform System of Citation*, 19th ed. (2010). Cambridge, MA: Harvard Law Review Association.

1

The Historical Background
of the U.S. Constitution

The U.S. Constitution is a document beloved by the American people and emulated by other nations. Most people find the U.S. Constitution to be synonymous with our national identity. Yet it didn't start out that way at all.

When the United States declared independence from Britain in 1776, there was no national government. The Declaration of Independence was signed by the representatives of 13 sovereign states, rather than by a single country. Each former colony was considered to be a separate nation, although they all worked together for the common cause. As historian Lewis M. Hacker pointed out, "between 1776 and 1781, the Continental Congress acted with no more formal authority than its own assertion and the cooperation of the several states—in whatever degree they chose to give that cooperation."[1]

A quick glance at the list of signers will reveal that Vermont was not even a party to the Declaration of Independence or the Continental Congress. The famed Green Mountain Boys, formed by Ethan Allen in 1770, were more interested in defending Vermont from claims by New York and New Hampshire, rather than opposing the British.[2] It was not until 1777 that Vermont declared its independence from Britain, although in 1775 the Green Mountain Boys stopped attacking their neighbors and supported the fledgling United States in its battle against the British. Vermont became the 14th state of the United States on March 4, 1791.[3]

The Articles of Confederation

Those who were assembled in the Continental Congress did wish the new countries to be united, though each state retained its sovereignty. As a result, the Continental Congress proposed the *Articles of Confederation* on July 12, 1776, 8 days after the signing of the Declaration of Independence.[4] Nonetheless, the new states were very concerned about submitting their independence to a new central government, and at first many states refused to ratify the Articles.[5]

As the war progressed, it quickly became apparent that the fate of each former colony would rest upon its neighbors retaining their independence. As a result, various states began to support and ratify the Articles of Confederation. On November 15, 1777, the Congress adopted the Articles of Confederation, although the last state (Maryland) didn't ratify until March 1, 1781.[6]

The Articles of Confederation did not establish a very strong central government. Article II established that: "Each state retains its sovereignty, freedom, and independence, and every power, jurisdiction, and right, which is not by this Confederation expressly delegated to the United States, in Congress assembled."[7] Article III stated that: "The said States hereby severally enter into a firm league of friendship with each other, for their common defense, the security of their liberties, and their mutual and general welfare, binding themselves to assist each other, against all force offered to, or attacks made upon them, or any of them, on account of religion, sovereignty, trade, or any other pretense whatever."[8] In reality, the Articles were worded more like a treaty between sovereign nations than the establishment of a new nation. In the late 1930s (before the United Nations was created), historian Lewis Hacker compared the Articles of Confederation to the League of Nations and stated that: "As the joint executive of a group of allied sovereigns, the Confederation Congress might have been considered adequate. As the government of a nation, it was pitiable."[9]

A. The "Chaos Clause"[10]

From the very day that they were passed, the Articles were seen as being inadequate. Alexander Hamilton warned that the "uncontrollable sovereignty in each state" would prove to be a problem, and John Witherspoon proposed an amendment to give Congress power over commerce.[11] The young Madison was especially concerned with the Articles, and had serious doubts as to whether they would allow Congress to conduct its necessary business.[12] According to historian Irving Brant, the biggest concern was the requirement that nine out of the thirteen states must agree to decisions involving "war or peace, to treaties, to requisitions of money from the states, to appropriations, borrowings, currency emissions or coinage. That meant that with nine states present, one could outvote eight. With eight present, Congress could not vote."[13]

In addition to the nine-state provision, the Articles also forbade the Congress from conducting any business (other than a motion to adjourn) "unless by the votes of a majority of the United States, in Congress assembled."[14] In other words, a majority must first vote to allow business to be conducted, then the debates could occur and a vote could be taken. But what constituted a majority? This section of the Articles led to a six-day battle among those who interpreted the section to mean that a numerical majority on that day was sufficient (as was done in the British Parliament and in corporations), versus those who said that it must be a majority of the states that was present. James Duane and James Madison were the leaders of the simple majority group, and Thomas Burke was the spokesperson for the state sovereignty block.

Burke's view was that seven states had to vote in favor of a bill before it could be formally introduced and debated in Congress, and that both members of the state delegation must be present in order for the state to be considered present. After a vigorous debate, Congress voted in favor of Burke's interpretation. "[A]s an effective lawmaking and executive body, the United States in Congress Assembled died right then, at the age of six days."[15]

There were many problems with the Articles of Confederation as a result of the nine-state and majority provisions. If one member of a delegation voted yes and another voted no, the state's vote was recorded as being no. Walking out of the convention meant that the state was voting no on everything, and became a favorite tactic. If nine states were present with 18 delegates, three delegates could cause a no vote, even if the other 15 were in favor of the legislation. Brant calls this provision the "chaos clause."[16]

The fight over the "chaos clause" was nothing compared to the problems that the country would face under the Articles of Confederation. Congress had no power to regulate, no power to instruct diplomats, no power to collect taxes. The next major episode in the slow implosion of the Articles took place over the issue of land ownership—an issue that gave the young Madison a chance to show true leadership.

B. The Fight Over Western Lands

Even before the start of the Revolutionary War, competing claims to land by various states and land speculation companies caused major grief. Connecticut claimed northeastern Ohio, New York and New Hampshire both claimed Vermont, and there were opposing claims to the territory that subsequently became Tennessee. Madison obtained a declaration from Virginia disclaiming Tennessee, Ohio, and Indiana, provided that the lands that now constitute West Virginia and Kentucky were recognized as being part of Virginia. A large part of the issue was the conflict between states that wanted to control the Western lands, and land speculators who wished to be in control so that they could sell lands off to anyone.

The Virginia cession was so unpopular that the "chaos clause" was used extensively. The Articles and the enfeebled Congress were almost deadlocked, but Madison helped to craft a compromise to take care of the situation. The fight over territory did not only cover the West; Vermont was also caught up in this dispute.

As mentioned above, Vermont was not at this time part of the United States. The famed Green Mountain Boys, formed by Ethan Allen in 1770, were more interested in defending Vermont from claims by New York and New Hampshire, rather than opposing the British.[17] It was not until 1777 that Vermont declared its independence from Britain, although in 1775 the Green Mountain Boys stopped attacking their neighbors and supported the fledgling United States in its battle against the British.

The Vermont declaration of independence from Britain effectively made it an independent and sovereign nation. When the Revolutionary War ended, Britain recognized the sovereignty of Vermont along with the other 13 colonies. Hence, everyone—except for New York and New Hampshire—recognized Vermont as a sovereign nation. Although there was significant sentiment towards allowing Vermont to join the United States, these claims, along with periodic raids by one or the other state, prevented its admission. Eventually New

Hampshire made its peace, and supported the admission of Vermont as another state that would help the region oppose the influence of New York.

The Vermont quest for independence became tied up with the controversy surrounding the Virginia cession. The Congress was divided between those who wished to see the states take control of the Western lands, and those who wished to see the entity known as the United States take title. The states that opposed Virginia were in favor of Vermont, and vice versa.

Because of the dispute of the Western lands, diplomats trying to negotiate a peace treaty with England had a difficult time. The U.S. laid claim to what later became the Northwest Territory (Ohio, Michigan, Indiana, Illinois, Wisconsin, and a small parcel of land east of the Mississippi River in Minnesota that would subsequently become the city of St. Paul. However, the diplomats were having a very difficult time with the British because of the competing claims. The British negotiators were exploiting this division to help bolster their claims and to avoid having to cede this land.

Another issue that was tied up with the Western land claims was United States access to navigation on the Mississippi. The U.S. had numerous issues with the French over rights to the Mississippi. Not only did the ownership issue mean that the French did not know with whom to negotiate, but it also prevented Congress from being able to give instructions to the delegates.[18]

The dispute caused much pain to James Madison, who saw the Congress degenerating into a free-for-all and therefore unable to transact any business. Madison and his fellow delegate Edmund Randolph attempted to provide a compromise. Believing that the importance of federal sovereignty was paramount, the two men came up with a unique proposal that took the debate out of the realm of the ordinary and showed that a little "thinking outside the box" could drastically change the status quo. Madison and Randolph proposed that title to the Western lands was derived from the British Crown, and therefore was passed by the cessation of Crown rule to the federal government. Eventually Congress passed the compromise with a statement that "if Virginia would make a cession comfortable to its own terms, Congress would accept it."[19] Madison hoped to preserve the Virginia claims to Kentucky as part of this compromise. The very idea of Kentucky being a federal land rather than part of the state was anathema in Virginia. However, as it turned out, Kentucky would not stand in the way of Madison's compromise. After the drafting of the Constitution, Vermont became the 14th state on March 4, 1791, and Kentucky the 15th state on June 1, 1792.

It was with the Western land debates that James Madison honed his abilities as a leader, visionary, and solver of conflicts, skills which he was to make use of later in the creation of the Constitution. According to historian Brant:

> Madison's leadership in the three-year struggle was not of the spectacular variety. Had it been, he would have met defeat. Far more difficult, his task was to draw together two sets of truculent extremists. Passionate devotees of state policy, land speculators hiding their self-interest under a mountain of moral-

ity—these, or a majority torn from their fringes, must be won to a compromise which satisfied neither passion nor self-interest. Madison knew that Maryland's demand for common possession of the Western lands, no matter how grievously it was misused by speculators, voiced nevertheless the universal need and right of the American people. Ardent as he was in defense of Virginia's title, he placed the interest of the nation first and did not flinch from political risk in upholding it.

The trend of events made it certain that federal title to the Northwest would ultimately be enforced. What would have happened, though, had that claim been forcibly asserted? With Virginia, the Carolinas and Georgia holding everything from the Ohio River to the Floridas, and their general economic interests in conflict with the North, it might have been the one move needed to split the United States into two confederacies. Blending political skill with devotion to principle, Madison not only averted this danger to the Union, but gave it the cementing bond of a national heritage of Western lands.[20]

The fight over the Western lands was Madison's chance to show his unique conflict resolution style of leadership. This was no ordinary delegate, but a true leader. By thinking outside the box, Madison was able to find a solution that was acceptable to both sides—a trait that would have even more impact a few years later.

C. Shays' Rebellion

Since the Articles of Confederation did not give the federal government the ability to raise taxes, the states were supposed to pay requisitions to the federal government. However, little money was actually collected, since the Congress had no way to enforce these requisitions. Although the right of coinage was reserved for the states, they had agreed in 1776 to allow Congress to create Continental bank notes. The only means by which the federal government could pay its debts was by printing more money. Naturally, this led to inflation and the devaluation of the currency, and is the source of the expression "not worth a Continental."[21]

At the same time, the supposedly sovereign states were also having similar problems. In Virginia, a courthouse was burned to destroy tax records, and Pennsylvania suffered under the threat of succession because of a threatened collection of taxes. States coined their own money, but this soon led to further devaluations. Meanwhile, the old pay vouchers that had been given to army officers during the war had been dishonored and were not worth the paper they were written on. In Western Massachusetts, the situation became very grim:

"[A] wave of farm foreclosures . . . swept the young republic to its first episode in class struggle. . . ." Daniel Shays, a revolutionary war veteran, led an armed uprising to close the courts and prevent them from foreclosing property. "It is true, that government had not caused, nor could it cure, the wide spread distress which occasioned this formidable insurrection: but still as the immediate pressure was necessarily felt, through the officers of the Law, enforcing the

judgements [sic] of the Courts, in the sale of property, at sacrifices simply ruin-
ous for the collection of debts and taxes, it was easy for demagogues to represent this as an attempt on the part of the State to oppress the people, and of the
rich to reduce the poor to virtual slavery."[22]

Shays' Rebellion, as the insurrection became known, showed the weakness
of the confederate system of government. The central government had no powers to put down the insurrection, leaving the entire matter to Massachusetts.
General Benjamin Lincoln was nominally in charge, but his aide-de-camp, Major Royall Tyler,[23] did most of the actual work.[24]

Having first closed the courts to prevent foreclosure, the insurgents then
attacked jails to release their fellow debtors. This was followed by a failed attack
on the federal armory in Springfield on January 25, 1787. By mid-February of
1787, the rebellion had been suppressed, but Daniel Shays and the ringleaders
had escaped to neighboring states with a vow to assemble more men and return.
Major Tyler immediately set out in pursuit of the rebels, and began diplomatic
missions to the neighboring states to seek their assistance in capturing the ringleaders.

Because each state was a sovereign unit, Major Tyler was not able to simply
pursue the fugitives. He had to ask permission from each state before anything
could be done. This was especially problematic with regard to Vermont, whose
status had still not been settled. It was especially difficult because the route of
the fugitives was right along the New York-Vermont border, and required simul-
taneous operations in both states.

At this time, "New-York [sic] claimed Vermont as a revolted Province of
her own: while the latter had proclaimed itself an independent State: had elected
. . . its Governor; and had chosen a Legislative Council, and House of Representatives, now in session at Bennington. It had applied for admission to the Confederacy; but Congress had not yet acknowledged its independence by receiving
it as a state."[25] As a result, Major Tyler spent a great deal of time and effort trying to not offend Vermont while not acknowledging it as a separate state or as
an independent nation.

The rebels were ultimately captured and sentenced to death, but the insurgents were later pardoned and released. Nonetheless, Shays' Rebellion pointed
out a number of weaknesses. The inability of the states to agree on anything was
the primary cause of the economic crisis, but even more important was the pa-
ralysis that the central government felt when rebellion struck. The central government had no power to raise an army, leaving the matter solely to the already-
impoverished states. Major Tyler had to visit each neighboring state separately
in order to convince them to arrest the ringleaders.

There were no mechanisms for cooperation; it was as if each state was an
independent nation. Indeed, Major Tyler initially failed in Vermont when the
governor vetoed the original resolution empowering the arrest of the insurgents.
This resolution was, however, subsequently passed and signed by the governor.

The prospect of armed insurgents rising against a paralyzed government caused many who had previously been opposed to central government to take stock of the situation and reconsider. According to political scientist Jack Rackove: "Had a convention to amend the Articles assembled in 1785 rather than 1787, the essential structure of the confederation would probably have been left intact. The putative reformers of the mid-1780s tended to think in terms of adding specific, limited powers to those that Congress already claimed, if only formally; they evinced little interest in the separation-of-powers issues that preoccupied the convention of 1787. The transformation of Congress into a bicameral assembly, the adoption of some scheme for proportional representation, the establishment of an independent executive and judiciary: all of these innovations would have remained beyond the acceptable range of debate in 1785. . . . Two years later the situation was entirely different."[26] Along with the economic crisis and trade issues, Shays' Rebellion has taken center stage in the history of that era. For that reason, the work of Daniel Shays is far more important than the courthouses he shut down or the few debtors he freed from jail. Indeed, it was the rebellion led by Daniel Shays that helped pave the way for a new Constitution.

D. Trade Problems and the Annapolis Convention

The Congress also had large and bitter debates over the issue of trade. The federal government was unable to assert control over tariffs, imposts, and duties. Various states had separate measures, some of which pertained to international trade, but some of which were applicable to trade with another state. The merchants were angry over this lack of uniformity and the inability of the Congress to take control. Meanwhile, the federal government was not getting any revenue from these tariffs and imposts—money that the government desperately needed. There were many attempts to have Congress take control over trade, but these were defeated by the state sovereignty contingent.

Once again, Madison came to the rescue by thinking outside the box. Although the two sides were totally entrenched in their diametrically opposed positions, Madison was able to come up with a "third way." Along with John Tyler, Madison proposed a conference on trade known as the Annapolis Convention. The motion was titled "Resolution of Mr. Tyler," so there has been some debate over who actually wrote it. However, Madison and Tyler both later claimed that it was Madison's work, and Tyler's son, President John Tyler, concurred.[27]

Knowing that it would be amended to death, Madison and Tyler waited until the last day of the session to put forth the proposal. The proposed commissioners included both members who were in favor of federal trade regulation, and members who were opposed. The strategy of bringing up an unorthodox and surprising compromise at the very end of the session worked. The resolution reads as follows:

Resolved, That Edmund Randolph, James Madison Jr., Walter Jones, St. George Tucker, Meriwether Smith, esquires be appointed commissioners, who, or any three of whom shall meet such commissioners as may be appointed by the other states in the Union at a time and place to be agreed on, to take into consideration the trade of the United States; to examine the relative situations and trade of the said states; to consider how far a uniform system in their commercial regulation may be necessary to their common interest and their permanent harmony; and to report to the several states such an act relative to this great object as when unanimously ratified by them will enable the United States in Congress effectually to provide for the Same.[28]

The commerce convention took place in Annapolis, Maryland, in September 1786. Although eight states had appointed delegates, not all of the appointed commissioners actually attended the meeting. With the exception of New Jersey, the state sovereignty contingent boycotted the meeting. Most of the 12 delegates present were in favor of a strong federal government, while the delegates from New Jersey sought federal relief in order to break the restrictions imposed by New York.[29]

It was at the Annapolis convention that a second convention was proposed, with the intention of getting support from the Congress so that delegates would actually attend. The report of the convention therefore became a solution that was different from the original problem that led to the meeting. In this situation, Madison made use of what later theorists would call the "garbage can" principle.[30]

Cohen, March, and Olsen coined the garbage can principle in 1972 as a way of explaining decision-making in higher education administration.[31] According to Cohen, March, and Olsen, "[a]ny decision can become a *garbage can* for almost any problem. The [issue] discussed in the context of any particular decision depends less on the decision or problems involved than on the timing of their joint arrivals and the existence of alternative arenas for exercising problems."[32] What this means in practicality is that solutions can become attached to problems other than those that they were originally proposed for. "One of the complications in accomplishing something in a garbage can decision-making process is the tendency for any particular project to become intertwined with a variety of other issues simply because those issues exist at the time the project is before the organization."[33] For example, a proposal to build a new building can lead to discussions on historic preservation, the environment, or social justice.

Indeed, in 1984 the garbage can principle led political scientist John Kingdon to apply the work of Cohen, March, and Olsen to policy formulation.[34] Kingdon's revision is called *Multiple Streams Theory*,[35] and is like a fly fisher sitting on the bank of a stream. When the fly is cast into the stream, something will be caught—but we don't know what it is. The fly fisher may catch a trout or a piece of trash floating by. Every once in awhile, however, the fly fisher may see beauty in something unexpected that he or she caught, such as a piece of driftwood suitable for carving. Similarly, a policy entrepreneur reaching into the solution stream can snag a loosely coupled solution floating by—and it isn't always what might be expected.

James Madison took advantage of the multiple streams/garbage can principle (even though it wouldn't be called that for nearly 200 years) by using the Annapolis convention to call for a gathering with increased powers to study amending the Articles of Confederation. March, Cohen, and Olsen[36] suggest that leaders provide garbage cans to dump projects into. This way the solutions can come out when needed, even if they are not immediately related to the problems. The grander the scale, the better the garbage can becomes, as it can then accommodate more solutions. Madison's idea of a convention with expanded powers was a very grand garbage can indeed.

Although Madison was the primary proponent of a new convention, the restrictions on his appointment prevented him from proposing it. Most of the states—including Virginia—had restricted the power of the delegates to negotiate on matters involving trade. However, the New Jersey commissioners were empowered by their state to act on *any* matter. Consequently, the New Jersey delegates were the only ones who could propose a motion for a convention to amend the Articles of Confederation.

Alexander Hamilton wrote the report proposing a constitutional convention. However, his wording was so strong that the delegates were afraid it would immediately cause state sovereignty advocates to reject the call. After Hamilton rewrote the draft, with the assistance of Madison, it asked for a second convention "for the same and such other purposes" as public affairs require.

The convention document also requested that the commissioners receive the kinds of broad negotiating powers that the New Jersey contingent had been granted, noting that there might be other areas of the Articles that would need adjustment.[37] The document proposed that this convention take place the following year in Philadelphia in order to:

> [D]evise such further provisions as shall appear to them necessary to render the constitution of the federal government adequate to the exigencies of the Union; and to report such an act for that purpose to the United States in Congress assembled, as when agreed to by them, and afterwards confirmed by the legislatures of every state, will effectually provide for the same.[38]

The stage was now set for the delegates to meet, creating what one scholar called the "Miracle at Philadelphia."[39]

The Creation of the U.S. Constitution

James Madison knew right away that a national convention would only be successful if it included General Washington. The general would lend credibility, both nationally and at home in Virginia. Madison was finally able to persuade the general to be one of the delegates from Virginia. The Virginia government had endorsed the idea of a convention, but it would still take an act of Congress to make it happen. As Congress debated the plan, the topic of Shays' Rebellion was in the forefront.

Delegates from Massachusetts who were opposed to the convention tried to block it by submitting a bill for a rival convention. However, Madison had anticipated this trick, and handled it by considering the Massachusetts plan to be an amendment to his own. By doing so, Madison all but assured the eventual passage of the convention bill.[40]

As the convention approached, Madison created a document entitled *Views of the Political System of the United States*.[41] This essay discussed some of the issues and problems that were raised by the Articles of Confederation, including:

♦ Failure of the States to comply with the Constitutional requisitions.

♦ Encroachment by the States on the federal authority.

♦ Violations of the law of nations and of treaties.

♦ Trespasses of the States on the rights of each other.

♦ Want of concert in matters where common interest requires it.

♦ Want of Guaranty to the States of their Constitutions and laws against internal violence.

♦ Want of sanction to the laws, and of coercion in the Government of the confederacy.

♦ Want of ratification by the people of the articles of Confederation.

♦ Multiplicity of laws in the several States.

♦ Mutability of the laws of the States.

♦ Injustice of the laws of the States.[42]

Madison went on to write that:

> The great *desideratum* in Government is such a modification of the sovereignty as will render it sufficiently neutral between the different interests and factions, to controul [sic] one part of the society from invading the rights of another, and at the same time sufficiently controuled [sic] itself, from setting up an interest adverse to that of the whole Society. In absolute Monarchies the prince is sufficiently neutral towards his subjects, but frequently sacrifices their happiness to his ambition or his avarice. In small republics, the sovereign will is sufficiently controuled [sic] from such a sacrifice of the entire Society, but is not sufficiently neutral towards the parts composing it. As a limited monarchy tempers the evils of an absolute one, so an extensive Republic meliorates the administration of a small Republic.[43]

The Philadelphia convention was called for the purpose of negotiating an agreement on trade and fixing any other necessary provisions of the Articles so that Congress could conduct its business. Even many of those who were supporters of the convention, such as Edmund Randolph, believed that any changes coming out of the meeting should be amended onto the Articles. Madison was definitely in favor of Hamilton's plan for a new constitution, but to say so out loud in public would have been an act of political suicide. Madison knew, however, that once the delegates were assembled, it might just be possible to get them to think outside the box. In order to prepare for that eventuality, Madison spent several weeks before the convention studying as much in the way of political theory as he could lay his hands on. This study encompassed both classical and modern theories, and included practical analysis of many constitutions.[44] This study was continued after the starting date of the convention, as there were not enough delegates to go forward.

By May 25, 1787, seven states had delegates present in sufficient numbers to be able to vote. The convention therefore began by unanimously electing Washington as the chair, and Major William Jackson as the secretary. The convention therefore began to debate and create their rules. One of the most important rules was that a quorum would consist of seven states (half plus one), rather than the nine states necessary under the Articles of Confederation. In addition, Madison was able to get the group to adopt a rule stating that a majority vote among states with a quorum of their own delegates would count as the vote of the state. "This was a departure from the fatal 'chaos clause' of the Articles of Confederation. . . . It put into practice the rule which Madison argued for, on March 5, 1781, as the proper interpretation of the Articles themselves. Had he won then, there might have been no need to write a new constitution."[45]

Although the convention business was to be kept secret until its report was finalized, Madison kept a complete journal of the debates and speeches. These were published after his death, and (along with the contributions of a few others such as John Lansing and Robert Yates) now provide a complete record of the convention.

A. The Virginia Plan

The cornerstone of what became the Constitution was the Virginia Plan, authored by Madison and presented by Edmund Randolph on May 29, 1787. The preamble suggested that the Articles of Confederation be amended. Changes included two houses of Congress—one elected according to financial contributions of the states and one nominated by state legislatures—along with a national executive (to be chosen by the Congress), a national judiciary, and the ability to pass laws, preempt state action, and call forth an army. A special council of revision could veto bills, but the legislature could override the veto.[46]

Some details of the Virginia Plan were known ahead of time. The French Charge-d'Affaires described the Virginia Plan to his government, and divided the American people into four distinct groups:

♦   Those who desired to establish a government based on . . . the Virginia Plan.

♦   Those who believed it impossible, under existing conditions, to reunite all members of the Confederation under a single head. With the North devoted to fisheries and commerce, the Middle States to farming and the South to great plantations, they would break the country into three independent confederacies, allied for defense.

- ♦ The Cincinnati. These old army officers, despairing of any other means of giving value to their defaulted pay certificates, were said to favor throwing the states into one mass under the rule of General Washington.

- ♦ Those who wanted nothing done at all. This strong party, which included Governor Clinton and Samuel Adams, pointed to the steady increase in population, the clearing of vast forests, the growth of commerce and industry, as evidence that political evils were overstressed. Why risk subjecting the people to despotism?[47]

In the Constitutional convention, although there was some support for each of these positions, most delegates felt that something needed to be done short of removing the states or breaking up the confederation. The Virginia Plan quickly became the basis of debate within the convention. Almost immediately, the preamble was changed to ask for a new, supreme national government. The big battle to come was over the power of the government. This led to a debate between large states and small states. "Madison was engaging in power politics—trying to fuse two groups of delegates, those from populous states and those from states which expected to become populous, into a common front for the abolition of state equality."[48] This was not a case of north versus south; South Carolina, New Jersey, and Connecticut were equally part of the small-state block, which was in favor of state equality. Meanwhile, New York, Massachusetts, and Virginia were pretty much on the same page in terms of national sovereignty. It was at that point that Madison suggested enumeration of the powers of the government. By doing this, he obtained support from both the national power block and the state equity block.[49]

B. The New Jersey Plan

The question of national power versus state equity came to a head over the question of legislative representation. This led to the creation of the New Jersey plan, which consisted of amending the Articles of Confederation to add more powers for Congress, a plural federal executive, and a supreme court. However, Madison was able to knock out the New Jersey plan by pointing out that it didn't fix the problems that the Congress had under the Articles of Confederation. According to Madison:

- ♦ The New Jersey plan provided no mechanism for enforcing treaties.
- ♦ "[E]ncroachments on the federal authority . . . was an evil inherent in all confederated republics, ancient and modern. Witness the illegal interstate commercial compacts, the unlawful raising of troops by Massachusetts, the refusal of New Jersey to comply with requisitions, the bribery of Connecticut to accept the territorial decree against her, the Indian wars, and treaties entered into by Georgia."[50]
- ♦ The New Jersey plan would not have given the central government the power to put down the rebellion in Massachusetts.
- ♦ Because there was no ratification by the people, there would be no supremacy over state constitutions.

♦ The federal judiciary had appellate jurisdiction, but not original jurisdiction.[51]

The defeat of the New Jersey plan left Madison's Virginia plan as the basis for debate. Connecticut then proposed that the House be elected by proportional representation, while the Senate was formed by state equality. By July 5, the proposed constitution included proportional representation in the House, including the counting of three-fifths of the slaves, and equal representation in the Senate. All money bills were to originate in the House, to be accepted or rejected by the Senate without amendment. Although Madison advocated direct election, the convention adopted election by the state legislatures. It was not until the Seventeenth Amendment was ratified in 1913 that popular election of the Senate became a reality.

The old issue of Western lands came back once again during the convention. Madison advocated a clause whereby no new states could be created from existing states without the consent of their legislature and Congress. This was a controversial proposal, as some of the states were still fighting the battle to retain their Western land claims. However, the work that Madison and the Congress had previously done helped to carry the day on this proposal.

One important provision of the new Constitution was that it did away with the need for unanimity with regard to amendments. The Articles of Incorporation had already witnessed a problem with amendments when Rhode Island withheld its consent on an amendment to raise revenue for the central government.[52] Instead of giving each state veto power over changes to the new Constitution, the document allowed new amendments to take effect once three-fourths of the states had ratified the proposal.[53]

C. Compromise and the Committee on Unfinished Parts

As the summer drew to a close, the convention used a parliamentary maneuver to keep things rolling along. Any provision that seemed to be difficult or controversial was referred to a Committee on Unfinished Parts. This procedure allowed the main group—the Committee of the Whole—to keep working on sections that could be done without controversy, while postponing the hard choices until later. "Appointed by ballot, it was made up of powerful leaders. Madison, Morris and King went on from the three big states. Sherman, Brearly and Dickinson came from the small-state bloc, with Gilman of New Hampshire unallied. Carroll reflected Maryland's mixed interests, and Williamson, Butler and Baldwin represented the Deep South. These men would make the ultimate decisions on the structure, strength and energy of the national government."[54] It was from the Committee on Unfinished Parts that the following provisions came about:

♦ The President was made elective by the people, through the Electoral College, to serve four years and be eligible to re-election.

+ Power to make treaties and appoint ambassadors and judges was transferred from the Senate to the President, subject to senatorial approval.
+ The General Welfare spending power was established.
+ The Senate was allowed to amend but not originate revenue bills.[55]

The last big battle was over the election of the president. Although most of the convention agreed to the Electoral College compromise, there was considerable disagreement over what to do if there was not a majority in the Electoral College. The small-state bloc proposed that the Senate elect the president. Madison felt that a one-third majority in the Electoral College should be sufficient. It was Sherman that suggested using the House of Representatives with equal votes by state delegation.

With the draft almost complete, Madison had one more compromise to suggest. There was a debate between those who wanted the Senate to be able to remove the president, and those who wished the president to be imperious to Congress. Madison proposed instead that the House should impeach and the Senate try the president. He was able to defeat a motion to suspend the president between the impeachment vote in the House and the trial in the Senate by explaining to the convention that:

> The President is made too dependent already on the legislature, by the power of one branch to try him in consequence of an impeachment by the other. This intermediate suspension will put him in the power of one branch only. They can at any moment, in order to make way for the functions of another who will be more favorable to their views, vote for a temporary removal of the existing magistrate.[56]

Madison's compromise "saved the country from ills whose effects can only be guessed at. Had he lost on these two points, easy impeachment and automatic suspension might have become a debauching instrument of congressional cabal, or a routine method of getting rid of a President whenever Congress showed up with a hostile majority."[57]

The delegates were divided between those who advocated a republican form of government to avoid tyranny of the governing, and those who feared that popular mobs—such as the group led by Daniel Shays—would take over the government and create tyranny of the majority. It was this division that led to the solution of putting into the government "a balance of powers that exploited cross-splitting divisions among men, and to do so by contriving selections processes, terms of office, and powers of position so that the natural disharmonies of persons would be converted into friction and conflict in government. Thus the rulers could go about their business of securing order and acting for the general welfare but would not be capable of converting their powers and energies against the people's liberty."[58]

Madison's leadership was instrumental in creating a government of checks and balances. "[Madison] clearly discerned the evolving needs of the American people, and his political experience and political reading had left him with no illusions as to the nature of man. He analyzed the political situation in terms of a conflict theory—the tendency of popular governments toward the violence of faction, with resulting confusion, instability, and injustice. He examined the root causes of faction and found them not in superficial or ephemeral forces but 'sown in the nature of man.' These forces erupted in religious, political, leadership, and above all economic conflict. . . ."[59]

Instead of trying to remove the sources of conflict, which he believed were an inevitable part of human nature, Madison's strategy was to remove the effects of this conflict through governmental checks and balances. This strategy meant that the different branches of the government "by their mutual relations, be the means of keeping each other in their proper place."[60] Each branch had its own powers and its own constituency. This prevented one branch from dominating the others, thereby preventing both tyranny of the governing and tyranny of the majority.

The final entry in Madison's *Journal of the Constitutional Convention* involves the signing of the finished document. It reads as follows:

> The Constitution being signed by all the members, except Mr. Randolph, Mr. Mason and Mr. Gerry, who declined giving it the sanction of their names, the Convention dissolved itself by an adjournment sine die.
> Whilst the last members were signing, Doctor Franklin, looking towards the President's chair, at the back of which a rising sun happened to be painted, observed to a few members sitting near him, that painters had found it difficult to distinguish in their art, a rising, from a setting, sun. I have, said he, often and often, in the course of the session, and the vicissitudes of my hopes and fears as to this issue, looked at that behind the President, without being able to tell whether it was rising or setting; but now at length, I have the happiness to know, that it is a rising, and not a setting sun.[61]

Having signed the Constitution, the delegates adjourned to dinner at the City Tavern. Brant asks the question:

> What would have been the verdict of these men on one another, had they undertaken to apportion credit for their achievement during the final festivities at the City Tavern? There is enough in the writings of the period to indicate that they would have given first place to Madison. . . . His fundamental gift to the Constitution was the concept of national supremacy and local autonomy in a federal republic ruled by the people, with checks and balances to guard against legislative or executive tyranny and against impetuous legislation. He proposed, supported and helped to secure such a government, organized for energy, and freed of dependence on the jealous and ambitious state political systems.
> Madison and Wilson stand out as the constructive statesmen of the convention. Both had a profound knowledge of public law, drawn from the history of it. Both were high nationalists. Both were committed to rule by the people under moderate safeguards against the passions and impetuousness of democracy. They formed a mighty team against the veiled monarchism of Hamilton, the rule of propertied aristocracy sought by the two Pinckneys, the prostrating

weakness (especially of the executive) which Mason and Randolph mistook for liberty. They won a fifty-per-cent victory in form, but far more than that in effect, in limiting small-state hegemony to state equality in the Senate. And they lost where they deserved to lose, in their effort to bring all state laws under the control of Congress and the Federal executive. . . .

In the field of actual construction, Madison's leadership began with the formulation of the Virginia Plan, followed by effective championship of its main provisions. . . . As the work went on, he showed the utmost skill in judging what would achieve and what would upset the balance between the great departments of government. Finally, he was a swift detector of flaws in superficially plausible proposals, and never lacked a remedy.[62]

Ratification of the Constitution

Madison's leadership did not end with the Philadelphia convention. Because the new Constitution called for a much stronger central government, many within the States were opposed to its adoption. In supporting ratification of the new Constitution, a group consisting of Alexander Hamilton, James Madison, and John Jay wrote a series of essays on the need for a new Constitution. These essays, now known as the *Federalist Papers*, also contained interpretations of the provisions within the document itself. Because the authors were prominent members of the group that created the Constitution, their interpretations are the preeminent source for Constitutional interpretation. This makes the *Federalist Papers* valuable to lawyers, as well as historians and political scientists. The U.S. Supreme Court considers the *Federalist Papers* to be "an authoritative contemporary interpretation of the meaning of its provisions."[63]

The *Federalist Papers* are not the only sources that are looked to for an understanding of the U.S. Constitution. The debates at the Constitutional convention are also available, and are quite authoritative, both for lawyers and for historians. For example, in determining why the U.S. has adopted a bicameral legislature, one need only look to the words of Pennsylvania convention delegate James Wilson, who stated that:

> Despotism comes on Mankind in different Shapes, sometimes in an Executive, sometimes in a Military, one. Is there no danger of a Legislative despotism? Theory & practice both proclaim it. If the Legislative authority be not restrained, there can be neither liberty nor stability; and it can only be restrained by dividing it within itself, into distinct and independent branches. In a single House there is no check, but the inadequate one, of the virtue & good sense of those who compose it.[64]

Madison wrote 29 of the *Federalist Papers* urging ratification of the Constitution. It was due to his skillful handling of the ratification process in Virginia that the state agreed to ratify the document.[65] In fact, Madison's pledge to work in the new Congress for a Bill of Rights convinced five states to ratify the Constitution with reservations (Rhode Island and North Carolina did not ratify until the Bill of Rights had been submitted).[66]

Although some Antifederalists called for a second convention to create the Bill of Rights, Madison realized that this was in fact nothing more than a ruse to create yet another Constitution. "By championing a bill of rights, he could prove that the Constitution was a friend of liberty and concomitantly undercut the popular appeal of the Antifederalists. He suspected, correctly it turned out, that most Antifederalists were not so much proponents of individual rights as they were jealous of their own states' powers—that is, of *states*' rights. . . . By vigorously pursuing a bill of rights, Madison could call their bluff."[67]

Madison did not win all the arguments, either in the Constitutional Convention or with the Bill of Rights. His plan to allow the federal government to veto state laws was not passed, and he was opposed to the equal representation of the states in the Senate. Two of the proposed amendments—a proposed change in the proportion of representatives to state population and a clause concerning Congressional compensation—were not passed. (The defeated proposal on compensation was subsequently revived, and was ratified as the 28th Amendment on May 7, 1992.) Yet many of the proposals that Madison made were adopted (with modifications) and became part of our national Constitution. Many of Madison's compromises were made by way of new proposals that involved looking at the situation through a different lens. Many of the techniques he used—creating many different proposals, finding new ways of thinking about issues, and applying moral leadership—are the subject of modern studies in leadership.

James Madison was a solver of problems and conflicts. He accomplished this through the use of unorthodox thinking outside the box, trying to reconfigure conflicts in order to reduce dissention. From the Virginia Declaration of Rights to the fight over Western lands, and from the creation of the United States Constitution to the proposal of the Bill of Rights, Madison always looked beyond the traditional viewpoints in order to find the "third way." Madison's leadership gave us a legacy of enduring gifts, not only in the Constitution he helped create, but also with a model of conflict resolution that has critical importance for leadership. By thinking outside the box and finding the "third way," Madison showed the world how leaders can resolve conflicts. These were important gifts that Madison left humankind.

The Bill of Rights

During the debate over ratification, several states noted the need to add a Bill of Rights. In order to deal with these criticisms, the new Congress proposed a series of 12 amendments that would help to retain individual liberties against encroachment by the strong central government. The first two proposed amendments, dealing with the U.S. Congress, were not adopted by the states in 1789. The other ten proposed amendments, known collectively as the *Bill of Rights*, were ratified between 1789 and 1791.

One of the rejected amendments—proposed Amendment II—read as follows: "No law varying the compensation for the services of the Senators and Representatives shall take effect, until an election of Representatives shall have intervened."[68] During the ratification of the Bill of Rights, only six of the thirteen states ratified this proposal, and it was declared to be a failed amendment. The states that had ratified this proposal were Maryland (December 19, 1789), North Carolina (December 22, 1789), South Carolina (January 19, 1790), Delaware (January 28, 1790), Vermont (on November 3, 1791, eight months after becoming the 14th state), and Virginia (December 15, 1791).[69] Virginia was the last state to ratify this proposal as part of the Bill of Rights.

Nearly a century later, however, the idea of regulating Congress' ability to grant itself a pay raise began to regain popularity. On May 6, 1873, Ohio became the first state in 82 years to ratify proposed Amendment II.[70] However, the movement to revive the proposal sputtered for another 105 years until March 6, 1978, when Wyoming ratified the proposed amendment.[71] In the next 13 years, a series of state governments ratified the proposal. The third time turned out to be the charm, as the proposed amendment was ratified by the following states:

- 1983: Maine (April 27).
- 1984: Colorado (April 22).
- 1985: South Dakota (February 21); New Hampshire (March 7); Arizona (April 3); Tennessee (May 28); Oklahoma (July 10).
- 1986: New Mexico (February 14); Indiana (February 24); Utah (February 25).
- 1987: Arkansas (March 13); Montana (March 17); Connecticut (May 13); Wisconsin (July 15).
- 1988: Georgia (February 2); West Virginia (March 10); Louisiana (July 7).
- 1989: Iowa (February 9); Idaho (March 23); Nevada (April 26); Alaska (May 6); Oregon (May 19); Minnesota (May 22); Texas (May 25).
- 1990: Kansas (April 5); Florida (May 31).
- 1991: North Dakota (May 25).
- 1992: Alabama (May 5); Missouri (May 5); New Jersey (May 7); Michigan (May 7).[72]

On May 7, 1992, Michigan became the 38th state to ratify the amendment, carrying it past the threshold of being ratified by three-fourths of the states. Later that same day, New Jersey ratified, becoming the 39th state to ratify what became the 27th Amendment. However, Michigan is considered to be the state that brought the amendment into being.[73] This formerly failed amendment, proposed by James Madison in 1789 as part of the Bill of Rights, was the proposal that wouldn't go away.[74]

Documents and Sources on the
Articles of Confederation

A. The Library of American Civilization Series

Although microform now seems quaint and antiquated, there are still large collections of documents in libraries all over the country. Regrettably, not all microform series are included in library catalogs or listed on OCLC. However, those libraries that have these microform collections have a wealth of primary sources on the Constitution and the early republic. There are two main sets, namely the Library of American Civilization (LAC) and the Early American Imprints series. Other microform series, such as the Civil War oriented Lost Cause Press, also contain primary documents on the Constitution.

The Library of American Civilization was compiled in the early 1970s. The company—called Library Resources—made a tragic decision to print the series on microcards, which require a special reader. Some of the microforms of the Early American Imprints series also used this format. Unfortunately, there was no way to print from these readers, and beginning in the 1980s the equipment itself became unavailable. The LAC itself subsequently went out of print. However, in the past decade Indus International[75] has begun to produce microcard and ultrafiche readers. An optional attachment allows the images to be scanned to a computer, where they can be printed or downloaded. This equipment has given new life to the Library of American Civilization and to those copies of the Early American Imprints that are printed on microcards.

The LAC "is a collection of primary source materials relating to virtually all aspects of American life & literature up to World War I. Primary source material includes books, pamphlets, periodicals, biographies and autobiographies, fictional works, poetry, collections of various kinds, and selected federal, state, and local documents. Some non-U.S. materials are included."[76] While some LAC materials are cataloged in OCLC, the most complete list is contained in the index to the set, which is entitled the Microbook Library of American Civilization.[77] Terry Ballard, a librarian at Qunnipiac University, has compiled a list of Library of American Civilization titles available free on the web.[78] Primary sources relating to the Constitution and the early republic available in the Library of American Civilization series include the following titles:

◆ Bradley, Stephen Row. (1780). *Vermont's Appeal to the Candid and Impartial World Containing, A Fair Stating of The Claims of Massachusetts-Bay, New-Hampshire, and New-York*; the right the state of Vermont has to independence; with an address to the honorable American Congress, and the inhabitants of the thirteen United States. Hartford: Hudson & Goodwin. Library of American Civilization, LAC 40102.

♦   Clinton, Sir Henry. (1794). *Observations on Mr. Stedman's History of the American War*. London: J. Debrett. Library of American Civilization, LAC 40080.

♦   Coxe, Tench. (1794). *A View of the United States of America*, in a series of papers, written at various times, between the years 1787 and 1794 interspersed with authentic documents, the whole tending to exhibit the progress and present state of civil and religious liberty, population, agriculture, exports, imports, fisheries, navigation, ship-building, manufactures, and general improvement. Philadelphia: William Hall/Wrigley & Berriman. Library of American Civilization, LAC 10190.

♦   Coxe, Tench. (1787). *An Enquiry Into The Principles On Which A Commercial System For The United States Of America Should Be Founded To Which Are Added Some Political Observations Connected With The Subject*, read before the Society for Political Enquiries, convened at the house of His Excellency Benjamin Franklin, Esquire, in Philadelphia May 11th, 1787. Philadelphia: Robert Aitken. Library of American Civilization, LAC 40106.

♦   Fay, Jonas, & Allen, Ethan. (1870). *A Concise Refutation of the Claims of New Hampshire and Massachusetts-Bay, To the Territory of Vermont With Occasional Remarks on The Long Disputed Claim Of New-York To The Same*. Hartford: Hudson and Goodwin. Library of American Civilization, LAC 40102.

♦   Franklin, Benjamin. (1878). *Philosophical and Miscellaneous Papers*. London: C. Dilly. Library of American Civilization, LAC 15314.

♦   Hazard, Ebenezer. (1792-1794). *Historical Collections Consisting Of State Papers, And Other Authentic Documents, Intended As Materials For A History Of The United States of America*. Philadelphia: T. Dobson. Library of American Civilization, LAC 23452-53.

♦   Jackson, Jonathan J. (1788). *Thoughts Upon The Political Situation Of The United States Of America In Which That Of Massachusetts Is More Particularly Considered*; with some observations on the Constitution for a federal government: addressed to the people of the Union. Worcester, MA: I. Thomas. Library of American Civilization, LAC 15267.

♦   Jones, Absalom. (1794). *A Narrative Of The Proceedings Of The Black People During The Late Awful Calamity In Philadelphia, In The Year 1793; And A Refutation Of Some Censures, Thrown Upon Them In Some Late Publications*. Philadelphia: P. William W. Woodward. Library of American Civilization, LAC 40128.

♦   Lee, Richard Henry. (1787). *Observations Leading To A Fair Examination Of The System Of Government Proposed By The Late Convention*; and to several essential and necessary alterations in it, in a number of letters from the Federal Farmer to the Republican. Library of American Civilization, LAC 40119.

♦   Lendrum, John. (1795). *A Concise And Impartial History Of The American Revolution To Which Is Prefixed, A General History Of North And South America, To-*

gether With An Account Of The Discovery And Settlement Of North America. Boston: Thomas and Andrews. Library of American Civilization, LAC 20828.

♦   McHenry, James. (1906). Papers of Dr. James McHenry on the Federal Convention of 1787. *American Historical Review, 11(3)*, 595-624. Library of American Civilization, LAC 40119.

♦   Muir, James. (1795). *An Examination Of The Principles Contained In The Age Of Reason In Ten Discourses*. Baltimore: S. & J. Adams. Library of American Civilization, LAC 14262.

♦   Smith, William Loughton [also attributed to Alexander Hamilton]. (1792). *The Politicks And Views Of A Certain Party, Displayed*. "An attack on Jefferson for his opposition to Hamilton's views." [Description from OCLC record.] Library of American Civilization, LAC 40066.

♦   State of Pennsylvania. (1789). *Minutes of the Convention of the Commonwealth of Pennsylvania* which commenced at Philadelphia, on Tuesday the twenty-fourth day of November, in the year of Our Lord one thousand seven hundred and eighty-nine, for the purpose of reviewing, and if they see occasion, altering and amending, the constitution of this state. Philadelphia: Z. Poulson. Library of American Civilization, LAC 15578.

♦   Stedman, Charles. (1794). *The History of the Origin, Progress, and Termination of the American War*. Dublin: Messrs. P. Wogan and P. Byrne. Library of American Civilization, LAC 22619-20.

♦   Stokes, Anthony. (1783). *A View Of The Constitution Of The British Colonies In North America And The West Indies, At The Time The Civil War Broke Out On The Continent Of America*. London: B. White. Library of American Civilization, LAC 15980.

♦   Sullivan, James. (1791). *Observations Upon The Government Of The United States of America*. Boston: Samuel Hall. Library of American Civilization, LAC 23453 and LAC 40149.

♦   *Official Opinions of the Attorneys General of the United States*, advising the President and heads of departments in relation to their official duties. (1791-1869). Washington, DC: R. Farnham. Library of American Civilization, LAC 21684-94

♦   *The Public Statutes at Large of the United States of America, 1789-1845*. Washington, DC: Government Printing Office. Library of American Civilization, LAC 22035-36.

♦   Warren, Mercy Otis [also attributed to Elbridge Gerry]. (1788). *Observations on the New Constitution, and on the Federal and State Conventions*. Boston, printed; New-York re-printed. Library of American Civilization, LAC 40119.

♦   West, Samuel. (1793). *Essays On Liberty And Necessity In Which The True Nature
    Of Liberty Is Stated And Defended, And The Principal Arguments Used By Mr. Ed-
    wards And Others For Necessity Are Considered.* Boston: Samuel Hall. Library of
    American Civilization, LAC 40034.

B. The Early American Imprints Series

The Early American Imprints series is based on Charles Evans' *American
Bibliography.*[79] The publications described in Evans are available on opaque
microcard as part of the Early American Imprints series (produced by the
American Antiquarian Society),[80] as well as on the Readex/Newsbank Digital
Evans series. The items in both the microform and online series are arranged by
the accession number in Evans' bibliography. The opaque microcards (but not
the online version) also contain materials from the supplement by Rodger Bristol,[81] as well as *American Bibliography, A Preliminary Checklist for 1801-1819,*
compiled by Ralph R. Shaw and Richard H. Shoemaker.[82] The documents are
now also available as a digitized online image database from News-
bank/Readex.[83] The following list contains some of the most important items in
the series related to the Articles of Confederation:

♦   *Articles of Confederation and Perpetual Union Between the states of New Hamp-
    shire, Massachusetts Bay, Rhode Island And Providence Plantations, Connecticut,
    New York, New Jersey, Pennsylvania, Delaware, Maryland, Virginia, North Caro-
    lina, South Carolina and Georgia.* Various drafts are available in the *Early Ameri-
    can Imprints* first series with the following *Evans* numbers:
    o   Early American Imprints, first series, no. 15148.
    o   Early American Imprints, first series, no. 15619.
    o   Early American Imprints, first series, no. 15620.
    o   Early American Imprints, first series, no. 15622.
    o   Early American Imprints, first series, no. 15623.
    o   Early American Imprints, first series, no. 15624.
    o   Early American Imprints, first series, no. 15625.
    o   Early American Imprints, first series, no. 15626.
    o   Early American Imprints, first series, no. 15627.
    o   Early American Imprints, first series, no. 43388.
    o   Early American Imprints, first series, no. 43488.

♦   Constitutional Convention. (1787). *Supplement to the Independent Journal,* Satur-
    day, September 22, 1787: copy of the result of the deliberations of the Federal Con-
    vention. New York: J. M'Lean and Co. Early American Imprints, first series, no.
    20812.

♦   Drayton, William Henry. (1778). *The Speech of the Hon. William-Henry Drayton,
    Esquire, Chief Justice of South-Carolina.* Delivered on the twentieth January, 1778.
    In the General Assembly resolved into the Committee of the Whole; upon the Arti-

cles of Confederation of the United States of America. Early American Imprints, first series, no. 15785.

♦ Jay, John. (1788). *Extract From An Address To The People Of The State Of New York, On The Subject Of The Federal Constitution.* Early American Imprints, first series, no. 45277 and 45065.

♦ Lee, Richard Henry. (1787-1788). *Letters From The Federal Farmer To The Republican.* "Attributed to R.H. Lee. Originally published anonymously in 2 separate pamphlets, printed by T. Greenleaf, New York (1787 and 1788, respectively), and paged continuously; the 1st pamphlet with title: Observations leading to a fair examination of the system of government proposed by the late convention; and the 2d with title: An additional number of letters from the Federal farmer to the Republican." [Description from OCLC Record.]
   o   Early American Imprints, first series, no. 21197.
   o   Early American Imprints, first series, no. 20454.
   o   Early American Imprints, first series, no. 20455.
   o   Early American Imprints, first series, no. 20456.

♦ Martin, Luther, & Deye, Thomas Cockey. (1788). *The Genuine Information, Delivered To The Legislature Of The State Of Maryland, Relative To The Proceedings Of The General Convention, Lately Held At Philadelphia.* Philadelphia: Eleazer Oswald. Early American Imprints, first series, no. 21220.

♦ *Observations On The Articles Of Confederation Of The Thirteen United States Of America, Entered Into In July, 1778, And Ratified And Completed [Sic] The 1st Of March, 1781.* (1787). Early American Imprints, first series, no. 20600.

♦ Pinckney, Charles. (1787). *Observations On The Plan Of Government Submitted To The Federal Convention, In Philadelphia, On The 28th Of May, 1787.* New-York: Francis Childs. Early American Imprints, first series, no. 20649 and 20650.

♦ Randolph, Edmund. (1787). *To The Printer.* Sir, the inclosed letter contains the reasons of His Excellency Governor Randolph for refusing his signature to the proposed foederal constitution of government submitted to the several states by the late convention at Philadelphia, 1787. Early American Imprints, first series, no. 20669.

♦ *Remarks On A Pamphlet, Entitled "A Dissertation On The Political Union And Constitution Of The Thirteen United States Of North-America."*(1784). "By a citizen of Philadelphia." With some brief observations, whether all the western lands, not actually purchased or conquered by the crown of Great-Britain, antecedent to the late cession, made to the thirteen United States of North-America, ought not to be considered as ceded to the thirteen states jointly——and whether all the confiscated estates of those people, by some termed Loyalists, are to be considered as forfeited to the states in which they were resident, or to all the states included in the confederation. Early American Imprints, first series, no. 18782.

♦   State of Maryland. (1778). *A Declaration Whereas The General Assembly Of Mary-land Hath Heretofore Resolved . . . That The United States In Congress Assembled Should Have Full Power To Ascertain And Fix The Western Limits Of Those States, That Claim To The Mississippi Or South Sea.* Printed by Frederick Green, 1778. "Protesting those portions of the Articles of Confederation which allowed only certain states to accrue benefits from the sale and settlement of western lands. 'Read and assented to' by the House of Delegates and Senate, December 15, 1778. [Description from OCLC Record.] Early American Imprints, first series, no. 43488.

♦   State of New-York. (1788). *The Debates And Proceedings Of The Convention Of The State Of New-York*: assembled at Poughkeepsie, on the 17th June, 1788, to deliberate and decide on the form of federal government recommended by the General Convention at Philadelphia, on the 17th September, 1787 New-York: Francis Childs. Early American Imprints, first series, no. 21310 and 21242.

♦   State of New-Hampshire. (1783). *In The House Of Representatives, June 20th, 1783.* An Address To The People Of The State Of New-Hampshire. Whereas The United States In Congress Assembled, Have Taken Into Consideration So Much Of The Eighth Article Of The Confederation. . . . "Concerning the acceptance by the state of New Hampshire of the amended article of Congress fixing the ratio of payment, according to population, to be apportioned the states for expenses incurred in the common defense. Includes reasons for the alteration, from an address of Congress. 'In Council the same day, read and concurred. . . .'" [Description from OCLC Record.] Early American Imprints, first series, no. 18046.

♦   State of New-Hampshire. (1783). *In The House Of Representatives, June 20th,* 1783 the committee on the recommendations of Congress, report as their opinion, that the following resolutions of Congress and consequent requisition of the General Court, be printed in hand bills and directed to the selectmen of the several towns, parishes and places within this state. Early American Imprints, first series, no. 18047.

♦   State of North-Carolina. (1787). *An Act For Appointing Deputies From This State, To A Convention Proposed To Be Held In The City Of Philadelphia In May Next, For The Purpose Of Revising The Foederal Constitution.* New Bern, NC: Hodge & Blanchard. Early American Imprints, first series, no. 45116.

♦   State of Virginia. (1786). *An Act For Appointing Deputies From This Commonwealth To A Convention Proposed To Be Held In The City Of Philadelphia In May Next, For The Purpose Of Revising The Foederal Constitution.* Richmond: John Dunlap and James Hayes. Early American Imprints, first series, no. 20101.

♦   Sullivan, James. (1791). *Observations Upon The Government Of The United States Of America.* Boston: Samuel Hall. Early American Imprints, first series, no. 23812.

♦   *To The People Of Maryland Give Me Leave To Address You Upon A Subject Of The Greatest Importance To You And Your Posterity; A Subject Which Essentially Concerns The Welfare, Happiness And Grandeur Of This State, And Therefore Worthy Of Your Most Deliberate And Candid Consideration; I Mean The Expediency Of*

Your Acceding To The Confederacy Proposed To You By Congress, And Now Adopted And Ratified By Ten Of The Thirteen States Of America. (1779). "Signed: An American. Possibly by Luther Martin. . . . Date of publication supplied by Shipton & Mooney; erroneously dated 1776 by Evans." [Description from OCLC Record.] Early American Imprints, first series, no. 15112.

♦ United States Continental Congress. (1786, March 8). *A Motion Of Mr. Dane, That A Committee Of Five Be Appointed To Examine How Far The Several States Have Complied With And Adopted The Alteration Of The Eighth Article Of The Confederation And Perpetual Union, Recommended By Congress, April 18, 1783, And To Consider And Report, What Further Measures Are To Be Adopted By Congress, For Carrying Into Effect A Federal Rule For Apportioning Federal Taxes On The Several States.* Early American Imprints, first series, no. 20069.

♦ United States Continental Congress. (1786, July 14). *On The Report Of A Committee Consisting Of Mr. Lee, Mr. King, And Mr. Kean: Resolved, That, Congress Consider The Confederation As A Compact Between The Several States For Mutual Good.* Early American Imprints, first series, no. 20047.

♦ United States Continental Congress. (1785). *The Committee Consisting Of [Blank] To Whom Was Referred The Motion Of Mr. Monroe, Submit The Following Report That The First Paragraph Of The Ninth Of The Articles Of Confederation Be Altered.* Early American Imprints, first series, no. 19301.

♦ United States Continental Congress. (1787). *The Committee, Consisting Of Mr. Dane, Mr. Clark, Mr. Varnum, Mr. Lee, And Mr. Grayson, To Whom It Was Referred To Consider What Officers In The Civil Department Are Become Unnecessary; And To Whom Also Was Referred A Motion Of Mr. Dane, Respecting The Department Of The Treasury—Report The Following Resolutions.* Early American Imprints, first series, no. 20767.

♦ United States Continental Congress. (1786). *The Grand Committee, Consisting Of Mr. Livermore, Mr. Dane, Mr. Manning, Mr. Johnson, Mr. Smith, Mr. Symmes, Mr. Pettit, Mr. Henry, Mr. Lee, Mr. Bloodworth, Mr. Pinckney And Mr. Houstoun [Sic], Appointed To Report Such Amendments To The Confederation, And Such Resolutions As It May Be Necessary To Recommend To The Several States, For The Purpose Of Obtaining From Them Such Powers As Will Render The Federal Government Adequate To The Ends For Which It Was Instituted; Beg Leave To Submit The Following Report To The Consideration Of Congress.* "Report recommending seven new articles to the Articles of Confederation, given Aug. 7, 1786." [Description from OCLC Record.] Early American Imprints, first series, no. 44996.

♦ United States Continental Congress. (1787). *The United States In Congress Assembled, Friday, September 28, 1787.* Congress having received the report of the Convention lately assembled in Philadelphia, resolved unanimously, that the said report, with the resolutions and letter accompanying the same, be transmitted to the several legislatures, in order to be submitted to a convention of delegates. Philadelphia: Dunlap & Claypoole. Early American Imprints, first series, no. 20790.

C. Books on Constitutional Research

♦   Alexander, John K. (1990). *The Selling of the Constitutional Convention: A History of News Coverage.* Madison, WI: Madison House.

♦   Amar, Akhil Reed. (2005). *America's Constitution: A Biography.* New York: Random House.

♦   *The Anti-Federalists.* (1985). Cecelia M. Kenyon. Boston: Northeastern University Press.

♦   Bernstein, Richard B., & Rice, Kym S. (1987). *Are We to Be a Nation? The Making of the Constitution.* Cambridge, MA: Harvard University Press.

♦   Bowen, Catherine Drinker. (1986). *Miracle at Philadelphia: The Story of the Constitutional Convention, May to September.* Boston: Little, Brown.

♦   Burns, Edward McNall. (1968). *James Madison: Philosopher of the Constitution.* New York: Octagon Books.

♦   Collier, Christopher. (1987). *Decision in Philadelphia: The Constitutional Convention of 1787.* New York: Ballantine Books.
    o   [2nd ed.] Collier, Christopher, & Collier, James Lincoln. (2007). *Decision in Philadelphia: The Constitutional Convention of 1787.* New York: Ballantine Books.

♦   *Constitutional Chaff: Rejected Suggestions of the Constitutional Convention of 1787 With Explanatory Argument.* (1941). Jane Butzner (Ed.). Columbia University Press.

♦   Dickinson, John, & Lee, Richard Henry. (1999). *Letters from a Farmer in Pennsylvania; Letters from the Federal Farmer.* Indianapolis, IN: Liberty Fund.

♦   *Documentary History of the Ratification of the Constitution.* (2008). John P. Kaminski et al. (Eds.). Charlottesville, VA: Rotunda Press of Virginia, *available at* http://rotunda.upress.virginia.edu/founders/RNCN.html.
    "This landmark work in historical and legal scholarship draws upon thousands of sources to trace the Constitution's progress through each of the thirteen states' conventions. The digital edition allows users to search the complete contents by date, title, author, recipient, or state affiliation and preserves the copious annotations of the print edition" [Description from website.]

♦   Donovan, Frank Robert. (1965). *Mr. Madison's Constitution: The Story Behind the Constitutional Convention.* New York: Dodd, Mead.

♦   Eidelberg, Paul. (1968). *The Philosophy of the American Constitution: A Reinterpretation of the Intentions of the Founding Fathers.* New York: Free Press.

◆ *The Essential Bill of Rights: Original Arguments and Fundamental Documents.* (1998). Gordon Lloyd & Maggie Lloyd (Eds.). Lanham, MD: University Press of America.

◆ Farrand, Max, & Matteson, David Maydole. (1986). *The Records of the Federal Convention of 1787.* New Haven: Yale University Press.

◆ Farrand, Max. (1914). *The Framing of the Constitution of the United States.* New Haven: Yale University Press.

◆ *The Federalist Papers.* (1787-1788). Although all of the *Federalist* essays were signed as "Publius," it is generally agreed that the authors were Alexander Hamilton, James Madison, and John Jay. There are many editions of the *Federalist Papers*, both in print and online. One recent version produced by BN Publishing in 2006 contains both the *Federalist Papers* and the *Antifederalist Papers*, and a good online edition is found at http://www.foundingfathers.info/federalistpapers.

◆ *The Framers and Fundamental Rights.* (1991). Robert A. Licht (Ed.). Washington, DC: AEI Press.

◆ Frisch, Morton J. (1991). *Alexander Hamilton and the Political Order: An Interpretation of His Political Thought & Practice.* Lanham, MD: University Press of America.

◆ Goldwin, Robert. (1987). *From Parchment to Power: How James Madison Used the Bill of Rights to Save the Constitution.* Washington, DC: AEI Press.

◆ Hoar, George Frisbie. (1903). *The Connecticut Compromise: Roger Sherman, the Author of the Plan of Equal Representation of the States in the Senate, and Representation of the People in Proportion to Numbers in the House.* Worcester, MA: Press of C. Hamilton.

◆ Independence National Historical Park. (1987). *1787: The Day-to-Day Story of the Constitutional Convention.* New York: Exeter Books.

◆ Janosik, Robert J. (1991). *The American Constitution: An Annotated Bibliography.* Lanham, MD: Scarecrow Press.

◆ Jefferson, Thomas. (1939). *Thomas Jefferson on Democracy.* Saul K. Padover (Ed.). New York: Mentor/New American Library.

◆ Jillson, Calvin C. (1988). *Constitution Making: Conflict and Consensus in the Federal Convention of 1787.* New York: Agathon Press.

◆ Ketcham, Ralph Louis. (2003). *The Anti-Federalist Papers and the Constitutional Convention Debates.* New York: Signet Classic.

♦   Lansing, John. (1967). *The Delegate from New York, or Proceedings of the Federal Convention of 1787, From the Notes of John Lansing, Jr.* Port Washington, NY: Kennikat Press.

♦   *Light on the First Ten Amendments from the Correspondence of Madison.* (1935). C. R. Williams (Ed.). Washington, DC: Legislative Reference Service.

♦   Madison, James
   o   *The Constitutional Convention: A Narrative History, from the notes of James Madison.* (2005). Edward J. Larson & Michael Winship (Eds.). New York: Modern Library.
   o   *The Debates in the Federal Convention of 1787: Which Framed the Constitution of the United States of America.* (2007). Amherst, NY: Prometheus Books.

♦   Matson, Cathy D., & Onuf, Peter S. (1990). *A Union of Interests: Political and Economic Thought in Revolutionary America.* Lawrence: University Press of Kansas.

♦   McDonald, Forrest
   o   *Novus ordo seclorum: The Intellectual Origins of the Constitution.* (1985). Lawrence, KS: University Press of Kansas.
   o   *We the People: The Economic Origins of the Constitution.* (1958). Chicago: University of Chicago Press.

♦   Mee, Charles L. (1987). *The Genius of the People.* New York: Harper & Row.

♦   Meigs, William Montgomery. (1987). *The Growth of the Constitution in the Federal Convention of 1787: An Effort to Trace the Origin and Development of Each Separate Clause.* Littleton, CO: F. B. Rothman.

♦   Miller, William Lee. (1992). *The Business of May Next: James Madison and the Founding.* Charlottesville: University Press of Virginia.

♦   Morgan, Robert J. (1988). *James Madison on the Constitution and the Bill of Rights.* New York: Greenwood Press.

♦   *The Origins of the American Constitution: A Documentary History.* (1986). Michael G. Kammen (Ed.). New York: Penguin.

♦   *Papers of the Continental Congress, 1774-1789.* (1943-1971). Washington, DC: National Archives.

♦   *The Philosophy of Freedom: Ideological Origins of the Bill of Rights.* (1993). Samuel B. Rudolph (Ed.). Lanham, MD: University Press of America.

♦   Prescott, Arthur Taylor. (1941). *Drafting the Federal Constitution: A Rearrangement of Madison's Notes Giving Consecutive Developments of Provisions in the Constitution of the United States, Supplemented by Documents Pertaining to the*

Philadelphia Convention and to Ratification Processes, and Including Insertions by the Compiler. Baton Rouge, LA: Louisiana State University Press.

♦ Reid, John Phillip. (1986). *Constitutional History of the American Revolution.* Madison, WI: University of Wisconsin Press.

♦ Richardson, Hamilton P. (1985). *The Journal of the Federal Convention of 1787 Analyzed.* Littleton, CO: F.B. Rothman.

♦ Rossiter, Clinton
   o *Alexander Hamilton and the Constitution.* (1964). New York: Harcourt, Brace & World.
   o *Seedtime of the Republic: The Origin of the American Tradition of Political Liberty.* (1953). New York: Harcourt, Brace.
   o *The Political Thought of the American Revolution.* (1963). New York: Harcourt, Brace & World.
   o *1787: The Grand Convention.* (1966). New York: Macmillan. Republished (1987) New York: W.W. Norton.
   o *Six Characters in Search of a Republic: Studies in the Political Thought of the American Colonies.* (1964). New York: Harcourt, Brace & World.

♦ Rutland, Robert Allen. (1987). *The First Great Newspaper Debate: The Constitutional Crisis of 1787-88.* Worcester, MA: American Antiquarian Society.

♦ Scott, James Brown. (1918). *James Madison's Notes of Debates in the Federal Convention of 1787 and Their Relation to a More Perfect Society of Nations.* New York: Oxford University Press.

♦ St. John, Jeffrey. (1987). *A Child of Fortune: A Correspondent's Report on the Ratification of the U.S. Constitution and the Battle for a Bill of Rights.* Ottawa, IL: Jameson Books, 1990. Originally published as *Constitutional Journal: A Correspondent's Report from the Convention of 1787.* Ottawa, IL: Jameson Books.

♦ Steiner, Bernard Christian. (1915). *Connecticut's Ratification of the Federal Constitution.* Worcester, MA: American Antiquarian Society.

♦ Story, Joseph. (2008). *Commentaries on the Constitution of the United States.* Clark, NJ: Lawbook Exchange.
   Written by U.S. Supreme Court Justice Joseph Story in 1833, this work is considered to be very authoritative because it is one of the earliest commentaries on the Constitution.

♦ Thach, Charles C., Jr. (2007). *The Creation of the Presidency, 1775-1789: A Study in Consitutional History.* Indianapolis, IN: Liberty Fund.

♦ Van Doren, Carl. (1948). *The Great Rehearsal: The Story of the Making and Ratifying of the Constitution of the United States.* New York: Viking Press.

♦ Vile, John R. (2005). *The Constitutional Convention of 1787: A Comprehensive Encyclopedia of America's Founding.* Santa Barbara, CA: ABC-CLIO.

♦ Watkins, William J., & Rosenfeld, Richard N. (2004). *Reclaiming the American Revolution: The Kentucky and Virginia Resolutions and Their Legacy.* New York: Palgrave Macmillan.

♦ Wehmann, Howard H., & DeWhitt, Benjamin L. (1989). *A Guide to Pre-Federal Records in the National Archives.* Washington, DC: National Archives and Records Administration.

♦ Wood, Gordon S. (1998). *The Creation of the American Republic, 1776-1787.* 2nd ed. Chapel Hill, NC: University of North Carolina Press.

♦ *The World's Greatest Debate.* (1940). Glenn Clark (Ed.). St. Paul, MN: Macalester Park Publishing.

D. Articles and Websites on Constitutional Research

♦ Adkison, Danny M. (2004). The Ninth Amendment and the Negative Pregnant. *Forum: A Journal of Applied Research in Contemporary Politics, 2(3),* 1-6, *available at* http://www.bepress.com/forum/vol2/iss3/art5.

♦ Aldrich, John Herbert, & Grant, Ruth Weissbourd. (1993, May). The Antifederalists, the First Congress, and the First Parties. *Journal of Politics, 55(2),* 295-326.

♦ *The American Founding Era Collection* (Rotunda Press, University of Virginia) http://www.rotunda.upress.virginia.edu/index.php?page_id=Founding%20Era %20Collection "The American Founding Era Collection brings together original digital works with digital editions of the papers of major figures of the early republic, many of them decades in the making. These digital editions will present all material from the published volumes, including editorial annotations and careful transcriptions of hundreds of thousands of documents, in a fully searchable and interoperable online environment." [Description from website.]

♦ Arnold, Richard S. (1997, May). How James Madison Interpreted the Constitution. *New York University Law Review, 72(2),* 267-293.

♦ *The Avalon Project* http://avalon.law.yale.edu/default.asp Created by the Lillian Goldman Law Library at Yale University, the Avalon Project contains many historical documents in the areas of law, history, economics, politics, diplomacy, and government. The site includes a number of historical items related to the Articles of Confederation, the adoption of the Constitution, and the Early Republic. Some of the documents on this site include:
o   The Articles of Confederation.

o   Documents, journals, and resolutions of the Continental Congress.

o   Documents from the Annapolis Convention.

o   All known journals of the Constitutional debates, including those by James Madison, Alexander Hamilton, William Pierce, Rufus King, William Paterson, Robert Yates, and James McHenry.

o   Variant resolutions and proposals from the Philadelphia convention.

o   Messages, speeches, and papers of the U.S. presidents.

o   The constitutions of the states.

o   The *Federalist Papers.*

o   Notes and debates of the ratification process in the various states.

◆   Bailey, Jeremy David. (2004). Executive Prerogative and the "Good Officer" in Thomas Jefferson's Letter to John B. Colvin. *Presidential Studies Quarterly, 34(4),* 732-754.

◆   Black, Hugo L. (1960, April). The Bill of Rights. *New York University Law Review, 35(4),* 865-881.

◆   Bolt, William K. (2004, Fall). Founding Father and Rebellious Son: James Madison, John C. Calhoun, and the Use of Precedents. *American Nineteenth Century History, 5(3),* 1-27.

◆   Brennan, William J., Jr. (1961, April). The Bill of Rights and the States. *New York University Law Review, 36(4),* 761-778.

◆   *A Century of Lawmaking for a New Nation: U.S. Congressional Documents and Debates*
http://memory.loc.gov/ammem/amlaw/lwabout.html
This digital collection on the Library of Congress American Memory website contains records of the Continental Congress (1774-1788) and the 1st through 43rd Congresses (1889-1875). Documents on the website include:

o   *Journals of the Continental Congress* (1774-89).

o   *Letters of Delegates to Congress* (1774-89).

o   *Records of the Federal Convention of 1787 (Farrand's Records).*

o   *Debates in the Several State Conventions on the Adoption of the Federal Constitution* (1787-88) *(Elliot's Debates).*

◆   Corley, Pamela C., Howard, Robert M., & Nixon, David C. (2005, June). The Supreme Court and Opinion Content: The Use of the *Federalist Papers. Political Research Quarterly, 58(2),* 329-340.

◆   *Documents from the Continental Congress and the Constitutional Convention*
http://memory.loc.gov/ammem/collections/continental
Part of the Library of Congress American Memory website. "The Continental Congress Broadside Collection (253 titles) and the Constitutional Convention Broadside Collection (21 titles) contain 274 documents relating to the work of Congress and the drafting and ratification of the Constitution. Most broadsides are a single page-

length; others range from 1 to 28 pages. [Many] contain manuscript annotations not recorded elsewhere that offer insight into the delicate process of creating consensus. In many cases, multiple copies bearing manuscript annotations are available to compare and contrast." [Description from website.] These collections include:

o   Extracts of the journals of Congress.

o   Resolutions, proclamations, and committee reports.

o   Treaties.

o   Early printed versions of the United States Constitution and the Declaration of Independence.

♦   Dougherty, Keith L., & Heckelman, Jac C. (2006). A Pivotal Voter from a Pivotal State: Roger Sherman at the Constitutional Convention. *American Political Science Review, 100(2)*, 297-302.

♦   Dube, Ann Marie. (1996). *A Multitude of Amendments, Alterations and Additions.* Washington, DC: National Park Service, *available at* http://www.nps.gov/history/history/online_books/dube/inde1.htm.
    Created by the National Park Service, this work "traces the textual evolution of U.S. founding documents, ·including the Declaration of Independence, the Articles of Confederation, and the Constitution. Evaluates these documents' cultural impact on the lives of 19th and 20th century Americans." [Description from website.]

♦   Finkelman, Paul. (1990). James Madison and the Bill of Rights: A Reluctant Paternity. *Supreme Court Review, 1990*: 301-347.

♦   Greene, F. (1994). Madison's View of Federalism in *The Federalist*. *Publius: The Journal of Federalism, 24(1)*, 47-62.

♦   History Central. *The United States as a New Nation.*
    http://www.historycentral.com//NN
    Contains numerous documents on the history of the United States and the Early Republic, including the *Journal of the Continental Congress.*

♦   Liebman, James S., & Garrett, Brandon L. (2004, May). Madisonian Equal Protection. *Columbia Law Review, 104(4)*, 837-974.

♦   Lutz, Donald. (1992). The State Constitutional Pedigree of the U.S. Bill of Rights. *Publius: The Journal of Federalism, 22(2)*, 19-45.

♦   McHenry, James. (1906). Papers of Dr. James McHenry on the Federal Convention of 1787. *American Historical Review, 11(3)*, 595-624. [Also available in the Library of American Civilization, LAC 40119.]

♦   Madison, James. (1787, April). *Notes on the Confederacy.* Harrisonburg, VA: James Madison Center, James Madison University, *available at* http://www.jmu.edu/madison/gpos225-madison2/constitution.htm.

♦ Marshall, Terence E. (1998). The Constitutional Purpose of the Bill of Rights, *Review of Politics, 60(1)*, 171.

♦ Pierce, William. (1898, January). Notes of Major William Pierce on the Federal Convention of 1787. *American Historical Review, 3(2)*, 310-334.

♦ *Policies and Problems of the Confederation Government*
http://memory.loc.gov/ammem/ndlpedu/features/timeline/newnatn/confed/confed.html
Part of the Library of Congress American Memory website. "Provides an overview of the Confederation Government and links to related documents." [Description from website.]

♦ Prindle, David. (2004, September). The Invisible Hand of James Madison. *Constitutional Political Economy, 15(3)*, 223-237.

♦ Rakove, Jack N. (1992, Fall). James Madison and the Bill of Rights: A Broader Context. *Presidential Studies Quarterly, 22(4)*, 667-677.

♦ Robertson, David Brian. (2005, June). Madison's Opponents and Constitutional Design. *American Political Science Review, 99(2)*, 225-243.

♦ Schofield, Norman. (2002). Evolution of the Constitution *British Journal of Political Science, 31(2)*, 1-20.

♦ Slonim, Shlomo. (2000). Securing States' Interests at the 1787 Constitutional Convention: A Reassessment. *Studies in American Political Development, 14(1)*, 1-19.

♦ Sorenson, Leonard R. (1992). Madison on the Meaning of the "General Welfare," the "Purpose" of Enumerated Powers, and the "Definition" of Constitutional Government. *Publius: The Journal of Federalism, 22(2)*, 109-121.

♦ Sorenson, Leonard R. (1995). Madison on the "General Welfare" of America: His Consistent Constitutional Vision. Lanham, MD: Rowman & Littlefield.

♦ Squire, Peverill. (2005). The Evolution of American Colonial Assemblies as Legislative Organizations. *Congress & the Presidency, 32(2)*, 109-131.

♦ Squire, Peverill. (2006). Historical Evolutions of Legislatures in the United States. *Annual Review of Political Science, 9*, 19-44.

♦ Taylor, Quentin P. (2002). Publius and Persuasion: Rhetorical Readings of the *Federalist Papers. Political Science Reviewer, 31*, 236-282.

♦ Weber, Paul J. (1988, Spring). Madison's Opposition to a Second Convention. *Polity, 20(3)*, 498-517.

♦   Zuckert, Michael P. (1992). Completing the Constitution: The Fourteenth Amend-
      ment and Constitutional rights. *Publius: The Journal of Federalism, 22(2)*, 69-91.

E. Dissertations and Theses on the Constitution and Articles of Confederation

Doctoral dissertations and Master's theses are two of the most under-used
sources of information. Yet many times dissertations contain or analyze primary
sources. These are tremendous resources that should be consulted by serious
researchers. Dissertations and theses may be ordered from ProQuest using the
publication numbers listed below. Some of these items may also be available in
ProQuest's *Dissertations & Theses Full Text* database.

♦   Aranda, Ted. (2009). *Democracy and Revolution: The Athenian Political System
      and the Anglo-American Constitutional Struggle* (unpublished Ph.D. dissertation,
      University of Illinois at Chicago) (available from ProQuest Dissertations & Theses,
      Publication No. AAT 3327393).

♦   Bintz, Irene Clare. (1989). *Foreign Trade and the Emergence of American National-
      ism* (unpublished Ph.D. dissertation, Wayne State University) (available from Pro-
      Quest Dissertations & Theses, Publication No. AAT 9022374).

♦   Bonn, Franklyn George, Jr. (1964). *The Idea of Political Party in the Thought of
      Thomas Jefferson and James Madison* (unpublished Ph.D. dissertation, University of
      Minnesota) (available from ProQuest Dissertations & Theses, Publication No. AAT
      6507832).

♦   Cahill, Edward Charles. (2001). *The Republican imagination: Aesthetics, Literary
      Form, and American National Formation* (unpublished Ph.D. dissertation, Rutgers –
      The State University of New Jersey) (available from ProQuest Dissertations & The-
      ses, Publication No. AAT 3038360).

♦   Constantinescu, Maria. (2009). *A Humean Reading of the American Constitution*
      (unpublished Ph.D. dissertation, New York University) (available from ProQuest
      Dissertations & Theses, Publication No. AAT 3380178).

♦   Curry, Thomas John. (1983). *The First Freedoms: The Development of the Concepts
      of Freedom of Religion and Establishment of Religion in America From the Early
      Settlements to the Passage of the First Amendment to the Constitution* (unpublished
      Ph.D. dissertation, Claremont Graduate University) (available from ProQuest Dis-
      sertations & Theses, Publication No. AAT 8321047).

♦   Dougherty, Keith L. (1997). *Collective Action under the Articles of Confederation:
      The Impact of Institutional Design on the Provision of Public Goods* (unpublished
      Ph.D. dissertation, University of Maryland – College Park) (available from ProQuest
      Dissertations & Theses, publication No. AAT 9736552).

◆   Downes, Paul Bernard. (1996). *The Spell of Democracy: Literature and Politics in the Post-Revolutionary United States* (unpublished Ph.D. dissertation, Cornell University) (available from ProQuest Dissertations & Theses, Publication No. AAT 9637470).

◆   Duncan, Christopher Mark. (1992). *Men of a Different Faith: The Anti-Federalists and the Idea of Public Happiness in Early American Political Thought* (unpublished Ph.D. dissertation, Wayne State University) (available from ProQuest Dissertations & Theses, Publication No. AAT 9310645).

◆   Evans, Michael C. (2009). *The Republic and Its Problems: Alexander Hamilton and James Madison on the 18th Century Critique of Republics* (unpublished Ph.D. dissertation, University of Maryland – College Park) (available from ProQuest Dissertations & Theses, Publication No. AAT 3372842).

◆   Faber, Michael J. (2008). *Founding Expectations: American Politics and the Debate over the Constitution* (unpublished Ph.D. dissertation, Indiana University) (available from ProQuest Dissertations & Theses, Publication No. AAT 3337245).

◆   Farley, Brett Anthony. (2001). *American Federalism: Lockean Majoritarianism or Madisonian Republicanism* (unpublished M.P.P. thesis, Regent University) (available from ProQuest Dissertations & Theses, Publication No. AAT 1413957).

◆   Felt, Florence Agnes. (1914). *Formation of the Articles of Confederation* (unpublished A.M. thesis, University of Chicago) (available from ProQuest Dissertations & Theses, Publication No. AAT TM21189).

◆   Frazer, Gregg L. (2004). *The Political Theology of the American Founding* (unpublished Ph.D. dissertation, Claremont Graduate University) (Publication No. AAT 3103770).

◆   Greer, David Alan. (2007). *Revolutionary—Federalist—Republican: The early life and reputations of William Hull* (unpublished Ph.D. dissertation, Texas Christian University) (available from ProQuest Dissertations & Theses, Publication No. AAT 3284079).

◆   Guerra, Darren P. (2005). *Article V: The Federal Amending Process and American Constitutionalism* (unpublished Ph.D. dissertation, Claremont Graduate University) (available from ProQuest Dissertations & Theses, Publication No. AAT 3192280).

◆   Hammons, Christopher Wade. (1997). *Madison's Theory of Constitutional Design: An Empirical Analysis* (unpublished Ph.D. dissertation, University of Houston) (available from ProQuest Dissertations & Theses, Publication No. AAT 9835728).

◆   Haynes, David Lee. (2008). *Our Government's Attenuation of the Fourth Amendment.* (unpublished D.A. dissertation, Idaho State University) (available from ProQuest Dissertations & Theses, Publication No. AAT 3322827).

♦ Horpedahl, Jeremy M. (2009). *The Growth of Government and Democracy in America, 1790-1860: Theory and History From an Economic Perspective* (unpublished Ph.D. dissertation, George Mason University) (available from ProQuest Dissertations & Theses, Publication No. AAT 3367069).

♦ Humphreys, Brooks. (2009). *The Missing Founding Fathers: The Need to Teach the Role of the Antifederalists in the Adoption of the Bill Of Rights* (unpublished M.A. thesis, Creighton University) (available from ProQuest Dissertations & Theses, Publication No. AAT 1474122).

♦ Iggulden, Emily. (2008). *The "Loyalist Problem" in the Early Republic: Naturalization, Navigation and the Cultural Solution, 1783-1850* (unpublished M.A. thesis, University of New Hampshire) (available from ProQuest Dissertations & Theses, Publication No. AAT 1459498).

♦ Jensen, Merrill M. (1935). *The Articles of Confederation* (unpublished Ph.D. dissertation, University of Wisconsin–Madison) (available from ProQuest Dissertations & Theses, Publication No. AAT 0112895).

♦ Kabala, James Stanley. (2008). *A Christian Nation? Church-State Relations in the Early American Republic, 1787-1846* (unpublished Ph.D. dissertation, Brown University) (available from ProQuest Dissertations & Theses, Publication No. AAT 3318336).

♦ Kasper, Eric T. (2007). *The Enjoyment of Life and Liberty: James Madison's Liberal Design for the Bill of Rights* (Unpublished Ph.D. dissertation, University of Wisconsin–Madison) (available from ProQuest Dissertations & Theses, Publication No. AAT 3261364).

♦ Kester, Scott. (2006). *Republican Hope with Auxiliary Precautions: James Madison's Vision and the United States Constitution* (unpublished Ph.D. dissertation, Lehigh University) (available from ProQuest Dissertations & Theses, Publication No. AAT 3215842).

♦ Kirkham, David M. (1989). *"Inflamed with study": Eighteenth Century Higher Education and the Formation of the American Constitutional Mind* (unpublished Ph.D. dissertation, George Washington University) (available from ProQuest Dissertations & Theses, Publication No. AAT 9009216).

♦ Kleinerman, Benjamin A. (2004). *The Place of Executive Power in the American Constitutional Republic* (unpublished Ph.D. dissertation, Michigan State University) (available from ProQuest Dissertations & Theses, Publication No. AAT 3146053).

♦ LaCroix, Alison Leigh. (2007). *A Well-Constructed Union: An Intellectual History of American-Federalism, 1754-1800* (unpublished Ph.D. dissertation, Harvard University) (available from ProQuest Dissertations & Theses, Publication No. AAT 3251290).

♦ Landi, Alexander R. (1973). *The Politics of James Madison* (unpublished Ph.D. dissertation, University of Dallas) (available from ProQuest Dissertations & Theses, Publication No. AAT 7418752).

♦ Lang, Daniel George. (1983). *The Law of Nations and the Balance of Power: The Influence of European Thought on the Founding Fathers* (unpublished Ph.D. dissertation, University of Virginia) (available from ProQuest Dissertations & Theses, Publication No. AAT 8402870).

♦ Lubert, Howard Leslie. (1999). *The Creation of American Federalism, 1765-1787* (unpublished Ph.D. dissertation, Duke University) (available from ProQuest Dissertations & Theses, Publication No. AAT 9928843).

♦ Madden, David P. (2007). *The Origins of the Eleventh Amendment* (unpublished M.A. thesis, University of Missouri–Kansas City) (available from ProQuest Dissertations & Theses, Publication No. AAT 1442054).

♦ Matthews, Marty Dale. (2001). *Charles Pinckney: A Forgotten Founder* (unpublished Ph.D. dissertation, University of South Carolina) (available from ProQuest Dissertations & Theses, Publication No. AAT 3036220).

♦ Mercieca, Jennifer Rose. (2003). *"We the People" and the Rhetorics of Republicanism in America, 1776-1845* (unpublished Ph.D. dissertation, University of Illinois at Urbana-Champaign) (available from ProQuest Dissertations & Theses, Publication No. AAT 3086138).

♦ Mogg, Jennifer A. (2006). *America's False Dichotomy: Sovereignty and the Federal/National Distinction at the Constitutional Convention of 1787* (unpublished Ph.D. dissertation, University of Houston) (available from ProQuest Dissertations & Theses, Publication No. AAT 3242258).

♦ Natelson, Robert G. (2010). *The Original Constitution: What It Actually Said and Meant.* CreateSpace (Print on Demand).

♦ Nedelsky, Jennifer Ruth. (1977). *Property and the Framers of the United States Constitution: A Study of the Political Thought of James Madison, Gouverneur Morris, and James Wilson* (unpublished Ph.D. dissertation, University of Chicago) (available from ProQuest Dissertations & Theses, Publication No. AAT T-26294).

♦ Olson, Gary Duane. (1968). *Between Independence and Constitution: The Articles of Confederation, 1783-1787* (unpublished Ph.D. dissertation, University of Nebraska–Lincoln) (available from ProQuest Dissertations & Theses, Publication No. AAT 6909639).

♦ Padula, Guy R. (1999). *Madison v. Marshall: Constitutional Theory and the Original Intent Debate* (unpublished Ph.D. dissertation, City University of New York) (available from ProQuest Dissertations & Theses, Publication No. AAT 9946208).

◆ Pfister, Jude M. (2007). *Constitutional Development in the United States Supreme Court During the 1790s* (unpublished D.Litt. dissertation, Drew University) (available from ProQuest Dissertations & Theses, Publication No. AAT 3284516).

◆ Povolish-Boudet, Angela M. (2008). *Establishment Clause Myths: Unveiling the Rhetoric of Original Intent* (unpublished Ph.D. dissertation, Southern Illinois University at Carbondale) (available from ProQuest Dissertations & Theses, Publication No. AAT 3311002).

◆ Prince, Charles Orbray. (2002). *The Meaning and Purpose of the Ninth Amendment to the United States Constitution* (unpublished D.A. dissertation, Idaho State University) (available from ProQuest Dissertations & Theses, Publication No. AAT 3042256).

◆ Rao, Gautham. (2008). *The Creation of the American State: Customhouses, Law, and Commerce in the Age of Revolution* (unpublished Ph.D. dissertation, University of Chicago) (available from ProQuest Dissertations & Theses, Publication No. AAT 3338505).

◆ Richard, Carl J. (1988). *The Founding Fathers and the Classics* (unpublished Ph.D. dissertation, Vanderbilt University) (available from ProQuest Dissertations & Theses, Publication No. AAT 8910868).

◆ Rudolph, Alonna. (2005). *A Student's Guide to the Constitution* (unpublished M.A. thesis, State University of New York Empire State College) (available from ProQuest Dissertations & Theses, Publication No. AAT 1425568).

◆ Sanders, Stefanie. (2005). *The Gene Pool of Pragmatism: Pragmatic Philosophy in the Federalist Papers* (unpublished M.A. thesis, California State University) (available from ProQuest Dissertations & Theses, Publication No. AAT 1428797).

◆ Schenker, Jeffrey. (2004). *James Madison: Consistent Defender of Republican Values* (unpublished D.Litt. dissertation, Drew University) (available from ProQuest Dissertations & Theses, Publication No. AAT 3146385).

◆ Shaw, Stephen Kent. (1986). *The Ninth Amendment: Preservation of the Constitutional Mind* (unpublished Ph.D. dissertation, University of Oklahoma) (available from ProQuest Dissertations & Theses, Publication No. AAT 8609827).

◆ Siegel, Neil Scott. (2001). *Intransitivities Protect Minorities: Interpreting Madison's Theory of the Extended Republic* (unpublished Ph.D. dissertation, University of California – Berkeley) (available from ProQuest Dissertations & Theses, Publication No. AAT 3019806).

◆ Slauter, Thomas Eric. (2000). *The State as a Work of Art: Politics and the Cultural Origins of the Constitution* (unpublished Ph.D. dissertation, Stanford University) (available from ProQuest Dissertations & Theses, Publication No. AAT 9995285).

♦ Span, Henry A. (1998). *Protecting Property from Democracy: Rights, Fairness, Utility, and the "Takings" Clause* (unpublished Ph.D. dissertation, University of California – Berkeley) (available from ProQuest Dissertations & Theses, Publication No. AAT 9902239).

♦ Stephens, Frank Fletcher. (1907). *The Transition from the Government Under the Articles of Confederation to That Under the Constitution* (unpublished Ph.D. dissertation, University of Pennsylvania) (available from ProQuest Dissertations & Theses, Publication No. AAT 0255672).

♦ Trees, Andrew Spencer. (1999). *"A Character to Establish": Personal and National Identity in the New American Nation* (unpublished Ph.D. dissertation, University of Virginia) (available from ProQuest Dissertations & Theses, Publication No. AAT 9948507).

♦ Uzzell, Lynn Elizabeth. (2008). *Because Men Are Not Angels: The Understanding of Human Nature Informing the United States Constitution* (unpublished Ph.D. dissertation, University of Dallas) (available from ProQuest Dissertations & Theses, Publication No. AAT 3312625).

♦ Vandemark, Rebecca Ann. (2005). *The Pastoral Influence on the Rhetoric of the Constitution for the Past and for Today* (unpublished M.P.A. thesis, Regent University) (available from ProQuest Dissertations & Theses, Publication No. AAT 1429519).

♦ Whitten, Dolphus. (1961). *The State Delegations in the Philadelphia Convention of 1787* (unpublished Ph.D. dissertation, University of Texas) (available from ProQuest Dissertations & Theses, Publication No. AAT 6104726).

♦ Zummo, Paul. (2008). *Thomas Jefferson's America: Democracy, Progress, and the Quest for Perfection* (unpublished Ph.D. dissertation, Catholic University of America) (available from ProQuest Dissertations & Theses, Publication No. AAT 3348469).

Notes

1. Lewis M. Hacker, *The Shaping of the American Tradition*. 210 (New York: Columbia University Press, 1947).
2. National Park Service, *Vermont Regional History*, National Register of Historic Places (2009), *available at* http://www.cr.nps.gov/nr/travel/centralvermont/vhistory1.htm.
3. *id.*
4. Hacker at 210.
5. Hacker at 210. See also, *The Articles of Confederation*, Ben's Guide for Kids to the U.S. Government (Last modified February 26, 2003), *available at* http://bensguide.gpo.gov/9-2/documents/articles.
6. *id.*
7. Articles of Confederation, Article II, *available at* http://www.yale.edu/lawweb/avalon/artconf.htm.
8. Articles of Confederation, Article III.
9. Hacker at 211.
10. The term "Chaos Clause" was used by historian Irving Brant in his four-volume biography of James Madison. Irving Brant, *James Madison* (Indianapolis: Bobbs-Merrill, 1941).
11. Brant at 105.
12. *id.*
13. *id.*
14. *id.*
15. *id.* at 107.
16. *id.* at 105.
17. National Park Service, *Vermont Regional History.*
18. "At this time, the Western borders of Kentucky and Tennessee were the Tennessee River rather than the Mississippi as they are now. This land was owned by the Chickasaw Indians, but was purchased by the U.S. in an 1818 treaty negotiated by the Revolutionary War hero Isaac Shelby and General Andrew Jackson. However, this land was treated for all practical purposes as if it was U.S. territory." *Jackson Purchase*, University of Tennessee at Martin, *excerpt* from The Kentucky Encyclopedia [ed. John E. Kleber] (Lexington, KY: University Press of Kentucky, 1992), *available at* http://www.utm.edu/departments/acadpro/library/departments/special_collections/wc_hist/jackpur.htm.
19. 2 Brant at 156.
20. *id.* at 156-157.
21. *Continental bank note*, HistoryWired, *available at* http://historywired.si.edu/object.cfm?ID=437.
22. Ada Lou Carson, *Thomas Pickman Tyler's "Memoirs of Royall Tyler": An Annotated Edition* (1985) at 32 (unpublished Ph.D. dissertation, University of Minnesota) (available from ProQuest Dissertations & Theses, Publication No. AAT 8526403).
23. Royall Tyler (1757-1826) was an important person in the field of law. He was also known as a playwright and novelist. He was appointed to the Supreme Court of Vermont in 1801, and was Chief Justice from 1807 to 1814. He also taught Jurisprudence at the University of Vermont from 1811 to 1814. Tyler was also the author of *Reports of Cases Determined and Argued in the Supreme Court of Judicature of the State of Ver-*

mont (1800-1810, 2 volumes). Known as "Tyler's Reports," the Bluebook citation is "Tyl." The full text of Tyler's Reports is available on *Google Books*.

Tyler was also an important playwright and literary figure. His play *The Contrast*, which was the first professionally produced play in the United States, was staged in Philadelphia in 1787 during the time of the Constitutional Convention. *See*, Carson; *See also*, Ada Lou Carson and Herbert L. Carson, *Royall Tyler* (Boston: Twayne Publishers, 1979); Paul P. Reuben, *Royall Tyler*, PAL: Perspectives in American Literature—A Research and Reference Guide, *available at* http://web.csustan.edu/english/reuben/pal/chap8/tyler.html.

24. Carson at 34.

25. Carson at 39.

26. Jack Rakove, *The Legacy of the Articles of Confederation*, 12 Publius: The Journal of Federalism 45, 53 (Autumn, 1982).

27. 2 Brant at 381-382.

28. *id.* at 381.

29. *id.* at 383-385.

30. The garbage can is part of *organized anarchy theory*, which was first proposed in 1972 by Cohen, March, & Olsen to help explain decision making in the administration of higher education. Michael D. Cohen, James G. March, J., & Johan P. Olsen, *A garbage can model of organizational choice*, 17 Administrative Science Quarterly 1 (March, 1972). According to the theory of an organized anarchy, the goals or objectives are problematic; there is disagreement over what the goals are or how they are defined. "It can be described better as a loose collection of ideas than as a coherent structure." *id.* at 1. The technology and processes by which these goals are obtained is unclear; "its own processes are not understood by its members." *id.* Finally, participation within the system is fluid, and changes over time. *See*, Robert Birnbaum, *How Colleges Work: The Cybernetics of Academic Organization and Leadership*, San Francisco: Jossey-Bass, 1988 at 154). In a bureaucracy, lines of communication and authority are tightly coupled and can be found on an organization chart. However, an organized anarchy is more of a loosely coupled system. Each part of the anarchy flows in streams "through an organization as the Gulf Stream flows through the Atlantic Ocean." Birnbaum at 159-160. Within the organization, several types of streams flow independently, namely problems, solutions, and participants. These streams are accompanied by decision points at which the participants must make a policy determination. *id.* at 161.

The model of higher education decision-making proposed by Cohen, March, & Olsen involves placing the problems, solutions, and participants together inside a garbage can. As the can is shaken, problems and solutions stick together and in turn stick to participants. "In the garbage can, it is possible for almost any problem, any solution, and any participant to become tightly coupled with any decision, and it is often impossible to predict with any degree of accuracy which it will be. . . . What becomes tightly or loosely coupled in this symbolic system is related to a mixture of collegial interactions, bureaucratic structures, ongoing coalitions, chance, and cognitive processes by which people make inferences and judgments under conditions of uncertainty." Birnbaum at 164-165.

31. Birnbaum.

32. Michael D. Cohen, James G. March, J., & Johan P. Olsen, Leadership in an organized anarchy, *in ASHE Reader on Organization snd Governance in Higher Education* (Lexington, MA: Ginn, 1986), 399 at 406.

33. *id.* at 408.

34. John Kingdon, Agendas, Alternatives, and Public Policies, Boston: Little Brown (1984).

35. Kingdon's variation on the garbage can, *Multiple Streams Theory*, involved characterizing the Federal government as an organized anarchy. (Indeed, we know from the problems with Brant's "Chaos Clause" that the government under the Articles of Confederation was barely organized, and was almost a complete anarchy.) In this theory, the preferences of the public are problematic, the means to attain them are unclear, and there is fluid participation due to changing committee memberships, varying interest, and the cycle of elections. Three separate streams consisting of problems, policies (solutions), and politics are constantly flowing through the government. The streams "flow through the governmental system largely independent of one another and each according to its own unique set of internal dynamics and rules. The *problem stream* consists of those conditions which policymakers have chosen to interpret as problems." Problems are developed "(1) through systematic indicators; (2) dramatic events; and, (3) feedback based on programs, citizen input, and previous experience." Eric C. Ness, Deciding Who Earns HOPE, PROMISE, and SUCCESS: Toward a Comprehensive Model of the Merit Aid and Eligibility Policy Process *at* 18, [Unpublished Doctoral dissertation] Department of Leadership, Policy, & Organizations, Vanderbilt University (2006).

"The *policy stream* consists of the various ideas and "solutions" developed by specialists in many different policy communities. The *politics stream* consists of changes or developments involving the national mood, interest group politics, and administrative or legislative turnover." [Emphasis in original.] Michael K. McLendon, *State governance reform of higher education: Patterns, trends, and theories of the public policy process*, 17 Higher Education: Handbook of Theory and Research, 57, 102-103.

The way in which the public views issues is always relevant to an elected official, and public opinion does have a valid place in policy analysis. Similarly, organized interest groups generally have some consensus and some conflicts. Kingdon at 157. And turnover of officials causes shifts in policy, as happened when Republicans took the House in 1994 and 2010, or when President Barak Obama was elected in 2008.

When the three independent streams converge, a *window of opportunity* may open, allowing a *policy entrepreneur* the opportunity to put policies and solutions together, "a brief moment in time to push attention to their pet problems or to push their pet solutions. However, because there is only loose coupling among the streams of activity, there is much variability in the ways in which *particular* problems, solutions, and political conditions become linked with one another." [Emphasis in original.] McLendon at 103. In Kingdon's model, "windows emerge in either the problem or political stream and thereby lead to participants coupling with the policy stream for alternatives or solutions." Ness at 19. Zahariadas revised the theory stating that "unlike problem windows, which he agrees leads to coupling with the policy stream, political windows lead to the reverse—coupling with the problem stream upon which to apply an existing solution." Ness at 19.

36. Leadership in an organized anarchy at 408-409.

37. 2 Brant at 386-387.

38. *id.* at 387.

39. Catherine Drinker Bowen, Miracle at Philadelphia: The Story of the Constitutional Convention, May to September. Boston: Little, Brown (1986).

40. 2 Brant at 392.

41. James Madison, *Views of the political system of the United States*, *in* Louis M. Hacker & H. S. Zahler, (Eds.), The Shaping of the American Tradition, New York: Co-

lumbia University Press (1947) at 212.

42. Hacker at 212-215.

43. Madison at 212-215.

44. Edward McNall Burns, James Madison: Philosopher of the Constitution, New York: Octagon Books (1968) at 9.

45. 3 Brant at 19.

46. *id.* at 24-25.

47. *id.* at 25.

48. *id.* at 32-33.

49. *id.* at 36.

50. *id.* at 73.

51. *id.* at 73-74.

52. Historical Note at XIV.

53. U.S. Constitution, Article V.

54. 3 Brant at 134.

55. *id.* at 136.

56. *id.* at 146.

57. *id.*

58. James McGregor Burns, Leadership, New York: Harper & Row (1978) at 155.

59. J. M. Burns at 155-156.

60. *id.*

61. James Madison, The Constitutional Convention: A Narrative History, from the notes of James Madison, ed. Edward J. Larson & Michael Winship, New York. Modern Library (2005) at 763.

62. Brant at 154-158.

63. Historical Note at XVIII.

64. *Comments of James Wilson,* The Debates in the Federal Convention of 1787 (Notes of James Madison), (June 16, 1787), *available at* http://elsinore.cis.yale.edu/lawweb/avalon/debates/616.htm.

65. James McGregor Burns & L. Martin Overby, Cobblestone leadership: Majority rule, minority power, Norman, OK: University of Oklahoma Press (1990) at 8.

66. *id.* at 20.

67. *id.* at 21.

68. U.S. Constitution, Amendment XXVIII.

69. Amendments to the Constitution at 44.

70. *id.*

71. *id.*

72. *id.*

73. *id.*

74. *See generally, 1789 Pay Raise Amendment Returns to Haunt Congress,* 50 Congressional Quarterly Weekly Report 1230 (1992); *James Madison Gets His Way as Congress Ducks Issue: Leaders Reluctantly Ignore 203-Year Time Period in Ratifying 27th Amendment on Pay Raises,* 50 Congressional Quarterly Weekly Report 1323 (1992); *Both Chambers Rush to Accept 27th Amendment on Salaries,* 50 Congressional Quarterly Weekly Report 1423 (1992).

75. The company website is http://www.indususa.com.

76. This description came from a San Francisco State University Library research guide entitled "History Research: Library of American Civilization," *available at*

http://www.library.sfsu.edu/research/guides/lac.html.

77. The Microbook Library of American Civilization (Chicago: Library Resources, 1971-72).

78. Terry Ballard, Library of American Civilization titles available free on the Web. Hamden, CT: Quinnipiac University, *available at* http://www.quinnipiac.edu/x1849.xml.

79. Charles Evans, American Bibliography: A Chronological Dictionary of All Books, Pamphlets, and Periodical Publications Printed in the United States of America from the Genesis of Printing in 1639 Down To and Including the Year 1820 (P. Smith, 1941-1959).

80. Early American imprints, 1639-1800 [microform], (American Antiquarian Society, 1984); *available on* opaque microcard.

81. Rodger P. Bristol, *Supplement* to Charles Evans' American bibliography (University Press of Virginia, 1970).

82. Ralph R. Shaw and Richard H. Shoemaker, American bibliography, a preliminary checklist for 1801-1819 (Scarecrow Press, 1958-1966).

83. The company website is http://www.newsbank.com/Readex/index.cfm.

2

Finding Legal Materials:
The U.S. System of Law and Government

The legal system in the United States is a complicated and complex mishmash of different entities, jurisdictions, and governmental bodies. What is legal in one jurisdiction is illegal in another. This apparently disconnected structure tends to confuse and frighten people. However, the legal system is in fact fairly logical, once you learn how it works. The different branches of government don't just produce overlapping laws; rather, each part of the government produces a unique type of law. There are well-defined relationships between the federal government and the state governments and between each jurisdiction's governmental branches. These relationships help to make sense of our legal system.

This chapter will provide a basic overview of our legal system. I will discuss how to read a legal citation. The chapter will also include a bibliography of books, websites, and online databases for starting legal research.

As we all know, the basic structure of our government is made up of three branches—legislative, executive, and judicial. The legislative branch includes the Congress in Washington, D.C., and the state legislature in each state. The executive branch consists of administrative agencies, such as the U.S. Department of Labor or the state Departments of Transportation, as well as independent boards and agencies such as the Institute for Museum and Library Services (IMLS). The judicial branch consists of all of the courts that hear cases. Each branch produces its own type of law. The legislative branch produces *statutes*, the executive branch produces *administrative regulations*, and the judicial branch produces *case law*.

In addition to the three branches of government, we also have the system known as *Federalism*. Each state or territory has its own sovereign government. Each state decides how to apply its laws, subject only to the state constitution, the U.S. Constitution, and a very narrow band of laws that are passed by Congress. However, as we discuss the structure of the government, keep in mind that there are many similarities between the federal and state legal systems. Each branch of government (and the type of law the branch produces) is analogous.

How to Read a Legal Citation[1]

Like any other subject area, the ability to conduct legal research is dependent upon good references and good citations. The basic building block of legal citation is *A Uniform System of Citation*, also known as the *Harvard Bluebook*.[2] The *Bluebook*—compiled by the editors of the *Columbia Law Review, Harvard Law*

45

Review, University of Pennsylvania Law Review, and *Yale Law Review*—has
been published since 1926.

Many of the main style formats, such as the *American Psychological Association* (APA) and *Modern Language Association* (MLA) handbooks, refer users
to the *Bluebook* for legal citations. The *Chicago Manual of Style* also suggests
that writers consult the *Bluebook* when citing legal materials. When it comes to
non-legal materials, however, the *Bluebook* style is vastly different from any of
the other style guides. As a result, annotations for books, articles, and websites
found in the text are cited in the APA format, while materials in the endnotes are
in *Bluebook* format. For more information on this issue, see the introduction for
A Note on Citation Formats.

The basic foundation of the legal citation is the abbreviation. Each of the
standard legal research series has a standardized abbreviation. For example, the
United States Reports (the official publication which contains cases from the
U.S. Supreme Court) is always designated as *U.S.*

Cases and statutes are often published in more than one location. When that
happens, the official publication put out by the government is always listed first.
Privately published series are listed *after* the official publication information. It
is not considered improper to give a citation to the official set, even if you have
used an unofficial version. In fact, it is recommended. Since the text of the case,
statute, or regulation is always the same in each version, you should provide the
citation to the official source. Citing the unofficial sources is optional.

Whenever you see a legal citation, the number before the abbreviation is the
volume number, and the number after the abbreviation is the page number. A
legal citation may look like the following:

> United States v. American Library Association, 539 U.S. 194; 123 S. Ct. 2297;
> 156 L. Ed. 2d 221; 2003 U.S. LEXIS 4799; 71 U.S.L.W. 4465 (2003), *avail-
> able at* http://laws.findlaw.com/us/000/02-361.html.

There are various different parts to this citation. However, each part will
always be consistent. Once you learn the different parts, you should be able to
interpret all types of legal citations. This citation breaks down as follows:

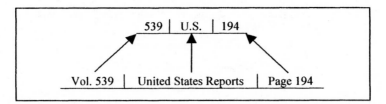

After the case name (United States v. American Library Association), the
first citation is to the official publication. In volume 539 of the *United States*

Reports, the case will begin on page 194. The other citations that follow are privately published series that also include this case:

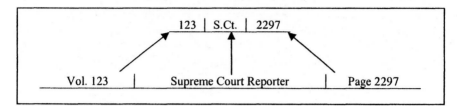

The *Supreme Court Reporter* is published by West Group, and contains the full text of all Supreme Court opinions. This series also contains a number of editorial enhancements, including a classification system (similar to the Library of Congress Classification System) for legal principles found in each case. Similarly, LexisNexis publishes the *United States Supreme Court Reports, Lawyer's Edition*, which also contains the full text of the Supreme Court opinion and editorial enhancements. The *Lawyer's Edition* began re-numbering the volumes again in a second series, hence the 2d in the citation.

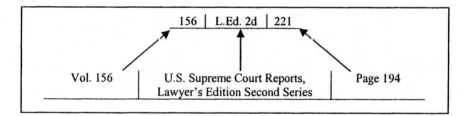

Many researchers find the *Lawyer's Edition* to be useful because it provides cross-references to other research tools—such as the U.S. Code Service (U.S.C.S.)—which are also published by LexisNexis. These cross-references are very helpful.

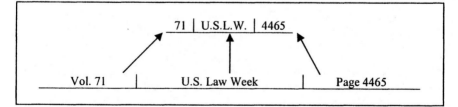

Published weekly, the *U.S. Law Week* contains the full text of cases from federal courts, state courts, and administrative agencies. The editors publish all U.S. Supreme Court cases, as well as cases from other courts that "establish new precedents, address new statutes, contribute to emerging legal doctrines, tackle current controversies, or [cause] splits in the Circuits."[3]

The citation example of United States v. American Library Association also contains some references to fee-based electronic products. The premier databases for legal research are LexisNexis and Westlaw, although other fee-based services (such as Loislaw and Versuslaw) can be used. In the citation for United States v. American Library Association used earlier, *2003 U.S. LEXIS 4799* refers to the LexisNexis database. The listed website, which is part of a comprehensive free legal research site called Findlaw, also contains the full text of this case.

Like LexisNexis, Westlaw also has a unique identifier number for cases. The Westlaw citation for the United States v. American Library Association case is *2003 WL 21433656*. Westlaw's current policy is to remove the WL number once the official citation (to the *U.S. Reports*) is available. However, if you find an item that still has the WL number, you can enter that number into the database and retrieve the case.

Statute citations are also very important. To illustrate how a statute citation is created, I will use the Library Services and Technology Act as an example. The name "Library Services and Technology Act" is called the *Popular Name* because this is how the statute is referred to in general terms. The popular name is not actually part of the official statute citation. Official statute citations only provide finding information, not the name of the act. However, you will often see the popular name added to the official citation in order to enhance understanding. The entire statute (as passed by Congress) is cited as follows:

The Library Services and Technology Act, P.L. 104-208

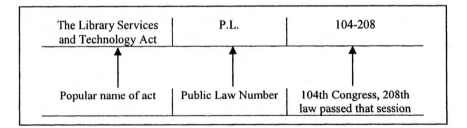

The Library Services and Technology Act	P.L.	104-208
Popular name of act	Public Law Number	104th Congress, 208th law passed that session

The next example contains the same statute after it has been codified. (Codification puts the sections of the law together with other laws on the same subject.) The citation contains the symbol § (like a double letter S). In legal citations, the symbol § means "section number." A citation containing multiple section numbers is often shown by using §§. In addition, if a statute includes multiple code sections in a row, legal citations often use the phrase *et seq.* after the initial section number. (*et seq.* may or may not be italicized, but it is always written in lowercase letters). Finally, the volume numbers for codes are often called "Titles." For example, copyright law is contained in Title 17 of the *U.S. Code*. Here is an illustration of the proper citation for a statute:

The Library Services and Technology Act, 20 U.S.C. § 9121 *et seq.*

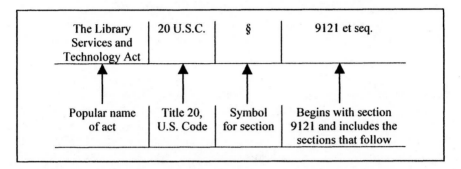

With this information, you should be able to read legal citations. The ability to interpret legal citations will help librarians and archivists find statutes and judicial rulings. Even more important, this skill will translate into better service for our clients.

Starting Legal Research

Just as with any field of research, you have to start somewhere. Researching legal materials tends to overwhelm clients (and sometimes librarians). However, the same principles apply to legal research that you would use to help clients in any other area. As with any topic, start first with subject-specific (in this case legal) encyclopedias and dictionaries. (See section A, General Resources, below.) Once the client has read a general overview of the subject, he or she will have an idea of which terms to use for further research. The legal encyclopedias not only provide an overview, but they also refer readers to appropriate cases, statutes, regulations, law journal articles, and books.

After using legal encyclopedias, the client should find some books or research series on the topic, along with articles in legal and non-legal journals. After that, the client will be able to go online and formulate a proper search with the appropriate terminology.[4]

Remember that the client must do his or her own research. Giving too much assistance can lead to charges of practicing law without a license. (For more information on this topic, see Bryan M. Carson, *The Law of Libraries and Archives*.)[5]

I have listed some of the general resources (both print and online) that clients should use to begin their research. In addition, I have tried to include in my endnotes as many citations to websites as possible in order to provide free resources for librarians and archivists. For more websites with library-related legal information, *see* Bryan M. Carson, (2002, January), Researching the Legal Issues Faced by Librarians, Publishers, and Book Distributors, *Against The Grain, 13(6)*, 63-66.

Documents and Sources on the
U.S. System of Law and Government

A. General Resources

Because of the changing nature of legal books, databases, and websites, it is important for me to include this disclaimer: Inclusion of a website or company in this book does not constitute an endorsement or recommendation. It is merely a listing. "This publication is designed to provide accurate and authoritative information in regard to the subject matter covered. It is sold with the understanding that the publisher is not engaged in rendering legal, accounting, or other professional service. If legal or other expert assistance is required, the services of a competent professional person should be sought."[6]

◆ *Black's Legal Dictionary*
   This work is the most popular single-volume legal dictionary. Some of the definitions give a citation to cases where the legal terms were originally defined.

◆ *Words and Phrases (West Group)*
   This multivolume series contains extended definitions of legal words and their usage. Entries range from one paragraph to several pages. All of the definitions quote cases and give the case citations. It is available online via Westlaw or through a separate subscription.

◆ *American Jurisprudence (Am. Jur.)*
   This legal encyclopedia contains excellent background material. The footnotes include references to cases, statutes, regulations, and law review articles. *American Jurisprudence* is the best legal encyclopedia for the general public. Because the articles are arranged by broad topic, it is necessary to use the index. This series is cited as *Am. Jur.* It is available online via Westlaw or through a separate subscription.

◆ *Corpus Juris Secundum (C.J.S.)*
   This legal encyclopedia is a bit more specialized than *American Jurisprudence*. Because lawyers don't like Latin, the work is usually known by its official citation abbreviation, *C.J.S.* Published by West Group, *C.J.S.* contains cross-references to other works published by West. It is vital to use the index, since articles are arranged by broad topic. It is available online via Westlaw or through a separate subscription.

◆ *American Law Reports (A.L.R.)*
   This series contains articles in the form of annotations about legal topics. The official citation is *A.L.R.* The editorial policy of *A.L.R.* is that each annotation will con-

tain every significant case on the topic. As a result, an *A.L.R.* annotation is extremely useful. The old saying is that once you find an *A.L.R.* annotation on your subject, your research is done. This is almost true, although you do have to check for more recent cases on your topic. It is available online via Westlaw or through a separate subscription.

◆ *Current Index to Legal Periodicals (C.I.L.P.)*
A weekly print service from the University of Washington Law School that indexes the contents of 175 major law reviews, including articles, comments, and case notes. C.L.I.P. is also available on Westlaw, and directly by subscription from the University of Washington.

◆ *Current Law Index (C.L.I.)*
Current Law Index (*C.L.I.*) is a paper index of legal journals that is produced by Information Access Company (IAC). It is the print version of LegalTrac. Articles are indexed using Library of Congress Subject Headings.

◆ *Current Law Journal Content*
http://lawlib.wlu.edu/CLJC
This free service is the newest index to law reviews and legal journals. It is a joint venture between the University of Texas Tarlton Law Library and the Washington & Lee Law School Law Library. The database consists of the Table of Contents (TOC) information from 1,353+ law journals from 2004 to 2011, with work underway to extend the TOCs back to 2000.

CLJC supports the Boolean connectors AND, OR, and NOT. Common fields (journal name, journal code, author, title, within the abstract, and publication date) are available as commands within the search box. Publication year, country of publication, date added, and profile ID are also options on the search screen. Truncation is supported, but not wildcard characters. Stop words are ignored. CLJC also has a citation report that ranks the impact of a particular journal, similar to that used by other services such as Journal Citation Reports.

◆ *Government Periodicals Index* (ProQuest)
This database indexes approximately 170 magazines and newsletters with substantial research value published by U.S. government agencies. Updated quarterly with indexing since 1988.

◆ *Indexes to Foreign Legal Periodicals*
This series indexes articles from over 360 foreign-language legal journals. Entries are in the original languages, with specialized subject, author, geographic, and book review indexes. Ovid has an online version available.

◆ *Index to Legal Periodicals (I.L.P.)*
Published by the H.W. Wilson Company since 1908, this series indexes articles in legal journals, law reviews, and *A.L.R.* annotations. The series also indexes legal newspapers, Bar Association journals, and law-related articles from general publications. The *Index to Legal Periodicals* is available online and in print.

◆ *Index to Periodical Articles Related to Law (I.P.A.R.L.)*
This title indexes law-related articles in social and behavioral sciences journals (including business). The series only indexes titles not included in the *Index to Legal Periodicals, Current Law Index, Index to Foreign Legal Periodicals, Legal Resource Index,* or *LegalTrac.* The series uses Library of Congress subject headings. I.P.A.R.L. is available on HeinOnline from 1958-2006, and may be searched by article title, article creator or author, journal title, and/or Library of Congress subject heading. The interface allows Boolean searching.

◆ *LegalTrac (Gale)*
The LegalTrac database indexes and abstracts 875 major law reviews, legal newspapers, Bar Association journals, as well as law-related articles from over 1,300 business and general publications. Also contains selected full text of around 100 publications. LegalTrac is available online only and does not have a printed counterpart.

◆ Leiter, Richard A. (2007). *National Survey of State Laws.* [6th ed. Revised.] Detroit: Cengage Gale.
"Cited in the majority opinions in three recent Supreme Court cases, the new edition of this lauded reference helps users make quick, state-by-state comparisons of current state laws—how they differ and how they're similar—for a range of relevant subjects. Entries are then referenced to a specific code or statute enabling the reader to access the detailed text of the law elsewhere." [Description from Gale catalog.]

◆ *Martindale-Hubbell Law Directory*
http://www.martindale.com
Published by LexisNexis, this directory lists law firms. It also contains biographical information on lawyers. However, the directory only includes those who return the forms, so it doesn't always include everyone. In recent years, some law firms have dropped *Martindale-Hubbell* because of the prevalence of web directories.

◆ *Martindale-Hubbell Law Digest*
Published by LexisNexis, this multi-volume series contains summaries of the laws of every U.S. state and territory and over 80 countries, along with summaries of international treaties and conventions. The series also contains summaries of uniform laws such as the *Uniform Commercial Code* and the *Uniform Residential Landlord and Tenant Act.* The *Martindale-Hubbell Law Digest* is useful for looking up brief answers. It is also useful for finding the citation to the proper statute. The *Martindale-Hubbell Law Digest* is available as part of the *Martindale-Hubbell Law Directory* series or by itself.

◆ *Restatements of the Law*
The *Restatements* are a series of works that tell users what the law is in a particular field. The *Restatements* are compiled from statutes and case law, and are produced by the American Law Institute. "Restatements are essentially codifications of common law judge-made doctrines that develop gradually over time because of the principle of *stare decisis.* Although Restatements are not binding authority in and of themselves, they are highly persuasive because they are formulated over several years with extensive input from law professors, practicing attorneys, and judges. . . .

[T]hey reflect the consensus of the American legal community as to what the law is (and in some areas, what it should become) . . . Courts are under no formal obligation to adopt Restatement sections as the law. But they often do, because such sections accurately restate the already-established law in that jurisdiction, or on issues of first impression, are persuasive in terms of demonstrating what is the current trend that other jurisdictions are following."[7]

In addition to the materials listed above, I recommend the following books for those who are interested in finding out more about legal research:

♦ Barkan, Steven M., Mersky, Roy M., Dunn, Donald J., et al. (2009). *Fundamentals of Legal Research*. New York: Foundation Press.

♦ Berring, Robert C., & Edinger, Elizabeth A. (2005). *Finding the Law*. St. Paul, MN: Thomson/West.

♦ Dykes, Christopher C. (2010). *Federal Income Tax Law: A Legal Research Guide*. Buffalo, NY: W.S. Hein.

♦ Hansell, R. Stephen, Hinderman, Tammy A., & Rhoades, Sarah J. (2010). *Find It Free and Fast on the Net: Strategies for Legal Research on the Web*. Eau Claire, WI: NBI.

♦ Karlin, Barbara H. (2009). *Tax Research*. Upper Saddle River, NJ: Pearson Education.

♦ Levitt, Carole A., & Rosch, Mark E. (2010). *Find Info Like a Pro*. 2 Vol. Chicago: American Bar Association.
Volume 1 is entitled "Mining the Internet's Publicly Available Resources for Investigative Research," and volume 2 consists of "Mining the Internet's Public Records for Investigative Research."

♦ Nagasankara Rao, Dittakavi, & Fishman, Joel. (2009). *Navigating Legal Research & Technology: Quick Reference Guide to the 1,500 Most Common Questions About Traditional and Online Legal Research*. Getzville, NY: Bridge Publishing Group.

♦ Olson, Kent C., & Cohen, Morris L. (2009). *Principles of Legal Research*. St. Paul, MN: West.

♦ Palfrey, John G. (2010). *Cornerstones of Law Libraries for an Era of Digital-Plus*. Cambridge, MA: Berkman Center for Internet & Society, Harvard Law School.

♦ Raabe, William A., Whittenburg, Gerald E., & Sanders, Debra L. (2009). *Federal Tax Research*. Mason, OH: Thomson/South-Western.

♦ Richmond, Gail Levin. (2010). *Federal Tax Research: Guide to Materials and Techniques*. New York: Foundation Press.

B. Subscription Databases

There are a number of subscription databases for researching law. Some are available to academic libraries, while others are geared more toward lawyers, law schools, or bar associations. Some providers, such as Westlaw and LexisNexis, have separate versions for different markets. While this is not a complete list, it should give a general idea of the big players in the field. Other database providers, particularly those that deal with business or tax information, also license products with legal content. For more information on this topic, I recommend using Mary Rumsey's excellent research guide from Globalex (New York University Hauser Global Law School Program), *A Guide to Fee-Based U.S. Legal Research Databases*, *available at* http://www.nyulawglobal.org/globalex/US_FeeBased_Legal_Databases1.htm.

◆ *Bloomberg Law*
  http://www.bloomberglaw.com
  One of the largest names in business research, *Bloomberg* has only recently expanded into legal research. The service provides over 100 years of case law, plus statutes, regulations, company information, realtime news, court dockets, SEC documents, and alerts for dockets. The materials are browseable by practice area and jurisdiction. The "Points of Law" feature is a summary of legal principles written by *Bloomberg* editors. Practice area law reports are available online or in print. *Bloomberg* has also created its own legal digest and legal citator products. The database supports full Boolean connectors (including proximity connectors), natural language searching, field searching, phrases, date restrictions, and truncation ("stemming"). Results can be sorted in multiple ways, including relevance, chronological, and reverse chronological order.[8]

◆ *BNA (Bureau of National Affairs)*
  http://www.bnai.com
  Provides stand-alone databases in such subject areas as taxation, environmental law, employee benefits, labor law, antitrust (competition), banking, bankruptcy, intellectual property, and media law. Each database contains primary statutes, cases, and regulations, along with editorial analysis. The products are arranged based on BNA loose-leaf publications.

◆ *Casemaker Online Research Library*
  http://www.casemaker.us
  Contains a collection of primary federal and state statutes, regulations, administrative decisions, and court opinions. The database has cases from the U.S. Supreme Court (1754 to present), Federal Court of Appeals decisions (1930 to present), Federal District Court cases (1932 to present), Court of Claims (1997 to present), Court of International Trade (1999 to present), U.S. Tax Court Decisions (1999 to present), and Federal bankruptcy cases (1979 to present). Federal administrative decisions include the Board of Immigration Appeals (1996 to present), Internal Revenue Service Revenue Rulings (1954 to present), and National Transportation Safety Board Decisions (2000 to present). *Casemaker* also includes current editions of the U.S. Code,

Code of Federal Regulations, and Federal Court Rules. State appellate cases are available for all 50 states; while the inception date varies, all states go back at least to 1950. (For example, Ohio goes back to 1893.) All jurisdictions also contain current constitutions, statutes, and regulations, and some state Attorney General opinions, court rules, and administrative opinions are also available. Several states (such as Ohio) include unreported opinions (1981 to 2002). The "authority check" feature is an automated citation "which shows a list of citing cases and the text where the citation occurs." *Casemaker* supports full Boolean connectors (including proximity connectors), natural language searching, field searching, phrases, date restrictions, and truncation ("stemming"). Results can be sorted in multiple ways, including relevance, chronological, and reverse chronological order.

◆ *CCH Intelliconnect*
http://tax.cchgroup.com/intelliconnect-tax-research/default.htm
A large database with federal, state, and international taxation (both individual and corporate), accounting and audit material, and information on financial and estate planning. The database also contains tax news, journals, and newsletters, as well as information on changes in the capital structure of companies, such as name changes, new stock issues, splits, and reverse splits.

◆ *CCH Tax Research NetWork*
http://tax.cchgroup.com/default
This is CCH's comprehensive tax service, and includes both primary and secondary materials on Federal, state, and international tax; financial and estate planning; accounting and audit; and pension and payroll. The product also contains the *Internal Revenue Code,* rulings, and tax treaties. Tax news includes the *Tax Tracker* and *Tax Highlights. Practical Tax Expert* and *Practical Tax Professional* provide editorial guidance and sample calculations. Many of the database products in Tax Research NetWork are also available with separate subscriptions.

◆ *Checkpoint (Thomson RIA)*
http://www.checkpoint.riag.com
RIA Checkpoint offers access to complete tax libraries in federal, state, and local tax, international tax, estate planning, financial reporting and management, pension and benefits, and payroll tax. The database includes court opinions and administrative decisions, current tax news, practice guides, tax statutes and regulations, and *U.S. Tax Treaties in Force.* The database contains the full text of the *Journal of Taxation* and *Journal of Corporate Taxation,* as well as administrative materials from the Internal Revenue Service. Some archival materials date back to 1860.

◆ *Courtport*
http://www.courtport.com
Provides information on civil, criminal, bankruptcy, and other court cases, including docket sheets, filings, rulings, calendars, motions, and related documents. The database contains criminal records, outstanding warrants, and sex offender registries. Other records include corporate and Uniform Commercial Code filings, vital records, trademarks, and property records. Records are available for all federal and state jurisdictions.

♦ *eCode360*
http://www.ecode360.com
This site contains municipal codes from across the country. Code sections can be
browsed by section number, or searched using Boolean keywords.

♦ *EBSCOhost Legal Information Reference Center*
http://www.ebscohost.com/thisTopic.php?marketID=6&topicID=1386
This consumer-oriented database "contains more than 310 full-text publications and
. . . legal forms. Many of the full-text legal reference books are provided through
Nolo. . . ." [Description from website.]

♦ *Fastcase*
http://www.fastcase.com
Contains primary federal and state court opinions. The database includes cases from
the U.S. Supreme Court (1754 to present), Federal Court of Appeals decisions (1924
to present), Federal bankruptcy cases, and Federal District Court cases (1932 to present). State appellate cases are available (1950 to present) for all 50 states. Cases can
be updated using the "authority check," an automated citator which shows a list of
citing cases and the text where the citation occurs. Although Fastcase does not provide statutes or regulations, it does link (and frame) Federal and state statute and
regulation sites. The database supports full Boolean connectors (including proximity
connectors), natural language searching, field searching, phrases, date restrictions,
and truncation ("stemming"). Results can be sorted in multiple ways, including relevance, chronological, and reverse chronological order.

♦ *Gale Legal Forms*
http://www.gale.cengage.com/LegalForms
A database of legal forms aimed at the general public rather than attorneys. The
forms are arranged by state, then by topic. Although created by lawyers, the forms
use plain English whenever possible. [Description from website.]

♦ *HeinOnline*
http://www.heinonline.org
A large historical and archival full-text database. Includes cases from the U.S. Supreme Court (1754 to present), U.S. Attorney General Opinions, English Reports
Full Reprint (1694-1867), and Israel Law Reports (1954-1996; Hebrew). The journal
collection has cover-to-cover full-page images for the complete run of over 1200 legal journals. The *Federal Register* and *Code of Federal Regulations* are available
back to v. 1 (1936 and 1938, respectively), along with U.S. Statutes at Large (1789
to present), the *Congressional Record* (1873 to present), the *Annals of Congress*
(1789-1824), *Register of Debates* (1824-1837), and *Congressional Globe* (1833-
1873). Session laws are available (1995 to present) for all 50 states and the Canadian
Parliament. HeinOnline is especially rich in international law and treaty research.
The database includes all U.S. treaties (in-force, expired, or not yet officially pub-
lished), including the *United States Treaties and Other International Agreements*
"Blue set," the *Foreign Relations of the United States* series, publications of the
American Society of International Law, many national Yearbooks, and the *Hague
Permanent Court of International Justice Series*. Also contains many United Na-

tions legal publications, including the complete collection of the *United Nations Treaty Series*, the *Monthly Statement of Treaties & International Agreements*, and the *United Nations Legislative Series*.

♦ *LexisNexis and LexisNexis Academic*
http://academic.lexisnexis.com
http://www.lexisnexis.com
LexisNexis Academic is a subset of the full legal database aimed at colleges and universities. Legal information in *LexisNexis Academic* includes U.S. Federal & State case law, statutes, codes, and regulations, legal news, full-text law reviews and journals (most are from the late 1980s or early 1990s forward), plus *Shepard's Citations* for updating cases and statutes. *LexisNexis Academic* also contains wire services (updated in real time), major and regional newspapers, transcripts from broadcast and foreign language news sources. Company, industry, and market information includes multiple business directories, as well as 10-K, 10-Q, and other SEC filings. Reference materials include Gallup Poll results and biographies. *LexisNexis Academic* also contains full-text materials on accounting, auditing, and taxation. The database supports full Boolean connectors (including proximity connectors), natural language searching, field searching, phrases, date restrictions, and truncation ("stemming"). Results can be sorted in multiple ways, including relevance, chronological, and reverse chronological order.

The *professional version* (lexis.com) contains everything in the *Academic version*, plus additional materials. There are many additional titles in the law review section, and a larger amount of foreign and international law (although some is available in the *Academic* product). The *professional version* also contains a number of monographs and treatises. Court docket information is available for a separate fee. For short-term research with no contracts, the company provides the LexisOne database, http://www.lexisone.com.

♦ *LawMoose*
http://www.lawmoose.com
LawMoose contains both a free site and a subscription service. The subscription site links to government websites, state bars and other legal associations, as well as industry and professional associations. LawMoose also contains a topical library of practice materials. In addition to Boolean and keyword searching, the subscription site uses a vocabulary system called MooseBoost, a polyhierarchical thesaurus-like approach to building relationships between legal words and concepts.

♦ *Loislaw*
http://www.loislaw.com
Contains a collection of primary federal and state court opinions. The database includes cases from the U.S. Supreme Court (1754 to present), federal Court of Appeals decisions (1924 to present), federal bankruptcy cases, and federal District Court cases (1999 to present). Federal District Court archives are available back to 1921 for an additional cost. State appellate cases are available, although the inception date varies by state. Federal and state statutes and regulations are also available. Loislaw also provides a number of specialized treatises and formbooks. Personal and corporate public records for all 50 states are provided by Acxiom, and include con-

tact information, asset ownership, bankruptcies, judgments, liens, criminal records, professional licenses, and Secretary of State corporate filings. GlobalCite, an automated citator feature, finds other documents on Loislaw that reference the statute, case, regulation, or state statute. The database supports full Boolean connectors (including proximity connectors), natural language searching, field searching, phrases, date restrictions, and truncation ("stemming"). Results can be sorted in multiple ways, including relevance, chronological, and reverse chronological order.

♦ *NationalLawLibrary*
http://www.itislaw.com
This database contains U.S. Supreme Court opinions (1754 to present), Federal Circuit Courts of Appeals (1879 to present), and federal statutes and regulations. Inception dates for state appellate cases vary, although some states date back to 1886. The product does not contain a citator for updating, although case citations can be typed into the search box. The database supports full Boolean connectors (including proximity connectors), natural language searching, field searching, phrases, date restrictions, and truncation ("stemming"). Results can be sorted in multiple ways, including relevance, chronological, and reverse chronological order.

♦ *TheLaw.net*
http://www.thelaw.net
Contains U.S. Supreme Court cases (1754 to present), Federal Circuit Courts of Appeals (1924 to present), cases from all 50 states (1950 to present), federal and state statutes and regulations. The database also contains rules of court and legal forms, legislative and executive agency materials, links to bar associations, news resources, and a portal to legal reference websites. The product does not contain a citator for updating, although case citations can be typed into the search box. The database supports full Boolean connectors (including proximity connectors), natural language searching, field searching, phrases, date restrictions, and truncation ("stemming"). Results can be sorted in multiple ways, including relevance, chronological, and reverse chronological order.

♦ *Ordinance.com*
http://www.ordinance.com
Contains municipal ordinances, with a particular emphasis on zoning and planning.

♦ *Pacer* (Administrative Office of the United States Courts)
http://pacer.uspci.uscourts.gov
Public Access to Court Electronic Records (PACER) contains "case and docket information from Federal Appellate, District and Bankruptcy courts, and from the U.S. Party/Case Index via the Internet. Links to all courts are provided from this web site. . . . Each court maintains its own databases with case information. [PACER] offers electronic access to case dockets to retrieve information such as:

o   A listing of all parties and participants including judges, attorneys, and trustees.

o   A compilation of case related information such as cause of action, nature of suit, and dollar demand.

o   A chronology of dates of case events entered in the case record.

   o   A claims registry.

   o   A listing of new cases each day.

   o   Appellate court opinions.

   o   Judgments or case status.

   o   Types of documents filed for certain cases.

   o   Imaged copies of documents.

   o   The U.S. Party/Case Index." [Description from website.]

♦ Public Documents Masterfile (Paratext)
http://www.paratext.com/public_document.html
This subscription database allows searching of the entire *GPO Monthly Catalog*, the *U.S. Congressional Serial Set*, and *Non-GPO Public Documents Held by the Library of Congress*, thus providing access to a large portion of U.S. government publications from 1774 to the present.

♦ *ProQuest Congressional*
http://www.proquest.com
ProQuest acquired this database from LexisNexis in December 2010. The Congressional database includes the full text of U.S. congressional publications, hearings, reports, prints, documents, and Legislative Histories, as well as the full text of proposed legislation and its status. The database also contains the *Congressional Record*, *Rules of Congress*, federal statutes, the *United States Code Service*, the *Federal Register*, and the *Code of Federal Regulations*. The *Congressional* database contains biographical and financial information on members of Congress, as well as a listing of each member's voting record. The *Congressional* database also includes congressional committee and Congressional Research Service reports, and abstracts from the CIS Index. Other research tools available for an additional cost include Congressional indexes (1789-1984), Statutes at Large (1789-present), the U.S. Serial Set and Serial Set maps (1789-1969), and Congressional hearings (1824-present).

♦ *Versuslaw*
http://www.versuslaw.com
Depending on subscription level, Versuslaw provides U.S. Supreme Court cases (1886 to present), Federal Circuit Courts of Appeals (1930 to present), Federal District Court cases (1950 to present), plus current federal and state statutes and administrative regulations. State appellate cases are available, although the inception date varies by state.
    Versuslaw also contains "opinions from the U.S. Tax Court, Board of Immigration Appeals, Court of Federal Claims, Court of International Trade, IRS Rulings, NTSB Aviation Accident Synopsis, U.S. Office of Government Ethics, U.S. Social Security Rulings, Federal Mine Safety & Health Review Commission, and the Occupational Safety & Health Review Commission." [Description from website.] The database supports full Boolean connectors (including proximity connectors), natural language searching, field searching, phrases, date restrictions, and truncation ("stemming"). Results can be sorted in multiple ways, including relevance, chronological, and reverse chronological order.

♦   *Westlaw* and *Westlaw Campus*
    http://west.thomson.com/products/services/campus-research/default.aspx?
    http://west.thomson.com/westlaw/default.aspx
    Westlaw Campus Research is a subset of the full legal database aimed at colleges
    and universities. Legal resources include all federal and state cases (from the Na-
    tional Reporter System) with headnotes from the West digests, the United States
    Code Annotated (USCA), Code of Federal Regulations (CFR), Federal Register, and
    a full-text collection of European Union law. The legal encyclopedia *American Ju-
    risprudence* (Am Jur) 2d edition and the *American Law Reports* (A.L.R.) series are
    very useful (although the encyclopedia interface is a bit clunky).
        Westlaw Campus contains business, trade, and professional journals, wire ser-
    vices (updated in real time), newspapers, and transcripts from broadcast and foreign
    language news sources. Over 800 full-text law reviews and journals are available,
    with most titles dating back to the late 1980s or early 1990s. *Westlaw Campus* in-
    cludes company information from multiple business directories, as well as 10-K, 10-
    Q, and other SEC filings. Cases and statutes can be updated using the *Keycite* prod-
    uct. *Westlaw Campus* supports full Boolean connectors (including proximity
    connectors), natural language searching, field searching, phrases, date restrictions,
    and truncation ("stemming"). Results can be sorted by relevance, chronological
    order, and reverse chronological order.
        The *professional version* contains everything in *Westlaw Campus*, plus addi-
    tional materials. There are additional titles in the law review section, a number of
    monographs and treatises, and a collection of foreign and international law. Court
    docket information is available for a separate fee.

C. General Legal Websites

There are three major types of websites that you should be aware of. The
first type of website that most people use is a web portal, such as Yahoo! The
second type of web service that people use is a search engine, and the third type
of website actually contains primary legal information or secondary articles relating to the law. These three types of sites are not necessarily mutually exclusive, since many portals include search engines, as well as primary and secondary legal materials.

A portal contains "information ABOUT a specific thing."[9] Portals usually
are arranged around a directory. When you click on one of the topics in the directory, you are given a screen with sub-headings. The topic narrows as you
click on each link, until eventually you find the materials you need. As the name
implies, portals are doors to further information, either on the same site or elsewhere on the web. One of the most important and well-known portals is Yahoo!
There are also "niche portals that lead you to information about a specific topic—for example, wine.com (for wine drinkers), dog.com (for dog lovers), and
javascript.com (for programmers)."[10]

One analogy that helps to explain portals is to compare them to that favorite
tool of librarians, the bibliography. Portals don't always contain the information
you are seeking; rather, they link you to relevant information on their website, to

other portals, or to websites which contain the desired information. In the same way, a bibliography "links" you to other bibliographies, or to books, articles, and websites that contain information about your topic.

I often compare the directory of a portal to a table of contents, and the search engine to an index; sometimes you use the table of contents to find information, and sometimes you use the index. By the same token, sometimes you need to use a portal, and sometimes you need to use a search engine.

There are several different kinds of search engines. Most people usually start with a general search engine such as Google or AllTheWeb. General search engines contain a catalog of sites. They allow you to do keyword searching of the websites in their catalog. A natural language search engine, such as Ask.com, allows you to enter a question. The natural language search engine then uses an algorithm to do keyword searching from your question.

As a librarian, I don't usually recommend natural language searching. The only exception is when I am just beginning to research a topic and I don't know enough about it to formulate keywords. In that situation, I find the natural language search to be helpful; once I find some information about the topic, I can formulate my keywords.

One valuable type of search engine is a meta-search engine such as Metacrawler,[11] Dogpile,[12] or Ixquick.[13] Meta-search engines that perform your search in a number of general search engines at the same time can be very helpful. The library at the University of California, Berkeley has compiled an excellent anno tated guide to meta-search engines.[14] The final type of search engine is the subject-specific search engine, such as Lawcrawler, which I will discuss in detail below.

One important factor that you must always remember is to evaluate the quality and reliability of websites. The information revolution and the Internet have made more knowledge readily accessible than ever before; at the same time, however, there are potholes on the information superhighway. It is very important to make sure that we remember that not all websites are accurate.

One advantage of the Internet is that anyone can create his or her own homepage; unfortunately, that is also a drawback. Since judging reliability is a prerequisite for using information, we must look at the following factors:

♦ Who sponsored the web page? Is the sponsor an expert in the field?

♦ Does the sponsor have a bias?

♦ Where did the information come from?

♦ Does the material give credit to a source?

♦ Is *that* source reliable?

♦ When was the information compiled?

♦ When was the web page updated?

♦ What is the potential audience for the site?

♦ How did you find the Internet site? Who wrote the web page that referred you?

As researchers, we do this type of evaluation every time we find a reference in our research. However, we need to be even more vigilant with websites. Be sure to watch out for second-level sources; sometimes you can start with a reliable site but then follow a link to an unreliable site.

The following websites provide good information. These are the sites[15] that legal and non-legal librarians usually advise researchers to use when beginning a search. I have also included several sites which contain legal research tutorials.

♦ *American Association of Law Libraries*
  http://www.aallnet.org
  This website contains links to legal directories, law journals, law library online catalogs, law schools, legal organizations, and law-related discussion lists.

♦ AALL/LISP. *How to Research a Legal Problem: A Guide for Non-Lawyers*
  http://www.aallnet.org/sis/lisp/research.htm
  Created by the Legal Information Services to the Public special interest section of the American Association of Law Libraries.

♦ *American Law Sources On-line*
  http://www.lawsource.com
  Links to freely accessible online sources of law for the United States and Canada, including free commentaries and practice aids. (The same company also maintains a site for Mexican legal research.)

♦ *Cornell Legal Information Institute*
  http://www.law.cornell.edu
  The first comprehensive legal site on the web, the Legal Information Institute (LII) contains all U.S. Supreme Court opinions since 1992 (plus over 600 historically important court decisions), the *U.S. Code*, the *Code of Federal Regulations*, Federal court rules, opinions of the New York Court of Appeals, and a basic guide to legal citation based on the *Bluebook* format. New opinions from the U.S. Supreme Court are posted simultaneously on the LII and on the Supreme Court's website. Topical explanatory pages provide overviews and links for approximately 100 areas of law.

♦ Feltes, Gretchen. (2005). *A Guide to the U.S. Federal Legal System: Web-based Public Accessible Sources.* New York: Columbia University Law Library, *available at* http://www.nyulawglobal.org/globalex/United_States.htm.
  Updated October 2010; *available at* http://www.nyulawglobal.org/globalex/United_States1.htm.
  This bibliographic essay provides an excellent overview of publicly-accessible sources for both primary and secondary U.S. legal information and materials.

♦ *Findlaw*
  http://www.findlaw.com (general website)
  http://lp.findlaw.com (legal practitioner's website)
  The top free commercial legal research site, *Findlaw* contains or provides links to statutes and administrative regulations for every U.S. jurisdiction, cases that are

available online, and forms (including tax forms). U.S. Supreme Court cases are included from 1893 to the present. *Findlaw* also includes a directory of lawyers, legal job listings, legal news, commentary, and editorials on current legal topics, as well as explanatory articles about specific areas of law.

♦ *Google Books* and *HathiTrust Digital Library*
http://books.google.com
http://catalog.hathitrust.org
Google has digitized a fair number of opinions, statutes, treatises, and legislative hearing records, mostly before 1923 (because of copyright law). While Google Books only returns a partial result list, the HathiTrust Digital Library (an alternative interface) returns all pages with the search term. Noted books include the 1914 edition of *Bouvier's Law Dictionary and Concise Encyclopedia*, the 1922 edition of *Corpus Juris*, *The Institutes of the Laws of England* by Sir Edward Coke, English legal commentaries by Sir William Blackstone and Thomas Cooley, *The Nature of the Judicial Process* by Benjamin Cardozo, and *A Sketch of English Legal History* by Frederic William Maitland, Francis C. Montague, and James Fairbanks. Other highlights include portions of the *Congressional Globe* and *Statutes at Large*, and numerous pre-1923 reporters, state statutes, and law journals.

♦ *Google Scholar*
http://www.scholar.google.com
Many researchers know *Google Scholar* as a free web-based search service for scholarly literature that links to full-text articles held by individual libraries. However, *Google Scholar* is also a free legal research site. A radio button on the search page allows searches for articles (including patents) or for legal opinions and journals. *Google Scholar* also generates basic "cited by" and "related articles" features, although they are hardly a replacement for *Shepard's Citations* or *Keycite*. While missing many features from subscription databases such as ranking results by date, this is still a good (free) option for the general public and for non-lawyers. It works especially well for searching articles from law reviews.

♦ *GovEngine.com*
http://www.govengine.com
This free portal links to statutes, regulations, and cases for federal, state, and territories, as well as courts, official government sites, and administrative agencies.

♦ *Internet Legal Research Group*
http://www.ilrg.com
Although ILRG emphasizes U.S. law, the portal contains over 4000 selected legal web sites in 238 jurisdictions "quality controlled to include only the most substantive legal resources online." [Description from website].

♦ *Justia*
http://www.justia.com
A legal web portal with lots of free case law, articles on legal topics, and links to law sites. The Justia blog contains useful analyses of the law.

♦   Orin S. Kerr, *How to Read a Legal Opinion: A Guide for New Law Students*, 11-1
    Green Bag 51 (2007), *available at* http://ssrn.com/abstract=1160925.
    This guide walks beginners through the basics of reading and understanding law
    cases by explaining judicial opinions, how they are structured, and what to look for
    when reading them. Although aimed at beginning law students, the article is acces-
    sible for anyone regardless of the level of legal knowledge.

♦   *Law Guru*
    http://www.lawguru.com
    This site links to many legal resources and provides a search tool for these websites.
    Law Guru contains forms, articles, legal news, discussion lists, and a law dictionary,
    as well as a legal bulletin board on which volunteer lawyers answer questions. The
    "Legal FAQ" section contains explanatory information on various areas of law.

♦   *LawHelp*
    http://www.lawhelp.org
    "LawHelp helps low and moderate income people find free legal aid programs in
    their communities, and answers to questions about their legal rights." [Description
    from website.] Contains sample forms and instructions, along with information on
    common legal topics such as government benefits, family law, landlord-tenant is-
    sues, and Power of Attorney documents. The laws of each state are located in sepa-
    rate state guides, such as http://www.washingtonlawhelp.org.

♦   *LawMoose*
    http://www.lawmoose.com
    The *U.S. House Internet Law Library* was a major website in the 1990s, but was dis-
    continued after a decade. At that point, LaVern Pritchard used the Internet Law Li-
    brary files to create a new the model. Although most of the site is no longer free and
    is aimed at lawyers, the public portal is still there with a subscription site on top.

♦   *'Lectric Law Library*
    http://www.lectlaw.com
    This website has all kinds of serious legal information, presented in a humorous
    fashion. The site includes an excellent legal dictionary ("The 'Lectric Law Lexi-
    con"), legal forms, and explanatory articles about legal topics.

♦   *LegalDockets.com*
    http://www.legaldockets.com
    This free public record site, run by Paul Bush, contains public record link resources,
    although it now also contains advertisements. LegalDockets' subscription site,
    Courtport (http://www.courtport.com/), contains additional public records. Courtport
    allows free access for academic users with an ".edu" email address.

♦   *Legal News Sources*
    http://www.earlham.edu/~peters/courses/cle/clelinks.htm
    Created by Peter Suber, a philosophy professor at Earlham College, this guide con-
    tains links to many legal news sources and legal search engines.

♦ *LexisOne Free Case Law*
http://www.lexisone.com/lx1/caselaw/freecaselaw
U.S. Supreme Court cases from 1781 to present, as well as federal and state cases decided within the last ten years.

♦ *LLRX*
http://www.llrx.com
One of the most important online free legal research journals since 1996, LLRX contains articles and guides discussing the process of legal research. The site contains links to legal research websites, court rules, forms, and dockets. LLRX also reviews websites for researchers, software and online legal applications and database services, and books on legal technology and library technology topics.

♦ *MegaLaw*
http://www.megalaw.com
This portal links to both U.S. and international primary law, as well as legal associations, legal forms, court rules, a directory for lawyers, and information for pre-law and law students. The LawBot search engine "is the only search engine built from the ground up to find law and only law. . . ."[16]

♦ *Municode.com*
http://www.municode.com
The website of the largest U.S. publisher of municipal codes.

♦ *National Federation of Paralegal Associations (NFPA)*
http://www.paralegals.org/displaycommon.cfm?an=1
Contains comprehensive links to federal and state agencies, courts, and statutes, as well as search engines and other legal directories, sites for specialty practice, associations and organizations, and law schools. The site also links to list services and law-related forums, sites for legal news, and international law materials.

♦ *Nolo Press*
http://www.nolo.com
A publisher of "self-help" legal books with some free information on the web site.

♦ *Public Records Free Directory*
http://publicrecords.onlinesearches.com
Contains links to state and county public record sites nationwide (both free and subscription), along with contact information for each agency.

♦ *Official City Sites*
http://www.officialcitysites.org
Contains links to the official websites for cities, states, counties, chambers of commerce, convention and visitor's bureaus, and other state, local, and regional sites.

♦ *Public Library of Law*
http://www.plol.org

A free website created by Fastlaw, the PLoL contains cases from the U.S. Supreme Court and Courts of Appeals, cases from all 50 states back to 1997, federal statutory law, and codes from all 50 states. The site also contains regulations, court rules, constitutions, and links to sites that sell legal forms.

◆   *Seattle Public Library's Municipal Codes Online*
    http://www.spl.org/default.asp?pageID=collection_municodes
    The Seattle Public Library has gathered links to freely searchable municipal codes from all over the U.S., plus links to companies that publish municipal codes.

◆   *Sterling Codifiers*
    http://www.sterlingcodifiers.com/
    A large publisher of municipal codes, Sterling Codifiers makes many of the codes it publishes available free online.

◆   *Tutorials and videos from the Harvard Law School Library*
    http://www.law.harvard.edu/library/research/tutorials/index.html
    These videos created by Harvard law librarians cover general topics including secondary sources, West digests, printed statutes in Print, bill tracking (with both *ProQuest Congressional* and *Thomas*), finding committee reports on *Thomas*, finding hearings and compiled legislative histories with *ProQuest Congressional*, and using the Popular Name Table on Westlaw.

◆   *USA.gov*
    http://www.usa.gov
    The federal government's web portal links to courts, agencies, and legal materials.

◆   *Washburn University Law Library*
    http://www.washlaw.edu
    A comprehensive legal site with links to business and law resources, directories, federal and state law cases, statutes, legal directories, and other general legal materials. This is also a good site for international law.

◆   Zimmerman's Research Guide
    http://www.lexisnexis.com/infopro/zimmerman
    Created by law librarian Andrew Zimmerman, this is a free legal encyclopedia and guide to research. The site has how-to training information, tutorials, and links to free legal websites.

D. Search Engines for Legal Research

◆   *AllTheWeb*
    http://www.alltheweb.com
    This search engine does keyword searches of html, pdf, Microsoft Word, Excel, and PowerPoint documents. The basic search will do partial Boolean searching using a plus sign (+) for required words and phrases and a minus sign (-) for excluded words. Quotation marks (" ") are needed for phrases; if no plus signs or quotation

marks are used, the search engine will look for *ANY* of your terms. The advanced search screen allows full Boolean searching, as well as domain name screening.

◆ *Bing*
http://www.bing.com
Microsoft's successor to *Windows Live*, the *Bing* search engine returns both crawled websites and real-time results. The simple search allows the basic AND/OR Boolean commands, as well as + and − . Full Boolean commands (including parentheses) can be used in the advanced search. However, the site is more focused on consumers and shopping than on scholarly results.

◆ *Bing vs. Google*
http://www.bing-vs-google.com
Run a single search, then compare the results side-by-side from Google and Bing.

◆ *Fee Fie Foe Firm*
http://www.feefiefoefirm.com
This search engine focuses on the websites of U.S. law firms. Indexed content includes profiles and biographical information, media releases, legal news and updates, and client seminars. Most helpful are case notes, newsletters, bulletins, and other publications using expert legal analysis. Separate searches are available for U.S., United Kingdom, Canada, Australia, New Zealand, Ireland, Singapore, and South Africa.

◆ *Google*
http://www.google.com
The most popular search engine, Google only allows partial Boolean searching by defaulting to AND, allowing OR, and using the minus sign (−) for excluded words. Google searches synonyms automatically, but using the plus sign (+) means "search exactly as is" (unlike most search engines, it does not denote a required term). Phrases should be placed in quotation marks. The order in which keywords or phrases are entered changes the results. Advanced search options allow customization, including better support for Boolean AND/OR searches. One disadvantage of Google is that it only searches the first 100 megabytes of a website, so search results can be inconsistent and searchers may miss results.

◆ *Index for US Legal Research*
http://gsulaw.gsu.edu/metaindex
"This page illustrates the use of searchable legal indexes on the World Wide Web. Only specifically legal indexes in the U.S. are included. Please note that many of the search tools here have additional search options available and that to derive full benefit from them you should visit the original sites directly." [Description from website.]

◆ *Infomine*
http://infomine.ucr.edu

Infomine provides a number of subject-specific search engines, including one for government information. Allows field searches, Boolean AND/OR searching, with quotation marks (" ") for phrases, and an asterisk (*) for truncation.

♦ *Lawcrawler*
Available at http://lawcrawler.findlaw.com or by clicking the link on Findlaw
Produced by Findlaw, this specialized search engine uses Google technology to index legal websites. Phrases must be placed in quotation marks (" "); required words need a plus sign (+); and excluded words must have a minus sign (-). Although full Boolean searching is not available, the + and - signs work fairly well.

♦ *Yippy Search*
http://search.yippy.com
Yippy is an unusual meta-search engine that groups similar results together into clusters by topic so users can "discover unexpected relationships between items." [Description from website.]

Whenever legal websites or search engines are used, you must evaluate the results carefully. Librarians should make a special effort to remind clients that the quality of the websites indexed by each search engine varies considerably. As one legal case (which hereafter will be referred to as the *Texas Web Case*) has noted:

> While some look to the Internet as an innovative vehicle for communication, the Court continues to warily and wearily view it largely as one large catalyst for rumor, innuendo, and misinformation. So as to not mince words, the Court reiterates that this so-called Web provides no way of verifying the authenticity of the alleged contentions that Plaintiff wishes to rely upon in his Response to Defendant's Motion. There is no way Plaintiff can overcome the presumption that the information he discovered on the Internet is inherently untrustworthy. Anyone can put anything on the Internet. No web-site is monitored for accuracy and nothing contained therein is under oath or even subject to independent verification absent underlying documentation. Moreover, the Court holds no illusions that hackers can adulterate the content on any web-site from any location at any time.[17]

This quote from the *Texas Web Case* provides an excellent statement of the need for website evaluation. The web is a great source of information, but it can also be a great source of misinformation. By viewing websites through a critical eye, it is possible to use the Internet without being misled.

Conclusion

Legal research is often perceived to be more difficult than it really is. The tools that are used for research in other areas—dictionaries, encyclopedias, and journal indexes—will help paralegals, librarians, and clients begin their research.

The most important questions to ask when looking for a legal resource are whether the item comes from the state or federal government, which branch of government created the item, and what is the court level. Legal research tools— both in print and online—are divided according to the source of the document.

Both print and online research tools are helpful. Many researchers automatically go to subscription databases such as Westlaw or Lexis, but these tools are not the only places to find information. It seems like every year brings another entry into the legal research marketplace, ranging from Bloomberg to LawMoose. Meanwhile, the open source movement includes free sites and search engines such as Google Scholar, MegaLaw, and Fee Fie Foe Firm.

However, this diversity of free legal research sources comes at a price. It is always important to evaluate your sources, but it becomes even more important when dealing with the World Wide Web. Be sure to always ask questions about your sources, and look for evidence of bias or lack of objectivity. Finally, remember that while some jurisdictions embrace open citation formats, others have rejected them. Be sure you always understand the local rules for the jurisdiction you work with.

There are a number of important web resources for law. This chapter has only scratched the surface of what is available. Many of these websites are authoritative and reliable. It is very important to remind clients of the need to evaluate the reliability of any website used for research. (As the *Texas Web Case* stated, "Anyone can put anything on the Internet.")[18] At the same time, we must be aware of our limitations in terms of the unauthorized practice of law.

The sources for legal research are sometimes confusing, but by creating an effective strategy it is possible to find your way through the maze of legal research. In the end, the reward of finding the answer you need justifies the difficulty in getting there. Just as any field of research has its peculiarities, so too does the law. But once you arrive at the necessary answer, all your efforts and your research will be worthwhile.

Notes

1. Portions of this section were previously published in Bryan M. Carson, The Law of Libraries and Archives (Lanham, MD: Scarecrow Press, 2007). [Used by permission.]

2. A Uniform System of Citation (17th ed., Harvard Law Review Association, 2000). Peter Martin has created an online citation manual based on Bluebook style; *see*, Peter W. Martin, Introduction to Basic Legal Citation (Cornell Legal Information Institute, 2003), *available at* http://www.law.cornell.edu/citation.

3. Bureau of National Affairs, U.S. Law Week Product Structure, *available at* http://www.bna.com/products/lit/uslw.htm.

4. The Cornell Law Library has produced a valuable overview of legal research. Cornell University Law Library, Basics of Legal Research, *available at* http://library .lawschool.cornell.edu/WhatWeDo/ResearchGuides/Basics.cfm.

5. Bryan M. Carson, The Law of Libraries and Archives (Lanham, MD: Scarecrow Press, 2007).

6. This language is from a *Declaration of Principles adopted jointly by a Committee of the American Bar Association and a committee of Publishers.*

7. American Law Institute, Wikipedia, *available at* http://en.wikipedia.org/wiki/ Restatement.

8. For a full review of Bloomberg Law, including pricing details, *see*, Robert J. Ambrogi, *Three's a Crowd? Bloomberg Law officially enters the high-end legal research service market*, Law Technology News (February 1, 2010), *available at* http://www.law .com/jsp/lawtechnologynews/PubArticleLTN.jsp?id=1202439542267&Threes_a_Crowd.

9. *What Is a Portal?* Portal King, Inc. (12 Nov. 2001), *available at* http://www .portalking.com/portal.htm.

10. *What Is a Portal?* InfoZen, Inc. (12 Nov. 2001), *available at* http://www.infozen .com/portal.html.

11. The URL for Metacrawler is http://www.metacrawler.com.

12. The URL for Dogpile is http://www.dogpile.com.

13. The URL for Ixquick is http://www.ixquick.com.

14. *Meta-Search Engines*, University of California Berkeley Libraries, *available at* http://www.lib.berkeley.edu/TeachingLib/Guides/Internet/MetaSearch.html.

15. I would like to thank a number of people for suggesting websites for inclusion in this book. A number of the sites were part of the 2008 Core Reference Tools created by Diane Kovacs of Kovacs Consulting. The complete list is available at http://www.kovacs.com/results08.html. Other results came from a question I posted on the Lawlib-L discussion list for librarians. I would like to thank the following people for making suggestions on the list: Damien MacRae, Betty Agin, Carol Bredemeyer, Dave Rodgers, Mary Lou Wilker, Rick Buckingham, Sid Kaskey, Robb Farmer, Mary Rice, Beverly Butula, Maria Sosnowski, Brian Raphael, Brad Small, LaVern Pritchard, and Paul Bush.

16. Big Search Engine Index, Directory of Law Search Engines, *available at* http://www.search-engine-index.co.uk/Reference/Law_Search.

17. St. Clair vs. Johnny's Oyster and Shrimp, Inc., 76 F.Supp.2d 773 (S.D.Texas, December 17, 1999).

18. *id.*

3

The Constitution:
The Supreme Law of the Land

The U.S. federal system depends, above all else, on the U.S. Constitution. It is the supreme law of the land, and no laws can be passed that are contrary to the Constitution. The Constitution applies to all of the branches of the federal government and to all state and territorial governments. No entity can make a law, regulation, or judicial decision that is contrary to the Constitution. Article VI of the Constitution (known as the "Supremacy Clause") states: "This Constitution, and the Laws of the United States which shall be made in Pursuance thereof; and all Treaties made, or which shall be made, under the Authority of the United States, shall be the supreme Law of the Land; and the Judges in every State shall be bound thereby, any Thing in the Constitution or Laws of any state to the Contrary notwithstanding."[1]

This chapter will discuss some of the issues relating to Constitutional interpretation including the concept of Federalism. There is a section on the meaning of the 14th Amendment, which for the first time applied many provisions of the original Constitution to the individual states. I will also discuss Due Process and the methodology used by the Supreme Court to scrutinize a law, and will provide a primer on how to read plurality decisions. The chapter will conclude with a listing of documents and sources on interpreting the U.S. Constitution.

A Federal System of Government

The U.S. Constitution established a federal system of government where power is shared between the central government and the states. On the surface a simple document, the complexities of the Constitution have occupied the Supreme Court for over 200 years. As the Supreme Law of the Land, all federal laws are subsidiary and must be enacted according to a specific power enumerated in the Constitution. (See the discussion of "enumerated powers" in Chapter 5, *Congress: The Legislative Branch*.) States are free to create their own statutes, subject only to the Constitution or to pre-emption by the federal government as part of a power granted by the Constitution.

The U.S. Constitution is primarily concerned with the power of the national government. Of the seven articles in the original Constitution, the first three are concerned with the selection, power, and relationships of the legislative, executive, and judicial branches. Article V is the provision that allows amendments, and Article VII spells out the procedure for ratification of the Constitution. The only parts of the Constitution that apply specifically to the states are Article IV, Article VI, and small parts of Article I (section 10) and Article III (sections 2(2)

– 2(3)). It is for that reason that almost all substantive law in the U.S. falls within the jurisdiction of the states.

The relationship between the central government and the states is known as a *federal* system of government. The Constitution provides for four types of governmental powers: "Those powers which belong exclusively to the States; powers which belong exclusively to the National Government; powers which may be exercised concurrently and independently by both; and powers which may be exercised by the States but only until Congress shall see fit to act upon the subject."[2]

The federal system of government, while still providing great power to the states, does vary greatly from the Articles of Confederation. The Articles of Confederation granted no exclusive and few concurrent powers to the national government. However, while the Constitution of 1787 is conservative by 21st-century standards, it certainly provided for a stronger central government than the Articles of Confederation. In an article entitled "Confederation and Federal Liberty," author Daniel J. Elazar explained the difference:

> [I]n federations, the federal government can reach out directly to its citizenry as well as through the constituent polities, while in a confederation, the confederal government must reach individual citizens only through the constituent polities. . . . [A] federation is more concerned with the preservation of individual liberty while a confederation places greater emphasis on the preservation of local liberties of its constituent polities.
>
> [Another] characteristic distinguishing federations from confederations is that the former have a common law of some scope which is enforceable throughout the federation, while the latter tend to leave matters of law to the constituent polities except as explicitly provided in limited areas determined to be of such general concern that they must be governed by a common law. This is a matter of the greatest importance; some might even say the heart of the matter. Federation is possible only where a sufficiently comprehensive common law binding all citizens of the constituent units is possible. By the same token, confederation is a viable means of establishing federal ties in situations where the parties to the bargain can only tolerate specific and limited common laws.[3]

Powers that are exclusively reserved for the federal government include such topics as interstate and international commerce, coining money, entering treaties, or going to war. The states regulate contracts, family law, business incorporations, and similar matters. The major questions involve concurrent powers which are exercised by both jurisdictions, along with powers that may only be exercised until the federal government pre-empts the field. If the area of law has traditionally been regulated by the states, the Supreme Court will presume (unless shown rebutting evidence otherwise) that the federal statute has not pre-empted the field.[4] The Court explained its interpretation of concurrent and pre-emptive powers in the case of Pacific Gas & Electric (PG&E) v. State Energy Resources Conservation and Development Commission:[5]

[W]ithin constitutional limits Congress may pre-empt state authority by so stating in express terms. Absent explicit pre-emptive language, Congress' intent to supersede state law altogether may be found from a "scheme of federal regulation . . . so pervasive as to make reasonable the inference that Congress left no room for the States to supplement it," because "the Act of Congress may touch a field in which the federal interest is so dominant that the federal system will be assumed to preclude enforcement of state laws on the same subject," or because "the object sought to be obtained by the federal law and the character of obligations imposed by it may reveal the same purpose." Even where Congress has not entirely displaced state regulation in a specific area, state law is pre-empted to the extent that it actually conflicts with federal law. Such a conflict arises when "compliance with both federal and state regulations is a physical impossibility," or where state law "stands as an obstacle to the accomplishment and execution of the full purposes and objectives of Congress." [Citations omitted.][6]

The PG&E case involved a nuclear power plant and questions of hazardous waste disposal under state or federal law. However, it is also instructive in showing how the jurisdictions work together. According to the Supreme Court:

Congress, in passing the 1954 [Atomic Energy] Act and in subsequently amending it, intended that the Federal Government should regulate the radiological safety aspects involved in the construction and operation of a nuclear plant, but that the States retain their traditional responsibility in the field of regulating electrical utilities for determining questions of need, reliability, cost, and other related state concerns.[7]

As interpreted by this case, the federal and state governments had concurrent powers under the Atomic Energy Act. On the other hand, some acts definitely pre-empt the field. One example that is often cited is the Employee Retirement Income Security Act of 1974 (ERISA). The language of the statute specifically states that it is pre-empting all state laws "insofar as they may now or hereafter relate to any employee benefit plan." The only laws that states may enact are those "which regulate insurance, banking, or securities."[8]

It is important to understand that the meaning of the term "Federalist" or "Federalism" in 1787 was somewhat different from the way in which the term is used today. In 1787, "Federalists" such as Hamilton or Madison were advocates of a strong central government which would have certain national powers; other powers would be handled by the states. Not even a strong federalist such as Hamilton would have advocated centralizing everything in one government; that would have been simply unacceptable for 13 previously separate colonies.

"The original constitutional division of power assumed that certain functions of government would be performed entirely by the central government and that other functions would be carried out by state or local governments. In this 'cake layer' federalism, or 'separation of powers model,' the majority of public activities were to be performed by subnational governments, while a limited number of functions, such as national defense and printing money, were to be the responsibility of the federal government."[9]

The separation of powers between federal and state governments was part of the protection from tyranny that the founders were concerned about. They wanted to ensure that none of the three branches of the federal government became too powerful, but they also wanted to be sure that neither the central government nor the state governments became too powerful either. However, through time federal and state governments began to perform overlapping activities. Author Guy Peters described the overlapping layers using the cake analogy:

> The cake layer then was transformed into a "marble cake," with the several layers of government still distinct, although no longer vertically separated from one another. . . . Federalism evolved further from a horizontal division of activities into a set of vertical divisions. Whereas functions were once neatly compartmentalized by level of government, the major feature of "picket fence" federalism is the development of policy subsystems defined by policy rather than by level of government. . . . It makes little sense to discuss federalism in its original meaning; it has been argued that contemporary federalism is as much façade as picket fence. A term such as *intergovernmental relations* more accurately describes the crazy quilt of overlapping authority and interdependence among levels of government than does a more formal, constitutional term such as federalism.[10]

Today the term federalism is often used to denote what Justice Sandra Day O'Connor called "the boundaries of federal pre-emption."[11] The current definition of federalism has been used many times to strike down U.S. laws in favor of the sovereign rights of the states. Starting in the 1990s, the Supreme Court struck down all or portions of the Gun Free School Zones Act of 1990,[12] the Religious Freedom Restoration Act,[13] the Age Discrimination in Employment Act,[14] and the Violence Against Women Act.[15] In each case, the Court found that the central government was interfering with the sovereignty of the states.[16]

The process of curbing national powers in favor of state sovereignty has been known, both in the press and in academic literature, as "federalism." The proponents of this school of thought ground their arguments (with some justification) in Madison, Jay, Hamilton, and the constitutional history of the 1787 Constitution. However, there are also grounds for those who believe that today's "federalists" would have been yesterday's advocates of state's rights.[17]

The 14th Amendment

The most often litigated portions of the U.S. Constitution are those having to do with the concept of *Privileges and Immunities*, the doctrine of *Due Process*, and the concept of *Equal Protection*. Part of Justice O'Connor's "boundaries of federal pre-emption" involves the relationship between federal and state governments and these doctrines. There are three places in the Constitution where privileges and immunities, due process, and equal protection are mentioned, namely:

♦ Article IV – The citizens of each State shall be entitled to all the privileges and immunities of citizens in the several States.

♦ 5th Amendment – No person shall be held to answer for a capital, or otherwise infamous crime, unless on a presentment or indictment of a Grand Jury, except in cases arising in the land or naval forces, or in the Militia, when in actual service in time of War or public danger; nor shall any person be subject for the same offense to be twice put in jeopardy of life or limb; nor shall be compelled in any criminal case to be a witness against himself, nor be deprived of life, liberty, or property, *without due process of law*; nor shall private property be taken for public use, without just compensation. [Emphasis added.]

♦ 14th Amendment – No State shall make or enforce any law which shall abridge the *privileges or immunities of citizens* of the United States; nor shall any State deprive any person of life, liberty, or property, without *due process of law*; nor deny to any person within its jurisdiction the *equal protection of the laws*. [Emphasis added.]

The Bill of Rights prevented the federal government from abridging the rights of its citizens, but said nothing about potential infringement by the states. As part of the Bill of Rights proposal, Madison attempted to include a provision stating that: "The equal rights of conscience, the freedom of speech or of the press, and the right of trial by jury in criminal cases shall not be infringed by any State."[18] However, Congress rejected this proposal, even though Madison stated that this provision was "the most valuable of the whole list."[19]

In the case of Barron v. Baltimore,[20] Chief Justice Marshall ruled that the Takings Clause of the Fifth Amendment only applied to the federal government, not to the states. After this, the Bill of Rights had no relevance to state laws. However, this changed with the 14th Amendment. Passed in the wake of the Civil War, the 14th Amendment changed the legal landscape completely.

Religion was one area in which the lack of applicability led to results that seem quaint by today's standards. Since the First Amendment didn't apply to the states, only the federal government was prevented from establishing an official religion. Nothing prevented the states from doing so. Most colonial ties with the Church of England were broken during the Revolution, but New Hampshire, Connecticut, and Massachusetts retained the Congregationalist Church as their established churches until 1790, 1818, and 1833, respectively.[21] Russell Kirk provided a good description of the evolution of the Establishment Clause:

The First Amendment, of course, was binding only upon the federal government, until 1925—when, in the case of Gitlow v. New York, the Supreme Court ruled that the Fourteenth Amendment brought the free-speech and free-press guarantees of the First Amendment within the cognizance of federal courts. In 1940, in the case of Cantwell v. Connecticut, this doctrine was specifically extended, also, to the religious-freedom clause of the First Amendment. Until [1940], then, the several states, in theory, could have established state Churches and in other ways have regulated religious observance.[22]

Some portions of the Bill of Rights have been applied to the states during the 20th century via a doctrine called *incorporation.* The following portion of the 14th Amendment is the basis of most of this change:

> No State shall make or enforce any law which shall abridge the privileges or immunities of citizens of the United States; nor shall any State deprive any person of life, liberty or property, without due process of law; nor deny to any person within its jurisdiction the equal protection of the laws.[23]

Rep. Robert Hale, who believed that the states were already bound by the Bill of Rights, gave one of the strongest statements from Congress.[24] On February 27, 1866, Hale explained his position during debate in the House over the 14th Amendment:

> [T]hese amendments to the Constitution, numbered from one to ten . . . constitute the bill of rights, a bill of rights for the protection of the citizen, and defining and limiting the power of Federal and State legislation. . . . [T]here has been from first to last, a violation of the provisions in this bill of rights by the very existence of slavery itself.[25]

However, the doctrine of incorporation is not without controversy. There are three main views of incorporation that have been articulated by Supreme Court Justices. Akhil Reed Amar provided a good summary of these three positions:

> The first, represented by Justice Frankfurter, insists that, strictly speaking, the Fourteenth Amendment never "incorporated" any of the provisions of the Bill of Rights. The Fourteenth requires only that states honor basic principles of fundamental fairness and ordered liberty — principles that might indeed happen to overlap wholly or in part with some of the rules of the Bill of Rights, but that bear no logical relationship to those rules. The second approach, championed by Justice Black, insists on "total incorporation" of the Bill of Rights . . . lock, stock, and barrel — at least if we define the Bill to include only the first eight amendments. Faced with these diametric views, Justice Brennan tried to steer a middle course of "selective incorporation." Under this third approach, the Court's analysis could proceed clause by clause, fully incorporating every provision of the Bill deemed "fundamental" without deciding in advance

whether each and every clause would necessarily pass the test.[26] [Citations omitted.]

These three views of 14th Amendment incorporation dominated 20th-century jurisprudence, but several other theories have also been advanced. Charles Fairman[27] proposed that the Bill of Rights was a product of its time and that it would have not been written the same way in 1866 when the 14th Amendment was passed. Therefore, he suggests that the requirements should not be unthinkingly imposed on states. More recently, Akhil Reed Amar proposed a "refined incorporation" model whereby:

> Instead of asking whether a given provision is fundamental or not, as Brennan suggests, we must ask whether it is a personal privilege — that is, a private right — of individual citizens, rather than a right of states or the public at large. . . . This question, or something like it, is obviously the filter we need once we remember that Section One incorporates "the privileges or immunities of citizens" declared in the original Constitution as well as the Bill of Rights. For how else could we filter out those Article I limitations that should be incorporated, like habeas, and separate them from those that should not, like capitation (a state right) or even bicameralism (a right of the public at large)? The same filter works for the Bill of Rights, and for the same reasons. Indeed, the filter nicely combines the respective strengths of Black's and Brennan's models of incorporation. With this filter, we can preserve the textual and historical support for Black's insistence that all the Bill's privileges or immunities are indeed incorporated while accommodating Brennan's intuition that perhaps not every provision of Amendments I-VIII sensibly incorporates. This synthesis offers a principled substitute to the seeming ad hocery [sic] of selective incorporation as now practiced.[28]

Whichever view of the incorporation question is chosen, it is clear that the 14th Amendment has become very important in American jurisprudence. Librarians doing legal research should therefore be familiar with the main arguments for and against incorporation.

Due Process of Law

The due process clause was first applied to the federal government by the 5th Amendment, but was subsequently brought to the states via the 14th Amendment. Due process, which deals with "how and why laws are enforced,"[29] can in turn be split into two doctrines, procedural due process and substantive due process. Procedural due process involves "the 'how'" of a law, while substantive due process is the "why."[30] The first questions for courts are (1) whether the procedures were properly complied with and the process fair, and (2) whether the person has been deprived of a protected "life, liberty, or property" interest.[31] If a statute does not permit challenge, presumes guilt, or is not applied fairly to everyone, it is subject to challenge on procedural due process grounds.

A statute can also run afoul of procedural due process by being too vague. According to the U.S. Supreme Court, "The terms of a penal statute . . . must be sufficiently explicit to inform those who are subject to it what conduct on their part will render them liable to its penalties . . . And a statute which either forbids or requires the doing of an act in terms so vague that men of common intelligence must necessarily guess at its meaning and differ **as** to its application, violates the first essential of due process of law." [Emphasis in original.][32]

Some of the questions that a court will ask in deciding a procedural due process case include:

> Is a law too vague? Is it applied fairly to all? Does a law presume guilt? A vagrancy law might be declared too vague if the definition of a vagrant is not detailed enough. A law that makes wife beating illegal but permits husband beating might be declared to be an unfair application. A law must be clear, fair, and have a presumption of innocence to comply with procedural due process.[33]

An excellent example of the role of procedural due process is the case of Thompson v. City of Louisville.[34] This case is extraordinary not only for the discussion of procedural due process, but also for the unusual route that it took to the U.S. Supreme Court. This case is (as far as I am aware) the only case to go directly from the lowest-level municipal court to the U.S. Supreme Court without being heard in any other courts along the way.

The case involved convictions for loitering and disorderly conduct. The defendant was fined $10 for each count. Under Kentucky law in effect at the time, there was no right of appeal if the only punishment was a fine of less than $20. This meant that there was no court that the defendant could appeal to—except for the U.S. Supreme Court. The local courts in Kentucky stayed imposition of the punishment while the case was appealed, and it went directly from the Police Court of Louisville to the U.S. Supreme Court. The lack of opportunity for appeal was a procedural issue in and of itself that the U.S. Supreme Court found problematic. But the underlying facts were equally egregious. Stewart Dean, whose father hired Sam Thompson for odd jobs, gave this personal account of the case [used by permission]:

> When I was a kid growing up in Louisville, KY, we had black help. My mother was almost completely paralyzed and my father was an eye surgeon. Our family only worked because of the kind-hearted, substantial and committed help of Queen Esther ("Queenie") Williams (who ran the house) [and] Willie Mae Fuqua (who did the laundry). On occasion, Sam Thompson would stop by to wax the floor or rake and burn the leaves in the autumn.
>
> Sam was a target for the local (white) police, perhaps because they learned that it was "fun" to push his button. They would lean on him, he would tell them to get off his back, and then they would throw him in jail for a week or two and fine him $10 on some [!@#$%^&*] pretext.
>
> I don't know that things got physical with the police. Louisville was hardly the Deep South, where a black man who stood up for himself was in mortal

mortal danger. But there was no recourse for Sam, because the Kentucky Constitution [didn't] allow appeals for a fine of [$20] or less! So the police would keep pushing Sam's button and doing it to him.

This happened time and again over the years, and, when I was 13 and Sam had been victimized like this for more than 50 times, Dad got Sam in touch with the KCLU to finally get him some recourse.

This time, Sam had been in a (black) bar waiting for the bus out of the cold. He had bought and paid for some food, the proprietor said he was welcome to be there, and Sam was sitting on a stool tapping his foot in time to the music on the juke box. The white police came in and did their usual number, and Sam was charged, fined and put in jail for dancing (shuffling his foot) in an establishment without a dancing permit.

Since there was no recourse from the KY State Supreme Court, the KCLU took the case to the Supreme Court of the United States, where the Louisville DA defending the City action got his [!@#] handed to him. And the police left Sam alone after that.[35]

The charge against Sam Thompson was loitering. However, when the police told him that he was under arrest, Thompson argued "vigorously" with the officer, saying that he was just waiting for a bus. For his efforts, Thompson was rewarded with the addition of a disorderly conduct charge.

At trial, evidence indicated that Sam Thompson had money in his pocket and a bus schedule showing that a bus going to his house would stop a block away at 7:30 that evening. A café waiter testified that he had served Thompson a dish of macaroni and a glass of beer. The manager testified that Thompson was a regular patron of the café, that he saw Thompson "patting" or "shuffling" his feet in time with the music, that there was no harm, and that Sam Thompson was welcome in his establishment. (Sam Thompson became known as "Shufflin' Sam" as a result of this testimony.) Time Magazine noted the following exchange during oral argument: "'What is a shuffle dance?' asked Justice William Brennan. Replied Louisville's uncomfortable assistant city attorney: 'I presume it is some sort of dancing that uses a system of shuffling.'"[36]

The Supreme Court found that there was no evidence whatsoever to uphold the conviction for loitering, and that the law was vaguely broad. As for the disorderly conduct charge, the Supreme Court noted that:

> The only evidence of "disorderly conduct" was the single statement of the policeman that after petitioner was arrested and taken out of the cafe he was very argumentative. There is no testimony that petitioner raised his voice, used offensive language, resisted the officers or engaged in any conduct of any kind likely in any way to adversely affect the good order and tranquility [sic] of the City of Louisville. The only information the record contains on what the petitioner was "argumentative" about is his statement that he asked the officers "what they arrested me for." We assume, for we are justified in assuming, that merely "arguing" with a policeman is not, because it could not be, "disorderly conduct" as a matter of the substantive law of Kentucky. Moreover, Kentucky law itself seems to provide that if a man wrongfully arrested fails to object to

the arresting officer, he waives any right to complain later that the arrest was unlawful. [Citations omitted.][37]

The "Shufflin' Sam" case therefore stood for three important propositions: (1) the law must actually state the offense, otherwise it is unconstitutionally vague; (2) arguing with an officer about being arrested is not disorderly conduct; and (3) there is *always* a right of appeal to the U.S. Supreme Court—even if the statute denies any right of appeal. While two $10 fines were minor in the scheme of things, this case was very important because the same statutes were used at the time to deal with civil rights protestors. After the Thompson case, loitering charges against civil rights protesters became more risky for Southern police.

The second part of the due process clause involves substantive due process. This concept was embraced by the Process Act of 1789, which was passed by the first Congress before the Bill of Rights.[38] Substantive due process involves life, liberty, and property. If the government is taking away any of the three, it must explain "whether the goal being pursued by the government constitutes a valid state interest, and whether there is a sufficient relationship between the means being used to reach that goal and the goal itself."[39] The Supreme Court defined substantive due process as follows:

> [I]t denotes not merely freedom from bodily restraint, but also the right of the individual to contract, to engage in any of the common occupations of life, to acquire useful knowledge, to marry, establish a home and bring up children, to worship God according to the dictates of his own conscience, and, generally, to enjoy those privileges long recognized at common law as essential to the orderly pursuit of happiness by free men.[40]

The way courts deal with substantive due process is to ask whether the rights involved are classified as being *fundamental* or *non-fundamental*. The rights mentioned above are considered fundamental. Other fundamental rights include interstate travel, access to the courts, the right to procreate,[41] and (with great controversy) the right to privacy.[42] For rights that are considered fundamental, the court will apply the strict scrutiny test. (See the next section below.)

Non-fundamental rights include economic issues, welfare legislation, employment, a driver's license suspension, etc. While these issues are still subject to the fairness concept in procedural due process, they are not considered to be fundamental freedoms. The courts will view challenges using the rational basis test. Strict scrutiny and rational basis will be discussed below, along with a concept called intermediate scrutiny.

How the Supreme Court Scrutinizes a Law[43]

Any time that the constitutionality of a law is challenged using Equal Protection or Due Process theories, the court must decide what kind of scrutiny to give that law. The Supreme Court will generally defer to the legislative branch on laws; however, not all laws are constitutional. In looking at laws that have been challenged, the Supreme Court has come up with three types of scrutiny that should be applied:

♦   *Strict scrutiny*: the law is unconstitutional unless it is the "least restrictive means" of serving a "compelling" government interest.

♦   *Intermediate scrutiny*: the law is unconstitutional unless it is "substantially related" to an "important" government interest.

♦   *Rational basis test*: the law is constitutional so long as it is "reasonably related" to a "legitimate" government interest.[44]

The Supreme Court has generally used *strict scrutiny* for laws that affect race and for government-imposed restrictions on the content of speech in public forums. In the case of Abrams v. United States,[45] the Supreme Court laid out the following rationale for freedom of speech:

> [W]hen men have realized that time has upset many fighting faiths, they may come to believe even more than they believe the very foundations of their own conduct that the ultimate good desired is better reached by free trade in ideas — that the best test of truth is the power of the thought to get itself accepted in the competition of the market, and that truth is the only ground upon which their wishes safely can be carried out. That at any rate is the theory of our Constitution.[46]

Restrictions on speech are only permitted if the law is narrowly tailored to further a compelling state interest.[47] Furthermore, the law must be the least restrictive alternative available. However, the marketplace of ideas is not absolute either. According to legal scholar Julie Hilden, "Just as Supreme Court First Amendment doctrine loves the 'marketplace of ideas,' it hates a 'captive audience' — an audience forced to listen to speech it doesn't want to hear."[48]

Intermediate scrutiny has been traditionally used for decisions involving gender (sex). (Note: The term "gender discrimination" came into general use in the late 1980s. Before that time, many cases used the terms "sex" or "sex discrimination.") Although many people do not realize it, gender discrimination also includes sexual harassment. When searching for laws about this topic, use the words "gender," "gender discrimination," or "sex discrimination," as well as "sexual harassment."

Most laws, however, are decided on the *rational basis test*. The results of the three tests are that the Supreme Court has never struck down a statute after finding a rational basis, while most laws that are examined with strict scrutiny will be found unconstitutional. That is why lawyers try to avoid the rational basis test and always urge Courts to apply strict or intermediate scrutiny.

Plurality Decisions

A plurality opinion is the most difficult type of decision to read and understand. In a traditional opinion, if a majority of the justices vote the same way, the opinion becomes law. If at least five out of nine justices agree, you have a straightforward majority opinion that announces a rule of law. However, sometimes there is a situation in which more than five justices agree on which party should win the case, but fewer than five justices agree on why that party should prevail. In that situation, you have a plurality opinion.[49]

In a plurality opinion, there may be separate parts of the decision. Five or more justices may join some parts, while fewer justices may join other parts. "Very often . . . the only way to determine the holding in a plurality decision is to head-count."[50]

In all court decisions, a majority of the justices must support "judgment X." Within that majority, the justices agreeing on judgment X may have different rationales for reaching that conclusion. If five or more justices out of the nine on the Supreme Court support judgment X and a particular given rationale, A, the court has established a majority decision. If less than five justices agree on the rationale (yielding rationales A and B, and conceivably as many as nine), then the Supreme Court has created a plurality decision. The plurality opinion, therefore, represents the minority rationales for the majority judgment.[51]

For example, five justices could support judgment X, and with that judgment-majority, three justices support rationale Z and two justices support rationale B. Further, assume four dissenting justices support judgment Y and agree on their dissenting rationale. The three justices supporting judgment X and rationale A will write the plurality decision. Although a plurality of (four) justices agrees on the dissenting rationale, a majority disagrees with the dissent's judgment. Accordingly, the group of three supporting judgment X and rationale Z writes the plurality decision for the Court.[52]

A justice may opt not to join an opinion, thereby preventing the establishment of a majority decision and instead establishing a plurality decision. In general, there are three reasons a justice might do this: to limit the plurality rationale, to expand the plurality rationale, or to provide an entirely different rationale for the majority judgment.[53]

There are important questions concerning the authority of a plurality decision, and whether it establishes a precedent for future cases. The Supreme Court attempted to answer this question in Marks v. United States.[54] In that case, the Supreme Court held that: "when a fragmented Court decides a case and no single rationale explaining the result enjoys the assent of five justices, 'the holding of the Court may be viewed as that position taken by those Members who concurred in the judgments on the *narrowest grounds* [the court will read the opinion to represent the most narrow possible rule]."[55] Nonetheless, there are still questions about plurality decisions, and the Supreme Court itself has not always followed the *Marks* rule.[56]

A recent example of a plurality decision occurred in the case of *United States et al. v. American Library Association*.[57] This case involved the question of whether it was constitutional to require libraries to use Internet filtering software on computers used by juveniles. The case involved the Children's Internet Protection Act[58] (CIPA), which requires that libraries receiving funding under the Library Services and Technology Act (LSTA) or receiving the E-rate (a discount on Internet service for schools, libraries, and museums) must use filtering software on their public Internet terminals.

In the CIPA case, there was no single majority opinion. Instead, there were five separate opinions in the case. Six justices believed that CIPA was constitutional. Chief Justice Rehnquist wrote the opinion of the Court, joined by Justices O'Connor, Scalia, and Thomas. Justices Kennedy and Breyer each filed separate opinions concurring in the judgment, but not agreeing upon the reasons. Justice Stevens wrote a dissenting opinion, and Justices Souter and Ginsburg each wrote a separate dissenting opinion. In order to determine what, exactly, the Court decided, we have to analyze each opinion and then do a head count. For a more detailed analysis of this case, see Bryan M. Carson, *The Law of Libraries and Archives*, Chapter 10, "Internet Use Policies and the Filtering Debate."[59]

One interesting provision of the plurality decision is that "the justices ultimately ruled that the law was constitutional only if adult library users were able to readily request and receive unfiltered access to the Internet."[60] This point was very important in getting the divergent justices to agree upon the results of the case, and was based on a provision in CIPA that allows libraries to disable the filtering software "to enable access for bona fide research or other lawful purposes."[61]

Because a head count shows that the three plurality opinions represented five justices, all of whom agreed that patrons have the right to request that the filtering software be disabled, this provision is the law of the land. A reading of the plurality opinions in the CIPA case, therefore, yields the requirement that laws pertaining to Internet filtering for libraries must allow the patron to request that the software be removed.

Another recent plurality case was Parents Involved in Community Schools v. Seattle School District No. 1.[62] The *Parents Involved* case dealt with race-based assignments in the public schools of Seattle, Washington, and Louisville, Kentucky. The rationale for each school was diversity and integration. Neither school was under any desegregation orders. Although a complete discussion of the case is beyond the scope of this book, we can use the scorecard method to determine who wrote which part:

♦   Part I—C. J. Roberts, J. Scalia, J. Thomas, J. Alito, and J. Kennedy. The statement of facts and underlying questions of law.

◆ Part II—C. J. Roberts, J. Scalia, J. Thomas, J. Alito, and J. Kennedy. This portion concerned the standing of the petitioners and the jurisdiction of the Court to hear the case.

◆ Part III-A—C. J. Roberts, J. Scalia, J. Thomas, J. Alito, and J. Kennedy. Establishes strict scrutiny as the applicable test.

◆ Part III-C—C. J. Roberts, J. Scalia, J. Thomas, J. Alito, and J. Kennedy. States that the schools' actions are not narrowly tailored and that there are other, less restrictive measures that could have been taken.

Non-majority opinions include:

◆ Part III-B—C. J. Roberts, J. Scalia, J. Thomas, and J. Alito. The issue of test scores and other outcomes of segregation or integration are not the business of the Court. Race can never be a factor.

◆ Justice Kennedy wrote an opinion concurring in part. He agreed that the Court had jurisdiction, that strict scrutiny was the appropriate test, and that the schools' plans did not satisfy the requirements of strict scrutiny. However, he felt that race could indeed be used on some occasions as a factor—but it should always be the last one considered.

◆ Justice Thomas joined all parts of C. J. Roberts' opinion, but also wrote a separate concurring opinion. Justice Thomas stated that re-segregation was not occurring in either Seattle or Louisville. According to Justice Thomas, housing patterns, employment practices, economic conditions, and social attitudes play no part whatsoever in integration, nor do the claimed educational or democratic benefits of diverse schools. He wrote that it is permissible for schools to be all black or all white, as long as the state isn't mandating racial separation.

◆ Justices Breyer, Stevens, Souter, and Ginsburg wrote a dissenting opinion. They would have upheld the schools' actions, arguing that the plans served a compelling state interest and were narrowly tailored. The dissent contains an appendix with statistical information on re-segregation trends.

◆ Justice Stevens joined in Justice Breyer's dissent, but also wrote a separate dissent. He took great issue with Chief Justice Roberts' opinion, particularly section III-B (which was not joined by Justice Kennedy, and thus did not have a majority).

The key to interpreting this case is the concurring opinion by Justice Kennedy. He used similar language in section III-C of his concurrence (and other language elsewhere in the opinion) to that used by Justice Breyer's dissent in section III-A, section V, and portions of section VI. However, nowhere did Justice Kennedy say that he was joining these sections in Justice Breyer's dissent, nor did the dissent state that they joined Justice Kennedy in section III-C.

Since three other justices joined Justice Breyer's dissent, Justice Kennedy would have made the fifth justice, forming a majority for those sections. Because, however, Justice Kennedy was not explicit, educators, lawyers, and legal scholars have been left to grapple with questions about what legal standard was really announced by the Supreme Court. It requires a word-by-word analysis comparing the writings of Justice Kennedy and Justice Breyer to determine the ruling of the Court.

My interpretation of this case is that Justice Kennedy's opinion is probably the true "opinion of the Court." A quick-and-dirty reading indicates that four other justices agree to the principles he espouses in each part of his concurrence. The best reading of this complicated opinion is to treat Justice Kennedy's concurring opinion as the ruling of the Court, allowing the use of socioeconomic class and open-enrollment policies to build as diverse a school as possible— using other factors first, and race only as the last factor considered.

Documents and Sources on U.S. Constitutional Interpretation

There are a number of excellent reference sources on the interpretation of the Constitution and its Amendments. The following list is a selected bibliography of items that I recommend for those who are interested in a broad overview of Constitutional interpretation.

◆ Amar, Akhil Reed
- o *America's Constitution: A Biography*. (2005). New York: Random House.
- o *The Bill of Rights: Creation and Reconstruction*. (1998). New Haven: Yale University Press.
- o Constitutional Rights in a Federal System: Rethinking Incorporation and Reverse Incorporation. (1995). *In* Terry Eastland (Ed.), *Benchmarks: Great Constitutional Controversies in the Supreme Court*. Washington, DC: Ethics & Public Policy Center.
- o Did the Fourteenth Amendment incorporate the Bill of Rights against states? Remarks at 14th annual Federalist Society symposium. (1996). *Harvard Journal of Law & Public Policy, 19(4)*, 443-450, *available at* http://islandia.law .yale.edu/amar/lawreview/1996Fourteenth.pdf.
- o Five views of federalism: Converse-1983 in context. (1994, October). *Vanderbilt Law Review, 47(5)*, 1229-1250, *available at* http://islandia.law.yale.edu/ amar/lawreview/1994Five.pdf.
- o The Bill of Rights and the Fourteenth Amendment. (1992, April). *Yale Law Journal, 101(6)*, 1193-1284, *available at* http://islandia.law.yale.edu/amar/ lawreview/1992Bill.pdf.
- o Of sovereignty and federalism. (1987, June). *Yale Law Journal. 96(7)*, 1425-1520.

◆ Antieau, Chester James. (1981). *The Original Understanding of the Fourteenth Amendment*. Tucson, AZ: Mid-America Press.

◆ Avins, Alfred. (1968). Incorporation of the Bill of Rights: The Crosskey-Fairman debates revisited. *Harvard Journal on Legislation, 6(1)*, 1, 17-26.

♦   Berger, Raoul
    o   Incorporation of the Bill of Rights in the Fourteenth Amendment: A nine-lived
        cat. (1981). *Ohio State Law Journal, 42(2)*, 435-466.
    o   *The Fourteenth Amendment and the Bill of Rights*. (1989). Norman, OK: Uni-
        versity of Oklahoma Press.

♦   Brennan, William J., Jr. (1961). The Bill of Rights and the states, *New York Univer-
    sity Law Review, 36(4)*, 761-778.

♦   *CQ Press Supreme Court Collection*
    http://www.cqpress.com/product/Supreme_Court_Collection.html
    A subscription database aimed at high school and college students with over 5,000
    case summaries and over 8,000 opinion-writing and voting results, along with con-
    textual framework and analysis of the Supreme Court and its decisions. The data-
    base analyzes "decisions within the context of our nation's history and the constitu-
    tion. Case summaries include related links to direct additional research about
    specific constitutional or public policy topics. . . . 'Case Boxscores' include date of
    decision, votes, opinion authors, and justice alignments and a link to the full-text of
    the case. Biographies of every justice include a detailed analysis of their judicial phi-
    losophies and 'case participation boxscores' with links to their opinions." [Descrip-
    tion from website.]

♦   Crosskey, William Winslow, & Jeffrey, William. (1953). *Politics and the Constitu-
    tion in the History of the United States*. Chicago: University of Chicago Press.

♦   Curtis, Michael Kent. (1986). *No State Shall Abridge: The Fourteenth Amendment
    and the Bill of Rights*. Durham, NC: Duke University Press.

♦   *Encyclopedia of the American Constitution.*
    o   [1st ed.] (1985). Leonard Williams Levy, Kenneth L. Karst, & Dennis J. Ma-
        honey (Eds.). New York: Macmillan.
    o   [2nd ed.] (2000). Leonard Williams Levy & Kenneth L. Karst (Eds.). New
        York: Macmillan.

♦   *Encyclopedia of the American Presidency.* (1994). Leonard W. Levy & Louis Fisher
    (Eds.). New York: Simon & Schuster.

♦   *Encyclopedia of the First Amendment.* (2008). John R. Vile, David L. Hudson Jr., &
    David Schultz (Eds.). Washington, DC: CQ Press.

♦   *Encyclopedia of the United States Congress*
    o   [1st ed.] (1995). Donald C. Bacon, Roger H. Davidson, & Morton Keller
        (Eds.). New York: Simon & Schuster.
    o   [2nd ed.] (2007). Robert E. Dewhirst & John David Rausch, Jr. (Eds.). New
        York: Facts On File.

♦ Fairman, Charles. (1949). Does the Fourteenth Amendment incorporate the Bill of Rights? The original understanding. *Stanford Law Review, 2(1)*, 5-139.

♦ Farber, Daniel A., & Sherry, Suzanna. (1990). *A History of the American Constitution*. St. Paul, MN: West.
A good source on the origin of the Constitution, this work contains both original essays and an annotated version of primary sources. The idea is that the primary sources will tell the story, with context provided by the essays. Although originally conceived as a college textbook, this is a good work for graduate and undergraduate libraries, as well as larger public libraries and law libraries.

♦ Farrelly, Stephen P. (2007). *Saying what the law is: A pragmatic theory of legal interpretation* (unpublished Ph.D. thesis, Emory University) (available from ProQuest Dissertations & Theses, Publication No. AAT 3279871).

♦ Flack, Horace E. (1965). *The adoption of the Fourteenth Amendment*. Gloucester, MA: P. Smith.

♦ Frankfurter, Felix. (1965). Memorandum on "Incorporation" of the Bill of Rights into the Due Process Clause of the Fourteenth Amendment. *Harvard Law Review, 78(4)*, 746-783.

♦ Haider-Markel, Donald P. (2009). Political Encyclopedia of U.S. States and Regions. 2 vols. Alexandria, VA: CQ Press.

♦ Kendrick, Benjamin B. (1914). *The Journal of the Joint Committee of Fifteen on Reconstruction*. New York: Columbia University.

♦ Linder, Doug. (2009). Exploring Constitutional conflicts: The incorporation debate, *available at* http://www.law.umkc.edu/faculty/projects/ftrials/conlaw/incorp.htm.

♦ Mansfield, Harvey C., Jr. (1991). *America's Constitutional Soul*. Baltimore: Johns Hopkins University Press.

♦ McGovney, D. O. (1918). Privileges or Immunities clause, Fourteenth Amendment, *Iowa Law Bulletin, 4(4)*, 219-244.

♦ Morrison, Stanley. (1949). Does the Fourteenth Amendment incorporate the Bill of Rights? The judicial understanding. *Stanford Law Review, 2(1)*, 140-173.

♦ Ng, Nora Y. (2009). *Strategic choice of legal instruments in the United States Supreme Court* (unpublished Ph.D. dissertation, Stanford University) (available from ProQuest Dissertations & Theses, Publication No. AAT 3343870).

♦ Rawle, William. (1825). *A View of the Constitution of the United States of America*. Philadelphia: H. C. Carey & I. Lea.

◆   Rossiter, Clinton. (1962). *The Three Pillars of United States Government: The Presidency, the Congress, the Supreme Court.* Washington: U.S. Information Service.

◆   Story, Joseph. (1833). *Commentaries on the Constitution of the United States.* Boston: Hilliard, Gray & Co.

◆   *Supreme Court Yearbook Series.* Washington, DC: CQ Press.
    This annual yearbook contains overviews of every Supreme Court term since 1989. The yearbook includes "case summaries of every opinion written during each court term . . . [e]ssays on the most significant cases from each year and the trends in each term . . . [and] tables and figures on voting patterns and constitutional law." This title is available as a stand-alone title (print or e-book) or as part of the Supreme Court Collection. [Description from website.]

◆   Wasserman, Rhonda. (2004). *Procedural Due Process: A Reference Guide to the United States.* Westport, CT: Praeger/Greenwood.

Speeches and debates in Congress provide a good source of information on the adoption of the 14th Amendment. These are available in the *Congressional Globe* (the predecessor to today's *Congressional Record*). Some of the debates and speeches in the *Congressional Globe* include the following:

◆   *Congressional Globe*, 39th Congress, 1st Session, 1064-65 (1866) (Remarks of Rep. Robert Hale).
◆   *Congressional Globe*, 39th Congress, 1st Session, 1065 (1866) (Remarks of Rep. John Bingham).
◆   *Congressional Globe*, 39th Congress, 1st Session, 1089 (1866) (Remarks of Rep. John Bingham).
◆   *Congressional Globe*, 41st Congress, 2nd Session, 1536 (1870) (Remarks of Sen. Samuel Pomeroy).

Some of the early (i.e., pre-14th Amendment) cases that discuss or interpret the relationship between the Bill of Rights and the states include:

◆   Barron v. Mayor & City Council of Baltimore, 32 U.S. (7 Pet.) 243 (1833).
◆   Livingston's Lessee v. Moore, 32 U.S. (7 Pet.) 469 (1833).
◆   Permoli v. First Municipality, 44 U.S. (3 How.) 589, 609 (1845).
◆   Fox v. Ohio, 46 U.S. (5 How.) 410 (1847).
◆   Smith v. Maryland, 59 U.S. (18 How.) 71 (1855).
◆   Withers v. Buckley, 61 U.S. (20 How.) 84 (1858).
◆   Pervear v. Massachusetts, 72 U.S. (5 Wall.) 475 (1867).
◆   Twitchell v. Commonwealth, 74 U.S. (7 Wall.) 321 (1869).

Notes

1. U.S. Constitution, Article VI.
2. Railroad Company v. Fuller, 84 U.S. 560; 21 L. Ed. 710; 1873 U.S. LEXIS 1397; 17 Wall. 560 (1873).
3. Daniel J. Elazar, *Confederation and Federal Liberty*, 12 Publius: The Journal of Federalism 1, 5 (Autumn, 1982).
4. Hillsborough County v. Automated Medical Laboratories, Inc., 471 U.S. 707, 716 (1985), *Quoted by* Robert Marchant, *Federal Preemption of State Law*, 3 Wisconsin Legislative Reference Bureau (May 2003), *available at* http://www.legis.state.wi.us/lrb/pubs/consthi/03consthiIII051.htm.
5. Pacific Gas & Electric Co. et al. v. State Energy Resources Conservation and Development Commission et al., 461 U.S. 190; 103 S. Ct. 1713; 75 L. Ed. 2d 752 (1983) (hereinafter PG&E).
6. PG&E at 204.
7. PG&E at 205.
8. Marchant, *quoting* 29 U.S.C. § 1144 (a), 29 U.S.C. § 1144(b)(2)(A).
9. B. Guy Peters, American Public Policy: Performance and Promise [5th ed.] (New York: Chatham House, 1999) at 22.
10. Peters at 23.
11. Sandra Day O'Connor, *On Federalism: Preserving Strong Federal and State Governments*, 35 Court Review 4 (Spring 1998).
12. United States v. Lopez, 514 U.S. 549 (1995).
13. City of Boerne v. Flores, 521 U.S. 507 (1997).
14. Kimel v. Florida Board of Regents, 528 U.S. 62 (2000).
15. United States v. Morrison, 529 U.S. 598 (2000).
16. Philip P. Frickey & Steven S. Smith, *Judicial Review, the Congressional Process, and the Federalism Cases: An Interdisciplinary Critique*, 111 Yale Law Journal 1707 (May, 2002).
17. *See*, Frickey & Smith.
18. Congressional Research Service, Library of Congress, *Amendments to the Constitution First Through Tenth Amendments*, U.S. Constitution Annotated *at* 1001 (Government Printing Office, 2002-2004), *available at* http://supreme.justia.com/constitution/018-bill-of-rights.html.
19. *id.*, quoting 1 Annals of Congress 755 (August 17, 1789).
20. Barron v. Mayor and City Council of Baltimore, 32 U.S. 243; 7 Peters 242 (1833), *available at* http://supreme.justia.com/us/32/243/case.html.
21. Russell Kirk, *The First Amendment and Religious Belief*, The Catholic World (April, 1958), *available at* http://www.ewtn.com/library/HOMELIBR/1STAMEND.TXT.
22. *id.*
23. U.S. Constitution, 14th Amendment.
24. Akhil Reed Amar, *The Bill of Rights and the Fourteenth Amendment*, 101 Yale Law Journal 1193, 1234 (April, 1992), *available at* http://www.saf.org/LawReviews/Amar1.html.
25. Robert Hale, *Statement of Rep. Robert Hale*, Congressional Globe, 39th Congress, 1st session at 1064-65 (1866).
26. Amar at 1196.

27. Charles Fairman, *Does the Fourteenth Amendment Incorporate the Bill of Rights*, 2 Stanford Law Review 5 (1949).

28. Amar at 1264-1265.

29. *Due Process*, Constitution.net, *available at* http://www.usconstitution.net/consttop_duep.html.

30. *id.*

31. Mathews v. Eldridge, 424 U.S. 319 (1976), *available at* http://supreme .justia.com/us/424/319/case.html. *See*, Rhonda Wasserman, Procedural Due Process: A Reference Guide to the United States (Praeger Greenwood, 2004).

32. Connally v. General Construction Co., 269 U.S. 385 at 391, 46 S.Ct. 126; 70 L.Ed. 322 (1926). *See*, S. I. Shuman, *Constitutional Law: Due Process: Vague and Indefinite Statute*, 51 Michigan Law Review 922 (1953). *See also*, Parker v. Levy, 417 U.S. 733 (1974).

33. Steven J. Mount, Constitutional Topic: Due Process, U.S. Constitution, *available at* http://www.usconstitution.net/consttop_duep.html.

34. Thompson v. City of Louisville et al., 362 U.S. 199; 80 S. Ct. 624; 4 L. Ed. 2d 654; 1960 U.S. LEXIS 1448; 80 A.L.R.2d 1355 (1960), *available at* http://supreme.justia .com/us/362/199.

35. Stewart Dean, My Politics Page, *available at* http://inside.bard.edu/~sdean/personal/pol/index.html (used by permission).

36. *Shufflin' Sam's Long Step*, 75 Time Magazine 15 (April 4, 1960), *available at* http://www.time.com/time/magazine/article/0,9171,869437,00.html.
In 2009, an interesting development in Britain reminded many of the "Shufflin' Sam" case, although from the perspective of intellectual property law. The incident began when the Performing Rights Society sent a cease-and-desist letter to a supermarket in Clackmannanshire, U.K. because the store was playing the radio without paying royalties. When the store complied and stopped playing the radio, store employee Sandra Burt began to sing out loud during her shifts. Soon after, the Performing Rights Society told Ms. Burt "that she would likely face fines for lost royalties for her 'performance.'"
However, the story had a happy ending after a BBC story on the threat caused "an overwhelming outpouring of public vehemence." The Performing Rights Society backed off. "They sent her a bouquet of flowers as an apology and said she had their permission to keep singing. The note read, 'We're very sorry we made a big mistake. We hear you have a lovely singing voice and we wish you good luck.'" Jackson Mick, *British Copyright Org Threatens Singing Store Employee Then Apologizes*, Daily Tech (October 23, 2009), *available at* http://www.dailytech.com/British+Copyright+Org+Threatens +Singing+Store+Employee+Then+Apologizes/article16592.htm.

37. Thompson at 205-206.

38. 1 Stat. 93 2 (1789). *See*, Andrew T. Hyman, *The Little Word "Due,"* 38 Akron L. Rev. 1 (2005).

39. *Substantive Due Process*, Pennsylvania Legislator's Municipal Deskbook [3d ed.] 47 (Harrisburg, PA: Local Government Commission, General Assembly of the Commonwealth of Pennsylvania, 2006), *available at* http://www.lgc.state.pa.us/ deskbook06/Issues_Citizens_Rights_04_Substantive_Due_Process.pdf.

40. Meyer v. State of Nebraska, 262 U.S. 390; 43 S. Ct. 625; 67 L. Ed. 1042; 1923 U.S. LEXIS 2655; 29 A.L.R. 1446 (1923).

41. Skinner v. Oklahoma, 316 U.S. 535; 62 S. Ct. 1110; 86 L. Ed. 1655 (1942).

42. Griswold v. Connecticut, 381 U.S. 479; 85 S. Ct. 1678; 14 L. Ed. 2d 510 (1965). *See*, Viktor Mayer-Schonberger, *Substantive Due Process and Equal Protection in the Fundamental Rights Realm*, 33 Howard Law Journal 287 (1990).

43. Portions of this section were previously published in Bryan M. Carson, The Law of Libraries and Archives (Lanham, MD: Scarecrow Press, 2007). [Used by permission.]

44. *See*, Brian A. Freeman, *Trends in First Amendment Jurisprudence: Expiating the Sins of Yoder and Smith: Toward a Unified Theory of First Amendment Exemptions from Neutral Laws of General Applicability*, 66 Missouri Law Review 9 (Winter 2001). *See also*, Edward C. Walterscheid, *Musings on the Copyright Power: A Critique of Eldred V. Ashcroft*, 14 Albany Law Journal of Science & Technology 309 (2004).

45. Abrams v. United States, 250 U.S. 616, 40 S. Ct. 17; 63 L. Ed. 1173; 1919 U.S. LEXIS 1784 (1919), *available at* http://caselaw.lp.findlaw.com/scripts/getcase.pl?court =us&vol=250&invol=616.

46. *id.* at 630.

47. "According to the plaintiffs, these content-based restrictions are subject to strict scrutiny under public forum doctrine, see Rosenberger v. Rector & Visitors of Univ. of Va., 515 U.S. 819, 837, 132 L. Ed. 2d 700, 115 S. Ct. 2510 (1995), and are therefore permissible only if they are narrowly tailored to further a compelling state interest and no less restrictive alternatives would further that interest, see Reno v. ACLU, 521 U.S. 844, 874, 138 L. Ed. 2d 874, 117 S. Ct. 2329 (1997)." American Library Association v. United States, 201 F. Supp. 2d 401, 407 (E.D. Pa. 2002).

The law of defamation in the U.S. is different from that of many other countries. The United Kingdom has become a destination for what is known as "Libel Tourism." Because of these differences, individuals in the U.S. sometimes have their hands tied by British courts.

The situation with the United Kingdom is based on two differences from U.S. law. First, there is no Constitutional Freedom of Speech issue, as there would be if a court in the U.S. ruled on this case. The First Amendment in the U.S. is stronger than any other country (even Canada). This right is nearly absolute for all protected speech, and an opinion is certainly protected. (Yelling "fire" in a crowded theater, on the other hand, is not considered to be protected speech.)

The government can impose time, place, and manner restrictions (such as requiring people to obtain a parade permit), but these restrictions are subject to strict scrutiny review. The government must show that there was a compelling governmental interest in restricting the speech, and that the imposed restriction was the least restrictive means of serving that compelling governmental interest. For parade permits, there are issues of traffic and pedestrian safety, the use of police officers to escort the parade, etc. That's why governments can ask for advance notice that a parade will take place.

The burden of proof is the other major difference between libel law in the U.S. and the U.K. In Britain, the defendant has the burden of proving that he or she did not defame the plaintiff. Unless the defendant proves this in court, he or she will automatically lose the case. By contrast, U.S. law puts the burden of proof on the plaintiff. The U.S. plaintiff must prove that there has been defamation; otherwise the court will automatically find for the defendant.

Because of the differences between British and U.S. defamation law, authors and publishers often have to retract poor reviews of a book or product. If John Doe writes a novel and I give it a bad review, I could be sued in a British court. Since defending the case would require me to lay out a substantial amount of money for a British solicitor and barrister, travel to Britain to testify in court, and in fact to prove that the book really was poorly written, it is much more sensible to retract the review, apologize, and write that the book is wonderful. It is these two differences between British and U.S. law that have led to the issue of libel tourism. *See,* Lynn Andriani, *New York Fights "Libel Tourism": New Bill Will Protect Authors from Foreign Lawsuits,* Publishers Weekly (January 21, 2008) at 12, *available at* http://www.publishersweekly.com/pw/print/20080121/1651-new-york-fights-e2-80-9clibel-tourism-e2-80-9d-.html.

48. Julie Hilden, *Television and the Marketplace of Ideas: What Role Will Developments Like TiVo and A La Carte Cable Play in Promoting Free Speech?* Findlaw's Writ (December 20, 2005), *available at* http://writ.news.findlaw.com/hilden/20051220.html.

49. *See,* Adam S. Hochschild, Note, *The Modern Problem of Supreme Court Plurality Decisions: Interpretation in Historical Perspective,* 4 Washington University Journal of Law & Policy 261, 271 (2000).

50. David C. Bratz, Comment, *Stare Decisis in Lower Courts: Predicting the Demise of Supreme Court Precedent,* 60 Washington University Law Review 87, 99 (1984).

51. Hochschild at 271 (2000).

52. Hochschild.

53. Hochschild.

54. Marks v. United States, 430 U.S. 188 (1977).

55. Marks at 193.

56. There have been many helpful articles written on this topic. For more information on plurality decisions, *see generally,* John F. Davis & William L. Reynolds, *Juridical Cripples: Plurality Opinions in the Supreme Court,* 1974 Duke Law Journal 59; Ken Kimura, *A Legitimacy Model for the Interpretation of Plurality Decisions,* 77 Cornell Law Review 1593 (1992); Burt Neuborne, *The Binding Quality of Supreme Court Precedent,* 61 Tulane Law Review 991 (1987); Laura Krugman Ray, *The Justices Write Separately: Uses of the Concurrence by the Rehnquist Court,* 23 U.C. Davis Law Review 777 (1990); Igor Kirman, Note, *Standing Apart to Be a Part: The Precedential Value of Supreme Court Concurring Opinions,* 95 Columbia Law Review 2083 (1995); Linda Novak, Note, *The Precedential Value of Supreme Court Plurality Decisions,* 80 Columbia Law Review 756 (1980); William G. Peterson, Note, *Splintered Decisions, Implicit Reversal and Lower Federal Courts: Planned Parenthood v. Casey,* 1992 Brigham Young University Law Review 289 (1992); William G. Peterson, Note, *Plurality Decisions and Judicial Decisionmaking,* 94 Harvard Law Review 1127 (1981); Comment, *Supreme Court No-Clear-Majority Decisions: A Study in Stare Decisis,* 24 University of Chicago Law Review 99 (1956); Mark Alan Thurmon, Note, *When the Court Divides: Reconsidering the Precedential Value of Supreme Court Plurality Decisions,* 42 Duke Law Journal 419 (1992); Ruth Bader Ginsburg, *Remarks on Writing Separately,* 65 Washington Law Review 133 (1990); Richard L. Revesz & Pamela S. Karlan, *Nonmajority Rules and the Supreme Court,* 136 U. Pa. L. Rev. 1067 (1988); Douglas J. Whaley, *A Suggestion for the Prevention of No-Clear-Majority Judicial Decisions,* 46 Texas Law Review 370, 371 (1968).

57. United States v. American Library Association, 539 U.S. 194; 123 S. Ct. 2297; 156 L. Ed. 2d 221; 2003 U.S. LEXIS 4799; 71 U.S.L.W. 4465 (2003), *available at* http://laws.findlaw.com/us/000/02-361.html. [Hereinafter "CIPA Case."]

58. 114 Stat. 2763A-335. The act is codified at 20 U.S.C. §§ 9134(f)(1)(A)(i) and

(B)(i) and at 47 U.S.C. §§ 254(h)(6)(B)(i) and (C)(i). Since the legal definition of a "minor" is a person under the legal age of 18, this provision applies to young adults, even though most of the discussion uses the term "children."

59. Bryan M. Carson, The Law of Libraries and Archives (Lanham, MD: Scarecrow Press, 2007).

60. Keith Michael Fiels, *ALA's Response to the CIPA Decision*, Posting to rusaaccess@ala.org (July 16, 2003), *available at* http://www.rpls.ws/Links/CIPA2.htm.

61. 20 U.S.C. § 9134(f)(3); 47 U.S.C. § 254(h)(6)(D). The E-rate allows disabling "during use by an adult." 47 U.S.C. § 254(h)(6)(D). Under the guidelines of the LSTA grant, any person is permitted to request that the filter be disabled. 20 U.S.C. § 9134(f)(3).

62. 127 S. Ct. 2738; 168 L. Ed. 2d 508; 2007 U.S. LEXIS 8670; 75 U.S.L.W. 4577, *available at* http://www.brownat50.org/brownCases/PostBrownCases/SeattleSchools.pdf.

The Enigma of International Law
in the U.S. Legal System

The Foreign Relations Power gives the Executive Branch the power to conclude treaties. After negotiation, treaties are sent to the Senate for ratification. Once a treaty has been ratified, it remains in effect unless there is an expiration provision or unless the U.S. government repudiates the treaty.

Once ratified, treaties become the law of the land, subject only to the Constitution. The "Supremacy Clause"of the Constitution (Article VI) states: "This Constitution, and the Laws of the United States which shall be made in Pursuance thereof; and all Treaties made, or which shall be made, under the Authority of the United States, shall be the supreme Law of the Land; and the Judges in every State shall be bound thereby, any Thing in the Constitution or Laws of any state to the Contrary notwithstanding."[1] However, it is not entirely clear how—or if—international law applies to domestic U.S. law. There are many questions (and some criticisms) about recent uses of international law in U.S. Supreme Court opinions. In a sense, this unsettled area of jurisprudence is a true enigma.

This chapter will explain the basis of international law and discuss the role of treaties in U.S. law. I will also address some of the criticisms of recent Supreme Court decisions. Finally, the chapter will contain resources for finding foreign and international law, treaties, and international tribunals.

Treaties and International Law

The Constitution proclaims in Article VI that treaties are the second most important "supreme" law of the land. Once a treaty has been passed, ratified, and executed, no federal or state statute, regulation, or judicial opinion can trump it—except for the provisions of the Constitution itself. Treaties and international law are therefore a very important part of the American legal system. However, because they represent a very different type of legal regime, it is important to understand the different types and sources of international law. While a complete discussion of international law is outside the scope of this work, the following section will provide a basic introduction. Readers who are interested in learning more should read a book or visit a website dealing specifically with public international law. Several such works are listed later in this chapter.

A. Public and Private International Law

There are two main types of international law. *Public International Law* deals with the relationship between nations and international organizations such as the United Nations, while *Private International Law* is concerned with the interactions of individuals or corporations across national boundaries. In the world of international law, nations and sovereign lands are usually referred to as "states." This terminology can be confusing to Americans, but is generally accepted. In the U.S., it would mean the federal government, as opposed to individual states within the U.S.

The definition of international law which is quoted most often comes from the *Restatement 3d of Foreign Relations Law*: "International law, as used in this Restatement, consists of rules and principles of general application dealing with the conduct of states and of international organizations and with their relations inter se, as well as with some of their relations with persons, whether natural or juridical."[2] In the comments, the *Restatement* distinguishes public and private international law as follows:

> International law, which in most other countries is referred to as "public international law," is often distinguished from private international law (called conflict of laws in the United States). Private international law has been defined as law directed to resolving controversies between private persons, natural as well as juridical, primarily in domestic litigation, arising out of situations having a significant relationship to more than one state. . . .
>
> Unless otherwise indicated, "international law" as used in this Restatement is law that applies to states and international (intergovernmental) organizations generally. It includes law contained in widely accepted multilateral agreements. Undertakings of a particular state or international organization under a particular international agreement — for example, the obligation of a state under a bilateral tax treaty with another state — are binding under international law, but the substantive content of such undertakings is not international law applicable generally. . . .[3]

Issues of war, peace, international relations, and trans-national organizations such as the United Nations or the Organization of African States are technically different than the questions of which laws apply to individuals, corporations, and non-governmental organizations. However, in reality there are many overlaps between the two. International treaties between nation-states (for example, tax treaties) can affect the rights of individuals, and private law can affect the way in which nations relate to one another. National laws dealing with asylum and refugees are examples of the latter situation. The Nutshell on Public International Law explains it as follows:

> On the domestic plane, international law is not a legal system. When we say in the U.S. . . . that international law is "the law of the land," we are in fact saying that it is a branch of our legal system, in much the same way that the law of torts or contracts is a branch of our legal system. . . . The question whether the individual invoking international law in an American court, for example, has rights or obligations under international law on the international plane . . . is for the most part irrelevant. The relevant question here is whether this or that

rule of international law is, as a matter of American law, appropriate to the resolution of the controversy before the court.[4]

International law is thus subject to—and enforced by—the domestic laws of each nation. However, this raises the question of where international law comes from. After all, there is no single body that creates international law. This makes international law vastly more difficult to determine than domestic laws within a nation. The most frequently consulted explanations of the origin of international law are the *Restatement*, and Article 38 of the United Nations statute establishing the International Court of Justice ("ICJ"), which states:

> The Court, whose function is to decide in accordance with international law such disputes as are submitted to it, shall apply:
> a.   international conventions, whether general or particular, establishing rules expressly recognized by the contesting states;
> b.   international custom, as evidence of a general practice accepted as law;
> c.   the general principles of law recognized by civilized nations;
> d.   subject to the provisions of Article 59, judicial decisions and the teachings of the most highly qualified publicists of the various nations, as subsidiary means for the determination of rules of law.[5]

The *Restatement* uses similar concepts with slightly different wording:

1)   A rule of international law is one that has been accepted as such by the international community of states
    a)   in the form of customary law;
    b)   by international agreement; or
    c)   by derivation from general principles common to the major legal systems of the world.
2)   Customary international law results from a general and consistent practice of states followed by them from a sense of legal obligation.
3)   International agreements create law for the states parties thereto and may lead to the creation of customary international law when such agreements are intended for adherence by states generally and are in fact widely accepted.
4)   General principles common to the major legal systems, even if not incorporated or reflected in customary law or international agreement, may be invoked as supplementary rules of international law where appropriate.[6]

Most international law today is made by treaties and international agreements. Just as a contract is binding on each party, a treaty between states is also considered binding.[7] Traditionally this meant bilateral treaties between two states. However, the 19th and 20th centuries saw large numbers of states join international organizations and conventions with multilateral treaties. In many cases, the rights granted by party states under these multilateral treaties allow activity that is reminiscent of legislative or administrative activity. In many cases, the rules and resolutions are binding on member states. Binding resolutions, such as those from the World Intellectual Property Organization or the International Monetary Fund, create international law.[8] The United Nations charter is similarly binding on its members, and in fact has obtained such a force of custom that it has also become customary international law.[9]

Treaties themselves are in fact governed by a multilateral agreement known as the *Vienna Convention on the Law of Treaties*.[10] This agreement was created in 1969 and became effective in 1980. The convention codifies the customary practices of negotiating and ratifying treaties. Although the U.S. signed the treaty in 1970, the Senate has never ratified it. Nonetheless, the State Department "considers many of the provisions of the Vienna Convention on the Law of Treaties to constitute customary international law on the law of treaties," and therefore complies with its provisions.[11]

Customary law is a more difficult concept to define. The nebulous nature of international law means that—unlike Justice Potter Stewart's definition of pornography—we *don't* know it when we see it.[12] Yet the comments to § 102 of the *Restatement* make a good starting point. Customary international law is created only when a state believes that it has a legal obligation to follow the rules.[13] One way in which this comes about is by the "Practice of states." The comments to § 102 define this as including "diplomatic acts and instructions as well as public measures and other governmental acts and official statements of policy, whether they are unilateral or undertaken in cooperation with other states, for example in organizations such as the Organization for Economic Cooperation and Development (OECD)."[14] These practices must be "general and consistent" and should have a wide following. If many states dissent, it prevents a principle from becoming customary law.[15]

Practice of states can range in the U.S. from enacted statutes, regulations, and opinions, all the way to pronouncements of the President or the State Department. These can all become customary international law if states feel that they are bound by the rules. One prominent example of customary law by presidential practice was the 1988 declaration by Ronald Reagan that the U.S. claimed 12 nautical miles of sea as part of its territory.[16] Since other states also claimed 12 nautical miles, this has become a practice of states.

"Secondary international law" consists of principles derived from the majority of domestic legal systems. The *Restatement* commentary uses Statutes of Limitations and rules against judicial conflict of interest as examples. In recent years, several U.S. Supreme Court cases have used secondary international law to invalidate or uphold statutes. Needless to say, this practice was considered controversial in some quarters.

In the case of Roper v. Simmons, the U.S. Supreme Court opinion prohibited execution of convicts who were minors at the time their crimes were committed.[17] Justice Kennedy's opinion was based upon both customary international law and secondary international law. First, the opinion noted that "Article 37 of the United Nations Convention on the Rights of the Child, which every country in the world has ratified save for the United States and Somalia, contains an express prohibition on capital punishment for crimes committed by juveniles under 18."[18] This analysis was a use of customary international law. The terms were not binding because the U.S. had not signed the agreement, but the widespread nature of its adoption led the Court to consider it customary international law.

In Roper v. Simmons, the Court also analyzed secondary international law by considering the actual laws of the rest of the world. Justice Kennedy explained that "only seven countries other than the United States have executed juvenile offenders since 1990: Iran, Pakistan, Saudi Arabia, Yemen, Nigeria, the Democratic Republic of Congo, and China. Since then each of these countries has either abolished capital punishment for juveniles or made public disavowal of the practice. In sum, it is fair to say that the United States now stands alone in a world that has turned its face against the juvenile death penalty." [Citation omitted.][19]

Roper v. Simmons was controversial because of its use of international law to invalidate U.S. law, but this case is not unique. During oral arguments in the cases of Gratz v. Bollinger[20] and its companion case, Grutter v. Bollinger, [21] Justice Ginsburg asked the Solicitor General for an understanding of international law. In her separate opinion for the Grutter case, Justice Ginsburg wrote that "affirmative action . . . must have a logical ending point . . . [that] accords with the international understanding."[22] Also, the U.S. Supreme Court struck down a state sodomy statute that made consensual homosexual sex illegal in Lawrence v. Texas.[23] The *Lawrence* opinion cited the evolving understanding of international law and cases from the International Court of Criminal Justice. Needless to say, this was also a very controversial decision.[24]

The Supreme Court itself indirectly addressed the controversy of using secondary international law in the case of Graham v. Florida.[25] This case involved the question of whether juveniles could be sentenced to life in prison without possibility of parole for crimes that did not include homicide. Before using secondary international law, the opinion included the following discussion:

> There is support for our conclusion in the fact that, in continuing to impose life without parole sentences on juveniles who did not commit homicide, the United States adheres to a sentencing practice rejected the world over. This observation does not control our decision. The judgments of other nations and the international community are not dispositive as to the meaning of the Eighth Amendment. But "[t]he climate of international opinion concerning the acceptability of a particular punishment" is also "not irrelevant." The Court has looked beyond our Nation's borders for support for its independent conclusion that a particular punishment is cruel and unusual. [Citation omitted.][26]

Because both customary and secondary international law are difficult to research and difficult to define, courts must use "evidence" to determine their existence.

Section 103 of the *Restatement* defines this evidence with the following wording:

1) Whether a rule has become international law is determined by evidence appropriate to the particular source from which that rule is alleged to derive (§ 102).
2) In determining whether a rule has become international law, substantial weight is accorded to
   a) judgments and opinions of international judicial and arbitral tribunals;
   b) judgments and opinions of national judicial tribunals;
   c) the writings of scholars;
   d) pronouncements by states that undertake to state a rule of international law, when such pronouncements are not seriously challenged by other states.[27]

The *Restatement* begins the process of clarifying the sources of international law, but the commentary provides more explanation. The comments note that while rulings of international tribunals are not binding on later cases, in practice most international courts do follow their previous decisions. Similarly, pronouncements of states interpreting international law may be taken as evidence of the law.

The Reporter's Notes for the *Restatement* also indicate that "the writings of scholars" is based upon the ICJ's wording in Article 38 that considers "the teachings of the most highly qualified publicists of the various nations. . . ." According to the Reporter's Notes:

> Such writings include treatises and other writings of authors of standing; resolutions of scholarly bodies such as the Institute of International Law (Institut de droit international) and the International Law Association; draft texts and reports of the International Law Commission, and systematic scholarly presentations of international law such as this Restatement. Which publicists are "the most highly qualified" is, of course, not susceptible of conclusive proof, and the authority of writings as evidence of international law differs greatly. The views of the International Law Commission have sometimes been considered especially authoritative.[28]

One of the best summaries of the sources of international law comes from a Columbia University Law Library research guide written by Kent McKeever. After analyzing the *Restatement* and the ICJ statute, he summarizes it as follows:

- ◆ Agreements Negotiated by the Affected Parties:
  - o Treaties
  - o Enactments by bodies established by treaties
  - o Resolutions of the United Nations General Assembly
  - o Directives of the European Union Commission
  - o Similar enactments by regional or subject-specific organizations

- o   Resolution of a dispute through mediation
- ♦   Deference to a Third Party Decision-Maker:
  - o   Case Law
  - o   International Courts of General and Limited Jurisdiction
  - o   International tribunals
  - o   National Courts, enforcing norms taken from international sources
  - o   Arbitral Decisions
- ♦   Academic Exposition, Synthesis, Persuasion, and Consensus:
  - o   Monographs
  - o   Articles
- ♦   Custom: Observation of What States Actually Do and Say:
  - o   Publications and information systems of the State Department and its foreign equivalents, IGO's, etc.
  - o   National yearbooks
  - o   International yearbooks
  - o   Truth & Reconciliation Commission Reports
  - o   The Restatement[29]

B. Treaties in the U.S. Legal System

Having now defined international law, we can begin to analyze their place in the U.S. legal system. Article II, Section 2 of the U.S. Constitution provides that "The President . . . shall have the power, by and with the advice and consent of the Senate, to make treaties, provided two-thirds of the Senators present concur. . . ." Through this provision, the power to negotiate treaties is reserved for the president, although it may be delegated to other members of the executive branch. It is the Senate, however, which must ratify a treaty.

There are two types of treaties in U.S. law, namely *self-executing* treaties and *non-self-executing* treaties. Unless the treaty is self-executing, enabling legislation is required for enforcement. "At a general level, a self-executing treaty may be defined as a treaty that may be enforced in the courts without prior legislation by Congress, and a non-self-executing treaty, conversely, as a treaty that may not be enforced in the courts without prior legislative implementation. . . . The doctrine of self-executing treaties thus serves to distinguish those treaties that require an act of the legislature to authorize judicial enforcement from those that require an act of the legislature to remove or modify the courts' enforcement power (and duty)."[30] The distinction between self-executing and non-self-executing treaties is important because of the Supremacy Clause.

As mentioned earlier, the Supremacy Clause stipulates that "this Constitution, and the Laws of the United States which shall be made in Pursuance thereof; and all Treaties made, or which shall be made, under the Authority of the United States, shall be the supreme Law of the Land; and the Judges in every State shall be bound thereby, any Thing in the Constitution or Laws of any State to the Contrary notwithstanding."[31] Thus a self-executing treaty does not require any follow-up (beyond Senate ratification) in order to become the "Supreme

Law of the Land." Once a self-executing treaty has been ratified, it trumps all contrary state *and* federal statutes, regulations, and decisions. Only the Constitution itself outweighs a validly ratified self-executing treaty.

If a treaty is non-self-executing, it requires an act of Congress to implement. In that case, it is the implementation act that outweighs contrary laws. However, this is subject to normal principles of statutory interpretation and pre-emption, as explained elsewhere in this book.

Naturally, there have been many attempts made to distinguish between self-executing and non-self-executing treaties. The U.S. Supreme Court first made this distinction in the 1829 case of Foster v. Neilson.[32] In an often-quoted passage, the Court ruled that:

> A treaty is in its nature a contract between two nations, not a legislative act. It does not generally effect, of itself, the object to be accomplished, especially so far as its operation is infra-territorial; but is carried into execution by the sovereign power of the respective parties to the instrument. In the United States a different principle is established. Our constitution declares a treaty to be the law of the land. It is, consequently, to be regarded in courts of justice as equivalent to an act of the legislature, whenever it operates of itself without the aid of any legislative provision. But when the terms of the stipulation import a contract, when either of the parties engage [sic] to perform a particular act, the treaty addresses itself to the political, not the judicial department; and the Legislature must execute the contract before it can become a rule for the court.[33]

The issue of whether a treaty is self-executing or requires enabling legislation is really a domestic question. Either way, the U.S. is still bound to its obligations under ratified treaties.[34] The Supremacy Clause operates to make self-executing treaties part of domestic law, but non-self-executing treaties will require *some* action on the part of Congress. This dual approach is based to some extent on the deference of federal courts toward the "political branches" (i.e., Congress and the Executive).[35]

Customary international law is more difficult for courts than treaties. The place of customary law has been vigorously debated. In *The Paquete Habana* (1900), the Supreme Court wrote:

> International law is part of our law, and must be ascertained and administered by the courts of justice of appropriate jurisdiction, as often as questions of right depending upon it are duly presented for their determination. For this purpose, where there is no treaty, and no controlling executive or legislative act or judicial decision, resort must be had to the customs and usages of civilized nations.[36]

What this provision means is that customary law can be used by domestic courts—but only if there is no contravening federal statute or regulation. The Supremacy Clause and the Foreign Relations Power make international law federal in nature, pre-empting state law. However, federal legislation can still override customary international law.[37]

The Supremacy Clause is controversial because some commentators believe it is outsourcing our law to outside groups. There has been criticism of several recent decisions using both treaty-based and customary international law.[38] In his confirmation hearing, Chief Justice Roberts responded to a question about the role of international law in domestic decisions by stating:

> [There are] a couple of things that cause concern on my part about the use of foreign law as precedent. . . . The first has to do with democratic theory. Judicial decisions in this country—judges of course are not accountable to the people, but we are appointed through a process that allows for participation of the electorate, the President who nominates judges is obviously accountable to the people. The senators who confirm judges are accountable to the people. In that way the role of the judge is consistent with the democratic theory. If we're relying on a decision from a German judge about what our Constitution means, no President accountable to the people appointed that judge, and no Senate accountable to the people confirmed that judge; and yet he's playing a role in shaping a law that binds the people in this country. I think that's a concern that has to be addressed.
>
> The other part of it that would concern me is that relying on foreign precedent doesn't confine judges. It doesn't limit their discretion [or] confine and shape the discretion of the judges. In foreign law you can find anything you want. If you don't find it in the decisions of France or Italy, it's in the decisions of Somalia or Japan or Indonesia or wherever. As somebody said in another context, looking at foreign law for support is like looking out over a crowd and picking out your friends. You can find them, they're there. And that actually expands the discretion of the judge. It allows the judge to incorporate his or her own personal preferences, cloak them with the authority of precedent because they're finding precedent in foreign law, and use that to determine the meaning of the Constitution. I think that's a misuse of precedent, not a correct use of precedent.[39]

However, other commentators believe that this position represents more of a "talking point" rather than a view of jurisprudence.[40] In an analysis of criticisms of the use of international law, Mark Tushnet comes to the following conclusions:

> [T]he criticisms are either irrelevant, not distinctive to the use of non-U.S. law, or seriously overstated. The structure of the irrelevance claim is simple: the validity of the criticism is entirely parasitic on some other argument—which is merely asserted, not defended—in the course of criticizing the references to non-U.S. law. The irrelevant criticisms apply other criticisms—deployed in a wide range of contexts, not just this one—of various judicial practices. The criticisms of references to non-U.S. law, that is, stand or fall with the validity of those other criticisms, and have little or no independent force. . . . [T]he target is not the actual practice of referring to non-U.S. law but to some

imagined practice that might develop out of the present one. Yet critics have provided no reasons why that development—which would involve the transformation of a practice that is defensible on its own terms into an indefensible one—will occur.[41]

An analysis of the *Roper* case by Harlan Grant Cohen declares that:

> Behind the rancorous war-of-words lay an assumption that, for better or for worse, the Court had in fact taken an "internationalist" or "transnationalist" turn and was increasingly willing to apply foreign and international law in reaching its decisions. What Roper and its reaction obscured, however, was that the assumption might not be true. Roper was only one of several recent Supreme Court decisions to touch upon issues of foreign law, international law, and the role of the Court in world affairs. A careful study of the 2003-2004 term—the term immediately preceding Roper and a term filled with cases of international import—yields a far more complex picture of the Supreme Court's international jurisprudence than that suggested by the war over Roper. In a wide range of opinions spanning topics as diverse as antitrust law and international human rights, the justices struggled—both with the legal materials and each other—to define the relationship between the United States and the world. Read together, those opinions begin to hint at a nascent Supreme Court theory of international law. That theory, far from adopting an internationalist or pro-international law position, reflects an unstable compromise between redressing international wrongs and protecting American sovereignty—a compromise that is far more respectful of American legal independence than criticism of Roper might suggest and which demonstrates both the potential and pitfalls of international law arguments before the Court.[42]

In the context of these criticisms, an analysis of the recent uses of international law in Supreme Court jurisprudence is helpful.[43] The most important recent cases were Hamdi v. Rumsfeld,[44] Rasul v. Bush,[45] and Medellin v. Texas.[46]

The *Hamdi* case involved a petition for *Habeas Corpus* after a U.S. citizen was held without charge as an enemy combatant. In deciding the case, both the Fourth Circuit and the Supreme Court considered the Geneva Convention (III) Relative to the Treatment of Prisoners of War,[47] along with "longstanding law-of-war principles."[48] The decision was a plurality opinion. The Opinion of the Court was written by Justice O'Connor and joined by Chief Justice Rehnquist, Justice Kennedy, and Justice Breyer. These four justices stated in the Opinion of the Court that the convention was not self-executing. However, these justices ruled that Hamdi was entitled to contest his classification as an enemy combatant in front of a neutral decision maker, as required by the Geneva Convention. Justice Souter (joined by Justice Ginsburg) concurred in part and dissented in part, agreeing with the result but for different reasons. Because, however, Justices Souter and Ginsburg also found that the government was not acting in accordance with the Geneva Convention, this six-person plurality makes the Geneva Convention the law of the land.[49]

The *Rasul* case involved non-U.S. citizens who were detained as enemy combatants. The question before the Supreme Court was whether they could challenge their detention. The Court found that there was a right to judicial challenges. The majority opinion by Justice Stevens relies solely on domestic law in the body of the opinion. However, "[a] different opinion . . . lurks beneath the surface. Hidden within the footnotes is a deep discursion on the historical scope of habeas corpus under the British Empire. . . ."[50] Notes 11-14 discuss a slough of cases involving customary international law. Harlan G. Cohen explains that:

> The cases cited tell the story of eighteenth-century captured French priva-teers, "a 'native of South Africa' allegedly held in private custody," a British citizen held in Northern Rhodesia, and Chinese nationals held in the British controlled territory at Tietsin. Do these footnotes explain Justice Stevens' adoption of such an expansive interpretation of the habeas statute? The footnotes appear to create an implicit analogy between the British Empire and the United States' new role in the world. Is Justice Stevens calling on the United States to recognize the great responsibility that comes with its growing power? Or are these footnotes meant to narrow Justice Stevens' opinion, providing examples of when habeas rights should and should not attach? Either way, the picture painted by this part of the opinion is the same: Rights are being spread around the world, not by international law, but by American law following American troops. Whether the U.S. government likes it or not, American Constitutional rights are marching in lockstep with American forces.[51]

Even though these references are in the footnotes rather than the body of the opinion, it is easy to see why many commentators find *Rasul* to be an important turning point in U.S. application of international jurisprudence.[52]

The *Medellin* case dealt with capital punishment and treaty obligations. The Vienna Convention on Consular Relations requires that foreign nationals convicted of crimes be given the ability to contact their consulate for legal assistance immediately upon arrest. The reason that this has become an issue in U.S. law is because a number of illegal immigrants from Mexico have been convicted of crimes. Some have been given the death penalty.

The Mexican government complained that its citizens have not been given access to Mexican consulates. This is important because the Mexican government has made a practice of providing legal and forensic assistance to defendants in capital cases. However, in each of these cases the defendants were represented by overworked and underfunded public defenders. It is thus possible that some defendants who were convicted would have won acquittal if private lawyers funded by the Mexican government had represented them.

In 2004, in a decision entitled *Case Concerning Avena and Other Mexican Nationals*, the Mexican government won a judgment against the United States in the International Court of Justice.[53] In 2004, the Oklahoma Court of Criminal Appeals gave a stay of execution to Osbaldo Torres, a convict whose execution was scheduled to proceed. The court in Oklahoma relied upon the *Avena* decision. The parole board subsequently recommended that the death sentence be commuted, which the governor then did. Both the parole board and the governor also relied upon the *Avena* case.[54]

On February 28, 2005, President Bush wrote a memorandum to the attorney general directing full U.S. compliance with the *Avena* decision.[55] However, the Texas courts refused to follow *Avena*. The next defendant who was scheduled to die was José Medellin. He challenged the execution under the *Avena* case and President Bush's memorandum.[56] However, the Supreme Court ruled in the *Medellin* case that the Vienna Convention on Consular Relations was a non-self-executing treaty that could only become binding domestic law if Congress passed enabling legislation. Since Congress had not done so, the Court declined to stop the execution.[57]

The *Medellin* case shows the issue of whether a treaty is self-executing or non-self-executing. It also shows the importance of enabling legislation for non-self-executing treaties. As such, it stands as a cautionary tale on the status of treaties as the supreme law of the land. The role of international law in domestic jurisprudence is still unsettled,[58] but it is clear that there has been—and will continue to be—a connection between domestic and international law in American courts.

Documents and Sources on International and Foreign Law and Treaties

The following list contains some of the most often used resources for researching international law, foreign law, and treaties. Subsection A contains books on international and foreign law, with websites found in subsection B. Subsection C contains links to international judicial bodies and tribunals such as the International Court of Justice. Articles and websites on treaty research are found in subsection D, and subsection E contains links to sources which list treaties in force or which contain the full text of treaties.

A. Books and Articles on International and Foreign Law

♦ Aust, Anthony. (2010). *Handbook of International Law*. Cambridge, UK: Cambridge University Press.

♦ Boczek, Boleslaw A. (2010). *The A to Z of International Law* [The A to Z Guide Series #134]. Lanham, MD: Scarecrow Press.

♦ Boyle, Alan. (2007). *The Making of International Law*. Oxford, UK; New York: Oxford University Press.

♦   Brierly, James. (1963). *The Law of Nations: An Introduction to the International Law of Peace*. Oxford, UK; New York: Oxford University Press.

♦   Brownlie, Ian. (2008). *Principles of Public International Law*. Oxford, UK; New York: Oxford University Press.

♦   Cassese, Antonio. (2005). *International Law*. Oxford, UK; New York: Oxford University Press.

♦   Danner, Richard A., & Bernal, Marie-Louise. (1994). *Introduction to Foreign Legal Systems*. Dobbs Ferry, NY: Oceana Publications.

♦   Evans, Malcolm D., & Capps, Patrick. (2009). *International Law*. Burlington, VT: Ashgate.

♦   *Guide to International Legal Research*. (2009). Newark, NJ: LexisNexis Matthew Bender.

♦   *International Law*. (2006). Evans, Malcolm (Ed.). Oxford, UK; New York: Oxford University Press.

♦   Louis-Jacques, Lyonette, & Korman, Jeanne. (1996). *Introduction to International Organizations*.New York: Oceana Publications.

♦   Lowe, Alan V. (2007). *International Law*. Oxford, UK; New York: Oxford University Press.

♦   Malanczuk, Peter, & Akehurst, Michael B. (2002). *Akehurst's Modern Introduction to International Law*. London, UK; New York: Routledge.

♦   Max Planck Institute for Comparative Public Law. (2003). *The Encyclopedia of Public International Law*. Bernhardt, Rudolf (Ed.). Amsterdam: Elsevier.

♦   Moynihan, Daniel P. (1990). *On the Law of Nations*. Cambridge, MA: Harvard University Press.

♦   *Oppenheim's International Law*. [9th ed.] (1992–). Jennings, Robert, & Watts, Arthur (Eds.). London, UK: Longmans.

♦   Posner, Eric A., & Sunstein, Cass R. (2006, October). The law of other states. *Stanford Law Review, 59*: 131-179.

♦   Schaffer, Ellen G., & Snyder, Randall. (1997). *Contemporary Practice of Public International Law*. Dobbs Ferry, NY: Oceana Publications.

B. Websites, Research Guides, and Online Articles on International and Foreign Law

♦ Bowman, M.J., & Harris, D.J. (1984). *Multilateral Treaties: Index and Current Status*. St. Paul, MN: Butterworth.

♦ Burnett, Anne E. (2003). Around the World in Twenty Minutes: International Legal Research on the web. Athens, GA: University of Georgia Law Library, *available at* http://digitalcommons.law.uga.edu/speeches/20.

♦ *Council on Foreign Relations*
http://www.cfr.org
The Council on Foreign Relations is an independent nonpartisan "think tank." Its website contains a wealth of material on treaties and foreign relations.

♦ *Electronic Information Systems for International Law*
http://www.eisil.org
A research guide created by the American Society for International Law. The site links to primary sources for international law. Modified Boolean searching is available.

♦ *EUR-Lex*
http://eur-lex.europa.eu/en/index.htm
A free database with European Union law and public documents, available in the 23 official languages of the European Union. Contains daily editions of the Official Journal of the European Union and Tenders Electronic Daily, along with treaties, international agreements, legislation in force, preparatory acts, case law, parliamentary questions, and the Directory of Community Legislation in Force. Documents date back to 1951. Although it has a wealth of materials, the interface is very primitive and difficult to use. The simple search uses unusual commands and does not support full Boolean. Instead of using OR, users need to put a comma (,) after each optional word. Use the word WITH for required terms, and EXCEPT for excluded terms. Nonetheless, this is a very rich database of materials dealing with E.U. law.

♦ *Foreign and International Law (Academic Info)*
http://www.academicinfo.net/lawforeign.html
An annotated research guide to foreign and international law. Includes both primary and secondary sources.[59]

♦ *Foreign and International Law (Law Library of Congress)*
http://www.loc.gov/law/help/foreign.php[60]

♦ *Foreign and International Law (WashLaw ForIntLaw)*
http://www.washlaw.edu/forint
Part of *WashLaw*, this website contains links to laws by region and country, or by subject area.

♦ *Foreign, Comparative & International Law*
http://www.law.uiowa.edu/library/fcil.php
Annotated links to a variety of primary foreign and international legal resources.[61]

♦ *Foreign, International, & Transnational Law Resources*
http://www.law.yale.edu/library/research/foreign&intl/grid.html
Created by Yale University Law School Library, this large portal contains links to treaties, tribunals and case law, and statutes. The site is arranged by jurisdiction, with some topical links.[62]

♦ *Global Legal Information Network*
http://www.glin.gov
The Global Legal Information Network (GLIN) is a public database of official texts of laws, regulations, judicial decisions, and other complementary legal sources contributed by governmental agencies and international organizations. These GLIN members contribute the full texts of their published documents to the database in their original languages. Each document is accompanied by a summary in English and, in many cases, in additional languages, plus subject terms selected from the multilingual index to GLIN. All summaries are available to the public, and public access to full texts is also available for most jurisdictions. [Description from website.]

♦ *GlobaLex* (Hauser Global Law School Program, New York University School of Law)
http://www.nyulawglobal.org/globalex
GlobaLex is a website dedicated to research in international and foreign law. Bibliographic essays contain both research and teaching resources, and are written by scholars who are familiar with research in the specific subject or country being discussed.

♦ Harms, Wiltrud. (2007). *Selected U.N. Resources and Research Tools: Overview and Search Tips for Legal Research.* New York: Columbia University Law Library, *available at* http://www.nyulawglobal.org/globalex/UN_Resources_Research_Tools.htm.

♦ *Hieros Gamos Guide to International Law*
http://www.hg.org/international-law.html
Created by a consortium of over 125 law firms worldwide, this large portal has links to both international and foreign law. The site also provides its own content, including e-books of practice materials and indexing for law journal articles. The site is famous for its *Doing Business Guides*, which discuss business law in various countries.

♦ *International and Foreign Jurisdictions*
http://www.uwe.ac.uk/library/resources/law/intfor.htm
Created by the law library at the University of the West of England (Bristol), this research guide contains links to a variety of primary and secondary sources for international and foreign law.[63]

♦   *International Legal Research Tutorial*
    http://www.law.duke.edu/ilrt
    A comprehensive guide to international and foreign legal research created by Marci
    Hoffman at the University of California Berkeley School of Law and Katherine To-
    pulos at Duke University School of Law. Highlights include:
    o   *Foreign & Comparative Law*
        http://www.law.duke.edu/lib/researchguides/foreign
    o   *International Law*
        http://www.law.duke.edu/lib/researchguides/internationallaw
    o   *Treaties*
        http://www.law.duke.edu/lib/researchguides/treaties
        http://www.law.duke.edu/ilrt/treaties_1.htm

♦   *Institute for Transnational Law* (University of Texas College of Law)
    http://www.utexas.edu/law/academics/centers/transnational/work
    "This site is a resource for French, German, Italian, Austrian and Israeli legal mate-
    rials in the fields of constitutional, administrative, contract and tort law. The English
    translations of decisions from Germany and France include cases from the Reichsge-
    richt, the Bundesverfassungsgericht, the Bundesgerichtshof, the Conseil Constitut-
    ionnel, the Conseil d'Etat and the Cour de Cassation." [Description from website.][64]

♦   *LawMoose World Legal Resource Center*
    http://www.lawmoose.com/index.cfm?cks=worldlaw
    The site contains numerous links to foreign and international law materials. The site
    also includes "a specialty search engine indexing a selection of valuable legal re-
    search sites." [Description from website.][65]

♦   *Legaltree*
    http://www.legaltree.ca/node/85
    This Canadian web page links to many legal sites, both in Canada and worldwide.
    Legaltree also contains user-contributed content, including research articles and e-
    books.

♦   *Lexadin* - The World Law Guide
    http://www.lexadin.nl/wlg
    Links to legal sites in over 160 countries.

♦   Maddex, Robert L. (1995). *Constitutions of the World*. Washington, DC: Congres-
    sional Quarterly.

♦   *Martindale-Hubbell International Law Digest*
    Published by LexisNexis, this series contains summaries of the laws of over 80
    countries, along with summaries of international treaties and conventions. The series
    also contains summaries of uniform laws such as the *Uniform Commercial Code* and
    the *Uniform Residential Landlord and Tenant Act*. The Martindale-Hubbell Interna-

tional Law Digest is useful for looking up brief answers and finding source citations to the proper statute. The Martindale-Hubbell Law Digest is available as part of the Martindale-Hubbell Law Directory series, as a stand-alone product, or on *LexisNexis* (professional version).

♦ *National Federation of Paralegal Associations*
http://nfpa.affiniscape.com/displaycommon.cfm?an=1&subarticlenbr=11
The NFPA site contains links to materials on both foreign and international law, including journals, articles, primary materials, and secondary materials on international legal research. The site also links to primary treaty materials from international organizations.

♦ Overy, Patrick. (2008, November/December). European Union travaux preparatoires: A guide to tracing working documents. *GlobaLex, available at* http://www.nyulawglobal.org/Globalex/European_Union_Travaux_Preparatoires.htm.
This bibliographic essay provides resources for finding government documents in the European Union.

♦ Reynolds, Thomas H., & Flores, Arturo A. (1989-2007). *Foreign Law: Current Sources of Codes and Basic Legislation in Jurisdictions of the World.* Buffalo, NY: Hein. Originally a looseleaf service in print, this series is now a continually updated electronic subscription database, *available at* http://www.foreignlawguide.com.

♦ Tashbook, Linda. (2005). *Researching the United Nations: Finding the Organization's Internal Resource Trails.* New York: Columbia University Law Library, *available at* http://www.nyulawglobal.org/globalex/United_Nations_Research.htm. Updated 2009, *available at* http://www.nyulawglobal.org/globalex/United_Nations_Research1.htm.

♦ *U.S. Tax Treaties (Internal Revenue Service)*
http://www.irs.gov/pub/irs-pdf/p901.pdf or
http://purl.access.gpo.gov/GPO/LPS39050

♦ *vLex*
http://vlex.com
"Largely a subscripton (fee) based system (though there is a small selection of free materials). There are some English language materials, and there is an English-language interface, but the vast majority of what you will find will be in the language of the originating country. Includes Spain, USA, France, Italy, Portugal, Colombia, Argentina, Andorra, EU, and some international materials. . . ."[66] The database includes current case law from the originating countries.

♦ *World Legal Information Institute*
http://www.worldlii.org
Links to legal sites all over the world, organized by country. While it does have some case law, most materials are in each country's official language.

C. Links to International Judicial Bodies and Tribunals

◆ *European Court of Human Rights*
   http://cmiskp.echr.coe.int/tkp197/search.asp?skin=hudoc-en

◆ *European Court of Justice*
   http://eur-lex.europa.eu/JURISIndex.do?ihmlang=en

◆ *Inter-American Court of Human Rights*
   http://www.oas.org/oaspage/humanrights.htm
   The Inter-American Court of Human Rights is an autonomous judicial institution whose purpose is the application and interpretation of the American Convention on Human Rights. [Description from website.]

◆ *International Criminal Court of Justice*
   http://www.icc-cpi.int
   An independent, permanent court that tries persons accused of the most serious crimes of international concern, namely genocide, crimes against humanity and war crimes. [Description from website.]

◆ *International Court of Justice*
   http://www.icj-cij.org
   "The International Court of Justice (ICJ) is the principal judicial organ of the United Nations. . . . [T]he Court is at the Peace Palace in The Hague (Netherlands). Of the six principal organs of the United Nations, it is the only one not located in New York. The Court's role is to settle, in accordance with international law, legal disputes submitted to it by States and to give advisory opinions on legal questions referred to it by authorized United Nations organs and specialized agencies. . . . Its official languages are English and French." [Description from website.]

◆ *Permanent Court of Arbitration*
   http://www.pca-cpa.org
   The PCA, established by treaty in 1899, is an intergovernmental organization providing a variety of dispute resolution services to the international community. [Description from website.]

◆ *United Nations*
   http://www.un.org

◆ *World Intellectual Property Organization*
   http://www.wipo.int
   "The World Intellectual Property Organization (WIPO) is a specialized agency of the United Nations. It is dedicated to developing a balanced and accessible international intellectual property (IP) system, which rewards creativity, stimulates innovation and contributes to economic development while safeguarding the public interest." [Description from website.]

◆ *World Trade Organization*
http://www.wto.org
The World Trade Organization (WTO) is a global international organization dealing with the rules of trade between nations. The WTO helps to negotiate and enforce international trade agreements. The *WTO Dispute Settlement Decisions* are available in print from Bernan Press.

D. Articles and Websites on Treaty Research

◆ *ASIL Guide to Electronic Resources for International Law Treaties*
http://www.asil.org/erghome.cfm
The American Society for International Law created this web page, which contains links to many sites on international law.

◆ *Electronic Information System for International Law*
http://www.eisil.org
This is the sister site of the *ASIL Guide to Electronic Resources*. It contains many links to primary sources of international law.

◆ Engsberg, Mark. (2006). *An Introduction to Sources for Treaty Research*, New York: Columbia University Law Library, *available at* http://www.nyulawglobal.org/globalex/Treaty_Research.htm.

◆ Feliú, Vicenç. (2008). *Introduction to Public International Law Research*. New York: Columbia University Law Library, *available at* http://www.nyulawglobal.org/globalex/Public_International_Law_Research.htm.

◆ Hoffman, Marci. (2001). Researching U.S. Treaties and Agreements. *LLRX*, *available at* http://www.llrx.com/features/ustreaty.htm.

◆ Louis-Jacques, Lyonette. (1998, June 8). *Fundamentals of Treaty Research: U.S. and Non-U.S. (Electronic Resources)*, Address at the Special Libraries Association Conference, *available at* http://www.lib.uchicago.edu/~llou/treaties.html.

◆ Majak, R. Roger. (1977). *International Agreements: An Analysis of Executive Regulations and Practices*. Washington, DC: Library of Congress Congressional Research Service.

◆ McKeeve, Kent. (2006). *Researching Public International Law*. New York: Columbia University Law Library, *available at* http://library.law.columbia.edu/guides/Researching_Public_International_Law.

◆ Pratter, Jonathan. (2005). *À la Recherche des Travaux Préparatoires: An Approach to Researching the Drafting History of International Agreements*. New York: Columbia University Law Library, *available at* http://www.nyulawglobal.org/globalex/Travaux_Preparatoires.htm. Updated 2008, *available at* http://www.nyulawglobal.org/globalex/Travaux_Preparatoires1.htm.

♦ Sahl, Silke
  o (2007). *Researching Customary International Law, State Practice and the Pronouncements of States Regarding International Law*. New York: Columbia University Law Library, *available at* http://www.nyulawglobal.org/globalex/Customary_International_Law.htm.
  o (2008). *Top Resources for Treaty Research*. New York: Columbia University Law Library, *available at* http://library.law.columbia.edu/guides/Top_Resources_for_Treaty_Research.

♦ *Treaties International—Legal Research (Washlaw)*
  http://www.washlaw.edu/forint/alpha/t/treaties.html

♦ Weigman, Stefanie. (2001). Researching Non-U.S. Treaties. *LLRX, available at* http://www.llrx.com/features/non_ustreaty.htm.

♦ Williams, Beth. (2006). *Guide to Researching Historical Treaties*. New York: Columbia University Law Library, *available at* http://library.law.columbia.edu/guides/Historical_Treaties.

E. Full Text and Status of Treaties to Which the U.S. Is a Party

Because the U.S. Senate must ratify a treaty before it becomes effective, the full texts of treaties are available with Senate documents. Key sources include:

♦ *Congressional Record*
  http://www.gpoaccess.gov/crecord/index.html
  Also available on Lexis, Westlaw, ProQuest, and HeinOnline.

♦ *Senate Executive Reports*
  http://www.gpoaccess.gov/serialset/creports/index.html
  This link contains documents for the most recent two Congresses. Older materials are available through the Serial Set on microform, or as a subscription database from ProQuest.

♦ *Senate Treaty Documents*
  http://www.gpoaccess.gov/serialset/cdocuments/index.html

♦ *Thomas (Library of Congress)*
  http://thomas.loc.gov/home/treaties/treaties.htm
  Contains information on treaties beginning with the 94th Congress (1975-1976).

♦ *United States Statutes at Large*
  http://memory.loc.gov/ammem/amlaw/lwsl.html
  From 1789 to 1947, all treaties were printed in *Statutes at Large*. This link contains the first 18 volumes, which cover the period between 1789 and 1875.

The following is a selective but representative list of sources that contain either listings of treaties or the full text. For more sources, refer to the research guides by Sahl and Williams listed in Section D.

♦ *Listing of Selected International Tax Conventions and Other Agreements Reprinted in the IRS Cumulative bulletin, 1913-1990.* (1991). Washington, DC: Government Printing Office.

♦ Department of the Army. (1976). *Selected International Agreements.* [DA pam 27; 24.] Washington, DC: Department of Defense.

♦ Library of Congress Congressional Research Service. (2001). *Treaties and Other International Agreements: The Role of the United States Senate.* Washington, DC: Government Printing Office, *available at* http://purl.access.gpo.gov/GPO/ LPS11657.

♦ Department of State. (1997–). *Treaty Actions.* Washington, DC: Government Printing Office, *available at* http://www.state.gov/s/l/treaty/c3428.htm.

♦ Department of State. (1991–). *United States Treaties and Other International Agreements.* Washington, DC: Government Printing Office. Available on *HeinOnline* and on microfiche.

♦ Department of State. (1941–). *Treaties in Force: A List of Treaties and Other International Acts of the United States in Force.* Washington, DC: Government Printing Office. [Previously known as *List of Treaties and Other International Acts of the United States of America in Force.*]
The latest issue of *Treaties in Force* is available at http://purl.access.gpo.gov/GPO/ LPS4126 or http://www.state.gov/s/l/treaty/tif/index.htm. Archived issues are available on the GPO website at http://purl.access.gpo.gov/GPO/LPS4127 or http://permanent.access.gpo.gov/lps4127.

There are also three commercially published guides to U.S. treaties prepared by Igor Kavass and published by W. H. Hein. All three are available as books, CD-ROMs, or via *HeinOnline.*

♦ Kavass, Igor. (1991–). *Kavass's Guide to the United States Treaties in Force* [sic]. Buffalo, NY: Hein.
Contains lists of bilateral and multilateral treaties and agreements arranged numerically, by subject, and by country, along with a chronological index and a directory of multilateral treaties by country and international organization.

♦ Kavass, Igor. (1994–). *Hein's U.S. Treaty Index: 1776–.* Buffalo, NY: Hein.
Lists bilateral and multilateral treaties to which the U.S. is a party. The index may be browsed by treaty number, subject, date, country, or international organization.

♦   Kavass, Igor. (1991–). *Kavass's Current Treaty Index*. Buffalo, NY: Hein.
    Indexes U.S. treaties and international agreements and treaties that have not yet ap-
    peared in TIAS.

F. Full Text and Status of Multilateral and Foreign Treaties

♦   *Avalon Project: Documents on Law, History, & Diplomacy (Yale University)*
    http://avalon.law.yale.edu/default.asp
    Contains historical treaties from antiquity to the 21st century.

♦   *The Flare Index to Treaties (University of London Institute of Advanced Legal Stud-
    ies)*
    http://193.62.18.232/dbtw-wpd/textbase/treatysearch.htm
    "A searchable database of basic information on over 1,500 of the most significant
    multilateral treaties from 1856 to the present, with details of where the full text of
    each treaty may be obtained in paper and, if available, electronic form on the Inter-
    net." [Description from website.]

♦   *Human Rights Library (University of Minnesota)*
    http://www1.umn.edu/humanrts
    A large collection of information on international law, including treaties and other
    international instruments, plus documents from the United Nations and regional or-
    ganizations. The site also has a number of bibliographies and research guides on
    various topics in international law and human rights.

♦   *Multilateral Treaties for Which the U.S. Is Depositary*
    http://www.state.gov/s/l/treaty/depositary

♦   *UNILAW*
    http://www.unidroit.info
    Produced by the International Institute for the Unification of Private Law (Unidroit),
    the UNILAW Data Base contains information regarding uniform law conventions
    and other instruments in both English and French.

♦   *UNILEX*
    http://www.unilex.info
    Produced by the International Institute for the Unification of Private Law (Unidroit),
    UNILEX is a collection of international case law and bibliographies on two of the
    most important international instruments for the regulation of international commer-
    cial transactions, the *United Nations Convention on Contracts for the International
    Sale of Goods* (CISG), and the *UNIDROIT Principles of International Commercial
    Contracts*.

♦   *United Nations Treaty Collection*
    http://treaties.un.org
    A large full-text collection containing the status and text of multilateral treaties de-
    posited with the Secretary-General, the United Nations Treaty Series (14 December

1946–January 2005), the League of Nations Treaty Series (5 July 1920–3 October 1944), the Su*mmary of Practice of the Secretary-General as Depositary of Multilateral Treaties*, the U.N. *Treaty Handbook, Handbook of Final Clauses of Multilateral Treaties, Monthly Statements of Treaties and International Agreements*, Depositary Notifications by the Secretary-General, and the *United Nations Treaty Series Cumulative Index*. Treaties are published in their original language(s), along with translations into English and French. Originally a subscription database, the UNTC became free in 2009.

♦ *World Treaty Index Multilateral Treaties Project* (Fletcher School of Law and Diplomacy, Tufts University), *available at* http://fletcher.tufts.edu/multilaterals.html.

Notes

1. U.S. Constitution, Article VI.
2. Restatement of the Law, Third, Foreign Relations Law of the United States, § 101 (hereinafter *Restatement*).
3. *id.* at § 101(C), § 101(D).
4. Thomas Buergenthal & Harold G. Maier, Public International Law in a Nutshell [2d ed.], St. Paul, MN: West, 1990 at 4.
5. Statute of the International Court of Justice, Article 38 (1946), *available at* http://www.icj-cij.org/documents/index.php?p1=4&p2=2&p3=0.
6. *id.* at § 102.
7. Buergenthal & Maier at 7-8.
8. Buergenthal & Maier at 91-92.
9. *Restatement*, § 102(H).
10. Vienna Convention on the Law of Treaties, 1155 United Nations Treaty Series 331 (May 23, 1969), *available at* http://untreaty.un.org/ilc/texts/instruments/english/conventions/1_1_1969.pdf.
11. "The United States signed the treaty on April 24, 1970." U.S. Department of State, *Vienna Convention on the Law of Treaties, available at* http://www.state.gov/s/l/treaty/faqs/70139.htm.
12. Justice Potter's famous phrase reads as follows: "I have reached the conclusion . . . that under the First and Fourteenth Amendments criminal laws in this area are constitutionally limited to hard-core pornography. I shall not today attempt further to define the kinds of material I understand to be embraced within that shorthand description; and perhaps I could never succeed in intelligibly doing so. But I know it when I see it, and the motion picture involved in this case is not that." Jacobellis v. Ohio, 378 U.S. 184, 197; 84 S. Ct. 1676, 1683; 12 L. Ed. 2d 793, 803-804 (1964) (Justice Stewart, Concurring).
13. *Restatement*, § 102(D).
14. *Restatement*, § 102(C).
15. *id.*
16. Presidential Proclamation No. 5928, December 27, 1988.
17. Roper v. Simmons, 543 U.S. 551; 125 S. Ct. 1183; 161 L. Ed. 2d 1 (2005).
18. *id.* at 576.
19. *id.* at 377, *quoting* Brief for Respondent at 49-50.
20. Gratz v. Bollinger, 539 U.S. 244; 123 S. Ct. 2411; 156 L. Ed. 2d 257; 2003 U.S. LEXIS 4801; 71 U.S.L.W. 4480 (2003).
21. Grutter v. Bollinger, 539 U.S. 982; 124 S. Ct. 35; 156 L. Ed. 2d 694; 2003 U.S. LEXIS 5357; 72 U.S.L.W. 3146 (2003).
22. *Grutter* at 2347.
23. Lawrence v. Texas, 539 U.S. 558; 123 S. Ct. 2472; 156 L. Ed. 2d 508; 2003 U.S. LEXIS 5013; 71 U.S.L.W. 4574 (2003) (overruling Bowers v. Hardwick, 478 U.S. 186 (1986)).
24. *See*, Ana Peyro Llopis, *The Place of International Law in Recent Supreme Court Decisions* [Global Law Working Paper 04/05], New York University School of Law, *available at* http://www1.law.nyu.edu/nyulawglobal/workingpapers/GLWP0405 Peyro.rtf; Diane Marie Amann, *"Raise the Flag and Let It Talk": On the Use of External Norms in Constitutional Decision Making*, 2 International Journal of Constitutional Law

597 (2004); Roger P. Alford, *"Outsourcing Authority?" Citation to Foreign Court Precedent in Domestic Jurisprudence: Four Mistakes in the Debate on "Outsourcing Authority,"* 69 Albany Law Review 653, 670-71 (2006). Alford relies on the authority of Equal Employment Opportunity Commission v. Arabian American Oil Co., 499 U.S. 244, 248 (1991). *See also,* Foley Brothers, Inc. v. Filardo, 336 U.S. 281, 285 (1949), superseded by statute, Civil Rights Act of 1991, Pub. L. No. 102-166, 105 Stat. 1071, 1077-78 (codified as amended in scattered sections of 42 U.S.C.); F. Hoffman-La Roche Ltd. v. Empagran S.A., 542 U.S. 155, 164 (2004), cert. denied, 126 S. Ct. 1043 (2006); Murray v. Schooner Charming Betsy, 6 U.S. 64, 118 (1804). *See generally,* Jonathan Turley, *Dualistic Values in the Age of International Legisprudence,* 44 Hastings Law Journal 185, 211-17 (1993); Curtis A. Bradley, *The Charming Betsy Canon and Separation of Powers: Rethinking the Interpretive Role of International Law,* 86 Georgetown Law Journal 479 (1998); Ralph G. Steinhardt, *The Role of International Law as a Canon of Domestic Statutory Construction,* 43 Vanderbilt Law Review 1103 (1990).

25. Terrance Jamar Graham v. Florida, 2010 U.S. LEXIS 3881 (May 17, 2010).

26. *id.* at 54-55. The quote is from Enmund v. Florida, 458 U.S. 782, 102 S. Ct. 3368, 73 L. Ed. 2d 1140 (1982) at 796-797, n. 22. Other cases cited by the opinion include: *Roper* at 575-578; Atkins v. Virginia, 536 U.S. 304, 122 S. Ct. 2242, 153 L. Ed. 2d 335 (2002) at 317-318, note 21; Thompson v. Oklahoma, 487 U.S. 815, 826, 108 S. Ct. 2687, 101 L. Ed. 2d 702 (1988) (plurality opinion) at 836, note 24; *Thompson* at 850; *Thompson* at 830; Coker v. Georgia, 433 U.S. 584, 97 S. Ct. 2861, 53 L. Ed. 2d 982 (1977) at 596, note 10 (plurality opinion); Trop v. Dulles, 356 U.S. 86, 101, 78 S. Ct. 590, 2 L. Ed. 2d 630 (1958) at 102-103 (plurality opinion).

27. *Restatement,* § 103.

28. *Restatement,* § 103 (Reporter's Notes).

29. Kent McKeeve, *Researching Public International Law* (New York: Columbia University Law Library, 2006), *available at* http://library.law.columbia.edu/guides/Researching_Public_International_Law.

30. Carlos Manuel Vazquez, *The Four Doctrines of Self-Executing Treaties,* 89 American Journal International Law 695, 695-96 (October 1995).

31. U.S. Constitution, Article VI.

32. Foster v. Neilson, 27 U.S. (2 Pet.) 253 (1829).

33. *id.* at 314.

34. Ian Brownlie, Principles of Public International Law [3d ed.] (Oxford, UK; New York: Oxford University Press, 1987) *at* 52-53.

35. *See,* Llopis.

36. The Paquete Habana, 175 U.S. 677, 700 (1900).

37. Buergenthal & Maier at 209-210. *See also,* L. Henkin, *International Law as Law in the United States,* 82 Michigan Law Review 1555 (1984).

38. *See,* Harlan G. Cohen, *Supremacy and Diplomacy: The International Law of the U.S. Supreme Court,* 24 Berkeley Journal of International Law 101 (2006), *available at* http://www.csb.uncw.edu/people/eversp/classes/BLA361/Intl%20Law/Required%20Readings/2.Intl%20Law%20of%20US%20Sup%20Ct.ssrn.pdf.

39. Confirmation Hearing on the Nomination of John G. Roberts, Jr. to Be Chief Justice of the United States Before the S. Comm. on the Judiciary, 109th Cong. 200 at 200, 201 (2005); *quoted in* Mark Tushnet, *When Is Knowing Less Better Than Knowing More: Unpacking the Controversy over Supreme Court Reference to Non-U.S. Law,* 90

Minnesota Law Review 1275 (2005-2006), *available at* http://local.law.umn.edu/uploads/ images/3277/Tushnet_Final.pdf.

40. Tushnet at 1276.

41. Tushnet at 1277-1278. *See also*, Amann; Llopis; Alford; John K. Setear, *A Forest with No Trees: The Supreme Court and International Law in the 2003 Term*, 91 Virginia Law Review 579 (May, 2005); Daniel A. Farber, *The Supreme Court, the Law of Nations, and Citations of Foreign Law: The Lessons of History*, 95 California Law Review 1335 (2007), *available at* http://www.law.berkeley.edu/mishkin/papers/ Mishkinarticle(Farber)10-17.doc.

42. Cohen at 103.

43. *See*, Farber; Tushnet; Carlos Manuel Vázquez, *Treaties as Law of the Land: The Supremacy Clause and the Judicial Enforcement of Treaties*, 122 Harvard Law Review 600 (2008), *available at* http://hlr.rubystudio.com/media/pdf/vazquez.pdf. *See also*, Cohen.

44. Hamdi v. Rumsfeld, 542 U.S. 507, 124 S. Ct. 2633, 159 L. Ed. 2d 578 (2004) (hereinafter "Hamdi"), *available at* http://caselaw.lp.findlaw.com/scripts/getcase.pl ?navby=case&court=us&vol=542&page=507.

45. Rasul et al. v. Bush and Abdullah Fahad Al Odah et al. v. United States et al., 542 U.S. 466; 124 S. Ct. 2686; 159 L. Ed. 2d 548 (2004) (hereinafter "Rasul"), *available at* http://caselaw.lp.findlaw.com/scripts/getcase.pl?navby=case&court=us&vol=542& page=466.

46. Medellin v. Texas, 554 U.S. 491, 129 S. Ct. 360, 171 L. Ed. 2d 833 (2008), *available at* http://laws.findlaw.com/us/000/06-984.html.

47. Geneva Convention (III) Relative to the Treatment of Prisoners of War, Aug. 12, 1949, 1955, art. 118, 6 U.S. T. 3316, 3406, T. I. A. S. No. 3364.

48. *Hamdi* at 521.

49. *Hamdi.*

50. Cohen at 137.

51. Cohen at 137-138.

52. *See*, Cohen; Llopis; Tushnet.

53. Case Concerning Avena and Other Mexican Nationals (Mexico v. United States of America), 2004 I.C.J. 128 (March 31, 2004), *available at* http://supreme.lp.findlaw .com/supreme_court/decisions/avena33104icj.pdf.

54. Sean D. Murphy, *Implementation of Avena Decision by Oklahoma Court*, 98 American Journal of International Law 581 (2004). *See also*, Noah Leavitt, *Is Oklahoma a New Human Rights Hot Spot? Why the State's Judges and Governor Were Right To Stop an Execution that Nearly Violated International Law*, Findlaw's Writ (May 24, 2004), *available at* http://writ.lp.findlaw.com/leavitt/20040524.html. *See also*, Stephen Yeazell, *When and How U.S. Courts Should Cite Foreign Law*, 26 Constitutional Commentary 59 (Fall 2009).

55. George W. Bush, *Compliance with the Decision of the International Court of Justice in Avena*, Memorandum for the Attorney General (February 28, 2005), *available at* http://www.debevoise.com/publications/pdf/Annex2oftheBriefAmicusCuriaeofthe UnitedStatesinsupportofRespondentPresidentialDirective_v1.PDF.

56. *Medellin v. Texas.*

57. John R. Crook, *Supreme Court Overturns Presidential Directive Seeking to Implement ICJ Decision*, 102 American Journal of International Law 635 (2008); Edward

Lazarus, *A Recent Supreme Court Decision on the Vienna Convention Reaffirms That Justice Stevens, at Eighty-Eight, Remains a Force to Be Reckoned With*, Findlaw's Writ (Mar. 27, 2008), *available at* http://writ.news.findlaw.com/lazarus/20080327.html.

58. *See*, Julian G. Ku, *Customary International Law in State Courts*, 42 Virginia Journal of International Law 265, *available at* http://www.hofstra.edu/pdf/law_ku _customary_international.pdf; Jack Goldsmith & Daryl Levinson, *Law for States: International Law, Constitutional Law, Public Law*, 122 Harvard Law Review 1791 (2009), *available   at*   http://www.harvardlawreview.org/issues/122/may09/goldsmith _levinson.pdf.

59. This link was suggested by Ronald Huttner, a retired attorney in Australia who ran a website called Vid-e-Lex in the 1990s. These links were part of his site, and are used with permission.

60. Suggested by Ronald Huttner.

61. Suggested by Ronald Huttner.

62. This annotation came from a summary of answers to a question on the Law-Lib discussion list. Sibyl D. Marshall, Foreign Case Law - Answers Summary, posting to law-lib@ucdavis.edu, May 30, 2007 (used by permission).

63. Suggested by Ronald Huttner.

64. Suggested by Sibyl Marshall.

65. Suggested by Ronald Huttner.

66. Suggested by Sibyl Marshall.

5

Congress: The Legislative Branch

In the federal system, the legislative branch passes the laws. The Congress and its laws have supremacy over all legal matters except the Constitution and treaties. Both the power of Congress and the restrictions on Congress come from the Constitution. Article I of the Constitution not only provides details about how the members of the U.S. House and Senate are elected, but Article I, Section 8, also enumerates the kinds of laws that Congress can pass. The Constitution only allows Congress to pass statutes which concern:

- Taxes, import duties, and excise taxes.
- Coining money and creating bonds to borrow money on credit.
- "To regulate Commerce with foreign Nations, and among the several States, and with the Indian Tribes."
- Laws concerning naturalization and immigration, bankruptcy, standards for weights and measures, post offices, and post roads.
- Laws promoting "the Progress of Science and useful Arts, by securing for limited Times to Authors and Inventors the exclusive Right to their respective Writings and Discoveries."
- Laws creating courts below the Supreme Court.
- Certain types of criminal laws.
- Declaring war, creating an army and navy, calling up the state militia when necessary.
- Laws dealing with the District of Columbia and federal lands; Congress has complete authority over all federal lands, including the District of Columbia.
- Making "all Laws which shall be necessary and proper for carrying into Execution the foregoing Powers and all other Powers vested by this Constitution in the Government of the United States, or in any Department or Officer thereof."[1]

In addition to the above, the House of Representatives can pass a budget and send it to the Senate for consideration. (Note that the budget must begin in the House.)[2] Also, the Senate has the power to confirm officers for executive agencies, nominees to the Supreme Court, and ambassadors to other countries. Finally, the Senate has the power to ratify treaties that have been negotiated by the President or the executive branch, and can enact laws to implement these treaties.[3]

Congress is prohibited from passing any laws that do not fall within one of the categories listed above. Most of the laws passed by Congress fall within the *Commerce Clause*, the *Copyright Clause*, or the *Necessary and Proper Clause*. (These are the three clauses that I have quoted in their entirety in the list above.) As long as a statute passed by Congress falls within one of the required categories and does not contradict the U.S. Constitution or a treaty that has been ratified by the Senate, the law will be valid and enforceable.

The laws that Congress passes are called statutes. They fall into two categories, *Public Laws* (also called *Public Acts*) and *Private Laws* (also called *Private Bills, Special Laws*, or *Private Acts*). Most statutes are Public Laws, which "relate to the public as a whole."[4] Public Laws may be "(1) general (applying to all persons within the jurisdiction), (2) local (applying to a geographical area), or (3) special (relating to an organization which is charged with a public interest)."[5] Private Bills, on the other hand, consist of "Legislation for the special benefit of an individual or locality."[6]

A recent example of a Private Law occurred in 2005, when Congress passed a special act concerning Theresa Marie "Terri" Schiavo. Schiavo's doctors diagnosed her as being in a persistent vegetative state. Her husband wanted her feeding tube removed, but her parents did not. After the courts in the case had all ruled in favor of the husband, Congress passed "An Act for the relief of the Parents of Theresa Marie Schiavo."[7] This law granted jurisdiction to the federal courts to hear the case. Ultimately the federal courts also ruled for the husband; however, the law that opened up the federal courts was a Private Act, since it only applied to one person.

Sometimes two statutes conflict with one another. The general rule is that the more recent statute applies, since Congress is presumed to know that the earlier law was already on the books.

Research Sources for the Legislative Branch

When Congress passes a statute, it is published in a series of volumes called the *United States Statutes at Large*. The statutes are listed in the order that they are passed. The *Statutes at Large* series is published by the U.S. Government Printing Office (GPO), and is distributed to libraries through the Depository Library System. The *Statutes at Large* are also available online through a variety of vendors, including (among others) LexisNexis, Westlaw, HeinOnline, ProQuest, and Bloomberg.

There is also a series of statutes that is published privately by West Group. This source is called the *United States Code Congressional and Administration News (U.S.C.C.A.N.)*. The *U.S.C.C.A.N.* series is arranged by public law number and also contains the laws in the order that they were passed. *U.S.C.C.A.N.* also includes the text of private statutes passed by Congress, as well as legislative history materials. (Legislative history will be discussed in more detail below.)

Since the *Statutes at Large* and *U.S.C.C.A.N.* present laws in the order they were passed, subject searching is not available (unless you are using an online version). In addition, many acts passed by Congress will include unrelated provisions that may pertain to another subject, such as funding for a highway or bridge included in an unrelated bill.

In order to help facilitate research, public laws have been compiled by topic in a series called the *United States Code* (*U.S. Code*). The process of arranging the laws by topic is called *codification*. The resulting works are also known as codifications or as codes. Most lawyers, librarians, and researchers use a codification because of the subject arrangement. The *U.S. Code* is published by the GPO and distributed to the depository libraries.

In addition to the *U.S. Code*, there are two private publishers that put out codifications of the laws passed by Congress. West Group produces the *United States Code Annotated*, and LexisNexis produces the *United States Code Service*. Both of these codes include the full text of the *U.S. Code*, along with additional materials. Most researchers use one of these two private sources instead of the official code, even though citation rules call for citing the U.S. Code itself. Reasons for the popularity of the private compilations include the annotations and additional materials, better indexes, and quicker publication time. Since the text of the laws and the numbering system are the same in all three sources, a researcher using one of the annotated codes can still consult or cite to the official code. (This is not considered to be plagiarism; the legal citation system always asks for citations to the official set, even if the unofficial series is used.)

The main advantage of annotated codes is that the editors have searched for and included information on cases that have been decided in the courts. After each section, there is a listing of cases that have cited or interpreted that particular provision of the *U.S. Code*. Using the annotated codes is a very effective way of finding cases that interpret a particular statute.

One way in which to determine the meaning of a particular piece of legislation is to search for legislative history materials. Legislative history consists of "[t]he background and events, including committee reports, hearings, and floor debates, leading up to the enactment of a law."[8] An advantage of using the *U.S.C.C.A.N.* instead of the *Statutes at Large* is that, in addition to the public laws themselves, the *U.S.C.C.A.N.* also includes legislative history materials. These materials often help to illustrate the background of the law, and to explain what Congress was thinking when the statute was passed. The witness statements and committee reports are particularly helpful. While not in any way binding, legislative history materials help provide guidance to courts and the public in determining the meaning of particular statutes.

Another good source for legislative history materials is the free *Thomas* website created by the Library of Congress.[9] The site includes a variety of information, including summaries and full text of bills and their status, the *Congressional Record*, the U.S. Constitution, public laws since 1973, and a wide variety of congressional documents such as committee reports.

Congressional documents can also be found on the Government Printing Office's websites, *GPO Access* and FDsys.[10] *GPO Access* also includes committee prints, as well as reports from government agencies and official boards. Other materials in *GPO Access* include the *Weekly Compilation of Presidential Documents* (the official publication of presidential statements, messages, remarks, and speeches) and the *Public Papers of the Presidents.* Please note the *GPO Access* site will transition in 2011 to the new FDsys site, which is available at http://www.gpo.gov/fdsys.

Occasionally, when a bill is signed into law, the president will give a speech called a *signing statement* which discusses the meaning of the law and its importance. Although not official, signing statements often provide a context and rationale for the law. For a description of sources for signing statements, see Chapter 6 on the Executive Branch. For example, when the Sarbanes-Oxley Act was signed into law, President George W. Bush declared:

> This law authorizes new funding for investigators and technology at the Securities and Exchange Commission to uncover wrongdoing. The SEC will now have the administrative authority to bar dishonest directors and officers from ever again serving in positions of corporate responsibility. The penalties for obstructing justice and shredding documents are greatly increased. Corporate crime will no longer pay.[11]

Another source of legislative history is the *Congressional Record,* which is distributed to depository libraries by the GPO. The *Congressional Record* contains debates, bills, joint resolutions, treaties, and Presidential messages. One caveat that you should be aware of is that the items in the *Congressional Record* are not necessarily what was actually said on the floor of the House or Senate. Members of Congress have the right *to edit* their words before publication. If a member says something he or she later regrets, the words can be edited out of existence, and Members can add anything they wish. Sometimes members add a letter from a constituent, a poem, a commemoration, or even a short story, even though these selections may not have been read on the floor of the House or Senate. While the *Congressional Record* should be taken with a grain of salt, it nonetheless provides an insight into congressional thinking.

Major Research Tools for Statutory Research

Here is a summary of the major research tools for finding statutes, bills, and legislative history, along with their official citations:

♦ *United States Code (U.S.C.)*
  Published by the Government Printing Office, this series is the official compilation of federal statutes passed by Congress. The code is arranged by topic. The *U.S. Code* is the source that should always be cited, regardless of whether the researcher has used the official code or an unofficial code.

♦ *United States Code Annotated (U.S.C.A.)*
  West Group publishes this unofficial version of the *United States Code.* The arrangement of the statutes is identical to the *U.S. Code.* The section for each statute

contains references to cases that discuss that specific law. As a result, legal researchers often use the U.S.C.A. to find cases that discuss a specific statute.

♦ *United States Code Service (U.S.C.S.)*
This unofficial version of the *United States Code* is published by LexisNexis. The statutory arrangement is identical to the *U.S. Code*. In addition to providing references to cases that discuss each code section, the U.S.C.S. also provides cross-references to other publications produced by LexisNexis.

♦ *United States Statutes at Large (Stat.)*
This series contains the official text of statutes passed by Congress, in the order the statutes were passed. The *Statutes at Large* are also available online from a variety of vendors.

♦ *U.S. Code Congressional and Administrative News (U.S.C.C.A.N.)*
This series contains both an unofficial version of the *Statutes at Large* and Legislative History documents for each statute, arranged by *Public Law Number*.

♦ *Code of Federal Regulations (C.F.R.)*
Published by the Government Printing Office, this series contains administrative regulations created by federal administrative agencies, arranged by topic.

♦ *Federal Register (Fed. Reg.)*
Published daily by the GPO, this series contains new and proposed federal administrative regulations, standards, and grant programs.

In addition to the printed series listed above, there are also many good websites with information on legislation and legislative history. (Always keep in mind the quote from the *Texas Web Case* cited in Chapter 2.) The list below contains some sites that are considered authoritative and reliable:

♦ *A Century of Lawmaking for a New Nation: U.S. Congressional Documents and Debates*
http://memory.loc.gov/ammem/amlaw/lwabout.html
Part of the American Memory website from the Library of Congress. In addition to the Continental Congress, this website contains documents and debates from the 1st through 43rd Congresses (1889-1875). Documents on the website include:
o *Journals of the House of Representatives* (1789-1875).
o *Journals of the Senate* (1789-1875), including the *Senate Executive Journal* (1789-1875).
o *Journal of William Maclay* (1789-1791), senator from Pennsylvania in the 1st Congress.
o *Annals of Congress* (1789-1824).
o *Register of Debates* (1824-1837).
o *Congressional Globe* (1833-1873).
o *Congressional Record* (1873-1875).
o *American State Papers* (1789-1838).

o   Congressional bills and resolutions begin with the 6th Congress (1799) in the
    House of Representatives and the 16th Congress (1819) in the Senate.

o   Volumes 1 through 3 of the *Congressional Record.* More recent *Congressional
    Record* volumes are on THOMAS, the Library of Congress's legislative infor-
    mation website.

♦   *Congressional Bills*, 103rd Congress (1993) to present
    http://www.gpoaccess.gov/bills

♦   *Congressional Calendars*, 104th Congress (1995) to present
    http://www.gpoaccess.gov/calendars

♦   *Congressional Committee Prints*, 105th Congress (1997) to present
    http://www.gpoaccess.gov/cprints

♦   *Congressional Documents*, 104th Congress (1995) to present
    http://www.gpoaccess.gov/serialset/cdocuments

♦   *Congressional Hearings*, 105th Congress (1997) to present
    http://www.gpoaccess.gov/chearings

♦   *Congressional Record*, 1994 to present
    http://www.gpoaccess.gov/crecord

♦   *Congressional Record Index*, 1983 to present
    http://www.gpoaccess.gov/cri

♦   *Congressional Reports*, 104th Congress (1995) to present
    http://www.gpoaccess.gov/serialset

♦   *CQ Press Congress Collection*
    http://www.cqpress.com/product/CQ-Congress-Collection.html
    This subscription database contains "historical analysis of members of Congress,
    their legislative voting behavior, interest groups, and their interactions in crafting
    public policy. . . ." Features include floor votes since 1969, historical analysis since
    the 79th Congress (1945-1947), and member biographies including "presidential
    support, vote, participation, and party unity data." Data can be exported for statisti-
    cal analysis. [Description from website.]

♦   *FDsys* (Government Printing Office)
    http://www.gpo.gov/fdsys
    FDsys is the next-generation replacement for GPO Access, and is scheduled to be
    released in 2011. According to the GPO, this site will use "a single search box," and
    will contain "advanced search capabilities with robust metadata about each publica-
    tion with the ability to construct complex search queries using advanced Boolean
    and field operators." The site will also allow "searching publications to a more
    granular level to locate more targeted topics within publications[,] refining and nar-

rowing searches by filtering, sorting, and searching within search results[, and] brows[ing] features by collection, Congressional committee, and date." Training manuals, tutorials, presentations, and other materials on FDsys are available at
http://www.gpo.gov/help/fdsys_user_manual.htm
http://www.gpo.gov/fdsysinfo/tutorials.htm
http://www.gpo.gov/fdsysinfo/presentations.htm
http://www.gpo.gov/fdsysinfo/outreach.htm

♦   *Findlaw*
http://www.findlaw.com/casecode
This is an effective interface for the *U.S. Code*. Information can be retrieved by title and section, searched by keyword, or browsed by title and section. Findlaw also contains a good interface for the *Code of Federal Regulations* and the *Federal Register*. The site allows keyword searching and browsing. For searching, use quotation marks (" ") for phrases and plus sign (+) for required terms.

♦   *Govtrac.us* (Civic Impulse, LLC)
http://www.govtrac.us
Searches legislation from the 106th Congress (1999) and tracks bills from the 103rd Congress (1993) to the present. Also contains information on members of Congress including district maps and congressional committees. Voting records are available since 1990 for the House and 1989 for the Senate. The site contains articles and RSS feeds dealing with current legislation, and is available as a mobile phone application for iPhone and Android.

♦   *GPO Access* (Government Printing Office)
http://www.gpoaccess.gov
Contains a wealth of information on legislation and legislative history. Many links are listed separately in this bibliography, but the site also includes congressional bills from the 103rd Congress (1993) to present, as well as history of bills from the 98th Congress (1983) to present. Please note the GPO Access site will transition in 2011 to the new FDsys site, which is available at http://www.gpo.gov/fdsys.

♦   *Public and Private Laws*, 104th Congress (1995) to present
http://www.gpoaccess.gov/plaws

♦   Public Documents Masterfile (Paratext)
http://www.paratext.com/public_document.html
This subscription database indexes the *Journals of the Continental Congress* (1774-1789), *Annals of Congress* (1789-1824), *Register of Debates* (1824-1837), and the *Congressional Globe* (1833-1873).

♦   Robinson, Gary J. (2007, March). *Overview of United States Federal Legislation*, *available at* http://content.glin.gov/summary/195571.
Written by a legal reference librarian at the Law Library of Congress, "[t]his article is an introduction to legislative materials produced by the United States Congress, including legislation, proposed legislation that does not pass, and documents relevant to researching legislative history. It discusses forms of legislative action, public

laws, the United States Code, techniques for verifying the currency of legislative language, legislative history, and bill tracking." [Description from GLIN.]

♦ *Thomas: Legislative Information on the Internet* (Library of Congress)
http://www.thomas.gov
Contains a variety of information on congressional actions, including calendars of floor debates and the full text of bills (can be searched or browsed) from the 101st Congress (1989) to the present. The database also contains bill summaries and status as well as public laws from the 93rd Congress (1973) to the present. Thomas includes House votes from the 101st Congress 2nd Session (1990) to the present and Senate votes from the 101st Congress 1st Session (1989) to the present. In addition, Thomas has the *Congressional Record* from the 101st Congress (1989) to the present, and committee reports from the 104th Congress (1995) to the present.

♦ *U.S. Code (Cornell Legal Information Institute)*
http://www.law.cornell.edu
Contains the *U.S. Code*, the *Code of Federal Regulations*, and an online version of the Congressional Research Service's Annotated U.S. Constitution. The interface allows users to retrieve a section by citation, browse the entire code, or search each title separately. Full Boolean searching capability (AND, OR, NOT) is available. Use quotation marks (" ") for phrases; if quotation marks or Boolean operators are not used, the search engine will default to AND.

♦ *U.S. Code (GPO Access)*
http://www.gpoaccess.gov/uscode
The GPO version of the *U.S. Code* contains the most current version, as well as previous versions since 1994. The Code can be browsed or searched. Searches include *U.S. Code* Citation, popular Name, Public Law Number, *Statutes at Large* Citation, or the Legislation that Amends a U.S. Code Section. Searching includes the Boolean operators AND, OR, NOT, and ADJ (the second query term follows the first within 20 characters). Use quotation marks (" ") for phrases and parentheses ( ) for complex searches. The GPO Access site will transition in 2011 to the new FDsys site, which is available at http://www.gpo.gov/fdsys.

Conclusion

The Constitution gives Congress both duties and powers. The House has the duty to initiate appropriation bills and budgets. The Senate has the duty to ratify treaties and to approve judges, ambassadors, and cabinet members.

The powers of Congress are laid out in Article I, Section 8 of the Constitution. However, the broadest powers of Congress come from the provisions known as the "commerce clause" and the "necessary and proper clause." Basing a statute on one of these two clauses is not without controversy. However, these two clauses are among the most often cited constitutional foundations for congressional action.

Statutory research involves not only seeking the laws that were passed but also their context and meaning. What did the legislators intend when they passed the statute? To answer these questions, it is necessary to look for hearings, committee documents, and debates. Early drafts of bills are also helpful.

In many ways, the pursuit of legislative history is less about the law and more about history or political science. However, legislative history is not just the pursuit of scholars. This type of analysis is important to lawyers, paralegals, and librarians who work with legislative materials.

Congress is usually too busy to oversee the laws once they have been passed. As a result, statutes will often contain clauses that empower government agencies to administer the law. These agencies will be the focus of the next chapter.

Notes

1. U.S. Constitution, Article I, § 8.

2. *id.*

3. For an article discussing the issue of whether Congress may enact laws under the power of a treaty that are otherwise beyond the scope of the limited areas reserved for Congress in Article I, § 8, *see,* Nicholas Quinn Rosenkranz, *Executing the Treaty Power,* 118 Harvard Law Review 1867 (April 2005).

4. Black's Law Dictionary 1106 (5th ed. 1979).

5. *id.*

6. Black's Law Dictionary 1076 (5th ed. 1979).

7. Compromise bill 686 (S. 686); (passed March 20, 2005; signed by the President, March 21, 2005).

8. Black's Law Dictionary 810 (5th ed. 1979).

9. Library of Congress, Thomas: Legislative Information on the Internet, *available at* http://thomas.loc.gov.

10. Government Printing Office, GPO Access, *available at* http://www.access.gpo .gov. In 2011, GPO Access will transition to a new service, FDsys, *available at* http://www.gpo.gov/fdsys.

11. President George W. Bush, *Signing Statement for Sarbanes-Oxley Act,* U.S.C.C.A.N. (July 30, 2002), *available at* http://www.whitehouse.gov/news/releases/ 2002/07/20020730.html.

6

Executive and Administrative Agencies

When Congress passes a law, it has the power to create an executive agency to administer that law. In order to administer the statute, the executive agency issues administrative regulations. These regulations have almost the same effect as a statute passed by Congress. Most regulations have the force of law as long as the regulations do not contradict the Constitution, a treaty provision, or a statute passed by Congress. However, the regulations must be within the scope of the authority that Congress has granted to the agency.

There are three types of administrative bodies. One type of agency is directly within the Executive Office of the President. These agencies help the president to develop and implement policies. The head of each agency reports directly to the president. An example of this type of organization is the Office of Management and Budget.

A second type of administrative body consists of those executive departments that are part of the president's cabinet. These departments are headed by a secretary who can set policy to a much greater extent than the head of a presidential office. The U.S. Department of Education is an example of this second type of organization.

The third type of governmental body consists of independent agencies that are not part of either the Executive Office of the President or a cabinet-level department. Examples of this type of organization include the Institute of Museum and Library Services (IMLS), the National Commission on Libraries and Information Science, and the National Archives and Records Administration. In addition to regular agencies, there are U.S.-chartered companies (such as Amtrak) and boards (such as the Merit Systems Protection Board).

All of the activities of these administrative agencies, whichever type they are, flow in some fashion from statutes and programs passed by Congress. For example, Congress passed the Museum and Library Services Act of 1996, P.L. 104-208 (re-authorized in 2003 by P.L. 108-81), which created the IMLS. The 2003 re-authorization included a program called "Librarians for the 21st Century," which "supports efforts to recruit and educate the next generation of librarians and the faculty who will prepare them for careers in library science. It also supports grants for research related to library education and library staffing needs, curriculum development, and continuing education and training."[1] The IMLS created rules and regulations for this program under the authority of the statute passed by Congress.

The power of an agency always flows back to a mandate by Congress. The regulations passed by an agency must be within the scope of the power that Congress delegated. Regulations that are outside of the scope of the statutes passed by Congress are considered to be an unconstitutional exercise of the legislative branch's power, and will be struck down by the courts.

Administrative Regulations

Administrative agencies not only administer the laws passed by Congress. They can also create rules and regulations that have the force of law. These regulations are considered to be part of the agency's mission in enforcing its congressional mandates. An administrative regulation must be created pursuant to a grant of power by Congress, and must not contradict any statute that Congress has passed. In addition, administrative regulations must not be contrary to the provisions of a treaty or of the U.S. Constitution.

Some examples of administrative regulations are the provisions relating to creating an Individualized Education Plan (known as an IEP) for students with disabilities. Schools across the country must adhere to this rule on IEPs. School librarians often work with teachers on assisting students with IEPs. The Department of Education has created rules stating:

> Each public agency shall ensure that within a reasonable period of time following the agency's receipt of parent consent to an initial evaluation of a child—
> (i) The child is evaluated; and
> (ii) If determined eligible under this part, special education and related services are made available to the child in accordance with an IEP.[2]

Another type of administrative regulation concerns forms that are to be filled out. For example, we all know about the Internal Revenue Service's form 1040, the individual income tax return. The establishment of this form by the IRS is a type of administrative regulation. Also, rules relating to grant programs such as the Librarians for the 21st Century are considered to be administrative regulations.

Administrative Proceedings and Hearings

In addition to creating regulations, agencies also make decisions and hold hearings. "These kinds of proceedings can range from a decision to award a grant to a full-scale hearing with lawyers and witnesses."[3] Examples of informal hearings include such decisions as license applications, claims for benefits, and awards of grants. Even an application for a driver's license is an informal agency proceeding. Another example of an informal decision that is applicable to libraries and archives is a Freedom of Information Act request. (For more information on the Freedom of Information Act, see the next section.) "In informal proceedings clients demonstrate compliance with agency standards and regulations; often this compliance is simply filling out the applicable forms truthfully and in a timely manner."[4]

The agency must always follow its own procedures, and must also fulfill the Constitutional requirements of providing *Due Process*. The *procedural due process* rights are contained in the 5th and 14th Amendments to the U.S. Constitution. These Constitutional provisions require that, before a person is deprived of liberty or property, he or she will be given *due process of law*. "Before a person is deprived of a protected interest, he must be afforded opportunity for some kind of a hearing, 'except for extraordinary situations where some valid governmental interest is at stake that justifies postponing the hearing until after the event.'"[5]

Libraries and archives often apply procedural due process when terminating problem employees, since working is considered to be a property interest.[6] A property interest can also include such library procedures as suspension of borrowing privileges. If a library does not follow its own written procedures, the patron can sue for a violation of procedural due process.[7] (For more information on these topics, see my book *The Law of Libraries and Archives*.)[8]

In order to help assure fairness in the administrative branch, Congress passed the Administrative Procedures Act (the APA).[9] The APA provides a standardized set of rules by which agency decisions should be made and agency hearings should be conducted. The APA governs, among other things, "investigations, adjudications, rulemaking, licensing, and open meeting and disclosure requirements."[10] The APA also includes the Freedom of Information Act, which is discussed in more detail below. Many states have also adopted similar acts. In order to help standardize these state acts, the Revised Model State Administrative Procedure Act was created in 1961 and revised in 1981.[11]

Although most agency decisions are informal, there are also formal agency decisions which can approximate a trial. An administrative law judge generally hears formal agency decisions, and a much stricter type of due process is necessary. For all practical purposes, these hearings are trials; they simply are in front of an agency judge instead of a court.

The procedural rules in an administrative proceeding are somewhat simpler than the formal rules of court. For example, some administrative proceedings may simplify the rules of evidence in order to provide the most favorable possible conditions for the person who is challenging the agency.

Government agencies generally have a specified set of procedures for administrative hearings, along with a specified route of appeal. Once the administrative appeals have been exhausted, the person who is challenging the agency has the right to appeal the case to the courts. Before the courts can get involved, however, there must be a *final agency action*, also known as *exhaustion of administrative remedies*. This means that the challenger must have first used all the administrative options open to him or her before turning to the courts.

In the federal system, a challenge to a final agency action would generally be filed in U.S. District Court. Most appeals of administrative hearings go directly from the district court to the U.S. Court of Appeals for the District of Columbia Circuit. In the state system, judicial oversight of final agency action may be heard by general trial courts or by specialized courts that are set up by the state.

In the U.S., statutes, regulations, and presidential materials are widely available. These are the primary documents that would be used in a civil law system such as those found in most European and Latin American countries. However, it is important to remember the differences between the common law system and the civil law system:

> Civil-law countries have comprehensive codes, often developed from a single drafting event. The codes cover an abundance of legal topics, sometimes treating separately private law, criminal law, and commercial law. While common-law countries have statutes in those areas, sometimes collected into codes, they have been derived more from an ad hoc process over many years. Moreover, codes of common-law countries very often reflect the rules of law enunciated in judicial decisions (i.e., they are the statutory embodiment of rules developed through the judicial decision-making process).[12]

In the U.S. legal system, however, case law and the judiciary are as important as statutes and regulations. Indeed, the reasoning involved in passing statutes is very different due to the enhanced role of the common law judiciary.[13] I will discuss case law and judicial resources in Chapter 8, *The Judicial Branch*. At this point, however, it is important to remember that statutes and regulations are not the only sources of American law.

Sources for Administrative Research

When an agency wishes to pass a regulation, it must first publish a notice which includes the text of the proposed regulation. Similarly, agencies need to give notice when they are going to hold a hearing to create regulations or to make certain kinds of decisions. These notices and the proposed regulations are printed in the *Federal Register*. The *Federal Register* is published daily, except for national holidays, and is available to depository libraries. The *Federal Register* is also available online at http://www.gpoaccess.gov/fr/index.html.

In addition to printing all hearing notices and proposed regulations, the *Federal Register* also reports about proposed agency forms, and contains announcements of grant programs, and provides the full text of all final regulations, forms, and grants. The *Federal Register* also contains executive orders and other presidential documents.

Just as statutes are codified by subject, so too are administrative regulations. The *Code of Federal Regulations* is a subject arrangement for rules and regulations. The *Code of Federal Regulations* is updated yearly, and is available to depository libraries. The official version of the *Code of Federal Regulations* is available online at http://www.gpoaccess.gov/cfr/index.html. In addition, there is an unofficial version which is updated more regularly; this version is called the *Electronic Code of Federal Regulations*, and is available at http://www.gpoaccess.gov/ecfr.

The *Code of Federal Regulations* in print is very difficult to search. It has a very poor index, and librarians or patrons usually need to know the agency that the regulation comes from in order to find the information they are looking for. The online versions mentioned above (as well as commercial subscription versions such as LexisNexis or Westlaw) are much more useful due to the keyword searching capability. As a result, I recommend using an online version of the *Code of Federal Regulations* if at all possible.

Many administrative hearings are also available, both on agency websites and in print. For example, Commerce Clearing House (CCH) publishes the *Private Letter Rulings* from the Internal Revenue Service.[14] These rulings are written IRS decisions that interpret the law with respect to an individual's specific circumstances. These written determinations are binding on the IRS with respect to the individual taxpayer who requested the ruling. Although the IRS can change its interpretations at any time, Private Letter Rulings do provide a way for other taxpayers to see how the law was being interpreted at the time the decision was written. Other examples of agency reports that libraries and archives may find useful include *Copyright Decisions, Decisions and Orders of the National Labor Relations Board, Decisions of the Commissioner of Patents*, and the *Federal Communication Commission Reports*.

Presidential documents are also available, both online and in print. (The locations for these materials are listed below.) Presidential executive orders have the force of law and are generally directives by the president to an executive agency or official to take a specific action, including the establishment or amendment of agency procedures. For example, the creation of a plan of succession for the Department of Homeland Security was done by executive order.

Another type of presidential document is the signing statement, which was referred to earlier in the section on legislative history. Often the president will give a public statement when signing an important piece of legislation. Although the signing statement does not have the force of law, it can be a useful tool for reconstructing the legislative history of a law.

In recent years, the use of signing statements by the administration of President George W. Bush has caused some controversy. Certainly not all signing statements are benign. Nixon insider John Dean pointed out that "Presidents have long used them to add their two cents when a law passed by Congress has provisions they do not like, yet they are not inclined to veto it. Nixon's statements, for example, often related to spending authorization laws which he felt were excessive and contrary to his fiscal policies."[15] Nonetheless, many signing statements have been useful and complementary to the legislation. The controversy with the Bush administration has been its constant use of negative statements to challenge legislative power while enhancing executive authority.[16] Here is a summary of the situation:

> A variety of different types of constitutional objections were asserted by the George W. Bush administration, most on a relatively regular basis, although the scope of those objections increased over time. These powers were often asserted without supporting authorities, or even serious efforts at explanation. The administration interpreted its own powers, gave them the widest possible scope, and then interpreted the limitations it found on congressional authority, usually giving legislative powers the narrowest possible reading. It then declared its positions and often gave only general indications as to its intentions for the way in which it would implement the statute.[17]

The controversy over signing statements reached its peak in the fight over the Detainee Treatment Act of 2005. There are actually two separate detainee acts. The first was a clause that was added to an emergency appropriation after Hurricane Katrina, and the second was part of a Department of Defense appropriation bill.[18] When the president signed the bill, he used a controversial signing statement. While testifying before the Senate Judiciary Committee, Bruce Fein used the following description of the situation:

> The Act prohibits the Executive in all its branches and agencies from torture or cruel, inhumane, or degrading interrogations whether to obtain foreign intelligence or otherwise. After taking political credit for signing the bill, President Bush issued a statement declaring in substance that he would ignore it when he saw fit as an unconstitutional encroachment on his power to protect "the American people from further terrorist attacks." According to the signing statement, "The executive branch shall construe Title X in Division A of the Act, relating to detainees, in a manner consistent with the constitutional authority of the President to supervise the unitary executive branch and as Commander in Chief and consistent with the constitutional limitations on the judicial power which will assist in achieving the shared objective of the Congress and the President, evidenced in Title X, of protecting the American people from further terrorist attacks." While to the layman, the language of the signing statement may seem both Delphic and innocuous, to the initiated the words referring to a unitary executive and Commander in Chief powers clearly signify that President Bush is asserting that he is constitutionally entitled to commit torture if he believes it would assist the gathering of foreign intelligence. President Bush has nullified a provision of statute that he had signed into law and which he was then obliged to faithfully execute.[19]

Concern that the president was using signing statements to nullify congressional legislation or to create an alternative legislative history caused many people to think that these were somehow new or bad. This use of signing statements troubled presidential candidate John McCain, who, as a former detainee himself, had authored the Detainee Treatment Acts. During the 2008 campaign, Senator

McCain promised that he would "never, never, never, never" use any signing statements.[20]

However, many commentators have stated that banning signing statements altogether is an overly broad reaction, and that there are in fact many legitimate reasons for using them. This defense of the institution of signing statements has come even from some of President Bush's harshest critics, such as Dawn Johnsen (head of the Office of Legal Counsel in the Obama administration), and *Findlaw's Writ* columnist John Dean.[21] The statements themselves are only an adjunct to ordinary legislative history, and in some instances can be helpful.[22]

Malinda Lee reminds us that there are in fact many uses for statements: "A presidential signing statement . . . serves diverse purposes. Signing statements often are made for public relations or political purposes. Some statements are ceremonial and merely comment on the bill signed, praising its supporters or emphasizing that it meets some pressing needs. Signing statements also may express general policy views; for example, they frequently include reference to how the legislation does not go far enough toward solving the problem at issue."[23] The use of signing statements is neither good nor bad. It is the use that is made of them that is determinative.

Signing statements can be found in the *Weekly Compilation of Presidential Documents*, the White House website,[24] *U.S.C.C.A.N.*, the *Congressional Record*, and the *Public Papers of the Presidents*. (Always remember that you must use .gov for the White House website. Do not use .com, as that will send you to a pornographic site.) In addition, veto statements by the presidents can be found in all of the sources mentioned above except for the *U.S.C.C.A.N.*

Presidential proclamations are typically addressed to the nation as a whole and often relate to ceremonial or celebratory occasions, such as National Religious Freedom Day or the Centennial of the U.S. Forest Service. Proclamations can also have significant legal consequences, however, such as implementing a trade agreement.

In addition to the two general compilations of presidential documents described below (the *Weekly Compilation of Presidential Documents* and the *Public Papers of the Presidents of the United States*), the primary sources of presidential proclamations and executive orders are the *Federal Register* and Title 3 of the *Code of Federal Regulations*.

The following list contains some useful sources for administrative research, including both primary and secondary resources:

♦   Baggott, Vickey L., & Griffin, Luke. (2004). *Guide to Popular U.S. Government Documents*. Mobile, Ala Infosential Press.

♦   *Ben's Guide to U.S. Government for Kids*
     http://bensguide.gpo.gov
     The award-winning *Ben's Guide* is aimed at educators, parents, and students. The site contains information on how the government works, as well as links to age-

appropriate government materials. Topics include the Bill of Rights, the budget, obtaining American citizenship, and the electoral and lawmaking processes. This is also a good site to find information on symbols (such as the seal) of U.S. government.

♦   Berman, Evan M., & Rabin, Jack. (2008). *Encyclopedia of Public Administration and Public Policy*. New York: Taylor & Francis.

♦   *Code of Federal Regulations*
    Published annually since 1938, the C.F.R. is a codification by agency and subject of federal administrative regulations.

♦   DeLeo, John. (2008). *Administrative Law*. Clifton Park, NY: Delmar Cengage Learning.

♦   *FDsys*
    http://www.gpo.gov/fdsys
    The official site of the Government Printing Office, this is the single best source for administrative and executive branch research. The site has a variety of governmental documents available free of charge. Searching includes the Boolean operators AND, OR, NOT, and ADJ (the second query term follows the first within 20 characters). Use quotation marks (" ") for phrases and parentheses ( ) for complex searches. Please note the *FDsys* replaced *GPO Access* in 2011.

♦   *The Federal Register*
    Published daily since 1936, this is the first place that regulations, proposed regulations, and grant opportunities appear. The *Federal Register* also contains presidential proclamations.

♦   *FedThread.org* (Princeton University Center for Information Policy)
    http://www.fedthread.org
    Contains the *Federal Register* from 2000 to present, along with updates by email or RSS feed. The site also contains a number of advanced search options.[25]

♦   Fisher, Louis
    o   (2008). Domestic Commander in Chief: Early Checks by Other Branches. *Cardozo Law Review, 29(3)*, 961-999, *available at* http://loc.gov/law/help/usconlaw/pdf/cardozo_fisher.pdf.
    o   (2004). *The Politics of Executive Privilege*. Durham, NC: Carolina Academic Press, *available at* http://www.loc.gov/law/help/usconlaw/politics.php.

♦   *GPO Monthly Catalog of U.S. Government Publications*
    http://catalog.gpo.gov/F?RN=704736081
    Contains records for all types of government documents from 1976 to the present, plus links to many online documents. The catalog can be searched by agency, title, subject, or keyword, and includes a listing of depository libraries. Older print volumes of the *Monthly Catalog* (1895-1975) are available in depository libraries.

- Hill, Kathleen, & Hill, Gerald N. (2004). *Encyclopedia of Federal Agencies and Commissions*. New York: Facts on File.

- Hume, Robert J. (2009). *How Courts Impact Federal Administrative Behavior*. New York: Routledge.

- Jackson, Byron M. (1999). *Encyclopedia of American Public Policy*. Santa Barbara, CA: ABC-CLIO.

- *Justia Regulations Tracker*
  http://regulations.justia.com
  This site provides a free version of the *Federal Register*.

- *Managing Electronic Government Information in Libraries: Issues and Practices*. Morrison, Andrea M. (Ed.). Chicago: American Library Association.

- Morehead, Joe. (1999). *Introduction to United States Government Information Sources*. Englewood, CO: Libraries Unlimited.

- *OpenRegs.com*
  http://openregs.com
  "Offers RSS feeds of proposed rules with comment periods ending soon; recently opened comment periods; recently published final regulations; and recently published 'significant' regulations."[26]

- Pierce, Richard J. (2008). *Administrative Law*. St. Paul, MN: Thomson/West.

- *Public Papers of the Presidents of the United States*
  This series contains presidential speeches and press releases from Presidents Hoover, Truman, Eisenhower, Kennedy, Johnson, Nixon, Ford, Carter, Reagan, George H.W. Bush, Clinton, and George W. Bush. (The series does not include the papers of President Roosevelt; these are available separately on microfiche.) In addition, appendices to the *Public Papers* contain materials that were previously published in the *Weekly Compilation of Presidential Documents*.[27]

- *Regulations.gov*
  http://www.regulations.gov
  This is the main federal website for the *Code of Federal Regulations*, and where proposed regulations are posted for public comment.

- *RegInfo.gov*
  http://www.reginfo.gov
  "RegInfo.gov tracks the steps in agency and OMB regulatory review that happen outside of the Federal Register publication process, usually before a proposed regulation or final rule is published."[28]

♦   Rossiter, Clinton
    o   (1956). *The American Presidency.* New York: Harcourt Brace. Republished
        (1987) Baltimore: Johns Hopkins University Press.
    o   (1970). *The Supreme Court and the Commander in Chief.* Ithaca, NY: Cornell
        University Press.

♦   Sears, Jean L., & Moody, Marilyn K. (2001). *Using Government Information
    Sources: Electronic and Print.* Phoenix, AZ: Oryx Press.

♦   *Statutes at Large*
    Presidential proclamations, but not executive orders, are published in *Statutes at
    Large.*

♦   *USA.gov*
    http://www.usa.gov
    The federal government's web portal includes links to courts, agencies, and legal
    materials.

♦   *United States Code, United States Code Annotated,* and *United States Code Service*
    Significant proclamations and executive orders may be included in the *United States
    Code* and its unofficial counterparts. The proclamations and executive orders follow
    the statutory sections to which they relate. Each version of the Code has tables indi-
    cating where specific presidential proclamations and executive orders can be found.

♦   *Weekly Compilation of Presidential Documents*
    "The *Weekly Compilation of Presidential Documents* is published every Monday
    and is the official publication of presidential statements, messages, remarks, and
    other materials released by the White House Press Secretary. Published by the Of-
    fice of the Federal Register (OFR), a branch of the National Archives and Records
    Administration (NARA), the *Weekly Compilation of Presidential Documents* first
    began in 1965 and is available on *GPO Access* from 1993 forward."[29] Please note
    the GPO Access site will transition in 2011 to the new FDsys site, which is available
    at http://www.gpo.gov/fdsys.

♦   *Whitehouse.gov*
    The official website of the White House provides users with free access to the full
    text of every proclamation and executive order of the current administration, orga-
    nized chronologically. (Remember to use .gov, *NOT* .com.)

Conclusion

Administrative agencies are an important but often overlooked part of our legal
system. These agencies are based on a statutory grant of power by Congress,
which can either restrict or empower their scope. Generally Congress leaves the
day-to-day administration of the law to these agencies. Some are located within
the executive branch of government, in which case the president has influence

over policies. There are also independent agencies which are not part of the executive branch, such as the Federal Reserve or the Farm Credit Administration.

There are two main roles for administrative bodies. First, agencies create regulations. The rules created by the Department of Homeland Security or the National Labor Relations Board are no less a part of the law than congressional statutes (unless they go beyond the scope of the statutory grant of power).

Agencies also enforce the law (both statutes and regulations). Sometimes this involves court action (for example, prosecution by the Department of Justice). However, agencies can also hold hearings in front of administrative law judges. These proceedings are separate from enforcement, and the judges don't always rule in favor of the agency. These agency actions can range from very formal quasi-judicial proceedings (such as EPA's Environmental Appeals Board) to informal opinions (such as IRS private letter rulings). Nonetheless, these quasi-judicial proceedings have a very real power to affect individuals and organizations. Many administrative opinions are collected for publication, and are often distributed to law libraries and government document depositories.

A simple statement about executive agencies is that their role is to enforce the law. Yet their powers extend way beyond enforcement. Agencies create regulations that affect millions of people, and hold quasi-judicial administrative hearings which can affect the rights of individuals. In short, the executive branch is a full-fledged law-making part of our governmental system. Because of the importance of administrative agencies, it is vital for citizens to be able to obtain information. The next chapter will discuss the Freedom of Information Act and obtaining governmental records.

Notes

1. Institute of Museum and Library Services, Librarians for the 21st Century, *available at* http://www.imls.gov/grants/library/lib_bdre.htm.

2. 34 C.F.R. § 300.343(b)(1), (2004), *available at* http://a257.g.akamaitech.net/7/257/2422/14mar20010800/edocket.access.gpo.gov/cfr_2002/julqtr/34cfr300.343.htm. For more information on writing or implementing an IEP, *see*, My Child's Special Needs: A Guide to the Individualized Education Program (Washington, DC: U.S. Department of Education, 2007), *available at* http://www.ed.gov/parents/needs/speced/iepguide/index.html.

3. Georgetown University Law Library, *What Is an Agency Decision?*, Administrative Law Tutorial (2001), *available at* http://www.ll.georgetown.edu/tutorials/admin/7a_what.html.

4. Anne Adams, *Basic Administrative Law for Paralegals* 203 (2nd ed., Aspen Law & Business 2003).

5. Board of Regents v. Roth, 408 U.S. 564, 92 S. Ct. 2701, 33 L. Ed. 2d 548, 1972 U.S. LEXIS 131, 1 I.E.R. Cas. (BNA) 23 (1972); *quoting* Boddie v. Connecticut, 401 U.S. 371, 379 (1971).

6. Roth.

7. *See*, Hewlett-Woodmere Public Library v. Phyllis Rothman, 108 Misc. 2d 715; 438 N.Y.S.2d 730; 1981 N.Y. Misc. LEXIS 2278 (D.C.N.Y., Second District, Nassau County, May 1, 1981).

8. Bryan M. Carson, *The Law of Libraries and Archives* (Lanham, MD: Scarecrow Press, 2007).

9. 5 U.S.C. §§ 551 to 559.

10. 2 Am. Jur. 2d Administrative Law § 14 (2004).

11. American Law Institute, Model State Administrative Procedure Act (1961).

12. James G. Apple & Robert P. Deyling, A Primer on the Civil-Law System at 36 (Washington: Federal Judicial Center, 1995), *available at* http://www.fjc.gov/public/pdf.nsf/lookup/CivilLaw.pdf/$file/CivilLaw.pdf.

13. *id.*

14. Internal Revenue Service, Private Letter Rulings (New York: CCH 1956-).

15. John W. Dean, *The Problem with Presidential Signing Statements: Their Use and Misuse by the Bush Administration*, Findlaw's Writ (January 13, 2006), *available at* http://writ.lp.findlaw.com/dean/20060113.html.

16. President Obama has also been criticized for using signing statements to negate statutes. For an example of this criticism, *See*, Jonathan Strong, *Obama Signing Statement: Despite Law, I can do what I Want on Czars*, The Daily Caller (April 15, 2011), *available at* http://dailycaller.com/2011/04/15/obama-signing-statement-despite-law-i-can-do-what-i-want-on-czars/#ixzz1KNG1XCmn.

17. Phillip J. Cooper, *George W. Bush, Edgar Allan Poe, and the Use and Abuse of Presidential Signing Statements*, 35 Presidential Studies Quarterly 515, 521 (September 2005), *available at* http://www.pegc.us/archive/Articles/cooper_35_PSQ_515.pdf.

18. The first Act was part of the Department of Defense, Emergency Supplemental Appropriations to Address Hurricanes in the Gulf of Mexico, and Pandemic Influenza Act, Public Law 109-148 (December 5, 2005). The signing statement is available at http://www.coherentbabble.com/signingstatements/SSann2005.htm#2005-13. The second

Act was part of the National Defense Authorization Act for Fiscal Year 2006, Public Law 109-163 (January 6, 2006). The signing statement is available at http://www.coherentbabble.com/signingstatements/SSann2006.htm#2006-01.

19. Bruce Fein, *Statement of Bruce Fein Before the Senate Judiciary Committee*, Re: Presidential Signing Statements (June 27, 2006), *available at* http://www.fas.org/irp/congress/2006_hr/062706fein.html. *See also*, Louis Fisher, *Signing Statements: What to Do?*, 4-2 The Forum 7 (2006), *available at* http://www.bepress.com/forum/vol4/iss2/art7; Congressional Research Service [by Michael John Garcia], Interrogation of Detainees: Overview of the McCain Amendment (September 25, 2006), *available at* http://www.coherentbabble.com/signingstatements/CRS/CRS-L33655.pdf; Marc N. Garber & Kurt A. Wimmer, *Presidential Signing Statements as Interpretations of Legislative Intent: An Executive Aggrandizement of Power*, 24 Harvard Journal on Legislation 363 (1987); Frank B. Cross, *The Constitutional Legitimacy and Significance of Presidential "Signing Statements,"* 40 Administrative Law Review 209 (1988); Steven G. Calabresi & Daniel Lev, *The Legal Significance of Presidential Signing Statements*, 4 The Forum 8 (2006), *available at* http://www.bepress.com/forum/vol4/iss2/art8; Chad M. Eggspuehler, Note, *The S-Words Mightier Than the Pen: Signing Statements as Express Advocacy of Unlawful Action*, 43 Gonzaga Law Review 416 (2007-2008).

20. John W. Dean, *The Damaged Institution of the Presidency, How the Obama Administration Intends to Restore It, and What We Can Expect from New OLC Head Dawn Johnsen*, Findlaw's Writ (January 9, 2009), *available at* http://writ.lp.findlaw.com/dean/20090109.html.

21. *id.*

22. *See*, Malinda Lee, *Reorienting the Debate on Presidential Signing Statements: The Need for Transparency in the President's Constitutional Objections, Reservations, and Assertions of Power*, 55 UCLA Law Review 705 (2008), *available at* http://www.uclalawreview.org/articles/content/55/ext/pdf/3.2-1.pdf. *See also*, Memo from Walter Dellinger, Assistant Attorney Gen., Office of Legal Counsel, U.S. Dep't of Justice, to Bernard N. Nussbaum, Counsel to the President, regarding The Legal Significance of Presidential Signing Statements (Nov. 3, 1993), *available at* http://www.usdoj.gov/olc/signing.htm.

23. Lee at 709.

24. Please note that you must use .gov for the White House website. Do not use .com, as that will send you to a pornographic site. The official White House website is found at http://www.whitehouse.gov.

25. Peggy Garvin, *The Government Domain: New & Free Regulations Trackers*, LLRX (April 21, 2010), *available at* http://www.llrx.com/columns/govdomain45.htm.

26. Garvin.

27. Government Printing Office, *Public Papers of the Presidents: About* (July 6, 2005), *available at* http://www.gpoaccess.gov/pubpapers/about.html.

28. *id.*

29. Government Printing Office, Weekly Compilation of Presidential Documents (December 22, 2004), *available at* http://www.gpoaccess.gov/wcomp/index.html.

7

The Freedom of Information Act

Since the rules and decisions of administrative agencies are such a vital part of our lives, the public should be able to receive information about these agencies.[1] This access to information is even more vital for librarians, since our profession *is* information. In order to provide the maximum information possible, the federal government has passed the Freedom of Information Act (FOIA).[2] Some documents are also available under the Presidential Records Act[3] (which will be discussed below) and the Federal Advisory Committee Act.[4]

The Freedom of Information Act, first passed in 1966, is the federal version of what is often called a *Sunshine Law*. The theory behind FOIA and sunshine laws in general is the same as that behind the First Amendment guarantees of freedom of the press. According to constitutional scholar Douglas O. Linder, the main reasons generally given for the values served by protection of free speech in the First Amendment include:

1. The Discovery of Truth—"This value was first suggested by Milton, who . . . suggested that when truth and falsehood are allowed to freely grapple, truth will win out."
2. Facilitating Participation by Citizens in Political Decision-Making—"It has been suggested that citizens will not make wise and informed choices in elections if candidates and proponents of certain policies are restricted in their ability to communicate positions."
3. Creating a More Adaptable and Stable Community (The "Safety Valve" Function)—"It has been suggested that a society in which angry and alienated citizens are allowed to speak their mind—'vent'—will be more stable, as people will be less likely to resort to violence. It has also been pointed out that allowing the alienated and discontented to speak freely enables government to better monitor potentially dangerous groups who would otherwise act more clandestinely."
4. Assuring Individual Self-Fulfillment—"Free speech enables individuals to express themselves, create an identity—and, in the process perhaps, find kindred spirits. Freedom of speech thus becomes an aspect of human dignity."
5. Checking Abuse of Governmental Power—"As Watergate, Irangate, Clintongate (and all the other 'gates') demonstrate, freedom of the press enables citizens to learn about abuses of power—and then do something about the abuse at the ballot box, if they feel so moved."
6. Promoting Tolerance—"It has been argued that freedom of speech, especially through our practice of extending protection to speech that we find hateful or personally upsetting, teaches us to become more tolerant in other aspects of life—and that a more tolerant society is a better society."
7. Creating a More Robust and Interesting Community—"A community in which free speech is valued and protected is likely to be a more energized,

creative society as its citizens actively fulfill themselves in many diverse
and interesting ways."[5]

Several of Linder's principles provide the justification not only for freedom
of the press but also for the Freedom of Information Act. Perhaps the most relevant of Linder's principles are #1 (the discovery of truth), #2 (facilitating participation by citizens in political decision-making), and #5 (checking abuse of
governmental power).

An informed society is an empowered society, as has been shown many
times since the establishment of our nation. The importance of information in an
open society has been reiterated frequently, most recently with the fall of the
Iron Curtain in 1989. Being able to get information about governmental operations provides people with the ability to influence decisions and to prevent cor-
ruption. It is against this background that open meeting laws, sunshine laws, and
the Freedom of Information Act were created.

Some of the documents produced via FOIA requests include commonly
used materials for genealogy and legal research. Genealogy researchers have
used FOIA to obtain naturalization information filed after September 27, 1906,
from the U.S. Bureau of Citizenship and Immigration Services. (The agency has
created Form G-639 for this purpose.)[6] Refugee advocates have requested Immigration and Naturalization Service and State Department reports on social or
political events that may impact applications for asylum. For many years, the
Internal Revenue Service refused to release IRS Private Letter Rulings and Field
Service Memorandums without a FOIA request. Publishers wishing to compile
the Private Letter Rulings had to use FOIA every year to obtain these documents. In the 1980s, however, the IRS quit requiring requests and began releasing these records as a matter of course.

The FOIA applies only to the federal government. Although state governments have their own sunshine laws, the specifics vary from state to state. However, the federal statute provides a good overview of the topic. It is also important to remember that FOIA is only applicable to federal agencies; it does not
apply to Congress or to the courts. The best place to begin researching the Freedom of Information Act is the U.S. Department of Justice FOIA website at
http://www.justice.gov/oip/index.html.

The Presidential Records Act

Under the Presidential Records Act,[7] presidential and vice-presidential documents are to be placed in the custody of the National Archives and Records Administration. According to the statute:

> The term "Presidential records" means documentary materials, or any rea-
> sonably segregable portion thereof, created or received by the President, his
> immediate staff, or a unit or individual of the Executive Office of the President

whose function is to advise and assist the President, in the course of conducting activities which relate to or have an effect upon the carrying out of the constitutional, statutory, or other official or ceremonial duties of the President. Such term—

> (A) includes any documentary materials relating to the political activities of the President or members of his staff, but only if such activities relate to or have a direct effect upon the carrying out of constitutional, statutory, or other official or ceremonial duties of the President; but
> (B) does not include any documentary materials that are (i) official records of an agency (as defined in section 552(e) of title 5, United States Code; (ii) personal records; (iii) stocks of publications and stationery; or (iv) extra copies of documents produced only for convenience of reference, when such copies are clearly so identified.[8]

Personal records of the president are excluded from the act. This includes:

> (A) diaries, journals, or other personal notes serving as the functional equivalent of a diary or journal which are not prepared or utilized for, or circulated or communicated in the course of, transacting Government business;
> (B) materials relating to private political associations, and having no relation to or direct effect upon the carrying out of constitutional, statutory, or other official or ceremonial duties of the President; and
> (C) materials relating exclusively to the President's own election to the office of the Presidency; and materials directly relating to the election of a particular individual or individuals to Federal, State, or local office, which have no relation to or direct effect upon the carrying out of constitutional, statutory, or other official or ceremonial duties of the President.

On November 1, 2001, President George W. Bush issued an executive order defining the scope of the act and claiming privilege in many types of records. Many pro-information commentators are unhappy with this claim of privilege, and with similar claims of privilege that have been asserted under the Federal Advisory Committee Act.[9]

The pertinent part of the order reads as follows:

> The President's constitutionally based privileges subsume privileges for records that reflect: military, diplomatic, or national security secrets (the state secrets privilege); communications of the President or his advisors (the presidential communications privilege); legal advice or legal work (the attorney-client or attorney work product privileges); and the deliberative processes of the President or his advisors (the deliberative process privilege).[10]

Although the statute does not automatically include all emails, many email messages would be subject to the act. Michael Dorf pointed out the issue with email messages in a column in *Findlaw's Writ*:

> The problem of how to classify electronic messages has broader ramifications. Private firms sued in civil actions must produce relevant documents—

including records of emails and text messages—while they do not have to produce transcripts of face-to-face and telephone conversations, for the simple reason that the latter leave no record. But at least in the civil litigation context, the law in principle treats these categories the same. Absent a valid privilege, if asked about a relevant conversation that produced no permanent record, a party or party's agent must divulge the substance of that conversation, at least to the best of his ability to remember. Of course, this regime makes it easier for a bad actor to cover up purely oral conversations than to cover up email and other written communications, but for a law-abiding firm, there is no ex ante distortion of incentives for using various modes of communicating.

The Presidential Records Act, by contrast, draws a distinction between written and spoken words, even in principle. The White House keeps logs of who called or was called by the President but, as far as the public can tell, does not routinely record those calls (at least since the days of President Nixon). Accordingly, there is no legal requirement to preserve the contents of telephone conversations, even though there is a legal requirement—in the PRA—to preserve emails and text messages.[11]

Although there are questions about its scope and whether technology has brought a need for reform, the Presidential Records Act is an important part of the landscape for open records. The records kept by the National Archives are certainly an important piece of history, as they can sometimes help to shed light on executive orders, administrative regulations, and presidential understandings of congressional action.

Agency Records Defined

Perhaps this section should actually be titled "Agency Records Not Defined." The FOIA statute applies to agency records. Unfortunately, the statute does not give a good definition of this term. There are two necessary components for an agency record: there must be a "Record," and it must be created by an "Agency." Although FOIA does not define records, there is one statute that does. FOIA specialists generally look to the definition given by the Federal Records Act in 44 U.S.C. § 3301, which deals with items "made or received by an agency of the United States Government."[12] Under the Federal Records Act, these items must be preserved unless the Archivist authorizes destruction.

However, several court decisions have emphasized that the scope of a record is broader than that of the Federal Records Act, as did a 1980 article in *FOIA Update* (published by the U.S. Department of Justice).[13] Many court decisions have revolved around whether a particular item is an agency record, since "Congress contemplated that an agency must first either create or obtain a record as a prerequisite to its becoming an 'agency record' within the meaning of the FOIA."[14] As long as the item contains information in "language or other symbols," it can be a record.[15] The FOIA includes multimedia, electronic items, and "all tangible recordations of information regardless of whether they are records under 44 U.S.C. § 3301."[16]

Not everything that comes from an agency is automatically an agency record. The record must actually have been created by or be in the possession of the agency before it can be considered an agency record.[17] For example, records of private grant recipients awarded money by an agency are not "Agency Records" unless the agency has actually acquired possession of the material. In addition, employees sometimes create items for their own use; if these personal records are "[m]ade voluntarily [by agency employees], not circulated to nor used by anyone other than the authors, and are discarded or retained at author's sole discretion for their own individual purposes in their own personal files," they do not become agency records and are not subject to disclosure under FOIA.[18]

The second aspect of an agency record is that it must be made by an agency. FOIA does not apply to Congress or the judiciary. However, the following are all considered "agencies" for the purposes of FOIA:

♦ All executive branch agencies, such as the Department of Justice and the Department of Labor.

♦ The Executive Office of the President, including agencies such as the Office of Management and Budget and the Office of Science and Technology Policy.

♦ Independent agencies, such as the Social Security Administration, National Labor Relations Board, Institute of Museum and Library Services, and the National Archives and Records Administration.

♦ Government-created corporations, including the Tennessee Valley Authority and Amtrak.

♦ Quasi-official organizations such as the Legal Services Corporation.

♦ Boards and commissions such as the National Commission on Library and Information Science, the National Indian Gaming Commission, and the Fulbright Foreign Scholarship Board.[19]

Almost every government office is included in this list. Only a few agencies are not covered by FOIA. Because the statute only applies to the executive branch and not to Congress, neither the Library of Congress nor the General Accounting Office is subject to FOIA requests. All executive-branch agencies, however, are subject to the requirements of FOIA.

Exceptions to the FOIA

FOIA allows anyone who makes a request to a federal agency to receive the records that have been asked for. There are only nine exceptions to this right; however, these exceptions are the source of most of the litigation over the Freedom of Information Act. The exceptions are as follows:

♦ Classified national defense and foreign relations information.

♦ Internal agency rules and practices. However, rules and practices relating to how the agency does business with the general public or the outside world are available with FOIA (i.e., administrative staff manuals and instructions to staff that affect the public).

♦ Information that is prohibited from disclosure by another law.

♦ Trade secrets and other confidential business information. However, courts can intervene if it appears that this designation is being used as a smokescreen.

♦ Inter-agency or intra-agency communications that are protected by legal privileges.

♦ Information involving matters of personal privacy.

♦ Information compiled for law enforcement purposes related to ongoing criminal, espionage, or terrorism investigations.

♦ Information relating to the supervision of financial institutions. This is specifically for audit information. Other materials are available including decisions on bank applications.

♦ Geological information on wells.[20]

In addition to the list above, information relating to ongoing criminal, espionage, or terrorism investigations is excluded from coverage by the FOIA.[21]

Although internal agency rules and procedures are protected from disclosure, this exception does not cover all rules. Any rules and practices relating to how the agency does business with the general public or the outside world are available via FOIA. For example, administrative staff manuals and instructions to staff that affect the public are considered to be public documents. (In fact, these are often distributed via the Federal Depository program.)

A. Balancing Privacy and Public Interest

The most common reasons for denying requests involve national security and privacy issues. For example, if personal information is present in a document, the agency may decide not to fill the request, or may fill the request but redact the personal information. This type of personal information is also subject to various federal privacy laws.

The Freedom of Information Act involves striking a very delicate balance between the public's right to know and the individual's right to privacy. This consideration has become more important in recent years due to the amount of information that may be collected about individuals. Law professor Jeffrey Rosen pointed out the quandary:

> As thinking and writing increasingly take place in cyberspace, the part of our life that can be monitored and searched has vastly expanded. E-mail . . . becomes a permanent record that can be resurrected by employers or prosecutors. . . . [E]very Web site we visit, every store we browse in, every magazine we skim, and the amount of time we spend skimming it, creates electronic foot-

prints that can increasingly be tracked back to us, revealing detailed patterns about our tastes, preferences, and intimate thoughts.[22]

There have been several theories proposed to explain why privacy is important enough to counter the public's right to know. The philosophical concept of individual dignity is rooted in Aristotle's "distinction between the public sphere of political activity and the private sphere associated with family and domestic life."[23] The concept was developed and applied to law in 1890 by the future Supreme Court justice Louis D. Brandeis and his law partner, Samuel Warren. Together, they defined the legal right to privacy in a famous article in the *Harvard Law Review*.[24]

The general accumulation of personal information by governmental bodies has exasperated the division between open records and privacy. The more personal information that government has, the more difficult it is to satisfy both the goal of keeping personal information confidential while opening up the workings of government to the people.

> [I]t is impossible to escape these definitional issues because they have pervaded debates over privacy and information since the nineteenth century. Privacy is in many ways a matter of shared expectations and sensibilities; thus, controversy over its meaning has always been linked to clashing normative concerns about the flow of information and the social occasion, purpose, timing, and status of those gathering and using information. In 1890, concern about informational privacy focused primarily on the telegraph or census and mail (for example, the legitimacy of census questions about religion or marital status) or individual complaints about press publicity. Like others at the time, Warren and Brandeis depicted the problem as single, isolated acts of disclosure of private facts. Since the 1960s, the debate has shifted dramatically to questions involving the long-term accumulation and disclosure of vast amounts of intimate facts. Embedded in these shifts are contested senses of "the self" that privacy ought to protect. As commentators struggle to categorize the growing number of privacy claims, they have spawned a host of classifications such as aesthetic and strategic privacy, procedural and substantive privacy, or territorial, informational, and decisional privacy. As Mary Dunlap has argued, "in the seemingly inevitable fusion of the actual or descriptive personal with the normative personal, the right to privacy before a given court and in a given political era expands and contracts in significant part according to the subjective perspectives of judges on human nature."[25] [Internal citations omitted.]

The dichotomy between the private sphere and the public sphere is also broken down by such concerns as medical information and security. As philosopher Dwight Furrow explains:

> The reason for privacy's instability is that the point of privacy is not privacy itself but rather control over one's public presentation. Privacy is important because public scrutiny threatens the sphere of spontaneity and unpredictability that enables the richness and depth of personality. . . .[26]

[However], restricting the free flow of information through legislation and legal regulation has costs that may make these remedies unpalatable even to those whose privacy is protected. For example, though patients want to protect the confidentiality of medical records, they benefit in situations where emergency medical procedures require the ready accessibility of medical information. Similarly, numerous polls show the public is generally willing to accept the threat to privacy represented by the Patriot Act if it reduces the threat of terrorism. . . .[27]

While the philosophical dimensions of privacy are nice, they are not persuasive as to why information should not be released under FOIA. A more persuasive theory rests on the Constitutional issues of substantive and procedural due process. Some cases also use the right of association, which the Supreme Court has ruled is an inherent part of the First Amendment.[28] Another common privacy concern involves identity theft and stalking.

To decide whether a document with private information should be released, agencies and courts use a balancing test. The question is whether the individual's right to privacy is greater than the public's right to know. When privacy issues are alleged by the agency, the requestor has the burden of proof to establish that the public interest is served by disclosure. If no privacy interest is found, further analysis is unnecessary and the information must be disclosed. However, if a privacy interest is found, the public interest in disclosure must be balanced against privacy interest in nondisclosure.

The premier case on privacy versus public interest is United States Department of Justice v. Reporters Committee for Freedom of the Press.[29] In this case, a news organization requested criminal record files from the FBI. The U.S. Supreme Court ruled that "the public interest exception requires a requestor to show that the documents would 'shed light on an agency's performance of its statutory duties.'"[30] In this situation, while the information was known at the time the person was arrested, it is no longer common knowledge. According to the Court, information that was once public but is now hard to obtain is considered to be practically obscure and the individual now has an interest in keeping it private.[31]

While most personally identifiable information carries an expectation of privacy, there are some materials that do not have such an expectation and may therefore be released under FOIA. These exceptions include:

♦   Titles, grades, salaries, duty stations, qualifications for the position held, rank, awards and decorations, etc.
♦   Filing a FOIA request—The person who files a request does not have an expectation of privacy, although home addresses are protected.
♦   Information that is particularly well known.
♦   Information a person makes public on him/herself.
♦   Information on corporations and business associations, which are artificial persons with no expectation of privacy.

Courts have also found that surviving family members have a right to privacy with respect to death scene photographs, most notably in a case involving the suicide of Deputy White House Counsel Vincent Foster during the Clinton administration.[32] In general, the courts tend to rule in favor of individual privacy over public interest in FOIA cases:

> The Supreme Court has consistently found that the right to privacy outweighs the public's right to access. . . . The Court [has] concluded that even if an event is not wholly private, the individual may still have a privacy interest attached to it, and even more importantly, that the right may be greatly affected in today's society where a "computer can accumulate and store information that would otherwise have surely been forgotten long before."[33]

How to File a FOIA Request

All agencies are required to publish their own procedures for FOIA requests, including a FOIA contact to which requests should be sent. The Justice Department has a complete list of contacts for each agency on its website at http://www.justice.gov/oip/foiacontacts.htm. *Figure 7.1* contains a sample letter of request.

Each agency is required to maintain a FOIA Reading Room with final opinions and orders, agency policy statements, administrative staff manuals, and records disclosed in response to a FOIA request that "the agency determines have become or are likely to become the subject of subsequent requests for substantially the same records."[34] Records placed in a reading room after November 1, 1996, are available via the Justice Department's FOIA web page.[35] Requests are typically filed either in person or through the U.S. mail. You must identify the requested records as specifically as possible, since agencies will not do research for you.

Despite all the wonderful principles enumerated above, agencies generally regard FOIA requests as being a bothersome chore that they are mandated to perform; consequently, agencies will do as little as possible to identify a document. If you misidentify a record, the agency will not try to correct your mistake, but will simply inform you that the record you asked for does not exist. Thus it is important to provide as much information as possible in the initial FOIA request.

Once a request has been filed, the agency has 20 business days, not including weekends or holidays (1) to decide whether or not to release the material, and (2) to notify you of its decision. If the records are located in a field office, if the amount of material requested is "voluminous," or if the agency has to consult with another federal agency about the records, the amount of time required for a response may be extended to 30 days.[36]

If you do not receive a response within the specified time, or if you receive an unfavorable response, each agency has a procedure for appealing the decision. After this process has been followed and all administrative remedies have been exhausted, there is the option of filing a lawsuit in federal court. If you file a lawsuit before you have gone through the agency's appeals process, the court will dismiss your case. Only when you have exhausted all administrative options and have obtained a final agency action can you sue in federal court.

Figure 7.1. **Sample FOIA Request Letter.**[37]

Inside Address
Phone number
Fax number
Email address

Date

Freedom of Information Act Request
Agency Head or FOIA Officer
Name of agency or agency component
Address

Dear _____ :

Under the Freedom of Information Act, 5 U.S.C. § 552, I am requesting copies of [identify the records as clearly and specifically as possible].
If there are any fees for searching or copying these records, please let me know before you fill my request. [Or, please supply the records without informing me of the cost if the fees do not exceed $_____, which I agree to pay.]
If you deny all or any part of this request, please cite each specific exemption to justify your withholding of information. Please notify me of appeal procedures available under the law. If you have any questions about handling this request, you may telephone me at _____ (office phone) or at _____ (home phone).

Sincerely,
[4 blank spaces for signature]
Name
Job Title (optional)

Since denials often state that the request was too vague, sometimes it pays to reformulate a request to be more specific. Resubmission can help to avoid costly appeals and litigation.

Because of the volume of requests, sometimes agencies are simply not able to respond to a request within the allotted time period. If you sue for non-response, the court may stay the proceedings in order to allow the agency to respond if it has been shown that "exceptional circumstances exist and that the agency is exercising due diligence in responding to the request."[38] This provides a kind of "safety valve" that allows courts to retain jurisdiction while providing an opportunity for agencies to fill the request.

Agencies are allowed to charge standard commercial rates for document search, duplication, and review. Requestors have no right to receive documents for free, although charges may be lowered to a "reasonable" rate for non-commercial use.[39] The agency also has the option of reducing or waiving the fees "if disclosure of the information is in the public interest because it is likely to contribute significantly to public understanding of the operations or activities of the government and is not primarily in the commercial interest of the requester."[40]

The fee that is charged is only for initial search, review, and duplication of the records. If the case goes to court, legal costs are not charged against the complainant.[41] In fact, if the complainant ultimately prevails in court, the government may be ordered to pay the complainant's attorney fees and other litigation costs.[42] No fee is to be charged for the first two hours of search time, or for the duplication of the first 100 pages.[43] You are not required to pre-pay the fee unless you have previously failed to pay requested fees, or unless the request will cost more than $250.[44]

Unfortunately, there is no limit on the amount of time that an agency may take to copy requested materials. While agencies must respond within 20 or 30 business days (depending on the circumstances), they may take years to copy the documents. Since litigation is generally about whether to grant or not grant the request for documents, requesting parties are occasionally left waiting for long periods of time. However, this is unusual and there may be judicial recourse if it appears that an agency is trying to thwart requests by delaying copying procedures for an unreasonable period of time.

The FOIA and Lawsuits

Although I will discuss the issues of jurisdiction and venue in Chapter 8, "The Judicial Branch," it is necessary to say a few words at this point about cases involving the Freedom of Information Act. For a more full discussion of jurisdiction and venue, please refer to the material in Chapter 8.

In order to use the federal courts, you must satisfy the requirements of jurisdiction. There are three requirements that you must show before you can use the federal courts: that the agency has "[1] 'improperly'; (2) 'withheld'; (3) 'agency records.' Judicial authority to devise remedies and enjoin agencies can only be invoked, under the jurisdiction grant conferred by § 552, if the agency has contravened all three components of this obligation."[45] If you fail to include these three elements in your complaint, the case is subject to dismissal for "failure to state a claim upon which relief can be granted" under rule 12(b)(6) of the Federal Rules of Civil Procedure.[46]

If you do need to sue in federal court, make sure that your complaint is filed in the proper venue. The case should be filed either in the district where the complainant resides, the district where the complainant has his or her principal place of business, the district where the records reside, or the District Court for the District of Columbia. Cases are always properly filed if you use the District of Columbia as the venue. (But see the section below on cases against the Tennessee Valley Authority.) However, if you sue in another district, you must allege in your complaint "the nexus giving rise to proper venue in that jurisdiction."[47] Although non-resident aliens are treated the same as U.S. citizens for FOIA purposes, requestors that reside outside of the U.S. must use the District Court for the District of Columbia or the district where the records reside.

Cases can be transferred to another venue if necessary "for the convenience of parties and witnesses."[48] This is known as the doctrine of *forum non-conveniens*. It is most often invoked when the records are physically located in a district other than the one in which the case was filed. However, I always recommend not counting on having a court transfer venue. Therefore, cases should be filed initially in the proper forum.

One potential minefield with venue involves FOIA cases against the Tennessee Valley Authority (TVA). The TVA is a wholly owned government corporation, and thus is subject to FOIA. However, the enabling statute for the TVA specifies that the Northern District of Alabama is the exclusive venue for lawsuits against the corporation. This conflicts with the FOIA statute, which always allows suits to be brought in the District Court for the District of Columbia. Because the law is not settled as to whether the TVA is amenable to FOIA suit either in Washington, D.C., or else only in the Northern District of Alabama, it is probably best to avoid the D.C. District. (After all, no one wants to be the "test case.")

Once a case has been properly filed in court, the agency has the burden of proof for explaining why it is not releasing the information.[49] This means that the agency has "the necessity or duty of affirmatively providing a fact or facts in dispute. . . ."[50] If the agency can't explain to the court why it is refusing the request, the judge will order the records to be released.

If it is determined that the documents may be released, but that they contain some information that is subject to an exception, you may receive the record with some items blacked out (redacted). This redaction is also subject to appeal through the agency's processes, and ultimately can be litigated in the federal courts.

State Open Records and Meetings Laws

Although the FOIA only applies to the federal government, all 50 states have also adopted similar open records laws for their agencies. These sunshine laws often work in combination with open-meeting statutes which require that public bodies allow their decision-making meetings to be attended by the public. Most states permit these bodies to go into private session in order to consider confidential personnel matters.

It is worth noting that many states exempt library circulation records and membership lists from their open records laws. In some states, such as Michigan, general statutory sections on library privacy mandate this protection. Other states, such as Illinois, have provisions specifically naming library circulation records and membership lists as being exempt from the open records laws.

In recent years, there has been a lot of litigation surrounding email communications. The general rule for the federal FOIA is that email is considered an agency record and is treated the same as other records.[51] In some cases, messages sent from home accounts (AOL, etc.) to other officials within an agency may also constitute agency records if they involve the transaction of agency business. Similar questions about the nature of email have cropped up under the Presidential Records Act.[52] And in April 2010, the Library of Congress announced that it would archive every public tweet posted on *Twitter* since the service began in 2006, including those by government officials.[53] Of course, there are privacy concerns with the archiving of personal tweets, but the FOIA and the Presidential Records Act probably alleviate these concerns for government tweeters.[54]

Computer metadata is another hot topic of litigation in the states. This is information about a document, either created automatically (such as creation date) or added later (such as index terms and keywords). In a recent Arizona case, the state supreme court decided that metadata is subject to open records requests under state law.[55] (This is an important reminder that what we do on the computer leaves traces.)

Email and computer technology go beyond issues of open records, however. Several states have dealt with the issue of whether email constitutes a meeting subject to open meeting laws. Because state precedents vary considerably on what constitutes a meeting, serial conversations may constitute an illegal meeting in some jurisdictions[56] but not others.[57] The same issues also apply to telephone conference calls and open meeting requirements.[58]

The federal open meetings act is called the *Government in the Sunshine Act*.[59] While there are no precedents under federal law, some state courts have considered email communication to constitute illegal meetings. One case which holds that email exchanges *do* constitute a meeting is Wood v. Battle Ground School District.[60] According to the Washington Court of Appeals, if a majority or quorum is included and action is taken as a result of the email exchange, then the communication constitutes a meeting. However, another case has specified that it is not a meeting if the subject of the email exchange is business that would not come before the body for a vote, or if email was sent but there was no exchange.[61]

Meanwhile, Virginia has held that email does *not* constitute a meeting under the state open meetings and open records laws. The Virginia definition of an open meeting required assemblage of three or more members. In this case, emails were sent between Mayor, Vice Mayor, and three City Council members in Fredericksburg, VA. The replies ranged from 4 hours to 2 days. The Virginia Supreme Court held that this type of asynchronous communication is not a meeting, but left open the question of chat rooms and synchronous communication:

> Indisputably, the use of computers for textual communication has become commonplace around the world. It can involve communication that is functionally similar to a letter sent by ordinary mail, courier, or facsimile transmission. In this respect, there may be significant delay before the communication is received and additional delay in response. However, computers can be utilized to exchange text in the nature of a discussion, potentially involving multiple participants, in what are euphemistically called "chat rooms" or by "instant messaging." In these forms, computer generated communication is virtually simultaneous.[62]

I urge caution with email messages, whether as an agency or a requestor. Agencies should check whether their email messages might constitute meetings subject to open access. Be aware of the possible ramifications of serial conversations. The issue of chat rooms and IM is especially problematic, as this basically forms an online meeting when the participants are able to communicate simultaneously.

If you are requesting records from an agency, be sure to ask for any applicable email messages. Remember to be aware that some agency officials will use "home" email accounts for agency business. This is not always because people are trying to get away with something. After all, we have all used a different email address for work purposes. However, this is something to be aware of and address in a FOIA request if these records are important to your research.

Documents and Sources on
the Freedom of Information Act

There are a number of good websites dealing with the Freedom of Information Act. The following are some places to start your research:

♦ *Department of Justice Office of Information and Privacy*
  http://www.usdoj.gov/oip/oip.html
  This is the best place to start learning about FOIA issues. The site contains useful suggestions, contact information for each agency, and links to online reading rooms.

♦ *Reporters Committee for Freedom of the Press*
  http://www.rcfp.org
  This website contains a number of helpful tips along with links to statutes and case law. The most useful feature is an "Automatic Letter Generator." This is a wizard-

type template which allows users to input their information in response to prompts. The wizard then generates a FOIA letter automatically. It is located at http://www.rcfp.org/foi_letter/generate.php.

♦ *FOIA Advocates*
http://www.foiadvocates.com/intro.html
This is the website for a law firm, but it contains a number of helpful tips and links.

♦ *Coalition of Journalists for Open Government*
http://www.cjog.net/expert.html

♦ *Open Government Guide*
http://www.rcfp.org/ogg/index.php
Contains information about state open records and meetings statutes.

♦ *Electronic Privacy Information Center*
http://www.epic.org

♦ *Electronic Freedom Foundation*
http://www.eff.org

♦ *Federal Trade Commission Privacy Initiatives*
http://www.ftc.gov/privacy/index.html

♦ *National Freedom of Information Coalition*
http://www.nfoic.org

♦ *Privacy.Org*
http://www.privacy.org

♦ *CPL Freedom of Information Act Guide*
http://www.chipublib.org/008subject/006govinfo/foia.html

♦ *Your Right to Federal Records: Questions and Answers on the Freedom of Information Act and Privacy Act.* (2004). Pueblo, CO: U.S. General Services Administration and U.S. Department of Justice. *Available online at* http://www.pueblo.gsa.gov/cic_text/fed_prog/foia/foia.htm.

There are many cases dealing with venue. The best resource is the chapter on litigation considerations in the Justice Department's *Freedom of Information Act Guide*, available online at http://www.4uth.gov.ua/usa/english/media/foia/litigati.htm. The guide discusses both published and unpublished cases dealing with the issue of venue.

There are also several other statutes that supplement or interact with the Freedom of Information Act (5 U.S.C. § 552 et seq.). Major statutes include:

- *Driver's Privacy Protection Act of 1994*, 18 U.S.C. § 2721 et seq., making unauthorized access of driver's license information illegal.[63]

- *Family Education Rights and Privacy Act* (FERPA), 20 U.S.C. § 1232g, governs privacy and the release of records by educational institutions.

- *Federal Advisory Committee Act*, 5 U.S.C. § 556, pertains to records of advisory committees and boards. It contains an open records clause.

- *Financial Services Modernization Act* (FSMA), 15 U.S.C., §§ 6801-6809, prohibits the disclosure of personal information by financial institutions.

- *Government in the Sunshine Act*, 5 U.S.C. § 552(b) et seq., is the federal open meetings statute.

- *Health Insurance Portability and Accountability Act* (HIPAA), Pub. L. 104-191, governs privacy in healthcare. The final rules established by the Department of Health and Human Services are found in 45 C.F.R. part 160 et seq.

- *Presidential Records Act*, 44 U.S.C. § 2201 et seq., which pertains to the official papers and documents of the president.

- *Privacy Act of 1974*, 5 U.S.C. § 552 et seq.

There are many books and law review articles on the Freedom of Information Act. Interested readers should search the Current Index to Legal Periodicals, Index to Legal Periodicals, LegalTrac, or Current Law Journal Content. I have included a few recent articles and books dealing with issues covered in the text.

- *Access Denied: Freedom of Information in the Information Age.* (2000). Davis, Charles N., & Splichal, Sigman L. (Eds.). Ames, IA: Iowa State University Press.

- Russo, Michael. (2006, Winter). Are bloggers representatives of the news media under the Freedom of Information Act? *Columbia Journal of Law and Social Problems, 40(2)*, 225-268.

- Bemis, Lauren. (2005, Fall). Balancing a citizen's right to know with the privacy of an innocent family: The expansion of the scope of exemption 7(C) of the Freedom of Information Act under National Archives & Records Administration v. Favish. *Journal of the National Association of Administrative Law Judiciary, 25(2)*, 507-543.

- Hammitt, Harry A., & Leahy, Patrick. (2008). *Litigation Under the Federal Open Government Laws: Covering the Freedom of Information Act, the Privacy Act, the Government in the Sunshine Act, and the Federal Advisory Committee Act.* Washington, DC; Lynchburg, VA: EPIC Publications, James Madison Project; Access Reports.

♦   McCrann, Grace-Ellen. (2007). An examination of the conditions surrounding the passage of the 1966 U.S. Freedom of Information Act. *Open Government: A Journal on Freedom of Information, 3(1)*, available at http://www.opengovjournal.org/article/view/771/791.

♦   McKee, Kathleen A. (2006). Remarks on the Freedom of Information Act: The "national security" exemption in a post 9/11 era. *Regent Journal of International Law, 4(2)*, 263-279.

♦   Montague, Autumn. (2006, Winter). Do not disturb: Defining the meaning of privacy under the Freedom of Information Act. *Howard Law Journal 49(2)*, 643-667.

♦   O'Connor, John F., & Baratz, Michael J. (2004, Spring). Some assembly required: The application of state open meeting laws to email correspondence. *George Mason Law Review, 12*: 719-774.

♦   Schindler, Devin S. (2010, Fall). Between safety and transparency: Prior restraints, FOIA, and the power of the executive. *Hastings Constitutional Law Quarterly, 38(1)*: 1-48.

♦   Sheehan, Catherine F. (1994). Note: Opening the government's electronic mail: Public access to National Security Council records. *Boston College Law Review, 35*: 1145-1201.

♦   Spiegel, Richard William. (2007). *REDACTED: A look at the United States government system for classifying and releasing information and how the current state of legal and procedural quagmire might be improved.* (Unpublished M.A. Thesis, University of Colorado at Boulder) (available from ProQuest Dissertations & Theses, Publication No. AAT 1442913).

Conclusion

In order to serve our library clients, we need to use all of the tools at our disposal. Sometimes this means going beyond the items in a government documents depository and filing a Freedom of Information Act request. Presidential records and advisory commissions are also subject to certain open records requirements. However, laws have not kept up with technology. There are some questions about the applicability of FOIA, open meetings laws, and the Presidential Records Act when dealing with chat and instant messaging, and email messages (particularly those from personal accounts).

Open records provide many uses in our society, and it is useful to have a basic knowledge of the process. The librarian's toolbox contains many different implements. Let's use all of them to find necessary information.

Notes

1. In April 2005, I was privileged to attend an excellent presentation at the Kentucky Library Association Academic Section conference on this difficult but important topic. Jo Staggs-Neel of the Agriculture Information Center at the University of Kentucky did an excellent job of explaining the Freedom of Information Act. Jo Staggs-Neel, *The Freedom of Information Act*, Presentation to the Kentucky Library Association Academic Section Conference (April 2005). After I told several colleagues about this vital information, it was suggested to me that I should write a "Legally Speaking" column for *Against the Grain* about the Freedom of Information Act (FOIA), and how to write a FOIA request. Part of the material in this section was published as Bryan M. Carson, *How to File a Freedom of Information Act Request*, 17 Against the Grain 82 (June 2005). I would like to thank Jo Staggs-Neel for providing the inspiration for the column, and thus for this chapter.

2. 5 U.S.C. § 552 et seq.

3. 44 U.S.C. § 2201 – 44 U.S.C. § 2207.

4. 5 U.S.C. § 556.

5. Douglas O. Linder, Introduction to the Free Speech Clause, Exploring Constitutional Law (University of Missouri–Kansas City School of Law, 2005), *available at* http://www.law.umkc.edu/faculty/projects/ftrials/conlaw/firstaminto.htm.

6. U.S. Citizenship and Immigration Services, *Form G-639, Freedom of Information/Privacy Request* (February 4, 2009), *available at* http://www.uscis.gov/files/form/g-639.pdf.

7. 44 U.S.C. § 2201 – 44 U.S.C. § 2207.

8. 44 U.S.C. § 2201(2).

9. *See*, Catherine F. Sheehan, Note: *Opening the Government's Electronic Mail: Public Access To National Security Council Records*, 35 Boston College Law Review 1145 (1994); Jane E. Kirtley, *Transparency and Accountability in a Time of Terror: The Bush Administration's Assault on Freedom of Information*, 11 Communication Law and Policy 479 (2006); Jonathan Turley, *Presidential Papers and Popular Government: The Convergence of Constitutional and Property Theory in Claims of Ownership and Control of Presidential Records*, 88 Cornell Law Review 651 (2003); Mark J. Rozell, *Executive Privilege Revived? Secrecy and Conflict During the Bush Presidency*, 52 Duke Law Journal 403 (2002); Robert V. Percival, *Presidential Management of the Administrative State: The Not-So-Unitary Executive*, 51 Duke Law Journal 963 (2001); R. Kevin Bailey, Note: *"Did I Miss Anything?" Excising the National Security Council from FOIA Coverage*, 46 Duke Law Journal 1475 (1997). *But see*, Carolyn Bingham Kello, Note: *Drawing the Curtain on Open Government? In Defense of the Federal Advisory Committee Act*, 69 Brooklyn Law Review 345 (2003).

10. Executive Order No. 13233, 66 F.R. 56025 (2001), *available at* http://www.archives.gov/about/laws/appendix/13233.html.

11. Michael C. Dorf, *All the President's IMs: Are Federal Record-keeping Laws Out of Step with Modern Communications?* Findlaw's Writ (January 12, 2009), *available at* http://writ.lp.findlaw.com/dorf/20090112.html.

12. 44 U.S.C. § 3301.

13. U.S. Department of Justice, *What Is an Agency Record?* 2-1 FOIA Update (1980), *available at* www.usdoj.gov/oip/foia_updates/Vol_II_1/page3.htm.

14. Forsham v. Harris, 445 U.S. 169, 182; 100 S. Ct. 977; 63 L. Ed. 2d 293; 1980 U.S. LEXIS 27; 5 Media L. Rep. 2473 (1980).

15. Nichols v. United States, 325 F. Supp. 130 (D. Kan. 1971).

16. Save the Dolphins v. U.S. Dept. of Commerce, 404 F. Supp. 407 (N.D. Cal. 1975).

17. Forsham v. Harris, 445 U.S. 169, 182; 100 S. Ct. 977; 63 L. Ed. 2d 293; 1980 U.S. LEXIS 27; 5 Media L. Rep. 2473 (1980).

18. Porter County Chap., Etc. v. U.S.A.E.C., 380 F. Supp. 630, 633 (N.D. Ind. 1974).

19. The Government Documents librarian at Louisiana State University has compiled an excellent directory of federal agencies. It is available at http://www.lib.lsu.edu/gov/index.html.

20. The exceptions are contained in 5 U.S.C. § 552(b), Subsections 1-9. *See*, Your Right to Federal Records: Questions and Answers on the Freedom of Information Act and Privacy Act (Pueblo, CO: U.S. General Services Administration and U.S. Department of Justice, 2004), *available at* http://www.pueblo.gsa.gov/cic_text/fed_prog/foia/foia.htm.

21. 5 U.S. C. § 552(c), Subsections 1-3.

22. Jeffrey Rosen, The Unwanted Gaze: The Destruction of Privacy in America (New York: Random House, 2000) at 51.

23. Judith DeCrew, *Privacy, in* The Stanford Encyclopedia of Philosophy (2006), *available at* http://plato.stanford.edu/entries/privacy.

24. Samuel D. Warren & Louis D. Brandeis, *The Right to Privacy,* 4 Harvard Law Review 193 (1890), *available at* http://www.ilrg.com/download/4harvlrev193.txt.

25. Michael Grossberg, *Some Queries About Privacy and Constitutional Rights,* 41 Case Western Reserve Law Review 857, 858-59 (1990), *quoting* Dunlap, *Where the Person Ends, Does the Government Begin? An Explanation of Present Controversies Concerning "The Right to Privacy,"* 12 Lincoln Law Review 47, 49 (1981).

26. Dwight Furrow, *The Privacy Paradox,* 64 The Humanist 25, 27 (May/June 2004).

27. *id.*

28. NAACP v. Alabama ex rel. Patterson, 357 U.S. 449, 460-61 (1958). *See also,* Right of Association, *in* The Constitution of the United States of America: Analysis and Interpretation, Johnny H. Killian and George A. Costello (eds.) (Washington: Congressional Research Service, Library of Congress, 1992 [amended 1996, 1998, and 2000]), *available at* http://caselaw.lp.findlaw.com/data/constitution/amendment01/12.html.

29. United States Department of Justice v. Reporters Committee for Freedom of the Press, 489 U.S. 749; 109 S. Ct. 1468; 103 L. Ed. 2d 774; 1989 U.S. LEXIS 1574; 57 U.S.L.W. 4373; 16 Media L. Rep. 1545 (1989).

30. *id. See also,* Martin E. Halstuk, *When Is an Invasion of Privacy Unwarranted Under the FOIA? An Analysis of the Supreme Court's "Sufficient Reason" and "Presumption of Legitimacy" Standards,* 16 Florida Journal of Law and Public Policy 361 (2005). "Information that does not directly reveal the operations or activities of the federal government falls outside the ambit of the public interest that the FOIA was enacted to serve."

31. Reporters Committee for Freedom of the Press.

32. National Archives & Records Administration v. Favish, 541 U.S. 157; 124 S. Ct.

1570; 158 L. Ed. 2d 319; 2004 U.S. LEXIS 2546; 72 U.S.L.W. 4265; 32 Media L. Rep. 1545 (2004).

33. Victoria S. Salzmann, *Are Public Records Really Public? The Collision Between the Right to Privacy and the Release of Public Court Records Over the Internet*, 52 Baylor L. Rev. 355, 364 (2000); *quoting* United Reporters Committee for Freedom of the Press at 771 (1989).

34. 5 U.S.C. § 552(a)(2)(D).

35. U.S. Department of Justice, Freedom of Information Act, *available at* http://www.justice.gov/oip/index.html.

36. 5 U.S.C. § 552(a)(6)(B)(iii). *See also*, U.S. Department of Commerce, *FOIA Website* (2005), *available at* http://www.osec.doc.gov/omo/FOIA/FOIAWEBSITE.htm.

37. U.S. Department of Commerce, *Sample FOIA Letter*, FOIA Website, *available at* http://www.osec.doc.gov/omo/FOIA/FOIAWEBSITE.htm.

38. U.S. Department of Justice, Freedom of Information Act Guide at 944 (2007), *available at* http://www.usdoj.gov/oip/foia_guide07.htm. *See also*, Open America v. Watergate Special Prosecution Force, 547 F.2d 605 (D.C. Cir. 1976).

39. 5 U.S.C. § 552(a)(4)(A).

40. 5 U.S.C. § 552(a)(4)(A)(iii).

41. 5 U.S.C. § 552(a)(4)(A)(iv).

42. 5 U.S.C. § 552(a)(4)(B).

43. 5 U.S.C. § 552(a)(4)(A)(iv)(II).

44. 5 U.S.C. § 552(a)(4)(A)(v).

45. Kissinger v. Reporters Committee for Freedom of the Press, 445 U.S. 136, 150 (1980).

46. Federal Rules of Civil Procedure, *available at* http://www.law.cornell.edu/rules/frcp.

47. *Freedom of Information Act Guide* at 911.

48. 28 U.S.C. § 1404(a).

49. 5 U.S.C. § 552(a)(4)(B).

50. Black's Law Dictionary, Burden of Proof (5th ed. 1979).

51. Electronic Freedom of Information Act Amendments of 1996, P.L. 104-231, 110 Stat. 3048 (Amendments to 5 U.S.C. § 552). *See also*, Grand Central Partnership, Inc. v. Cuomo, 166 F.3d 474 (2nd Cir. 1999).

52. Michael C. Dorf, *All the President's IMs: Are Federal Record-keeping Laws Out of Step with Modern Communications?* Findlaw's Writ (January 12, 2009), *available at* http://writ.lp.findlaw.com/dorf/20090112.html.

53. Doug Gross, *Library of Congress to archive your tweets*, CNN (April 14, 2010), *available at* http://www.cnn.com/2010/TECH/04/14/library.congress.twitter/index.html.

54. Jill Jarvis Tonus & Catherine Lovrics, *Copyright and Privacy Questions Around Your Public Tweets and the New Library of Congress Archive and Google Replay*, Slaw.ca (April 27, 2010), *available at* http://www.slaw.ca/2010/04/27/copyright-and -privacy-questions-around-your-public-tweets-and-the-new-library-of-congress-archive -and-google-replay.

55. Lake v. City of Phoenix, 222 Ariz. 547; 218 P.3d 1004 (October 29, 2009), *available at* http://www.supreme.state.az.us/opin/pdf2009/CV090036PR.pdf. *See*, Wildman Harrold Allen & Dixon, *Court holds that metadata is a matter of public record* (December 2 2009), *available at* http://www.wildman.com/index.cfm?fa=resourcecenter

.briefingroomdetail&oid=6091&rss=1#page=1.

56. Booth Newspapers, Inc. v. Univ. of Mich. Bd. of Regents, 507 N.W.2d 422 (Mich. 1993).

57. Moberg v. Independent School District No. 281, 336 N.W.2d 510 (Minn. 1983).

58. In California, conference calls are illegal meetings; Stockton Newspapers, Inc. v. Members of the Redevelopment Agency of the City of Stockton, 214 Cal. Rptr. 561, 565 (Cal. Ct. App. 1985). When the supreme court of Virginia heard this issue, they decided that conference calls were *not* illegal meetings; Roanoke City School Board v. Times-World Corporation, 307 S.E.2d 256 (Va. 1983). However, the Roanoke case led to the statute being amended to include conference calls in the definition of a meeting.

59. Public Law 94-409, 90 Stat. 1241, 5 U.S.C. § 552(b) et seq.

60. Wood v. Battle Ground School District, 27 P.3d 1208 (Wash. Ct. App. 2001).

61. Eugster v. The City of Spokane, 114 P.3d 1200 (Wash. 2005).

62. Beck v. Shelton, 593 S.E.2d 195, 1999 (Va. 2004).

63. This statute was enacted after the murder of actress Rebecca Schaeffer. The stalker who killed her obtained her home address from her driver's license records. Congress subsequently made driver's license information subject to nondisclosure.

8

The Judicial Branch:
The Federal Court System

The judicial branch of the United States government is the place where the actions of the other two branches are adjudicated. The role of the judiciary is twofold. First of all, the courts exist to perform justice in individual cases. In addition, the courts interpret statutes, regulations, and Constitutional provisions.

Although the courts rule on general principles of law, they do so in the context of cases involving actual specific parties and actual specific controversies. Article III of the Constitution requires that the courts hear "cases and controversies."[1] The following definition helps to illustrate what is meant by that requirement:

> By cases and controversies are intended the claims of litigants brought before the courts for determination by such regular proceedings as are established by law or custom for the protection or enforcement of rights, or the prevention, redress, or punishment of wrongs. Whenever the claim of a party under the Constitution, laws, or treaties of the United States takes such a form that the judicial power is capable of acting upon it, then it has become a case. The term implies the existence of present or possible adverse parties whose contentions are submitted to the Court for adjudication.[2]

Certain types of cases are not capable of being resolved in court. The executive or legislative branches, rather than the judiciary, are supposed to deal with issues that are inherently political.[3] For example, the decision to terminate a treaty with another country is a political question. This is not an issue in which the courts should be involved. Another example would be cases challenging the U.S. involvement in Vietnam. The courts refused to hear the merits of these cases because whether to commit U.S. troops to a war is a political question.

Another issue is that of *standing*. Standing refers to whether or not the plaintiff is the proper party to file the lawsuit. For example, in the case of Elk Grove School District v. Newdow, the question was about the words "under God" in the Pledge of Allegiance. Was the use of these words Constitutional? The Supreme Court did not rule on the merits of the case; instead, the Court ruled that Mr. Newdow did not have *standing* to file the lawsuit because he did not have custody of his children, on whose behalf he was suing.[4]

The courts do not just go around looking for issues about which to declare law. The courts cannot rule until an actual case has been brought. As the late Chief Justice Rehnquist wrote, "The requirement of 'actual injury redressable by the court'[5] serves several of the 'implicit policies embodied in Article III [of the Constitution].'[6] It tends to assure that the legal questions presented to the court will be resolved not in the rarified atmosphere of a debating society, but in a concrete factual context conducive to a realistic appreciation of the consequences of judicial action."[7]

Jurisdiction and Venue

The federal courts can only hear specific types of cases. Before a lawsuit can be filed in federal court, the plaintiff must first meet the basic requirements of showing that the court has *jurisdiction* over the issue, and that the case has been filed in the proper *venue*. *Jurisdiction* is the question of whether the court is empowered to hear cases on the particular issue that is at stake. By contrast, *venue* is the question of whether the court that has been selected is the right one to hear the case.

The federal courts only have jurisdiction over cases which involve a federal issue. If the case does not involve a federal issue, the proper forum will be a state court. Generally this means that the case must involve a federal statute or regulation, a treaty provision, or a Constitutional issue. Since most legal matters fall within the jurisdiction of state law, most cases are heard in state courts. This jurisdictional limitation is known as the *Federal Question* principle; namely, if the case does not include a Federal Question, only state courts may hear it.

There are only a few exceptions to the Federal Question principle. The most important exception involves *diversity jurisdiction*. Article III of the Constitution allows the federal courts to hear cases where the parties are citizens of different states. The rationale for allowing federal courts to hear these cases (known as *diversity cases*) was because the founders of our nation were afraid that local courts would have a bias towards their own residents and would not give out-of-state residents a fair trial.[8]

For example, suppose that the Largetown Public Library is located in the state of Oregon. The library signs a contract to buy furniture from the Freddy Furniture Company, which is located in the state of Washington. The contract specifies that the library will pay 50% down, with the balance due after the furniture is delivered. The library pays the deposit, but Freddy Furniture defaults on the contract and does not deliver the furniture. The library's attorney decides to sue the furniture company to get back the deposit money. The Largetown Public Library may either sue in the state courts of Oregon, in the state courts of Washington, *or* in the federal courts.

Another example of diversity jurisdiction involves a citizen of California who is involved in a car accident while on vacation in the state of Florida. If the person who caused the accident was a citizen of Connecticut, the case could be filed in the state courts of California, Florida, or Connecticut. However, the case could also be filed in federal court.

Since the accident took place in Florida, the laws of that state would apply, no matter in which court the case is filed. If the case were filed in the state court of California or Connecticut, the judge would still apply the laws of the state of Florida. Similarly, if the case were filed in federal court, the judge would apply the laws of Florida to the case.

There are several other types of cases that can be heard in federal courts, including controversies that involve more than one state, admiralty and maritime cases, and cases involving foreign countries or foreign citizens.[9] However, most cases in the federal courts either involve Federal Question jurisdiction or diversity jurisdiction.

In the example of the Largetown Public Library and Freddy Furniture, the federal courts received jurisdiction because of the diverse citizenship of the parties. Having established jurisdiction to enter the federal courts, the library can either file its lawsuit in the federal court in Oregon (where the library is located) or in the federal court in Washington (where the furniture manufacturer is located). The library can't file the case in a federal court in the state of New York, since New York has no relationship to the parties or to the case. The proper venue would be the federal court in either Oregon or Washington.

In the other example, a federal court in Florida would be a proper venue for a lawsuit, since the automobile accident occurred in that state. The key to determining proper venue is that one of the parties must reside within the geographical area of the court, or the event triggering the lawsuit must have occurred within the geographical area of the court.

Trial Courts

In the federal court system, cases are first heard in the district court. Every state has at least one district; most states have more than one. There are a total of 94 districts in the federal system. Within a particular district, there may also be multiple courthouses. For example, the state of Kentucky has two districts—the Eastern District of Kentucky and the Western District of Kentucky. Within the Eastern District, the main courthouse is in Lexington, but there are branches in Ashland, Frankfort, Pikeville, London, and Covington. The Western District of Kentucky has its main offices in Louisville, but there are also courthouses in Bowling Green, Owensboro, and Paducah.

In addition to the district courts, there are also some specialized courts that have been set up by Congress, namely the *Court of International Trade* and the *Court of Federal Claims.* "The *Court of International Trade* addresses cases involving international trade and customs issues. The *United States Court of Federal Claims* has jurisdiction over most claims for money damages against the United States, disputes over federal contracts, unlawful 'takings' of private property by the federal government, and a variety of other claims against the United States."[10] [Emphasis added.]

When a case is heard at trial, there are two kinds of questions that need to be resolved—*questions of fact* and *questions of law.* A *question of fact* involves "the resolution of a factual dispute."[11] For example, in a car accident involving a traffic light, the question of fact may be whether the light was green or red. The jury decides questions of fact.

Occasionally the parties to a lawsuit will waive the right to a jury trial and ask the judge to hear the case without a jury. This is known as a *bench trial*. If there is a bench trial, the judge will decide the questions of fact as well as the questions of law.

A question of law is "an issue which involves the application or interpretation of a law. . . ."[12] The judge decides questions of law. Here are some examples of questions of law:

♦ Whether a search in a criminal trial was legal.

♦ Whether to dismiss a case or grant summary judgment.

♦ Whether a particular witness may testify as an expert witness.

♦ Whether particular evidence can be admitted in the case.

♦ Whether a particular statute or regulation is constitutional or unconstitutional.

♦ Whether to uphold or overrule an objection by one of the attorneys at trial.

♦ Decisions involving the legal standard of proof required for the particular case.

♦ Decisions involving whether the court has jurisdiction or whether the case was filed in the proper venue.

♦ Decisions involving the instructions that the judge gives to the jury.

Once the jury has resolved a question of fact (known as a *factual finding*), the finding becomes final. The judge cannot change the factual findings, and neither can a higher court on appeal. (The judge can find that the jury did not have enough evidence to make that finding, but this is a question of law.) The only issues that can be appealed to a higher court are the judge's rulings about questions of law.

One of the first issues that the judge often needs to resolve is whether the case should go to trial at all. Rule 56 of the *Federal Rules of Civil Procedure* allows parties to a civil action to file a motion for *summary judgment*. A motion for summary judgment is a request for the judge to end the case and make a ruling without a trial on the grounds that "there is no genuine issue of material fact and . . . the moving party is entitled to prevail as a matter of law. . . . In effect [the motion] argues that as a matter of law upon admitted or established facts the moving party is entitled to prevail."[13] Either party may file a motion for summary judgment, whether on a particular issue or on the entire case. The party that files the motion has the burden of proving to the court that no genuine issue of fact exists. Any issue of fact will be resolved *against* the moving party. "[T]he party opposing the motion is to be given the benefit of all reasonable doubts in determining whether a genuine issue exists."[14]

Cases and issues are often resolved by summary judgment. Since the decision to grant or deny a motion for summary judgment is a legal question, the issue of whether a genuine issue of fact exists can be appealed to a higher court.

A summary judgment usually comes before the beginning of a trial. By contrast, once a trial has begun the judge has the power to issue a *directed verdict*. A directed verdict occurs when the party with the burden of proof has not presented enough evidence for his or her case to go forward. In this situation, "the trial judge may order the entry of a verdict without allowing the jury to consider it, because, as a matter of law, there can be only one such verdict."[15]

Once a case has been tried and decided, the losing party may ask the judge to grant a new trial, or to issue a *judgment notwithstanding the verdict*, also known as a *judgment N.O.V.* (NOV stands for *non obstante veredicto*.) The judgment N.O.V. means that the judge finds, as a matter of law, that the decision of the jury was incorrect. The entry of a judgment N.O.V. can be appealed, since it is a matter of law.

It is vital to note that the district court must follow the decisions of higher courts. If the court of appeals or the Supreme Court has ruled on an issue, that precedent is binding upon the district court. The binding nature of precedent is known as *stare decisis* (Latin for "Let the decision stand.)" It is only if the issue is one that has not been ruled on by a higher court that the district court is free to make its own ruling.

What happens, though, if there has not been a ruling on the issue in federal court, but there has been a ruling on a similar issue in one of the state courts or in the courts of another country? In that situation, the judge can make note of the previous ruling, but has the option of either following it or not following it. Rulings from another jurisdiction are not binding as precedent; however, rulings from another jurisdiction are persuasive, and are frequently cited by lawyers in order to convince the judge to rule in a particular manner. (Some of the foreign cases most frequently cited are those from other "common law" countries such as Britain, Canada, Australia, New Zealand, and South Africa. See the section on "Diversity of State Laws" in Chapter 9 for an explanation of the common law system.) Most of the time, however, the trial court merely follows the precedent of a higher court, rather than breaking new ground. The court of appeals and the Supreme Court have much more discretion on cases, since they do not have to follow precedent blindly. Indeed, the decisions of these courts usually become precedent.

Appealing a Case

Television programs often depict the losing party in a case saying, "The decision was wrong. I'm going to appeal!" Usually, the losing party doesn't understand that the only issues that can be appealed are questions of law. When a case is appealed, it is because the losing party has claimed that the judge misapplied the law. For example, an appealing party might claim that the judge should (or should not) have admitted certain evidence, that the jury instructions were wrong, or that the judge should have ruled that the statute was unconstitutional.

Just as the district court must follow the precedent of a higher court, so too must the court of appeals. If the Supreme Court has already ruled on an issue, the circuit courts of appeals have no discretion to change that ruling. However, the circuit courts of appeals do have a great deal of power. If the Supreme Court has not ruled on a case, the court of appeals may make whatever decision it wishes, even if another circuit has ruled in a different way. In addition, a circuit court of appeals may overrule previous cases from its own circuit, as long as the Supreme Court has not heard any cases on the issue.

Cases in the federal system are appealed to the U.S. Circuit Court of Appeals. There are 12 regular circuits that hear appeals from federal district courts. The map in *Figure 8.1* will help to illustrate the boundaries of the courts of appeals. Here is a list of the circuit courts:

- ♦ 1st Circuit (Boston)—Hears cases from Maine, New Hampshire, Massachusetts, Rhode Island, and Puerto Rico.
- ♦ 2nd Circuit (New York City)—Hears cases from New York, Connecticut, and Vermont.
- ♦ 3rd Circuit (Philadelphia)—Hears cases from Pennsylvania, New Jersey, Delaware, and the Virgin Islands.
- ♦ 4th Circuit (Richmond, VA)—Hears cases from West Virginia, Virginia, Maryland, North Carolina, and South Carolina.
- ♦ 5th Circuit (New Orleans)—Hears cases from Mississippi, Louisiana, and Texas.
- ♦ 6th Circuit (Cincinnati)—Hears cases from Michigan, Ohio, Kentucky, and Tennessee.
- ♦ 7th Circuit (Chicago)—Hears cases from Illinois, Indiana, and Wisconsin.
- ♦ 8th Circuit (St. Louis)—Hears cases from Minnesota, Iowa, North Dakota, South Dakota, Nebraska, Missouri, and Arkansas.
- ♦ 9th Circuit (Sacramento)—Hears cases from California, Oregon, Washington, Nevada, Idaho, Montana, Arizona, Alaska, Hawaii, Guam, and the Commonwealth of the Northern Marianas.
- ♦ 10th Circuit (Denver)—Hears cases from Wyoming, Utah, Colorado, New Mexico, Kansas, and Oklahoma.
- ♦ 11th Circuit (Atlanta)—Hears cases from Georgia, Alabama, and Florida.
- ♦ D.C. Circuit—Hears cases from the District of Columbia, as well as many appeals involving administrative hearings.
- ♦ Court of Appeals for the Federal Circuit—Has nationwide jurisdiction to hear appeals involving patents, as well as appeals from the Court of International Trade and the Court of Federal Claims.

There are some exceptions to the rule that an appellate court can hear only questions of law. Some statutes allow the court to review the factual evidence *de novo*, which means that the court starts all over again to hear the issue. For example, many administrative hearings are tried *de novo* when appealed to U.S. District Court. The judge will hear all the evidence, and will not give any deference to the ruling of the lower court or the administrative agency (as the case may be). Another instance of *de novo* review in a lawsuit involves the award of *punitive damages* (damages intended to punish the defendant for bad behavior, rather than to remedy the plaintiff's economic losses). The circuit court of appeals has the power to hear this issue *de novo*.[16]

Panels with three judges hear most cases that are appealed to the circuit court. Once this panel has made a decision, the losing party has the option of (1) asking for a rehearing of the case or of (2) asking the Supreme Court to hear the case. When the court of appeals rehears a case, all of the judges on the Circuit Court hear the case rather than only a three-judge panel. This situation is known as a *rehearing en banc*. The full Court of Appeals can either uphold or overrule the three-judge panel. The losing party then has the right to petition the U.S. Supreme Court for review.

Figure 8.1. **Geographic Boundaries, U.S. Courts of Appeal and District Courts.**[17]

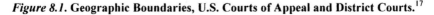

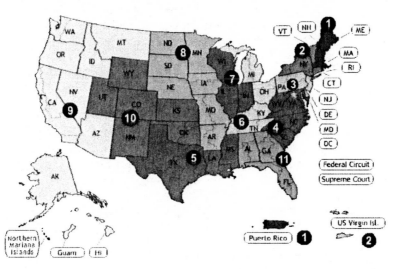

The U.S. Supreme Court

Once a case has been heard by the court of appeals, the losing party can petition the U.S. Supreme Court to review the decision. The process of asking the Supreme Court for a hearing is known as petitioning for a *Writ of Certiorari*. (Because lawyers don't like Latin, this is generally known as asking for *cert*.)

The U.S. Supreme Court does not have to hear all cases that request cert. In fact, most of the cases are turned down. The Supreme Court usually only hears

cases that present a unique and complicated issue. The Court will also sometimes hear cases when the circuit courts have split on a particular issue so that
the law is one way in one circuit and another way in another circuit.

Occasionally a case will skip directly from the district court to the Supreme
Court. This situation usually occurs only when the case contains an important
constitutional issue. The party that wishes to bypass the court of appeals can file
for cert., but it is up to the Supreme Court whether to accept the case at that time
or whether to wait until the court of appeals has heard the case. For example, the
American Library Association's challenge of the Children's Internet Protection
Act[18] went directly from the district court to the U.S. Supreme Court.[19]

Although the Court* usually hears cases after a decision has been rendered,
there are some situations in which a case may be appealed before trial. For instance, suppose that a judge excludes evidence from a case. Without that evidence, one litigant has grounds to move for summary judgment. In this situation,
the other litigant may then file an *interlocutory appeal*. The court of appeals and
the Supreme Court will have the power to decide this issue.

After the Supreme Court has heard a case, the case will be *remanded* back
to the court from which it came. This is necessary in order to finish litigating
any issues that still remain, and in order to implement the judgment. Sometimes
the interpretation will lead to further appeals, and some cases have come before
the U.S. Supreme Court more than one time.

One highly publicized example of the Court hearing a case multiple times
involved two drug rehabilitation counselors who were fired after they used peyote as part of a Native American religious ceremony. The counselors sued after
they were denied unemployment compensation. The Oregon Supreme Court
found in favor of the counselors on the grounds of the First Amendment principle of Freedom of Religion.[20] Since the case involved a federal constitutional
issue, the U.S. Supreme Court granted cert. After hearing arguments, the U.S.
Supreme Court realized that there was a dispute between the parties as to
whether peyote was in fact illegal in Oregon, so the U.S. Supreme Court remanded the case back to the Oregon Supreme Court in order to determine
whether peyote was illegal under Oregon law.[21] On remand, the Oregon Supreme Court found that the use of peyote was illegal in Oregon, but ruled the
First Amendment protected its use for religious purposes.[22] When the case re-
turned to the U.S. Supreme Court, the Court ruled that the Oregon Supreme
Court had misread the Constitution, and that the First Amendment did not protect the use of peyote for religious purposes.[23]

---

* The U.S. Supreme Court (or the state supreme court) is usually designated as "the
Court" with a capital C, while lower courts are usually designated as "the court" with a
lowercase c. The same situation applies to the word "Constitution." Generally, the word
"Constitution" with a capital C refers to the U.S. Constitution, while "constitution" with a
lowercase c usually refers to a state constitution.

The Supreme Court will often turn down petitions for cert. When this happens, the ruling of the lower court will stand. Denying cert. affects the parties in that particular case, but does not create a precedent that is binding on lower courts.

Often when the Supreme Court hears a case, there are interested parties who are not actually part of the lawsuit. These are people or groups that will be affected by the issues being litigated. In this situation, the interested parties can request permission to file a brief with the Court, explaining why they have an interest in the ruling and what they think the ruling should be. These briefs are called *Amicus Curiae* ("Friend of the court") briefs. Before an *Amicus* brief can be considered, the Supreme Court must approve it, and all of the parties to the litigation must agree to this filing.[24] The American Library Association often files *Amicus* briefs in cases involving access to information, even if the case does not involve traditional library services. For example, in 2005 the ALA filed a brief in the *Grokster/StreamCast* file-sharing case.[25]

One area in which federal and state courts interact is in terms of constitutional issues. When state courts hear a case that involves a federal issue, the U.S. Supreme Court has jurisdiction to hear an appeal from the highest state appellate court. In this situation, the U.S. Supreme Court will only hear the federal constitutional issue, and will not hear any state law issues relating to the case.

The U.S. Supreme Court is not bound by the decisions of any other court and has the power to establish new law or to overrule its own previous precedents. The only exception to this power is in diversity cases where the Supreme Court applies state law. Even there, however, if the state in question has not ruled on the issue, the Supreme Court is free to take judicial notice of decisions by other jurisdictions and to decide the issue whichever way it wishes.

Of course, if the issue subsequently arises in the state courts and does not involve a federal question, the state courts are free to overrule the U.S. Supreme Court on issues of state law that have been applied in a diversity ruling. The state courts may also change their interpretation of local law, even if the U.S. Supreme Court has made rulings under the old law in a diversity case.

Sources for Finding Cases

The main thing to remember when searching for cases is that they are published by jurisdiction and level of court. In the federal court system, there are separate series for each level of court. (Compilations that contain cases are called *reporters*.) The government officially publishes some reporters, while private publishers produce others. Each publication contains the exact same text of the opinions, but the private series contain editorial enhancements. You should always give a citation first to the official publication if possible. Some court opinions—such as the federal district courts—do not have an official reporter, in which case citing to the unofficial series is permitted. Here are some of the most important series, along with their citation abbreviations:

♦ *United States Reports (U.S.)*
An official publication from the U.S. government, this series provides the full text of decisions from the United States Supreme Court.

♦ *Supreme Court Reporter (S. Ct.)*
Published by West Group, this series contains the full text of cases from the United States Supreme Court, along with many editorial enhancements such as headnotes.

♦ *United States Supreme Court Reporter, Lawyers' Edition (L. Ed.)*
Published by LexisNexis, this series contains the full text of cases from the United States Supreme Court, along with many cross-references and other editorial enhancements.

♦ *Federal Reporter (First Series, Second Series, Third Series) (F., F.2d, F.3d)*
Contains cases from the U.S. Circuit Courts of Appeal and cases before 1932 from the U.S. District Courts. Published by West Group, this series also contains editorial enhancements including headnotes.

♦ *Federal Supplement (F. Supp.)*
Contains cases from the United States District Courts since 1932. Before 1930, these cases were published in the *Federal Reporter*. Since West Group has published the *Federal Supplement*, it includes headnotes and other editorial enhancements.

♦ *Federal Rules Decisions (F.R.D.)*
This series includes federal cases that discuss or interpret federal court rules, such as the Federal Rules of Civil Procedure or the Federal Rules of Evidence. The series includes the standard West Group editorial enhancements, including headnotes.

♦ *U.S. Law Week (U.S.L.W.)*
The Bureau of National Affairs (BNA) publishes this weekly summary of cases from state and federal courts.

♦ *U.S. Supreme Court Website*
http://www.supremecourtus.gov

♦ *U.S. Supreme Court Oral Arguments*
http://www.oyez.org/
A free multimedia archive of Supreme Court oral arguments from October 1955 to the present.

♦ US Courts Website
http://www.uscourts.gov

Official court sites are among the best places to find dockets, decisions, and orders of the courts. This website links to all federal courts, as well as the Administrative Office of the Courts.

A. The Key Number Classification System

One of the most difficult problems in legal research involves finding a case on a particular topic. Like the library researcher who needs to find a book, finding a case on a particular topic can be like searching for a needle in a haystack. Just as libraries arrange books using classification systems (Dewey, Library of Congress, SuDoc, etc.), the law can also be classified. The *West Key Number System* is an example of such a classification scheme.

The Key Number system is an ingenious invention. One of the advantages of using products produced by the West Group is that all of the publications contain the same enhancements. The editors at West Group read every case and write a summary of each separate point of law contained in the opinion. These summaries are called *headnotes*. [*Figure 8.2* contains an example of headnotes.]

Often a case will contain multiple points of law. A single case may involve issues of copyright law, civil procedure and evidentiary issues, and the First Amendment principle of free speech. One example of multiple points of law is the case of *The Wind Done Gone*.[26]

Within the Key Number system, each point of law in a case is assigned a topic. Within each topic, there is a *key number*. The key numbers can be very specific, much like an LC classification with a Cutter number. Since the Key Number system is standardized, every case uses the same classification system.

Cases published by the West Group print the headnotes before the actual text of the opinion itself. The summaries also include the Key Number topic and number. The case headnotes provide the classification for the points of law in the case. These headnotes in turn can be used to find similar cases.

West Group publishes many series called *digests* with collected summaries arranged by Key Number classification. Even in the online era, digests are an important way to find similar cases. There is at least one digest covering every U.S. jurisdiction. By using the Key Number system, a researcher can find published cases on his or her topic from every court in the country.

For example, researchers looking for cases on the fair use doctrine of copyright law would look under the topic *Copyrights and Intellectual Property*. Within this topic, Key Number 58 is for cases that discuss the fair use doctrine.[27] Once a user finds this section, he or she will see headnotes and citations concerning fair use. The Key Number system is a very powerful tool for legal researchers. *Figure 8.3* contains an example of Key Numbers in a digest.

The largest digest series published by West Group is called the *American Digest System*, which is made up of the *Century Digest*, the *Decennial Digest*, and the *General Digest*. All three publications contain the headnotes and citations for cases, arranged in the Key Number classification system. The *Century*

Digest contains the oldest materials, with citations and summaries of colonial, federal, and state cases from 1658 to 1896 using Key Number classification.

Figure 8.2. Headnotes for SunTrust Bank v. Houghton Mifflin Company, 268 F.3d 1257 (11th Cir. 2001).[28]

SUNTRUST BANK v. HOUGHTON MIFFLIN CO.   **1257**
Cite as 268 F.3d 1257 (11th Cir. 2001)

after the crime. Indeed, Appellant's attorneys reasonably decided to pursue the same general strategy at the Cook County case. Yet they neither subpoenaed, prepared, nor took any steps to ensure that any of the witnesses that testified at the Lowndes County trial would be available and ready to testify in Cook County. In fact, if Appellant's niece and sister hadn't happened to be in the gallery that day, Cook County counsel might not have been able to put on *any* relevant character witnesses at the sentencing phase. If this performance is rationalized as something a reasonable attorney might have done, we have rendered the word "reasonable" meaningless.

Given the unreasonable omission of relevant and available character evidence during the penalty phase of this case, the integrity of the death verdict is suspect. Appellant is likely on death row today because of the deficient performance by his attorneys at the sentencing phase of this case. I respectfully dissent.

KEY NUMBER SYSTEM

SUNTRUST BANK, as Trustee of the Stephen Mitchell trusts f.b.o. Eugene Muse Mitchell and Joseph Reynolds Mitchell, Plaintiff–Appellee,

v.

HOUGHTON MIFFLIN COMPANY, Defendant–Appellant.

No. 01–12200.

United States Court of Appeals, Eleventh Circuit.

Oct. 10, 2001.

Owners of copyright in novel "Gone With the Wind" brought action under Copyright Act, seeking temporary restraining order (TRO) and preliminary injunction to prevent publication and distribution of allegedly infringing book "The Wind Done Gone." The United States District Court for the Northern District of Georgia, No. 01-00701-CV-CAP-1, Charles A. Pannell, Jr., J., 136 F.Supp.2d 1357, granted preliminary injunction, and appeal was taken. The Court of Appeals, Birch, Circuit Judge, held that it was unlikely that plaintiff would be able to overcome defendant's fair use defense.

Vacated and remanded.

Opinion, 252 F.3d 1165, vacated.

Marcus, Circuit Judge, specially concurred, and filed opinion.

1. Federal Courts ⬤815
District court's grant of preliminary injunction is reviewed for abuse of discretion.

2. Federal Courts ⬤776, 850.1
Court of Appeals reviews decisions of law de novo and findings of fact for clear error.

3. Copyrights and Intellectual Property ⬤4.5
Copyright cannot protect idea, only expression of that idea.

4. Copyrights and Intellectual Property ⬤53.2
Copyright does not immunize work from comment and criticism.

5. Injunction ⬤138.3
Chief function of preliminary injunction is to preserve status quo until merits of controversy can be fully and fairly adjudicated.

6. Injunction ⬤138.1
Preliminary injunction movant must establish: (1) substantial likelihood of success on merits, (2) substantial threat of irreparable injury if injunction were not

Figure 8.3. **Headnotes from the 11ᵗʰ Decennial Digest.**[29]

⚷ 53(2). Reproduction in different medium.

S.D.N.Y. 2001. Copyright of protectable work protects against unauthorized copying not only in work's original medium but also in any other medium.— Oriental Art Printing, Inc. v. Goldstar Printing Corp., 175 F.Supp.2d 542, affirmed in part, appeal dismissed in part 34 Fed.Appx. 401.

S.D.N.Y. 2001. Seller of toy glove which was substantially similar to motion picture character's copyrighted glove with protruding razor blades had "access" to copyrighted glove, for purpose of proving infringement, even if seller did not actually see movie; seller had reasonable opportunity to see movie.—New Line Cinema Corp. v. Russ Berrie & Co., Inc., 161 F.Supp.2d 293.

D.Wyo. 2002. Film about monsters who met and were afraid of child was not substantially similar to, and thus did not infringe copyright in poem in which child monster recounted seeing human in his closet to his monster mother; any similarity between works was merely similarity of ideas, and not similarity in expression of those ideas.—Madrid v. Chronicle Books, 209 F.Supp.2d 1227.

⚷ 53.2. Fair use and other permitted uses in general.

Library references

C.J.S.   Copyrights and Intellectual Property
             §§ 45, 46, 48—50.

C.A.9 (Cal.) 2003. "Fair use" exception excludes from copyright restrictions those works that criticize and comment on another work. 17 U.S.C.A. § 107.— Mattel, Inc. v. Walking Mountain Productions, 353 F.3d 792, on remand 2004 W L 1454100.

Factors court considers in determine whether allegedly infringing work constitutes fair use are: (1) purpose and character of use, including whether such use is of commercial nature or is for nonprofit educational purposes; (2) nature of copyrighted work; (3) amount and substantiality of portion used in relation to copyrighted work as a whole; and (4) effect of use upon potential market for or value of copyrighted work. 17 U.S.C.A. § 107.—id.

Issue of whether allegedly infringing work is parody of copyrighted work is question of law, not matter of public majority opinion. 17 U.S.C.A. § 107.—id.

The *Decennial Digest* was published every 10 years from 1897 to 1975, and includes the headnotes for cases during that time period. Since 1980, the *Decennial Digest* has been published in two parts every five years. The *General Digest* comes out with a new volume every month, and contains all the cases since the publication of the last *Decennial Digest*. Most law libraries do not keep older volumes of the *General Digest* since these cases will be collected when the next *Decennial Digest* is published.

Besides the headnotes with case citations, the digests also contain a table of parties, a classified listing of the topics and key numbers, and a *words and phrases* section, which indexes the actual legal terms used in the headnotes. Each volume of the digest also contains a *table of statutes* for finding statutes discussed in cases listed in that volume. Most researchers who do not already know a topic and key number start with the *descriptive word index*, which is contained in each volume of the digest. The descriptive word index uses a controlled vocabulary to help researchers find cases using keywords.[30] The standardized terms give researchers a more precise search using the descriptive word index than is possible using the words and phrases section.

All of the digests published by West are arranged in the same manner. Once you have a topic and Key Number, you can look up that same topic and Key Number in every digest. For example, if I find a case from the U.S. Supreme Court, I can use the topic and Key Number from that case to find similar cases in New York, California, or wherever I want.

In the days before electronic searching, the *American Digest System* was the best way to find cases from all jurisdictions. Today, researchers often jump online and bypass this system, but the *American Digest System* still has value as the most complete collection of U.S. cases accessible by keyword. West also produces the *Federal Practice Digest* (containing headnotes for federal cases), digests for every state, and many regional digests, as well as digests for special topics, such as *West's Education Law Digest*.

A new service called CourtListener, http://courtlistener.com, provides a free email alert search for court cases. The service allows users to specify critera, including specific courts, case names, case numbers, and keywords. CourtListener uses Boolean logic, including wildcards and proximity searching. Matches are sent by email. The site searches all opinions (both published and unpublished) issued by the U.S. Supreme Court and the 13 federal circuits.

Updating Legal Research: *Shepard's Citations* and *KeyCite*

Once you have found a case, it is vital to make sure the case is still good law. Cases that have been overturned on appeal or overruled by a later case are worthless. In legal research, this task is performed using a product called *Shepard's Citations* or its more recent competitor *KeyCite*. *Figure 8.4* shows an example of *Shepard's Citations* in print, while *Figure 8.5* shows a screen from the online *Shepard's* product.

In the 1870s, a law book salesman in Chicago named Frank Shepard (1848-1900) noticed lawyers writing notes in the margins of cases to indicate whether they had been overturned on appeal or overruled by a later case. In 1875, Shepard began selling stickers that contained references to the later cases. This service evolved into the citator we are familiar with today. The philosophy behind *Shepard's Citations* is that "[r]ather than exercise editorial judgment on which cases 'affected' earlier cases (as lawyers did in their marginalia), the assumption was made that anytime one case is cited by another the link is worth noting."[31]

Currently published by LexisNexis, *Shepard's* is a bibliometric citation index[32] similar to the *Science Citation Index* created by the Institute for Scientific

Information and now published by Thomson Scientific as part of its *Web of Science* product. The *Science Citation Index* allows researchers to find articles that have cited a particular work. Similarly, *Shepard's* lets a user who has found a case on his or her topic discover other cases that have cited the initial case. Bibliometric searching has many useful purposes, including enabling the researcher to determine whether the initial case is still good law. The editors also analyze citing references (cases that cite other cases), which lets researchers track the history of their initial case and see if there have been further appeals. The process of updating research with *Shepard's Citations* is called *Shepardizing*, and using its more recent competitor is called *KeyCiting*. Improperly *Shepardizing* or *KeyCiting* a case is considered to be legal malpractice.

Figure 8.4. **Print Version of *Shepard's United States Citations*.**[33]

UNITED STATES REPORTS					Vol. 472
74Å405n	Fla	45F3d1488	807So2d13	11FS2d161	Cir. 7
81Å304n	514So2d1088	65F3d886	811So2d605	254FS2d228	783F2d62
10Å717n	Ill	222F3d1300	-) 811So2d630	Cir. 2	831F2d1299
-) 10Å733n	256IlА461	f) 668FS1492	823So2d49	f) 770F2d16	831F2d1330
-) 10Å755n	629NЕ102	Ala	825So2d216	818F2d282	856F2d956
-) 10Å789n	Iowa	489So2d711	835So2d1081	333F3d499	857F2d391
-) 10Å814n	d) 522NW87	491So2d1099	836So2d935	629FS364	859F2d1531
—353—	Mass	494So2d729	852So2d816	757FS5	j) 859F2d1538
Johnson v Bal-	401Mas431	503So2d880	859So2d1170	786FS381	j) 886F2d911
timore	517NЕ143	507So2d116	Del	829FS589	33F3d839
1985	N J	512So2d814	581A2d1102	d) 127FS2d389	43F3d343
(86LЕ286)	222NJS319	516So2d791	Idaho	f) 133FS2d244	141F3d772
(105SC2717)	536A2d1286	517So2d648	124Ida930	Cir. 3	154F3d751
a) 731F2d209	N Y	518So2d844	866P2d187	f) 768F2d516	193F3d901
a) 515FS1287	170NYM2d337	521So2d1013	La	768F2d517	j) 207F3d957
cc) 637FS903	648NYS2d514	521So2d1062	489So2d905	f) 768F2d518	627FS1556
Cir. 1	Wis	521So2d1384	Nev	829F2d393	877FS1188
f) 2F3d1227	d) 200Wis2d	534So2d633	107Nev255	829F2d394	f) 894FS1171
f) 811FS29	[725	534So2d660	810P2d767	f) 829F2d395	83FS2d972
254FS2d223	d) 547NW787	534So2d1140	Tex	830F2d483	Cir. 8
Cir. 2	100McL80	536So2d144	j) 70SW893	877F2d230	967F2d1199
f) 770F2d16	101YLJ428	540So2d772	86Cor1090	j) 877F2d236	645FS369
149F3d152	63АRF610s	542So2d1300	86Geo1814	54F3d1102	683FS714
612FS372	79АRF379n	545So2d216	87Geo1756	j) 181F3d500	793FS216
28FS2d90	79АRF398n	551So2d446	88Geo1560	2004USDist	864FS1530
Cir. 3	180АRF337n	553So2d633	89Geo1738	[LX14963	Cir. 9
f) 768F2d516	—372—	554So2d479	90Geo1838	620FS980	f) 806F2d1390
829F2d393	Baldwin v Ala-	554So2d1110	152PaL33	631FS1510	f) 843F2d1214
252F3d674	bama	554So2d1113	90LЕ1027n	631FS1514	843F2d1216
620FS980	1985	555So2d212	51LЕ886s	645FS1552	f) 843F2d1218
118FRD365	(86LЕ300)	555So2d230	63Å506n	648FS929	869F2d478
Cir. 4	(105SC2727)	555So2d1188	63Å525n	690FS1423	921F2d920
j) 868F2d1377	s) 456So2d129	556So2d745	63Å597n	950FS615	34F3d795
681FS332	cc) 526US1047	558So2d985	64Å778n	118FRD365	-) 34F3d797
Cir. 5	cc) 152F3d1304	562So2d558	64Å853n	Cir. 4	46F3d935
848F2d530	cc) 372So2d26	562So2d600	64Å886n	895F2d166	63F3d833
626FS186	cc) 372So2d32	564So2d286	65Å881n	53F3d662	272F3d1259
654FS1179	cc) 405So2d698	564So2d1004	65Å883n	67F3d1145	2003USDist
Cir. 6	cc) 405So2d699	564So2d1045	—400—	616FS1082	[LX18558
808F2d461	cc) 456So2d117	565So2d1222	Western Air	632FS905	622FS640
e) 860F2d669	cc) 539So2d	570So2d729	Lines, Inc. v	632FS907	f) 622FS646
121F3d1026	[1103	570So2d791	Criswell	732FS612	675FS1264
23Fed Appx	504US533	571So2d338	1985	314FS2d602	728FS1454
[366	505US1082	575So2d133	(86LЕ321)	Cir. 5	f) 728FS1460
671FS495	520US529	575So2d155	(105SC2743)	f) 837F2d1400	773FS210
696FS1175	e) 520US530	583So2d290	s) 709F2d544	f) 848F2d528	976FS1362
Cir. 7	Cir. 4	583So2d303	a) 868F2d1093	e) 848F2d534	149FS2d1161
j) 886F2d911	802FS1418	591So2d104	a) 514FS384	f) 873F2d98	Cir. 10
193F3d897	Cir. 5	600So2d362	cc) 869F2d449	j) 873F2d100	836F2d1553
82FS2d978	904F2d986	628So2d990	cc) 6F3d632	48F3d167	98F3d557
Cir. 8	363F3d554	629So2d17	472US362	d) 48F3d170	Cir. 11
873FS1316	Cir. 6	632So2d582	j) 492US192	626FS184	796F2d1413
Cir. 9	d) 231F3d329	678So2d283	e) 499US201	f) 654FS1179	e) 796F2d1416
d) 806F2d1392	Cir. 7	680So2d879	f) 499US201	967FS213	j) 796F2d1422
843F2d1214	754FS653	695So2d184	j) 501US475	Cir. 6	810F2d1101
843F2d1215	Cir. 9	705So2d860	507US611	859F2d25	817F2d1557
d) 128FS2d679	791F2d794	706So2d840	e) 528US86	860F2d668	j) 139F3d1448
165FS2d1126	839F2d454	717So2d12	e) 157LЕ1108	33F3d677	660FS1108
Cir. 11	j) 839F2d521	753So2d1181	e) 124SC1244	121F3d1024	660FS1110
d) 901F2d930	Cir. 11	758So2d599	Cir. 1	154F3d307	Cir. DC
Cir. Fed.	j) 769F2d1490	768So2d1006	798F2d528	227F3d639	649FS680
773F2d286	f) 811F2d1400	775So2d901	987F2d71	631FS721	Calif
779F2d673	828F2d663	788So2d193	987F2d73	f) 671FS495	218CA3d540
779F2d674	f) 864F2d1540	791So2d400	f) 2F3d1225	696FS1176	267CaR170
61F3d1567	918F2d1547	795So2d784	f) 2F3d1227	696FS1178	Colo
234F3d1382	941F2d1138	-) 797So2d1181	f) 811FS29	812FS118	736P2d845
	45F3d1487	805So2d742	870FS394		

Figure 8.5. Shepard's United States Citations
(Screen capture from LexisNexis Academic, 539 U.S. 166).[34]

⚠Western Air Lines, Inc. v. Criswell , 472 U.S. 400

Unrestricted Shepard's Summary

No subsequent appellate history.

Citing References:

⚠Cautionary Analyses: **Distinguished (2)**

Positive Analyses: Followed (22)

Neutral Analyses: Concurring Opinion (4),
Dissenting Op. (15), Explained (5)

Other Sources: Law Reviews (224), Statutes (5),
Treatises (110), Annotations (1),
Other Citations (2), Court
Documents (142)

LexisNexis Headnotes: HN1 (59), HN2 (26), HN3 (93),
HN4 (15), HN5 (20), HN6 (42),
HN7 (2), HN8 (8)

Show full text of headnotes

KeyCite is an online-only product developed by the West Group in the mid-1990s as a competitor to *Shepard's*. *KeyCite* is similar to other citation indexes in that it provides links to cases, articles, administrative decisions, and secondary materials that cite or discuss the original item. Citation searches can be performed on state or federal cases, federal statutes, and federal administrative opinions or regulations. *KeyCite* also uses "flags" to indicate whether a case is still good law.[35] Unlike *Shepard's*, which is available both online and in print, *KeyCite* is only available electronically. *KeyCite* has not yet caught up to *Shepard's* in popularity.

The newest entry in the legal citator market comes from Bloomberg Law. Its product is known colloquially as *BCIT* or *BCiting*. The citator contains direct case history and subsequent treatment with signals. The subsequent treatment section also uses a visual representation of the "strength" of the case using between one and five colored bars.[36]

Several online legal services contain automated citation checkers, including *Loislaw, Casemaker,* and *Fastcase*. Even *Google Scholar* does cited reference searching. However, it is important to remember that *Shepard's, KeyCite,* and *BCIT* are compiled by human editors. While computer-generated indexes such as *Google Scholar* have their place, they are not a replacement for products produced by humans. Legal research requires analysis with standardized criteria by legally trained editors.

Citators let researchers see whether a case has been overruled or distinguished by a subsequent case, and are also great tools for finding more cases on the same topic. *Shepard's* uses symbols (located inside the front and back covers of the print edition) to indicate the history of the case and its treatment by other cases, while *KeyCite* uses colored flags.

Because of the growing adoption of online research and the creation of *KeyCite*, the *Shepard's* series now emphasizes the online product. Use of the print copies has declined significantly, many law schools no longer teach the print, and some have stopped collecting printed copies.[37]

Both *Shepard's* and *KeyCite* provide important research tools. Anyone doing legal research should use one of these citators, either in print or online.[38] Together, citators and the West *Key Number system* provide powerful tools for anyone who is researching the law.

A. *Shepard's Citations*: History of Case Terminology

The terms that are used for the history of cases in *Shepard's Citations* are listed below. In the online world these terms are spelled out. In printed volumes, abbreviations (listed in parentheses) are used. There is generally a table of abbreviations inside the front or back cover of the book.

♦ **Published Connected Case (CC)**—The citing case is related to the case you are *Shepardizing*, arising out of the same subject matter or involving the same parties.

♦ **Modified (m)**—On appeal, reconsideration or rehearing, the citing case modifies or changes in some way, including affirmance in part and reversal in part, the case you are *Shepardizing*.

♦ **Reversed (r)**—On appeal, reconsideration or rehearing, the citing case reverses the case you are *Shepardizing*.

♦ **Same case (s)**—The citing case involves the same litigation as the case you are *Shepardizing*, but at a different stage of the proceedings.

♦ **Superseded (S)**—On appeal, reconsideration or rehearing, the citing case supersedes or is substituted for the case you are Shepardizing.

♦ **US Rehearing Denied (reh den)**—The citing order by the United States Supreme Court denies rehearing in the case you are *Shepardizing*.

♦ **US Rehearing Dismissed (reh dis)**—The citing order by the United States Supreme Court dismisses rehearing in the case you are *Shepardizing*.

♦ **Vacated (v)**—The citing case vacates or withdraws the case you are *Shepardizing*.[39]

B. *Shepard's Citations*: Subsequent Case Treatment

The terms used for treatment of cases in *Shepard's Citations* are listed below, with abbreviations in (parentheses).

♦ **Criticized (c)**—The citing opinion disagrees with the reasoning/result of the case you are *Shepardizing*, although the citing court may not have the authority to materially affect its precedential value.

♦ **Conflicting authorities (ca)**—Among conflicting authorities as noted in citing case.

♦ **Distinguished (d)**—The citing case differs from the case you are *Shepardizing*, either involving dissimilar facts or requiring a different application of the law.

♦ **Explained (e)**—The citing opinion interprets or clarifies the case you are *Shepardizing* in a significant way.

♦ **Followed (f)**—The citing opinion relies on the case you are *Shepardizing* as controlling or persuasive authority.

♦ **Harmonized (h)**—The citing case differs from the case you are *Shepardizing*, but the citing court reconciles the difference or inconsistency in reaching its decision.

♦ **Dissenting opinion (j)**—A dissenting opinion cites the case you are *Shepardizing*.

♦ **Concurring opinion (~)**—A concurring opinion cites the case you are *Shepardizing*.

♦ **Limited (L)**—The citing opinion restricts the application of the case you are *Shepardizing*, finding its reasoning applies only in specific limited circumstances.

♦ **Overruled (o)**—The citing case expressly overrules or disapproves the case you are *Shepardizing*.

♦ **Overruled in part (op)**—Ruling in the cited case overruled partially or on other grounds or with other qualifications.

♦ **Questioned (q)**—The citing opinion questions the continuing validity or precedential value of the case you are *Shepardizing* because of intervening circumstances, including judicial or legislative overruling.

♦ **Superseded (su)**—Superseded by statute as stated in cited case.[40]

C: *KeyCite* Status Case and Statute Treatment Flags

♦ **Red Flag**—"The case is no longer good law for at least one of the points of law it contains or that the statute or regulation has been amended by a recent session law or rule, repealed, superseded, or held unconstitutional or preempted in whole or in part."

♦ **Yellow Flag**—Use with caution. There is some negative history, although the opinion, statute, or regulation has not been reversed, amended, or overruled.

   o   For opinions, there is some negative history but the decision has not been reversed or overruled.

   o   For statutes, the Yellow Flag means that "the statute has been renumbered or transferred by a recent session law [or] that an uncodified session law or proposed legislation affecting the statute is available. . . ."

   o   For administrative regulations, a Yellow Flag means that "a proposed rule affecting the regulation is available [or] that the regulation has been reinstated, corrected, or confirmed. . . ."

   o   The Yellow Flag may also mean that "the statute or regulation was limited on constitutional or preemption grounds or its validity was otherwise called into doubt; or that a prior version of the statute or regulation received negative treatment by a court."

♦ **Blue H**—The opinion has some history.

♦ **Green C**—This means that there are "citing references but no direct history or negative citing references."[41]

D. *KeyCite* Cited Reference Depth of Treatment Signals

♦ ****** Examined**—The citing reference "contains an extended discussion of the cited case or administrative decision, usually more than a printed page of text."

♦ ***** Discussed**—The citing reference "contains a substantial discussion of the cited case or administrative decision, usually more than a paragraph but less than a printed page."

♦ **** Cited**—The citing reference "contains some discussion of the cited case or administrative decision, usually less than a paragraph."

♦ *** Mentioned**—The citing reference "contains a brief reference to the cited case or administrative decision, usually in a string citation."[42]

Conclusion

The judicial branch plays a much greater role in the Anglo-American legal system than elsewhere in the world. It is the courts that interpret and apply the law. But courts also themselves create legal principles.

Because of the importance of case law in the U.S., most of this chapter has been about using finding tools to discover relevant cases. The next chapter will deal with finding state legal materials. The same types of resources—reporters, digests, and citators—are also available for researching state case law. Finding judicial cases is really more about the process of searching than anything else.

Notes

1. U.S. Constitution, Art. III.

2. Johnny H. Killian, George A. Costello, and Kenneth R. Thomas, The Constitution of the United States of America: Analysis and Interpretation § 2 (Congressional Research Service 1992, amended 1996, 1998, 2000), *available at* http://caselaw.lp.findlaw.com/ data/constitution/article03/09.html#3, *quoting* in re Pacific Railway Commission, 32 F. 241, 255 (C.C. Calif. 1887).

3. Baker v. Carr, 369 U.S. 186 (1962), *available at* http://caselaw.lp.findlaw.com/ scripts/getcase.pl?court=us&vol=369&invol=186.

4. Elk Grove School District v. Newdow, 542 U.S. 1; 124 S. Ct. 2301; 159 L. Ed. 2d 98; 72 U.S.L.W. 4457 (2004), *available at* http://caselaw.lp.findlaw.com/scripts/getcase .pl?court=us&vol=000&invol=02-1624.

5. Valley Forge Christian College v. Americans United for Separation of Church and State, Inc., 454 U.S. 464, 472 (1982), *quoting* Simon v. Eastern Kentucky Welfare Rights Organization, 426 U.S. 26, 39, 41 (1976).

6. Valley Forge Christian College *at* 472, *quoting* Flast v. Cohen, 392 U.S. 83, 96 (1968).

7. Valley Forge Christian College *at* 472.

8. *See*, Debra Lyn Bassett, *The Hidden Bias in Diversity Jurisdiction*, 81 Washington University Law Quarterly 119 (Spring 2003), *available at* http://law.wustl.edu/ WULQ/81-1/p119%20Bassett.pdf. *See also*, Graham Lilly, *Making Sense of Nonsense: Reforming Supplemental Jurisdiction*, 74 Indiana Law Journal 181 (1998).

9. U.S. Constitution, Art. III.

10. Administrative Office of the Courts, *United States District Courts*, available at http://www.uscourts.gov/districtcourts.html.

11. Black's Law Dictionary 1122 (5th ed. 1979).

12. *id.*

13. Charles Alan Wright, Law of Federal Courts § 99 (St. Paul, MN: West, 1983). *See also*, Federal Rules of Civil Procedure 56, *available at* http://www.law.cornell.edu/ rules/frcp/Rule56.htm.

14. Wright.

15. Black's Law Dictionary 413 (5th ed. 1979).

16. Cooper Industries v. Leatherman Tool Group, 532 U.S. 424 (2001).

17. Administrative Office of the Courts Website, *available at* http://www.uscourts .gov/court_locator.aspx.

18. 114 Stat. 2763A-335, *codified at* 20 U.S.C. §§ 9134(f)(1)(A)(i) and (B)(i) and at 47 U.S.C. §§ 254(h)(6)(B)(i) and (C)(i).

19. United States v. American Library Association, 539 U.S. 194; 123 S. Ct. 2297; 156 L. Ed. 2d 221; 2003 U.S. LEXIS 4799; 71 U.S.L.W. 4465 (2003), *available at* http://laws.findlaw.com/us/000/02-361.html.

20. Black v. Employment Division, 75 Ore. App. 764, 707 P.2d 1274, 709 P.2d 246 (1985); *affirmed in part and modified in part*, 301 Ore. 221, 721 P.2d 451 (1986); *cert. granted*, Employment Division v. Smith, 480 U.S. 916, 94 L. Ed. 2d 684, 107 S. Ct. 1368 (1987), *motion denied*, 483 U.S. 1054, 97 L. Ed. 2d 816, 108 S. Ct. 28 (1987).

21. Employment Division v. Smith, 485 U.S. 660, 99 L. Ed. 2d 753, 108 S. Ct. 1444 (1988).

22. Smith v. Employment Division, 307 Ore. 68, 763 P.2d 146 (1988); *cert. granted*, Employment Division v. Smith, 489 U.S. 1077, 103 L. Ed. 2d 832, 109 S. Ct. 1526 (1989); *motion granted by* 490 U.S. 1045, 104 L. Ed. 2d 421, 109 S. Ct. 1951 (1989).

23. Smith v. Employment Division, 494 U.S. 872; 110 S. Ct. 1595; 108 L. Ed. 2d 876; 1990 U.S. LEXIS 2021; 58 U.S.L.W. 4433; 52 Fair Empl. Prac. Cas. (BNA) 855; 53 Empl. Prac. Dec. (CCH) P39,826; Unemployment Ins. Rep. (CCH) P21,933 (1990).

24. "An amicus curiae brief that brings to the attention of the Court relevant matter not already brought to its attention by the parties may be of considerable help to the Court. An amicus curiae brief that does not serve this purpose burdens the Court, and its filing is not favored." (Rule 37(1) of the Rules of the Supreme Court of the United States.) Rule 29 of the Federal Rules of Appellate Procedure also covers the filing of an amicus curiae brief. The rule reads:

A brief of an amicus curiae may be filed only if accompanied by written consent of all parties, or by leave of court granted on motion or at the request of the court, except that consent or leave shall not be required when the brief is presented by the United States or an officer or agency thereof, or by a State, Territory or Commonwealth. The brief may be conditionally filed with the motion for leave. A motion for leave shall identify the interest of the applicant and shall state the reasons why a brief of an amicus curiae is desirable. Save as all parties otherwise consent, any amicus curiae shall file its brief within the time allowed the party whose position as to affirmance or reversal the amicus brief will support unless the court for cause shown shall grant leave for a later filing, in which event it shall specify within what period an opposing party may answer. A motion of an amicus curiae to participate in the oral argument will be granted only for extraordinary reasons.

25. Metro-Goldwyn-Mayer Studios Inc. v. Grokster, Ltd., 162 L. Ed. 2d 781, 125 S. Ct. 2764 (2005), *available at* http://laws.findlaw.com/us/000/04-480.html.

26. SunTrust Bank v. Houghton Mifflin Company, 268 F.3d 1257 (11th Cir. 2001).

27. Georgetown University Law Library, *Basics: Finding a Case (Opinion)*, Cases and Digests Tutorial, *available at* http://www.west.thomson.com/documentation/ westlaw/wlawdoc/lawstu/lsdig02.pdf.

28. This is an actual scanned image from the Federal Reporter 3d series. SunTrust Bank v. Houghton Mifflin Company, 268 F.3d 1257 (11th Cir. 2001).

29. These headnotes were taken from *West's 11th Decennial Digest*, Part II, page 484 (2004). The font face and size were changed to make them more readable.

30. For more information on the American Digest System and how to use digests, *see*, Rod Borlase, *Anatomy of a West Judicial Opinion (with Correlations to Westlaw)*, Borlase Law Library and Legal Research Guides (1995, 1999), *available at* http://www.rodborlase.com/Guides/OpinionAnatomy.html. *See also*, Frank Houdek, *Using a West Digest to Find Cases by Subject*, Southern Illinois University School of Law Library (Fall 2005), *available at* http://www.law.siu.edu/lawlib/guides/ westdigests.htm; *Using the Digests* [tutorial with screen shots] (St. Paul, MN: West Group), *available at* http://www.west.thomson.com/documentation/westlaw/wlawdoc/ lawstu/lsdig02.pdf.

31. George S. Grossman, Legal Research: Historical Foundations of the Electronic Age 67 (New York: Oxford University Press, 1994).

32. "Bibliometrics is a type of research method used in library and information sci-

ence. It utilizes quantitative analysis and statistics to describe patterns of publication within a given field or body of literature. Researchers may use bibliometric methods of evaluation to determine the influence of a single writer, for example, or to describe the relationship between two or more writers or works." Ruth A. Palmquist, Bibliometrics, *available at* http://www.gslis.utexas.edu/~palmquis/courses/biblio.html.

33. Scanned image of United States Reports in 472 *Shepard's United States Citations*, page 851 (2004).

34. Western Air Lines, Inc. v. Criswell, 472 U.S. 400, 105 S. Ct. 2743, 86 L. Ed. 2d 321, 1985 U.S. LEXIS 107 (1985).

35. A *KeyCite* tutorial is available online at http://lawschool.westlaw.com/help/tourkeycite/menu.htm?Unit=menu. *KeyCite at a Glance*, a free brochure, is available at http://west.thomson.com/documentation/westlaw/wlawdoc/web/kcwlcqr6.pdf.

36. For a review of BCITE, *see*, Michael Robak, *The Bloomberg Citator: A First Look at BLAW's Citation Function*, 13 AALL Spectrum (July 2009), *available at* http://www.aallnet.org/products/pub_sp0907/pub_sp0907_Bloomberg.pdf.

37. *See, e.g.*, Rita Reusch, *By the Book: Thoughts on the Future of Our Print Collections*, 100 Law Library Journal 555, 557 (2008).

38. LexisNexis (which publishes *Shepard's*) has an excellent tutorial in pdf format on using *Shepard's Citations* at http://www.lexisnexis.com/Shepards/printsupport/shepardize_print.pdf.

39. The "Abbreviations Used in Shepard's Citations for History of Cases" is found inside the front cover of *Shepard's* print editions.

40. The "Abbreviations Used in Shepard's Citations for Treatment of Cases" is found inside the back cover of *Shepard's* print editions.

41. *Status Flags Used in KeyCite For Treatment of Cases and Statutes*, KeyCite at a Glance, *available at* http://west.thomson.com/documentation/westlaw/wlawdoc/web/kcwlcqr6.pdf.

42. *KeyCite Depth of Treatment of the Cited Reference*, KeyCite at a Glance, *available at* http://west.thomson.com/documentation/westlaw/wlawdoc/web/kcwlcqr6.pdf.

9

Federalism: The State Legal Systems

Most of this book so far has been devoted to the federal government. However, federal law is only one piece of the legal research puzzle. Each state has its own laws, which can range from corresponding with other states' laws to conflicting with other states' laws. Understanding the patchwork of state laws and state courts, as well as the relationship between federal and state laws, is crucial to performing legal research. These relationships can also help information professionals to assist clients.

In some circumstances, the federal government will pass a statute that completely preempts the field. In this situation, the states have no power to pass additional or contrary laws. In other situations, Congress has passed a statute, but has also allowed the states to have their own laws and regulations on the same subject. States can vary from having no legal regulation over a subject to having very tight regulation of that subject.

Patent law is an example of an area where the federal government has preempted the field. States are precluded from passing patent statutes. The federal trademark statute, however, has not preempted the states, and there are a variety of state laws relating to trademarks.

The legal structure of the states mirrors that of the federal system. All 50 states (plus two commonwealths,[1] American Samoa,[2] and the District of Columbia[3]) have a constitution. Two territories—Guam[4] and the U.S. Virgin Islands[5]—have Organic Acts passed by the U.S. Congress. These Organic Acts function as constitutions. Each jurisdiction has a legislative branch, an executive and administrative branch, and a judiciary. The structure of the branches may vary, but the basic concept remains the same. For example, most states, like the federal government, have two houses of the legislature. (However, Nebraska has a unicameral legislature with only one body. There are 49 state senators in Nebraska, which has been the only unicameral legislature in the nation since 1937.)[6]

Another difference between states involves the names of the courts. In some jurisdictions (such as Tennessee and Guam), the trial court of general jurisdiction is called the District Court. In other states (such as Kentucky and Michigan), the District Court is a court of limited jurisdiction, and the general trial court is the Circuit Court. Still other states (such as Ohio and Pennsylvania) use the term Court of Common Pleas. Courts of limited jurisdiction have names such as Municipal Court (Ohio), District Court (Kentucky and Michigan), or Recorder's Court (Georgia). The most unusual name is in New York, where the trial court of general jurisdiction is called the Supreme Court; the highest state appellate court is called the Court of Appeals. (New York also has an intermediate appellate court called the Appellate Division.)

191

Common Law, Civil Law, and the
Diversity of State Laws

State laws vary from considerable divergence to substantial uniformity to out-right imitation. For example, in 1952 the Guam Legislature adopted the California Code in its entirety.[7] In the 1980s, Guam adopted the Arkansas Insurance Code.[8]

There are also three states with the unique situation of having once been part of another state. As a result, Kentucky laws and decisions prior to 1793 and West Virginia laws and decisions prior to 1863 are found by looking at the legal documents of Virginia. Maine laws prior to 1820 are found by looking at the legal documents of Massachusetts.

However, the greatest diversity in state legal systems involves the laws of Louisiana and Puerto Rico. Although the U.S. legal system is based on the British Common Law system, Louisiana and Puerto Rico base many of their laws on Roman-Germanic legal traditions, known as the *Civil Law System*.[9]

Common Law is based on court decisions made by judges, while the Civil Law system is based primarily on statutes passed by the legislative bodies and contained in law codes. These statutes are much more detailed and complete than statutes passed in a Common Law jurisdiction. Civil Law statutes explain how they are to be interpreted in all situations.

A. The Common Law System

The English system of common law started with Henry de Bracton (1215—1268). Bracton collected the decisions of his court in a series entitled the *Note Books*. Bracton's work is commonly credited with beginning of the use of precedents and the rule of *stare decisis*.[10] Later, during the reign of Edward I (reigned 1272-1307), a new series of decisions was created. This new reporter was called the *Year Books*. The *Year Books* were published annually from 1291 to 1535.[11]

Statutory reform began during the time of Edward I, when the oral law was put into writing.[12] This process of codifying the oral law was prominent during the time of Edward I, but lost favor until the late 16th and early 17th centuries when Elizabeth I (reigned 1558-1603) and James I (reigned 1603-1625) revived the codified law. Sir Matthew Hale (1609-1676) noted that during the time of Edward I:

> We are therefore to know, That there are these several Kinds of Records of Things done in Parliament, or especially relating thereto, viz. I. The Summons to Parliament. 2. The Rolls of Parliament. 3. Bundles of Petitions in Parliament. 4. The Statutes, or Acts of Parliament themselves. And, 5. The Brevia de Par-

liamento, which for the most part were such as issued for the Wages of Knights and Burgesses. . . ."[13]

Initially, the *Year Books* and the statutes were limited by the difficulty of reproducing them. However, after the invention of the printing press, it became possible to make copies of these reports for dissemination to regional centers. It was not much later that individual authors began to publish treatises on the law.

During the period between 1523 and 1530, Christopher Saint Germain (1460?-1540) wrote *The Dialogue in English, between a Doctor of Divinity, and a Student in the Laws of England.*[14] This work consisted of "a dialogue between a doctor of the civil and canon law and a student of the common law, composed with the main object of contrasting the relations between equity and common law, but incidentally affording a good introduction to the principles of both."[15] *Doctor and Student* was published in 22 editions between 1530 and 1765, when *Blackstone's Commentaries* replaced Saint Germain's work as the standard text for lawyers and students.

Of course, the road to written law in England was not without a few bumps. In 1607, *The Interpreter* was published by John Cowell (1554-1611), who was Regius Professor of Law at Cambridge. *The Interpreter* was a law dictionary. However, Cowell put his own spin on the definitions of law terms. "[U]nder such words as 'king,' 'parliament,' 'prerogative,' 'subsidy,' [Cowell discussed] the theory of absolute monarchy. The champions of common law took alarm, caused Cowell to be reprimanded by the council, and his book to be burned by the hangman."[16] Cowell's dictionary was a good attempt to define the terms of law, but showed that legal dictionaries can also be subjective.

One of the most important works from this time period was *Maxims of the Law, and A Reading on the Statute of Uses*, by Sir Francis Bacon (1561-1626). The *Maxims* were a simplification of the existing laws. The principles that the *Maxims* espoused were scattered throughout the judicial and statutory law, but Bacon put them together in one place. Bacon's principal objective was to provide simple and memorable rules for deciding cases.[17]

Sir William Holdsworth (1871-1944), in his important work *A History of English Law*, recognized the importance of the *Maxims*. "'Many another lawyer could have stated legal propositions accurately. He [Bacon] alone had the philosophical capacity, the historical knowledge, and the literary taste needed to select the subject matter and to shape the form of the books in which English law was to be restated'. . . . While his contemporaries explained law in terms of antiquity and usage, Bacon worked from the basis of policy and principle."[18]

Bacon's *Maxims* were both a restatement and an oversimplification of the law. At the same time that the body of published law was growing, there was a reaction by the common law lawyers. Many lawyers wanted to be able to memorize the entire law. "[M]emory's growing salience and complexity as a cultural discourse ran parallel to its diminishing importance as a carrier of legal knowledge, with print contributing to both parts of the process."[19] The *Maxims* were memorized by unlucky law students from the 1600s through the first half of the 20th century. (Luckily for us, the only time that law students or paralegals must now learn the *Maxims* is if the student elects to take a Remedies class.)

One of the most prolific writers of the English law was Sir Edward Coke (1552-1634). Coke was chief justice of the King's Bench from 1613 to 1616. Coke's most famous books were the *Reports* and the *Institutes*. "In his *Reports* (eleven volumes, 1600-15), which are models of terse and vigorous statement, a highly authoritative and almost complete statement of contemporary common law is given. In his *Institutes* (four volumes, 1628-44), a mass of antique learning is brought to bear upon the explanation and defence [sic] of the English legal system. Coke's title to fame is that he adapted the medieval rules of common law to the needs of the modern state, and recast these rules in an intelligible form, collecting and condensing the obscure and chaotic dicta of the *Year Books* and the abridgments."[20]

One of the last writers to successfully put all of the law together in one great treatise was Sir William Blackstone (1723-1780). Blackstone's work *Commentaries on the Law of England* was a combination of general legal treatise, legal history text, and philosophical manifesto.[21] The *Commentaries* were "not only a statement of the law of Blackstone's day, but the best history of English law as a whole which had yet appeared."[22]

Blackstone's work delved deeply into the "law of nature" and the "law of revelation."[23] Within the law of nature, Blackstone identified those items that are *malum in se,* or bad because they are against the laws of nature. He also discussed acts that are *malum prohibitum,* or "bad because prohibited." Blackstone wrote: "An action that is *malum in se*, therefore, violates not only one's duty to God (to live life for His glory), but also violates duty to self in that it could potentially compromise one's health and well-being."[24] On the other hand, acts which are *malum prohibitum* are based on the laws that are established by the government. "Government has the authority to pass laws that set forth a rule of civil conduct only, and such laws must be in accordance with the law of nature."[25]

Blackstone's work relied heavily on the philosophy of John Locke (1632-1704). Locke's theory was that groups are influenced by three factors. These factors are *God, Government,* and *Public Opinion*. "God's authority derives from his status as creator, and natural or moral law is his benevolent will for us. Locke's political theory concerns the authority of governments, which he takes to be, at bottom, the right of all individuals to uphold natural law transferred to a central agency for the sake of its power and impartiality."[26]

Blackstone's judicial application of Locke's philosophy was tremendously influential in many ways. As works of philosophy and jurisprudence, the natural law theories of Locke and Blackstone were familiar to Thomas Jefferson and the founders of the United States. Jefferson was building on the work of Locke and Blackstone when he declared that "[w]e hold these truths to be self-evident, that all men are created equal, that they are endowed by their Creator with certain unalienable rights, that among these are life, liberty and the pursuit of happiness. That to secure these rights, governments are instituted among men, deriving their just powers from the consent of the governed."[27]

Another way in which Blackstone influenced American law and legal publishing was through the work of St. George Tucker (1752-1827), a law professor at The College of William and Mary. In 1803, Tucker produced an "American" edition of Blackstone entitled *Commentaries with notes of reference to the constitution and laws of the United States and of the state of Virginia*.[28] This book was one of the first works on the growing body of law in the United States, and was prized by legal practitioners for most of the 19th century. It was very widely distributed, not only in Virginia and Kentucky (which was part of Virginia until 1792), but also in many other states. Tucker's work was very useful because it applied the principles of English common law to the legal system of the United States.

B. The Civil Law System

Today's Common Law is based on broad codified statutes interpreted by judges.[29] Civil Law, on the other hand, is almost entirely a statutory system. In strict Civil Law systems, courts have no discretion; their only function is to apply the statutes as written, and decisions are binding only on the parties themselves. Civil Law codes resemble the cataloging codes of the library profession in that "the rule is the rule is the rule."

The Civil Law system began with the Roman law of the *Corpus Iuris Civilis*, which was compiled under the direction of the Emperor Justinian in A.D. 533.[30] (Ancient Latin did not have the letter J, so this work would today be spelled "Corpus Juris Civilis".) This great body of law was itself built on the past, claiming "to look back over fourteen hundred years of legal history."[31]

The *Corpus Iuris Civilis* contains four parts. These four parts are the *Novels*, the *Codex*, the *Digest*, and the *Institutes*. The *Novels* were pronouncements of the emperor, similar to *Presidential Proclamations* in the U.S., and contained items that came out after the completion of the *Codex*. The *Novels* are sometimes considered to be the beginning of Byzantine law, and are of much less importance than the other parts of the *Corpus Iuris Civilis*.[32]

The *Codex* consists of imperial orders from Justinian and his predecessors, and is sometimes mistakenly compared to a modern law code.[33] In fact, it would be more like the modern *Restatement of Laws* than anything else.[34] The *Digest* contains excerpts of classical jurisprudence; each entry contains the name of its author and where it came from, in much the same way that a modern digest contains excerpts of cases and their citations. The *Institutes* consist of a narrative format containing legal principles, and is most similar to the official commentary that accompanies certain modern codes such as the *Uniform Commercial Code*.

The importance of Justinian's *Corpus Iuris Civilis* is that ordinary people had the law accessible to them in a way that could be understood. Justinian's "code" was in many ways not like a modern code, but rather was a compilation of the laws.[35]

In the 19th century, the French emperor Napoleon created a commission to update the Roman law. The resulting code is a modern version of Justinian's Roman law, with modern assumptions but based upon similar principles. "The Code Napoleon . . . is based on scholarly research and the drafting of legal code which is passed into law by the legislative branch. It is then the judge's job to interpret that [legislative] intent more than to follow judicial precedent."[36]

Because the laws of Louisiana and Puerto Rico came in large part from the Napoleonic Code, these legal systems are in many respects very different from the rest of the nation. However, both jurisdictions (particularly Louisiana) have also been influenced by philosophies and events beyond their borders. In particular, the laws of neighboring jurisdictions, federal laws, and attempts to standardize through uniform and model laws have had great influence on these two legal systems.

One way in which Puerto Rico and Louisiana have been influenced by common law is in the area of court opinions. Although Civil Law cases are generally not precedential in nature, both jurisdictions follow their previous court decisions in accordance with the principle of *stare decisis*. The effect of common law is especially pronounced in Louisiana. Thus, the legal systems of these two jurisdictions have slowly begun to resemble the rest of the nation, although they both still retain measures of Roman and Napoleonic civil law.

C. Uniform and Model Laws

There have been a number of attempts over the years to create uniformity in state laws through the publishing of uniform and model laws. Some of these uniform and model laws have met with more success than others. Two of these models, the Uniform Commercial Code and the Uniform Computer Information Transactions Act, are discussed in detail in my book *The Law of Libraries and Archives*.[37]

Model acts are standardized laws that contain sample language. Organizations such as the American Law Institute (ALI), the National Conference of Commissioners on Uniform State Laws (NCCUSL), and the American Bar Association (ABA) will draft model laws in order to help state legislatures draft statutes for their states.[38] An example is the Model Business Corporation Act prepared by the Committee on Corporate Laws of the American Bar Association.[39]

On the other hand, *uniform laws* are proposals on topics of such great importance that the NCCUSL urges enactment in identical form in every state and territory. Uniform laws are routinely proposed, but are not effective until passed individually by each state legislature. Sometimes part but not all of a uniform law is adopted by a state. A uniform law is more likely to be passed than a model act.

The Uniform Commercial Code is the most successful uniform law. Beginning in 1943, the Uniform Commercial Code was created as a joint venture between the American Law Institute and the National Conference of Commissioners on Uniform State Laws.[40] The first draft of the UCC was completed in 1951. In 1953 Pennsylvania was the first state to adopt the Uniform Commercial Code as law. Since that time the UCC has been adopted with only a few variations by every state, as well as by the District of Columbia, Guam, and the Virgin Islands.[41] Only Louisiana[42] and Puerto Rico[43] have not adopted the Code.

Before a change or amendment to the UCC can become effective, *both* the American Law Institute *and* the National Conference of Commissioners on Uniform State Laws must approve the change. (However, states may make changes in their versions of the UCC.) For many years, the UCC has been the basis of commercial law in the United States concerning such important topics as secured transactions, commercial property, and contracts. Article 2 of the UCC deals with contracts, and was discussed in my book *The Law of Libraries and Archives*.

The most important fact to remember about model and uniform laws is that they are only guides. Each state is free to adopt or reject these laws. States are also free to make changes in the uniform or model laws, and to interpret them any way they wish. When researching state law, be sure to use the actual legal codes from the state itself rather than the uniform or model act.

Researching State Law

The basic point to remember when researching state law is that each jurisdiction has its own legislative code and administrative code, just as the federal system does. The popularity of the Internet has greatly improved access to state statutes and regulations. The comprehensive legal website *Findlaw* is a good place to begin if you are looking for online versions of these codes.

Another good place to start looking for state law is the legislative web page for each state. These sites frequently contain the state statutes, regulations, and bills. Some states also include minutes or agendas for legislative hearings. To find your state legislature, go to the National Conference of State Legislatures at http://www.ncsl.org.

State constitutions are also available, both online and in print. Oceana Publications produces a looseleaf service entitled *Constitutions of the United States, National and State*, which also has a subscription counterpart online.[44] The following websites contain links to state constitutions:

◆   *Constitution.org*
     http://www.constitution.org/cons/usstcons.htm

♦ *Findlaw*
   http://www.findlaw.com/11stategov/index.html

♦ *NBER/Maryland State Constitutions Project*
   http://www.stateconstitutions.umd.edu
   Produced by the National Bureau of Economic Research at the University of Maryland, this website contains "most of the roughly 150 state constitutions adopted
   since 1776, based on the original sources and thus correcting errors in the earlier
   printed collections. The site's goal is to provide searchable and indexed text for
   every one of the roughly 150 state constitutions since 1776, as well as quantitative
   databases on the characteristics of state constitutions. Historical state constitutions
   are also included in two major collections of worldwide scope, Constitutions of the
   World from the late 18th Century to the Middle of the 19th Century (Horst Dippel
   ed., 2005-date), available online as The Rise of Modern Constitutionalism, 1776-
   1849 http://www.modern-constitutions.de, and the microfiche Constitutions of the
   World 1850 to the Present (Horst Dippel ed., 2002-date)."[45]

Judicial cases are at the same time both relatively difficult and relatively
easy to find. On the one hand, most trial court cases and many cases from intermediate courts of appeals are unpublished. Some cases may be published only in
specialized reporters, such as *Ohio Miscellaneous Reports* (Bluebook citation:
Ohio Misc.) or *New York Miscellaneous Reports* (Bluebook citation: Misc.). The
rules for using unpublished cases vary from state to state, with many jurisdictions prohibiting their use.

For the first century of its existence, the United States relied on the case law
reporters of individual states. Nominative reporters such as *Tyler's Reports* in
Vermont or *Lockwood's Reversed Cases* in New York were the only way to find
the law. Then, in 1879, a Minnesota lawyer named John B. West created a revolution in the retrieval of law.

West's innovation was the creation of the "National Reporter System,"
which published cases from all over the country. His first publication was the
North Western Reporter, which covered cases from Minnesota and the north
central region of the United States. This reporter was followed by series for
other regions and for federal cases. "Until the advent of the *North Western Reporter. . .* the prompt publication of opinions was practically unknown to the
legal profession in this country. In each State lawyers were compelled to wait in
the first instance, on the convenience of their State reporter. . . and in the second
place, upon the delays incident to the conflicting business demands of the local
publishers."[46] West's publications "made it possible for lawyers to collect the
judicial opinions of all states easily."[47]

Since the inception of the West National Reporter System, most cases from
the highest state appellate courts (and some cases from intermediate appellate
courts) are published in the West Group's *Regional Reporters* (also known as
the *National Reporter System*). These reporters are also found on *Westlaw* and
Lexis. While the reporters themselves are not on all subscription products, many

of the cases are available. In addition, many recent cases are also available on the Internet via Findlaw and official court websites.

The National Reporter System contains cases from all 50 states, D.C., Puerto Rico, Guam, Virgin Islands, American Samoa, and the Northern Marianas. The jurisdictions are broken down into seven regions, and a series of reporters is published for each region. *Figure 9.1* shows a map of the Regional Reporters. The Regional Reporters cover the following jurisdictions:

- *Atlantic Reporter* (A., A.2d)—State appellate court decisions from Connecticut, Delaware, Maine, Maryland, New Hampshire, New Jersey, Pennsylvania, Rhode Island, Vermont, and Washington, D.C.

- *North Eastern Reporter* (N.E., N.E.2d)—State appellate court decisions from Illinois, Indiana, Massachusetts, New York, and Ohio.

- *North Western Reporter* (N.W., N.W.2d)—State appellate court decisions from Iowa, Michigan, Minnesota, Nebraska, North Dakota, South Dakota, and Wisconsin.

- *Pacific Reporter* (P., P.2d)—State appellate court decisions from Alaska, Arizona, California, Colorado, Hawaii, Idaho, Kansas, Montana, Nevada, New Mexico, Oklahoma, Oregon, Utah, Washington, and Wyoming.

- *South Eastern Reporter* (S.E., S.E.2d)—State appellate court decisions from Georgia, North Carolina, South Carolina, Virginia, and West Virginia.

- *South Western Reporter* (S.W., S.W.2d)—State appellate court decisions from Arkansas, Kentucky, Missouri, Tennessee, Texas, and Indian Territories.

- *Southern Reporter* (S., S.2d)—State appellate court decisions from Alabama, Florida, Louisiana, and Mississippi.[48]

In addition to the regional volumes, the National Reporter System also includes two state-specific reporters, the *California Reporter* (Bluebook citation: Cal. Rptr., Cal. Rptr. 2d) and the *New York Supplement* (Bluebook citation: N.Y.S., N.Y.S.2d). At one time these titles came as part of a complete subscription to the National Reporter System. However, in recent years they have become separate subscriptions. In fact, many libraries are now canceling these two titles because of economic considerations. Although most of the cases in these two reporters are also included in the regional reporter (*Pacific Reporter* and *North Eastern Reporter*, respectively), there are some cases that are only found in the *California Reporter* or the *New York Supplement*. The cases in these series are still available on Westlaw and Lexis, so many libraries that have canceled are still able to access the content online. However, depending on the library's contract, this may cause additional charges.

Figure 9.1. The National Reporter System for State Court Cases.[49]

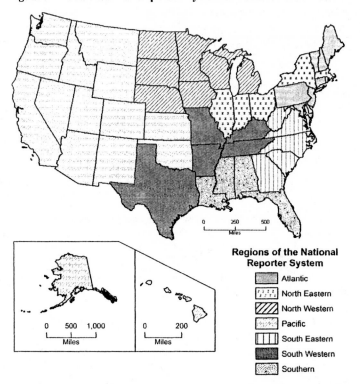

For details on researching specific states, I recommend the state bibliographies sponsored by the AALL Government Documents Special Interest Section. These bibliographies are published by Hein, and are available both in print and online; see their website at http://www.aallnet.org/sis/gd/stateb.html. The *Bluebook* is also a good resource because it identifies the sources for each jurisdiction. Other good resources for state legal research include the following:

♦   *Georgetown Library: State Law Resources*
     http://www.ll.georgetown.edu/states/

♦   *Legal Research Help for State Law* (Nolo Press)
     http://www.nolo.com/legal-research/state-law.html

♦   *Nyberg, Cheryl.* (Annual). *Subject Compilations of State Laws: An Annotated Bibliography.* Twin Falls, ID: Carol Boast and Cheryl Rae Nyberg. (Also available on the *HeinOnline* database.)

♦   *State Laws Listed by State* (Cornell Legal Information Institute)
     http://www.law.cornell.edu/states/listing.html

♦ *State Legislative History: Research Guides* (Indiana University Maurer School of Law Library)
http://www.law.indiana.edu/lawlibrary/research/guides/statelegislative/index.shtml
Compiled by Jennifer Bryan Morgan, this source provides guides for every state.

♦ Swindler, William Finley, Reams, Bernard D., Yoak, Stuart D., et al. (1987). *Sources and Documents of United States Constitutions.* London, UK: Oceana.

Please note that state rules for citations take precedence over general *Bluebook* format. In some cases, this represents an addition to *Bluebook*. For example, the *Bluebook* does not have a citation format for the *Florida Administrative Reports*, but rule 9.800(d) of the *Florida Rules of Appellate Procedure* gives the correct format.[50]

In recent years, several jurisdictions have adopted open citation formats. While the *Bluebook* has this information listed as of the time of publication, it is best to check the rules in each individual state. As of early 2010, jurisdictions using public domain citations include:

♦ Arkansas
♦ Louisiana
♦ Maine
♦ Mississippi
♦ Montana
♦ New Mexico
♦ North Dakota
♦ Northern Marianas
♦ Ohio
♦ Oklahoma
♦ Puerto Rico
♦ South Dakota
♦ Utah
♦ Vermont
♦ Wisconsin
♦ Wyoming

Advice from a Law Librarian
By Brad Small*

I'm a relatively new law librarian. Before working as a law librarian, I was a reference librarian at a public library. I think a good piece of advice for non-law

---

* I am very grateful to Brad Small, a law librarian at the Somerset County Law Library in Somerville, New Jersey. His advice is used by permission.

librarians is to take advantage of legal research tools and legal information produced by law schools, libraries, legal services, state entities and foundations in
their home state. For example, here are key New Jersey sites:

- Rutgers Law School Internet guides
  http://law-library.rutgers.edu
- Internet Law Guide, New Jersey Law Guide, Legal Service of New Jersey
  http://www.lsnjlaw.org
- New Jersey State Bar Foundation online publications
  http://www.njsbf.org/for-the-public/public-publications.html
- New Jersey State Library's legal research guide
  http://www.njstatelib.org/Research_Guides/Law/index.php
- New Jersey Judiciary
  http://www.njcourtsonline.com
- New Jersey Law Library Association
  http://www.njlla.org/displaycommon.cfm?an=2
- State of New Jersey website
  http://nj.gov

Another good tip for non-law librarians is to search their state website using
Google. For example, if a patron needs information on lemon laws in New Jersey, a good way to start the search is to type *lemon law site:nj.gov* in the Google
search box. Or, if a patron needs information on drunk driving laws in New Jersey, type in *drunk driving site:nj.gov*. Carrying this over to any state should
work well.

I'm a big believer in a click and mortar searching strategy . . . not just ran-
domly searching Google, but first identifying a real agency that you know
should have the information and starting there (like going to the state's consumer affairs website for consumer affairs laws). That way you are starting with
a known, legitimate resource.

Example: Researching Kentucky Law

Kentucky is a fairly typical state in its organization of legal materials. Nonetheless, like all jurisdictions, it has its own unique wrinkles. As with any jurisdiction, the best place to start is the *Bluebook*.

Kentucky government traces its formation to 1772, when "the Virginia
General Assembly created Fincastle County from western Botetourt County and
territory extending from the New and Kanawha Rivers to the Mississippi River,
including western Virginia and the present-day states of West Virginia and Kentucky."[51] The county seat was the town of Lead Mines (now known as Austin-
ville, Virginia), about 140 miles east of the present Kentucky-Virginia border.[52]
However, Fincastle County proved to be too large an area to administer effi-
ciently. On October 26, 1776, Thomas Jefferson introduced legislation to split
the area into three counties. This legislation was approved on December 7, 1776,

and signed by Governor Patrick Henry on December 31, 1776. Fincastle County was broken up into the new counties of Kentucky, Washington, and Montgomery. Harrodsburg was the county seat for Kentucky County.[53]

The new county of Kentucky was further subdivided into Lincoln County, Fayette County, and Jefferson County on November 1, 1780. County seats were established at Harrodsburg, Lexington, and Louisville, respectively. The original records, land entries, and survey books for Fincastle County, Virginia, are currently available in the courthouse of Montgomery County (Christiansburg), Virginia, while land patents in the Kentucky portion of Fincastle County are in the Kentucky Secretary of State Land Office (Frankfort, KY). Because all further subdivision occurred after Kentucky ceased to be part of Virginia, more recent records are kept with the state or the respective counties.[54]

A. Constitutional Research

Because Kentucky was part of Virginia until 1792, its laws were originally derived from the "mother state." However, Kentucky very quickly attained its own independence. The first constitution, written at the time of statehood in 1792, only lasted for seven years. In 1799 a second constitution was adopted which made substantial changes. The state's third constitution was adopted in 1850. Part of the problem that led to the adoption of numerous constitutions was that there were no provisions for amendment. This was finally fixed in the fourth constitution, which was promulgated in 1891 and is still effective today.

Because each of the four constitutions has substantially different provisions, it is important to determine which constitution was effective at the time being studied. This is important not only for constitutional research, but also when considering case law. A statute or regulation may be "constitutional" under one constitution but impermissible under another. I recommend that researchers begin by identifying which constitution was effective at the time, no matter what kind of research is being done.

♦ A Citizens' Guide to the Kentucky Constitution, Compiled by Laura Hromyak Hendrix and Edited by Tom Lewis, Research Report No. 137, Frankfort, KY: Legislative Research Commission, 2005, *available at* http://www.lrc.ky.gov/lrcpubs/ rr137.pdf.

♦ Text of act to create Fincastle County, Virginia (February 1, 1772). 8 The Statutes at Large: A Collection of All the Laws of Virginia 600-601 (1821), *available at* http://apps.sos.ky.gov/land/nonmilitary/coformations/countysearch1.asp?searchby =NEW+COUNTY&searchstrg=Fincastle.

♦ Text of act to create Kentucky County, Virginia (December 1, 1776). 9 Hening's Statutes at Large: Laws of Virginia 257-261 (1821), *available at* http://apps.sos.ky.gov/land/nonmilitary/coformations/countysearch1.asp?searchby

=NEW+COUNTY&keywordtype=AND&searchstrg=kentucky&page=&show=2&
sortby=&order=.

♦ Virginia Constitution (June 29, 1776), *available at* http://www.nhinet.org/ccs/docs/
va-1776.htm.

♦ Compact with Virginia (December 18th, 1789), *available at* http://courts.ky.gov/
NR/rdonlyres/CAD60C52-2381-4F7F-81EC-311F9344E1F7/0/CompactWith
Virginia.pdf.

♦ Act Admitting Kentucky into the Union (February 4th, 1791), *available at*
http://courts.ky.gov/NR/rdonlyres/5B9641C5-7BAF-44A5-A09F-7D9DDA47B398/
0/ActAdmittingKyIntoUnion.pdf.

♦ First Constitution of Kentucky (1792), *available at* http://courts.ky.gov/NR/
rdonlyres/7471028C-8BCC-41A2-BA80-02013D4FA550/0/1stKYConstitution.pdf.

♦ Second Constitution of Kentucky (1799), *available at* http://courts.ky.gov/NR/
rdonlyres/E5470543-A249-4265-8EDD-C0DDD6A7212/0/2ndKYConstitution.pdf.

♦ Third Constitution of Kentucky (1850), *available at* http://courts.ky.gov/NR/
rdonlyres/514E219E-9A7A-4D29-A862-C9BD00A3EC1/0/3rdKYConstitution.pdf.

♦ Present (Fourth) Constitution of Kentucky (1891), *available at* http://courts.ky.gov/NR/
rdonlyres/417875A5-340A-4600-A7C4-94B2C7D9B913/0/4thKYConstitution .pdf. The
current Kentucky Constitution is also available in a searchable format at
http://www.lrc.ky.gov/Law.htm.

B. Statutes, Regulations, and Legislative Research

Since 1944, both the Kentucky House and Kentucky Senate have produced
journals tracing action on all bills. These journals are an excellent source of information when compiling a legislative history. Audio recordings exist for many
recent legislative hearings and debates, with some committee hearings available
at the discretion of the committee chair. The tapes are not transcribed, although
hearing minutes serve as finding aids. Legislative floor sessions have been
videotaped since 1992. While not currently online, these recordings are available
for listening and purchase from the Legislative Research Commission library.

♦ *Guide to Kentucky Statutory Law*
http://www.law.louisville.edu/library/research/guides/ky-law/statutes
Created by the University of Louisville Brandeis School of Law Library.

♦ *Legislative Research Commission*
http://www.lrc.ky.gov/
The official repository for all legislative materials, this searchable site contains the

current versions of the Kentucky Revised Statutes, Kentucky Constitution, and Kentucky Administrative Regulations, as well as the legislative record (1987 to present) and filed bills (1997 to present). A free bill-watch service allows legislative tracking via email.

♦ *Peggy King Legislative Reference Library*
http://www.lrc.ky.gov/org_adm/libinfo.htm
Contains statutory, executive, and legislative history materials, including the *Interim Legislative Record* (1974 to present), the legislative and executive records, *Final Action Legislative Record* (1950 to present), *Kentucky Acts* (1820 to present), and House and Senate Journals (1944 to present). Copies of bills are kept for 14 years, and committee minutes for four years; older materials are available at the State Archives. Audio recordings of committee meetings are also available; interim tapes are destroyed after eight years, while session meeting tapes are transferred to the State Archives after four years. The library also contains videorecordings of the General Assembly (House) from 1992 to the present. Along with general reference materials, the library has copies of the current *Kentucky Revised Statutes*, *Kentucky Administrative Regulations*, and *Administrative Register of Kentucky*.

♦ Valentin, Ryan. (2009). *Kentucky Legislative History Research Guide*. University of Kentucky Law Library, *available at* http://www.law.uky.edu/files/docs/library/guides/KYLegHist.pdf.

C. Administrative Law and Regulations

The main source for administrative regulations in Kentucky is the *Kentucky Administrative Regulations* ("KAR"). The KAR is a codification arranged by agency into titles, chapters, and sections. It is available both in print and free online. New and proposed regulations are available via the *Administrative Register of Kentucky*.

♦ *Kentucky Administrative Regulations* (Legislative Research Commission)
http://www.lrc.state.ky.us/kar/frntpage.htm
Browse or search the KAR and the *Administrative Register of Kentucky*.

♦ *Board of Claims*
http://www.boc.ky.gov

♦ *Board of Tax Appeals*
http://www.kbta.ky.gov

♦ *Department of Financial Insititutions*
http://www.kfi.ky.gov/legalresources
Contains both advisory opinions and enforcement actions.

♦ *Department of Insurance*
http://insurance.ky.gov/AgreedOrders/Default.aspx

♦ *Energy and Environment Cabinet Office of Administrative Hearings*
   http://www.oah.ky.gov

♦ *Guide to Kentucky Administrative Law*
   http://www.law.louisville.edu/library/research/guides/ky-law/regulations
   Created by the University of Louisville Brandeis School of Law Library.

♦ *Opinions of the Attorney General* (OAGs)
   http://ag.ky.gov/civil/opinions.html
   Unlike many states, Attorney General opinions in Kentucky are binding on public
   officials. While not binding on private citizens, they are considered persuasive, and
   may be cited in court. Because these opinions represent the official position of the
   Office of the Attorney General, they are considered very persuasive. While the
   Attorney General also provides legal advice or information to public officials, these
   "are not published and do not receive the same detailed review as OAGs. They are
   not considered legal authority and should not be cited."[55]

♦ *Worker's Compensation Board Opinions*
   http://www.comped.net/opinions_board.php

In addition to the sites listed above, other administrative agency decisions
are also available online. As with most states, the best way to find administrative
decisions is to go to each individual agency from the general state website at
http://www.kentucky.gov.

D. Courts and the Judiciary

One unique issue in Kentucky research involves the highest appellate court.
Until 1976, Kentucky's high court was called the "Court of Appeals." Modern
reforms, however, created the Supreme Court of Kentucky, along with an inter-
mediate-level tribunal called the "Court of Appeals." Both Supreme Court justices and Court of Appeals judges are elected by district.

Unpublished cases may not be cited in Kentucky courts. As with many
states, a variety of individuals published opinions under their own names,
known as "nominal reporters." In some instances there were competing reporters. The following nominal reporters cover Kentucky opinions:

♦ 1785-1801—Hughes
♦ 1795-1821—Littell's Selected Cases
♦ 1801-1805—Sneed
♦ 1805-1808—Hardin
♦ 1808-1817—Bibb
♦ 1817-1821—A. K. Marshall
♦ 1822-1824—Littell
♦ 1824-1828—T. R. Monroe

- ◆ 1829-1832—J. J. Marshall
- ◆ 1833-1840—Dana
- ◆ 1840-1857—Ben Monroe
- ◆ 1858-1863—Metcalf
- ◆ 1863-1866—Duvall
- ◆ 1866-1879—Bush

Like most states, Kentucky eventually began publishing its own official reporter. The first state-published reporter was Kentucky Opinions (1864-1886). The Kentucky Law Reporter (1880-1908) overlapped with Kentucky Reports (1879-1951). However, these were discontinued in 1951 in favor of using West's South Western Reporter for official publication. The *Bluebook* (*A Uniform System of Citation*) is the best source for citation information.

There are a variety of Kentucky web pages that are useful for judicial and case law research. The list below gives some of the most important websites.

◆ *Guide to Kentucky Case Law*
http://www.law.louisville.edu/library/research/guides/ky-law/case-law
Created by the University of Louisville Brandeis School of Law Library.

◆ *Kentucky Appellate Court Briefs*
http://chaselaw.nku.edu/library/electronic_resources/briefs_search.php
A searchable website with the full text of Kentucky Supreme Court briefs since January 1999 and Kentucky Court of Appeals briefs since October 2005.

◆ *Kentucky Court of Justice*
http://courts.ky.gov
The official website for all state courts in Kentucky.
  o *The Supreme Court of Kentucky*
  http://courts.ky.gov/SupremeCourt
  The website contains opinions and orders, as well as the court docket.
  o *The Kentucky Court of Appeals*
  http://courts.ky.gov/courtofappeals
  The website contains opinions and orders, as well as the court docket.

◆ *Kentucky Trial Courts*
http://courts.ky.gov/districtcourt

◆ *Manuals for Court Clerks*
  o Clerks Accounting Manual
  http://courts.ky.gov/NR/rdonlyres/234326B2-08D8-4185-89EC-7DAC0AC9C7
  05/0/AOCAccountingManual052009final.pdf.
  o Clerks Manual
  http://courts.ky.gov/NR/rdonlyres/B75874F4-3EAF-473B-8F32-7799ABB54E
  02/0/ClerksManual.pdf

The following sources are available for those who are seeking court dockets:

♦ *Appellate Court and Supreme Court Dockets*
   http://apps.courts.ky.gov/dockets

♦ *Courtnet*
   http://courtnet.kycourts.net/courtnet/aocdefault.asp
   This site is limited to criminal justice professionals. Authorized users can check the status of cases and court appearances, find bail conditions, and determine compliance with court orders.

♦ *CourtNet-KBA* (Kentucky Court Records Online – Kentucky Bar Association)
   http://apps.courts.ky.gov/courtrecordsKBA
   Aimed at practicing lawyers, this site contains records and orders for pending trial court cases.

♦ *Kentucky Court Records Online*
   http://apps.courts.ky.gov/CourtRecords
   Aimed at the general public, this site contains an index of upcoming court cases.

♦ *Local Rules of Practice*
   http://apps.courts.ky.gov/localrules/localrules.aspx

♦ *Legal Forms from Kentucky Courts*
   http://courts.ky.gov/forms/default.htm

E. Law Libraries in Kentucky

♦ *Eastern Kentucky University Law Library*
   http://libguides.eku.edu/content.php?pid=9526&sid=66419

♦ *Eastern Kentucky University Justice and Safety Library*
   http://libguides.eku.edu/content.php?pid=9526&sid=66421

♦ *Kentucky Department for Libraries and Archives*
   http://www.kdla.ky.gov
   A combined state library and state archives, this agency is also responsible for records retention for the entire state government.

♦ *Northern Kentucky University, Chase College of Law Library*
   http://chaselaw.nku.edu/library

♦ *Peggy King Legislative Reference Library*
   http://www.lrc.ky.gov/org_adm/libinfo.htm

- *State Law Library of Kentucky*
  http://courts.ky.gov/research/sll

- *University of Kentucky Law Library*
  http://www.law.uky.edu/index.php?pid=37

- *University of Louisville, Brandeis School of Law Library*
  http://www.law.louisville.edu/library

- *Western Kentucky University, Government Documents & Law*
  http://www.wku.edu/library/dlps/gov_law.htm

F. Miscellaneous Kentucky Resources

- *Business and Corporate Records* (Kentucky Secretary of State)
  http://www.sos.ky.gov/business
  Like many states, Kentucky makes various business filings available to the general public through the Office of the Secretary of State. These records include annual reports, certificates of existence and authorization, and other documents on file with the Office of the Secretary of State. The office also maintains records of security interests recorded under the Uniform Commercial Code. The Secretary of State is also responsible for trademarks and service marks filed under state law.

- *Kentucky County Formations Home Page* (Kentucky Secretary of State)
  http://apps.sos.ky.gov/land/nonmilitary/coformations
  Use this page to determine the year each county was formed. This is especially important for finding records from the 18th and 19th centuries.

- *Kentucky Legal Research Links*
  http://chaselaw.nku.edu/library/electronic_resources/research_links.php

- *Kentucky Legal Research Websites* (University of Kentucky College of Law)
  http://www.law.uky.edu/index.php?pid=237

Example: Researching Massachusetts Law
By Laurel E. Davis, Esq.[*]

The vast majority of the Massachusetts legal resources listed here are free, online sources. However, some particularly important subscription-based or print sources have been referenced as well. The list is by no means complete but will hopefully provide researchers with good starting points.

[*] I am very grateful to Laurel E. Davis, Legal Reference Specialist for the Office of the Massachusetts Attorney General, for writing the section on Massachusetts legal research. Ms. Davis can be contacted at Laurel.Davis@state.ma.us.

Massachusetts legal research is fairly typical of the states, though it has a very rich colonial history that is often worth knowing and consulting when performing this research. The government of the Commonwealth of Massachusetts as it exists today originated as two distinct settlements of English immigrants: the Plymouth Plantation Colony, established by the Pilgrims in 1620, and the Massachusetts Bay settlement (centered in Boston) of the Puritans. The Mayflower Compact was the governing document of the Pilgrims, while the Massachusetts Bay Colony was governed by a royal charter. In 1691, William and Mary granted a new charter which essentially combined the Plymouth and Massachusetts Bay colonies and added new territory, including what is now Maine, parts of current-day Nova Scotia, and the islands of Nantucket and Martha's Vineyard.

Around the beginning of the American Revolution, Massachusetts colonists formed Provincial Congresses that governed without the consent of the English monarch. Talk soon began of the need for a formal constitution, particularly after the reading of the Declaration of Independence in 1776. Initially, the legislature (known in Massachusetts as the General Court) attempted to take on the task, but its efforts were to no avail. It was decided that a constitutional convention should be convened, with delegates representing the various towns and cities.

A. Constitutional Research

On September 1, 1779, the first meeting was held at the First Church in Cambridge. The illustrious attendees, including John Adams, John Hancock, Samuel Otis, and Samuel Adams, wanted to avoid gathering together in Boston because of rumors of an impending British attack.

Responsibility for drafting the document ultimately was handed to John Adams, who thus had the Massachusetts Constitution on his resume when he took on the task of drafting the United States Constitution less than a decade later. Two more sessions of the constitutional convention met before the constitution was distributed to the towns for final ratification.

At the fourth and final session, on June 15, 1780, the delegates officially adopted the *Constitution or Form of Government for the Commonwealth of Massachusetts*. It went into effect on October 25, 1780. Since then, the constitution has been amended 120 times. It is the oldest written constitution in the world that is still functioning.

◆   *Text of the Massachusetts Constitution*
    http://www.mass.gov/legis/const.htm.
    Indicates where original text has been affected by amendments. Note: Massachusetts Constitution is also printed in the official edition of the state statutory code, known as the General Laws of Massachusetts, as well as the two annotated codes: West's

Massachusetts General Laws Annotated and LexisNexis's Annotated Laws of Massachusetts.

♦ John Adams, *The Papers of John Adams, Volume 7 and 8, September 1778-February 1780* (Cambridge: Belknap Press of Harvard University Press, 1977).

♦ *Journal of the Convention for Framing a Constitution of Government for the State of Massachusetts Bay* (Boston: Dutton and Wentworth, 1832). Available online from Google Books.

♦ *Massachusetts, Colony to Commonwealth: Documents on the Formation of Its Constitution, 1775-1780.* (1961). Robert J. Taylor (Ed.). Chapel Hill: University of North Carolina Press.

♦ Samuel Eliot Morison, *The Formation of the Massachusetts Constitution*, 40 Mass. L.Q. n. 4, p. 1 (1955).

B. Statutes and Legislative Research

The legislative body in Massachusetts is known as the General Court, a term that reflects the colonial era when the legislature also wielded judicial powers. The legislature holds two-year sessions, which end in even-numbered years. However, the statutes (or session laws) passed in any given year are arranged in chronological order—based on the date signed by the governor—in an annual compilation known as the *Acts and Resolves of Massachusetts*.

Acts of a general and permanent nature are codified into the official *General Laws of Massachusetts*, published every two years. Additionally, there are two unofficial annotated statutory compilations, *Massachusetts General Laws Annotated* and *Annotated Laws of Massachusetts*, published by Thomson West and LexisNexis, respectively.

The State Library of Massachusetts is an invaluable resource for legislative research and provides many materials, including Acts & Resolves from 1692-1996, on its website. For legislative research involving bills from the 1980s through the current session, there is a good deal of information available online, especially if one ventures into fee-based services. However, for older statutory and legislative history research projects, a visit to the State Library (or an online reference request to one of the librarians) might be necessary.

♦ *General Court of Commonwealth of Massachusetts*
http://www.mass.gov/legis
The legislature's website provides session laws from 1997-present, as well as an unofficial, unannotated, online version of the *General Laws of Massachusetts.* Text of Senate bills from the current session of the legislature and one previous; text of House bills from the current session of the legislature and two previous sessions. Senate journals from 1998-present; House journals from 2001-present.

♦   *InstaTrac*
    http://www.instatrac.com
    Subscription-based service for legislative news and tracking Massachusetts bills. In-
    cludes bill histories and summaries, full-text of bills from 1995-current, witnesses,
    written testimony, access to recorded roll call votes, House and Senate calendars.

♦   *Legislative Broadcast Services*
    http://masslegislature.tv
    Formal sessions of the Massachusetts House and Senate, archived back to 2007.

♦   *State Library of Massachusetts*
    http://www.mass.gov/lib
    Free electronic access to the *Acts & Resolves of Massachusetts* from 1692 to current.
    website includes a "Guide to Tracing Massachusetts Law," an excellent reference
    source for anyone compiling a history of a Massachusetts bill or law. Print collection
    and reference services are vital tools for any research on the legislature or its history
    and procedures.

♦   *State House News Service*
    http://www.statehousenews.com
    Subscription-based service from reporters covering the legislature, including se-
    lected floor debates and committee hearings. Covers current session and includes ar-
    chives back to 1986. State Library provides free on-site access.

C. Administrative Law and Regulations

The Code of Massachusetts Regulations (CMR) is the administrative code
for the Commonwealth. Agency rules are promulgated pursuant to authority
granted under the Administrative Procedures Act (M.G.L. c. 30A). There have
been three editions of the CMR (1976, 1978, and 1987). The Massachusetts
Register, a biweekly publication, updates the CMR. Prior versions of regulations
can be obtained from the State Library of Massachusetts, some of the Trial
Court law libraries, or from the Secretary of the Commonwealth, Regulations
Division. websites for individual agencies and departments often provide regulations, proposed regulations, and administrative law decisions.

♦   Cella, Alexander J. (1986). *Administrative Law and Practice* (Massachusetts Prac-
    tice Series vol. 39). St. Paul, MN: West. Available in many libraries in print and on
    Westlaw [Database identifier: MAPRAC].

♦   *Massachusetts Trial Court Law Libraries*
    http://www.lawlib.state.ma.us
    At this time, there is no free access to an electronic version of the CMR. However,
    the MTCLL website provides links to many agency regulations and does its best to

keep up-to-date. Beware that the print version is usually the most up-to-date version of the CMR. Site also includes executive orders and links to many agency opinions.

♦ *Regulations Manual from Secretary of the Commonwealth*
http://www.sec.state.ma.us/spr/sprpdf/manual.pdf
Explains the process of drafting, proposing, and filing regulations.

♦ *State Library of Massachusetts*
http://www.mass.gov/lib
Access "Digital Collections" for most of the Annual Reports of the Attorney General from 1832 forward, which include Massachusetts Attorney General opinions.

♦ *Social Law Library*
http://www.socialaw.com
Members can access an administrative law database that includes decisions from such agencies as the Massachusetts Commission Against Discrimination, the Massachusetts Civil Service Commission, the Office of the Attorney General, and the Department of Industrial Accidents, among others. The CMR is also available.

D. Courts and the Judiciary

The Massachusetts court system consists of the Trial Court, the Appeals Court, and the Supreme Judicial Court. There are seven departments of the Trial Court: (1) the District Courts; (2) Probate and Family Courts; (3) Land Court; (4) Housing Court; (5) Juvenile Court; (6) Boston Municipal Court; and 7) Superior Court. For a great summary of the jurisdiction of each trial court department, visit the Court Reference web site at http://www.courtreference.com/Massachusetts-Courts.htm.

Selected opinions from the Superior Court since September 1993 are published in the *Massachusetts Law Reporter*. Note that there is an appellate division of the District Courts and Boston Municipal Court; the decisions of that division are published in the *Reports of the Massachusetts Appellate Division*.

The Appeals Court is Massachusetts' intermediate appellate court. This court of general appellate jurisdiction was created in 1972 in order to alleviate some of the Supreme Judicial Court's burden. Today, the Appeals Court has 25 statutory justices. The justices usually sit in three-member panels, though there is also a continuous single justice session with a separate docket. The *Massachusetts Appeals Court Reports* is the official reporter for this court.

The highest court in Massachusetts is the Supreme Judicial Court, which was established in 1692 by the General Court. Originally called the Superior Court of Judicature, it became the Supreme Judicial Court in 1780 with the adoption of the Massachusetts Constitution and remains the only Massachusetts court with constitutional status. The SJC consists of one Chief Justice and six Associate Justices. The official reporter of the SJC is the *Massachusetts Reports*, which dates from September 1804 to present. Decisions of the SJC and Appeals

Court also are published in the *North Eastern Reporter* and *Northeastern Reporter 2d*. *The Bluebook: A Uniform System of Citation* is the best source for citation information, particularly with regard to the early nominative reporters.

♦ *Reporter of Decisions of the Massachusetts Supreme Judicial Court and the Appeals Court*
  http://www.massreports.com
  Provides an opinion archive with decisions from the SJC and Appeals Court from 2001. Supplies biographies of the justices, as well as memorials for deceased justices.

♦ *Supreme Judicial Court and Appeals Court of Massachusetts Public Case Information*
  http://www.ma-appellatecourts.org
  Complete docket information on cases entered since January 1, 1992, in the SJC, and since January 1, 1988, in the Appeals Court. Many SJC briefs available from September 2007 to present.

♦ *Suffolk University Law School (SJC oral arguments)*
  http://www.suffolk.edu/sjc
  Provides live webcasts of oral arguments before the Supreme Judicial Court, plus archived webcasts since September 2005.

♦ *Social Law Library*
  http://www.socialaw.com
  This membership library offers many free features on its website, including judicial assignments and slip opinions for the past six months for the SJC and Appeals Court. Members can gain access to decisions of the SJC, Appeals Court, Land Court, Housing Court, and Superior Court.

E. Law Libraries in Massachusetts

Because of different admission and circulation policies, it is always prudent to contact a library before visiting. Some of the libraries listed, as a general matter, are not open to the public. There are also other libraries in Massachusetts that have significant legal collections, such as the Boston Public Library, even if they are not specifically "law libraries."

♦ *Boston College Law Library*
  http://www.bc.edu/schools/law/library/home.html

♦ *Boston University School of Law, Pappas Law Library*
  http://www.bu.edu/lawlibrary

♦ *Harvard Law School Library*
  http://www.law.harvard.edu/library

♦   *Library of the United States Courts in the First Circuit*
    http://www.ca1.uscourts.gov

♦   *Massachusetts School of Law Library*
    http://www.mslaw.edu/IR_Library.htm

♦   *Massachusetts Trial Court Law Libraries*
    http://www.lawlib.state.ma.us
    Note: There are 17 trial court libraries throughout Massachusetts.

♦   *New England Law | Boston Library*
    http://www.nesl.edu/library/index.cfm

♦   *Northeastern University School of Law Library*
    http://www.northeastern.edu/law/library/index.html

♦   *Social Law Library*
    http://www.socialaw.com

♦   *Southern New England School of Law*
    http://www.snesl.edu/maincontent.aspx?p=73&t=3

♦   *State Library of Massachusetts*
    http://www.mass.gov/lib

♦   *Suffolk University Law School, Moakley Law Library*
    http://www.law.suffolk.edu/library

♦   *Western New England College School of Law Library*
    http://www1.law.wnec.edu/library/index.cfm?selection=doc.4368

F. Miscellaneous Massachusetts Resources

The major legal treatise for Massachusetts is the *Massachusetts Practice Series*, a multivolume series from Thomson West that covers a wide range of topics, including family law, civil procedure, municipal law, administrative law, criminal law and criminal procedure, tort law, and employment law. Massachusetts Continuing Legal Education also publishes a wide variety of practice handbooks and other materials that are available in print from many libraries and online from Loislaw, Westlaw, and LexisNexis.

Another invaluable resource for librarians is: Mary Ann Neary et al., *Handbook of Legal Research in Massachusetts* (3rd ed., MCLE 2009). It provides detailed information about performing legal research in Massachusetts. Chapter topics include research on statutes, legislative history, the judicial system, mu-

nicipal law, administrative law, and court rules. Several other helpful websites
include:

♦   *Links to Massachusetts City and Town Bylaws or Ordinances*
    http://www.lawlib.state.ma.us/source/mass/bylaws.html

♦   *Massachusetts Archives*
    http://www.sec.state.ma.us/arc/arcidx.htm
    Although the site does not provide primary source materials, it gives information
    about the collections, available research services, and contact information.

♦   *Massachusetts Lawyers Weekly*
    http://www.masslaw.com
    Major legal newspaper for Massachusetts. Most online content is available only to
    print subscribers. Provides legal news, opinions and digests, information on judges
    and courts.

♦   *Secretary of the Commonwealth, Corporations Division*
    http://www.sec.state.ma.us/cor
    Searchable databases for corporate entities, trademarks, and rejected corporate fil-
    ings.

Shadow Federalism

There are more than 50 jurisdictions in the U.S. Along with the 50 states, there
is the District of Columbia, two incorporated Commonwealths (Puerto Rico and
the Commonwealth of the Northern Marianas), and two territories (Guam and
the Virgin Islands). The residents of each of these entities are U.S. citizens. In
addition, American Samoa is an unincorporated territory whose residents are
considered nationals (but not citizens) of the U.S. However, there is one additional type of jurisdiction that often escapes notice. These are the many Native
American nations found in the U.S.

Over the past 400 years, there have been a number of treaties between Native American groups and the U.S. While there is an unfortunate history of broken agreements, the U.S. government does currently uphold these treaties. For
some purposes these groups are treated as if they were separate states. The terminology used for this is "shadow federalism." The concept flows partially from
the treaties clause of the Constitution. Although a discussion of this issue is beyond the scope of this work, I have included several websites, books, articles,
and dissertations which deal with this issue.

♦   *American Indian Sovereignty and Law: An Annotated Bibliography.* (2009). Wade
    Davies & Richmond L. Clow (Eds.). Lanham, MD: Scarecrow Press.

♦ Burton, Otha, Jr. (1997). *Elastic Federalism: National Transportation Policies That Incorporate Tribal Governments as America's Fourth Level of Government* (unpublished Ph.D. dissertation, Mississippi State University) (available from ProQuest Dissertations & Theses, Publication No. AAT 9818674).

♦ Canby, William C., Jr. (2004). *American Indian Law in a Nutshell*. St. Paul, MN: Thomson West.

♦ Clinton, Robert N., Goldberg, Carole E., & Tsosie, Rebecca. (2007). *American Indian Law: Native Nations and the Federal System*, 5th Ed. Newark, NJ: LexisNexis.

♦ Cohen, Felix S., et al. (2005). *Cohen's Handbook of Federal Indian Law*. Nell Jessup Newton et al. (Eds.). Newark, NJ: LexisNexis. [Updated annually with supplements.]

♦ Deloria, Vine, Jr., & Little, Clifford M. (1998). *The Nations Within: The Past and Future of American Indian Sovereignty*. Austin: University of Texas Press.

♦ De Puy, Henry F. (1917). *Bibliography of the English Colonial Treaties with the American Indians Including a Synopsis of Each Treaty*. New York: Lenox Club. Also available as an e-book on *HeinOnline*.

♦ *Early Recognized Treaties with American Indian Nations*. Lincoln, NE: University of Nebraska Libraries Electronic Text Center, *available at* http://earlytreaties.unl .edu/index.html.

♦ *Encyclopedia of United States Indian Policy and Law*. (2009). Paul Finkelman & Tim Alan Garrison (Eds.). Washington, DC: CQ Press.

♦ Evans, Laura E. (2005). *Influencing Powerful Partners: American Federalism and Strategies of Tribal Governments* (unpublished Ph.D. dissertation, University of Michigan) (available from ProQuest Dissertations & Theses, Publication No. AAT 3163792).

♦ Hargrett, Lester. (1947). *A Bibliography of the Constitutions and Laws of the American Indians*. Cambridge, MA: Harvard University Press.

♦ Hennessey, Jessica Lynne. (2009). *Endogenous Institutional Change: The transformation of the State-Local Relationship in the United States* (unpublished Ph.D. dissertation, University of Maryland, College Park) (available from ProQuest Dissertations & Theses, Publication No. AAT 3372970).

♦ House of Representatives Committee on Indian Affairs. (2008). *Tribal Courts and the Administration of Justice in Indian Country*. Washington, DC: Government Printing Office.

◆ House of Representatives Committee on Interior and Insular Affairs. (1964). *List of Indian Treaties*. Washington, DC: Government Printing Office. Also available as an e-book on *HeinOnline*.

◆ *The Indian Reorganization Act: Congresses and Bills*. (2002). Vine Deloria Jr. (Ed.). Norman, OK: University of Oklahoma Press.

◆ Jarding, Lilias J. (2001). *"Shadow Federalism": Natural Resources, Native Americans, and National Interactions* (unpublished Ph.D. dissertation, Colorado State University) (available from ProQuest Dissertations & Theses, Publication No. AAT 3032684).

◆ Jarding, Lilias J. (2004). Tribal-State Relations Involving Land and Resources in the Self-determination Era. *Political Research Quarterly, 57(2)*, 295-303.

◆ Kanassatega, Joshua Jay. (2009, Winter). The Discovery Immunity Exception in Indian Country: Promoting American Indian Sovereignty by Fostering the Rule of Law. *Whittier Law Review, 31(1)*, 199-277.

◆ Kappler, Charles J. (1904-1971). *Indian Affairs: Laws and Treaties*. Norman, OK: Oklahoma State University, *available at* http://digital.library.okstate.edu/Kappler. Contains U.S. and American Indian treaties from 1778 to January 13, 1971. Also available as an e-book on *HeinOnline*.

◆ Koenig, Alexa, & Stein, Jonathan. (2007, November). Federalism and the State Recognition of Native American Tribes: A Survey of State-Recognized Tribes and State Recognition Processes across the United States. *Santa Clara Law Review, 48*: 79-153, *available at* http://works.bepress.com/cgi/viewcontent.cgi?article=1001 &context=alexa_koenig.

◆ McCulloch, Anne M. (1994, Summer). The Politics of Indian Gaming: Tribe/State Relations and American Federalism. *Publius: The Journal of Federalism, 24(3)*, 99-111.

◆ *Native American Law* (WashLaw)
http://www.washlaw.edu/doclaw/subject/nativ5m.html
Contains many links to federal and tribal agencies, judiciary (including some tribal court opinions), organizations, and primary materials.

◆ *National Indian Law Library* (Native American Rights Fund)
http://www.narf.org/nill/index.htm
"The National Indian Law Library (NILL) is a public law library devoted to federal Indian and tribal law. Our mission is to develop and make accessible a unique and valuable collection of Indian law resources and other information relating to Native Americans." [Description from website.]

♦ *Opinions of the Solicitor of the Department of the Interior Relating to Indian Affairs 1917-1974.* (1979). Washington, DC: Department of the Interior. Also available as an e-book on *HeinOnline.*

♦ Richotte, Keith Steven, Jr. (2009). *"We the Indians of the Turtle Mountain Reservation. . .": Rethinking Tribal Constitutionalism Beyond the Colonialist/Revolutionary Dialectic* (unpublished Ph.D. dissertation, University of Minnesota) (available from ProQuest Dissertations & Theses, Publication No. AAT 3360388).

♦ Roberts, Christopher. (2004). *The Autonomy of American Indian Nations and Constitutional Construction.* Paper presented at the annual meeting of the New England Political Science Association, Portsmouth, Maine, April 30, 2004, *available at* http://www.allacademic.com/meta/p89893_index.html.

♦ Rosen, Deborah A. (2007). *American Indians and State Law: Sovereignty, Race, and Citizenship, 1790-1880.* Lincoln, NE: University of Nebraska Press.

♦ Seielstad, Andrea M. (2002, Spring). The Recognition and Evolution of Tribal Sovereign Immunity under Federal Law: Legal, Historical, and Normative Reflections on a Fundamental Aspect of American Indian Sovereignty. *Tulsa Law Review, 37*: 661-776.

♦ Steinman, Erich. (2004). American Federalism and Intergovernmental Innovation in State-Tribal relations. *Publius: The Journal of Federalism, 34(2),* 95-114.

♦ Steinman, Erich. (2005). *Institutionalizing Tribes as Governments: Skillful Meaning Entrepreneurship Across Political Fields* (unpublished Ph.D. dissertation, University of Washington) (available from ProQuest Dissertations & Theses, Publication No. AAT 3178112).

♦ Steinman, Erich. (2006, November). (Mixed) Perceptions of Tribal Nations' Status: Implications for Indian Gaming. *American Behavioral Scientist, 50(3),* 296-314.

♦ *Treaties between the United States of America and the Several Indian Tribes, from 1778 to 1837.* (1837). Washington, DC: Langtree and O'Sullivan. Also available as an e-book on *HeinOnline.*

♦ Tribal Supreme Court Project
http://www.narf.org/cases/supctproj.html
The site is sponsored by the Tribal Sovereignty Protection Initiative, the National Congress of American Indians, and the Native American Rights Fund.

♦ Washburn, Wilcomb E. (1995). *Red Man's Land/White Man's Law* [2nd ed.]. Norman, OK: University of Oklahoma Press.

♦ Wilkins, David E., & Lomawaima, K. Tsianina. (2001). *Uneven Ground: American Indian Sovereignty and Federal Law.* Norman, OK: University of Oklahoma Press.

♦   Witmer, Richard, & Boehmke, Frederick J. (2007). American Indian Political Incor-
    poration in the Post-Indian Gaming Regulatory Act Era. *The Social Science Journal,
    44(1)*, 127-145.

Conclusion

The U.S. legal system appears at first glance to be an unconnected but repetitive
hodge-podge of sources of law. In addition to the federal system, there are 50
states, the District of Columbia, two commonwealths (Puerto Rico and the
Northern Marianas), two territories (Guam and the Virgin Islands), and one un-
organized territory (American Samoa). Multiple bodies and organizations make
laws, including the judiciary, the legislative branch, executive agencies, independent agencies, and quasi-governmental organizations. How can an ordinary
person make sense of it all?

However, this first chaotic impression is nothing more than an illusion. The
federal and state systems parallel each other in the ways they produce law. Each
jurisdiction has a legislative branch that passes statutes, an executive branch that
promulgates regulations, and a judicial branch that produces cases. Each branch
at the federal level, and each branch at the state level, has specific types of publications that it produces.

Remember that legal research has the same structure as any other subject
area. For the basics, start with (legal) dictionaries and encyclopedias. Search for
books and (law) journal articles using indexes, abstracts, and databases. Find
primary materials using references from secondary sources. A basic familiarity
with the structure of the U.S. government and the types of publications produced
by each branch—coupled with knowledge of the research process in general—is
sufficient to begin conducting legal research. Legal research, it turns out, is not
so different from other types of research.

Notes

1. Constitution of the Commonwealth of Puerto Rico (1952), *available at* http://welcome.topuertorico.org/constitu.shtml; Covenant to Establish a Commonwealth of the Northern Marianas Islands, Public Law 94-241, 90 Stat. 263 (1976), *available at* http://www.cnmilaw.org/covenant.htm; Constitution of the Commonwealth of the Northern Marianas (1978), *available at* http://www.cnmilaw.org/constitution.htm.

2. Revised Constitution of American Samoa (1967), *available at* http://www.asbar .org/asconst.htm.

3. The District of Columbia is somewhat different in that Congress fulfills the same role as a state legislature. There is a constitution for D.C.; however, it was passed by Congress. Incidentally, the D.C. constitution is entitled "Constitution of the State of New Columbia," and was written with the idea that it would be sufficient both to govern the territory and to govern a separate state. Constitution for the State of New Columbia (1987), *available at* http://198.187.128.12/dc/lpext.dll/Infobase/37f?fn=document-frame .htm&f=templates&2.0.

4. Organic Act of Guam (1950), 48 U.S.C. § 1421 et seq.

5. Revised Organic Act of the Virgin Islands (1984), 48 U.S.C. § 1391 et seq.

6. *See*, Nebraska Legislature, On Unicameralism: Facts, *available at* http://www .unicam.state.ne.us/uni/facts.htm.

7. [Guam] Office of the Attorney General, About the Guam Code Annotated, *available at* http://www.guamattorneygeneral.com/guam_code.php.

8. *id.*

9. *See*, William Tetley, Part I, *Mixed Jurisdictions: Common Law vs. Civil Law (Codified and Uncodified)*, 99 Uniform Law Review 591 (1999), *available at* http://www.unidroit.org/english/publications/review/articles/1999-3.htm.   *See also*, William Tetley, Part II, *Mixed Jurisdictions: Common Law vs. Civil Law (Codified and Uncodified)*, 99 Uniform Law Review 877 (1999), *available at* http://www.unidroit.org/ english/publications/review/articles/1999-4a.htm.

10. *Bracton, Henry de*, The Law Museum Hall of Fame (1999), *available at* http://www.wwlia.org/hallfame.htm.

11. *id. See also*, John Maxcy Zane, The Story of Law [2d ed.] (Indianapolis, IN: Liberty Fund, 1998) at 455-456.

12. *id.* at 456.

13. Matthew Hale, *The History of the Common Law of England: Part I*, Avalon Project (1997), *available at* http://www.yale.edu/lawweb/avalon/econ/hale01.htm.

14. Christopher Saint Germain, The Dialogue in English, between a Doctor of Divinity, and a Student in the Laws of England (1513), [transl. William Muchall] (Ann Arbor, MI: University of Michigan Library), *available at* http://name.umdl.umich.edu/ AGY1099.0001.001. According to the *OCLC WorldCat* record, "The 1st was published (in 1530?) under title: Hereafter foloweth a dyaloge in Englysshe bytwyxt a doctoure of dyuynyte and a student in the lawes of Englande, of the groundes of the sayd lawes and of conscyence. The 2nd was published in 1530 under title: The secu[n]de dyaloge in Englysshe bytwene a doctour of dyuynytye and a student in the lawes of Englande. Both dialogues published anonymously. Both are by Christopher Saint Germain. Cf. St. Germain's Doctor and student / edited by T.F.T. Plucknett and J. L. Barton. 1974. P. xvi-xviii and 12ff./ The first dialogue is a modified translation of the author's 'Dialogus

de fundementis legum Anglie et de conscientia.'"

OCLC also shows several alternate titles, including: Dyaloge in Englysshe bytwyxt a doctoure of dyvynyte and a student in the lawes of Englande; Dialogve in English, betweene a doctor of diuinitie, and a student in the lawes of England; Dialogue in English, betweene a doctor of divinitie, and a student in the lawes of England; Doctor and student (1598).

15. *Law Reports*, in 8 Cambridge History of English and American Literature: An Encyclopedia in 18 Volumes [1907–21] (New York: Bartleby.com) § 13-12 (1907-1921), *available at* http://www.bartleby.com/218/1312.html.

16. *id.*

17. George S. Grossman, *Legal Research: Historical Foundations of the Electronic Age* 117 Oxford University Press (1994).

18. Allen D. Boyer, *Francis Bacon*, 92 Michigan Law Review 1622-1636 (1994), *quoting* William Holdsworth, A History of English Law [2d ed.] 489 (1937), *available at* http://eel.st.usm.edu/paprzycka/spr97/sci/baconf.html.

19. Richard J. Ross, *The Memorial Culture of Early Modern English Lawyers: Memory as Keyword, Shelter, and Identity, 1560-1640*, 10 Yale Journal of Law and the Humanities 229 (1998). *See also*, Ross, *The Commoning of the Common Law: The Renaissance Debate over Printing English Law, 1520-1640*, 146 University of Pennsylvania Law Review 323 (1998).

20. *Equity and Common Law: Bacon and Cowell; Coke*, in 8 Cambridge History of English and American Literature: An Encyclopedia in 18 Volumes [1907–21] (New York: Bartleby.com) § 13-13, *available at* http://www.bartleby.com/218/1313.html.

21. Sir William Blackstone, Commentaries on the Laws of England [1st ed.] (Oxford, UK: Clarendon Press, 1765), *available at* http://www.exlaw.com/library/bla-102.shtml.

22. W. S. Holdsworth, The historians of Anglo-American Law 22 (New York: Columbia University Press, 1928; *reprinted* Lawbook Exchange, 1994).

23. Duncan Kennedy, *The Structure of Blackstone's Commentaries*, 28 Buffalo Law Review 205 (Spring 1979).

24. Richmond.

25. Richmond.

26. John Locke, *Routledge Encyclopedia of Philosophy* [CD-ROM Version 1.0] (London, New York: Routledge, 1997).

27. The Declaration of Independence, Paragraph 2, *available at* http://www.law.ou.edu/hist/decind.html.

28. St. George Tucker, Blackstone's Commentaries: Notes of Reference, to the Constitution and Laws, of the Federal Government of the United States; and of the Commonwealth of Virginia. In five volumes. With an Appendix to Each volume, Containing Short Tracts upon such subjects as appeared necessary to form a connected view of the Laws of Virginia, as a member of the Federal Union (Philadelphia, PA: William Young Birch and Abraham Small, 1803; *reprinted* Austin, TX: Constitution Society, 2000), *available at* http://www.constitution.org/tb/tb-0000.htm.

29. For more information on this topic, *see* two articles I wrote on the history of legal publishing: Bryan M. Carson, *Publishing the Law: The Origins of Legal Publishing*, 12 Against the Grain 68 (November 2000), and Bryan M. Carson, *Written Law from Gutenberg to the Internet: A Historical Perspective*, 12 Against the Grain 74 (December

2000/January 2001).

30. W. M. Gordon and O. F. Robinson, *Introduction* to Translation of The Institutes of Gaius 8 (Ithaca, NY: Cornell University Press, 1988).

31. Peter Birks & Grant McLeod, *Introduction* to Translation of Justinian's Institutes 7 (Ithaca, NY: Cornell University Press, 1987).

32. O. F. Robinson, The Sources of Roman Law: Problems and Methods for Ancient Historians 21 (London, New York: Routledge, 1997).

33. Birks & McLeod at 11.

34. *id.*

35. J. L. Barton, *Gentilis and the* interpretatio duplex, *in* The Roman Law Tradition [ed. A.D.E. Lewis and D. J. Ibbetson] (Cambridge, UK: Cambridge University Press, 1994) at 104.

36. *How the Code Napoleon Makes Louisiana Law Different: Louisiana Law, A Short History Lesson*, La-Legal.com, *available at* http://www.la-legal.com/history_louisiana_law.htm.

37. Bryan M. Carson, The Law of Libraries and Archives (Lanham, MD: Scarecrow Press, 2007).

38. Uniform and Model Acts, Martindale-Hubbell Law Digest (1995).

39. Model Business Corporations Act, Committee on Corporate Laws, Section of Corporation, Banking and Business Law, American Bar Association, *in* Martindale-Hubbell Law Digest (1995) at UMA-8.

40. William A. Schnader, *Introductory Remarks to the Uniform Commercial Code* (November 1, 1967), *in* Martindale-Hubbell Law Digest Uniform Commercial Code (1995) at UMA-62.

41. *id.*

42. Louisiana has adopted several portions of the Uniform Commercial Code, but with substantial changes. *See*, Louisiana Law Digest Commercial Code, Martindale-Hubbell Law Digest at LA8-9 (1995).

43. Puerto Rico Law Digest Commercial Code, Martindale-Hubbell Law Digest (1995) at PR-4.

44. Oceana Publications also publishes *Constitutions of the Countries of the World* and *Constitutions of Dependencies and Territories*. Their website is at http://www.oceanalaw.com.

45. Kent Olson, *Re: State Constitutions*, posting to law-lib@ucdavis.edu, March 19, 2010 (used by permission).

46. John B. West, *A Symposium of Law Publishers*, 23 American Law Review 396, 400 (1889), *excerpted in* Grossman at 74.

47. Grossman at 76.

48. Association of Legal Writing Directors, *West Regional Reporter Coverage*, Appendix to ALWD Citation Manual [2d ed.] (Gaithersburg, MD: Aspen, 2000) at 1A, *available at* http://www.alwd.org/cm/cmAppendices/FirstEditionAppendices/App1A.pdf.

49. Dr. Katie Algeo, Associate Professor of Geography & Geology at Western Kentucky University, drew the map for inclusion in this book. I am very grateful to her. Because there are seven non-contiguous regions that had to be represented in grayscale, this map took some time and skill to create.

50. Sarah K. C. Mauldin, *FOUND Florida Librarians - Citing to Florida Administrative Law Reports*, posting to law-lib@ucdavis.edu, May 14, 2010.

51. Kentucky Secretary of State, Frequently Asked Questions, *available at* http://www.sos.ky.gov/land/nonmilitary/coformations/faq.htm.

52. *id.*

53. *id.*

54. *id.*

55. [Kentucky] Office of the Attorney General, Opinions of the Attorney General (2010), *available at* http://ag.ky.gov/civil/opinions.html.

10

The Past and Future of Legal Research

In today's world, we don't even think twice about being able to find the law. As this book has shown, the law is all around us, published by governments, publishing companies, bar associations, and even libraries. The Internet and legal databases have greatly expanded our ability to find the law. In some ways, it seems as if we are drowning in laws. However, think about what the alternative is like. If we couldn't easily find the law, it would be much easier for dictatorships to be established. Instead, every citizen in our nation has access in some fashion to the published law, either through a library or on the web. As a result, people can easily find out what the law is.

A much-quoted (and often misquoted) line from Shakespeare's play *Henry VI* explains it all. In order to establish a dictatorship, a character named Dick says, "The first thing we do, let's kill all the lawyers."[1] A few lines later, a character named Cade asks of a clerk, "Dost thou use to write thy name? Or hast thou a mark to thyself, like a honest plain-dealing man. . . ."[2]

The moral of Shakespeare's play is that lawyers, literacy, and knowledge of the law are the basic components of our freedom. Take a moment to imagine what life would be like if we didn't have laws that were available to the public, and libraries to house these laws. Without publishers and libraries, our society would be totally different. This chapter is the story of how modern law and legal publishing have been influenced by these ancient principles.

The Beginning in Mesopotamia

In the history of humankind, there have been three major developments. Each one has had an immediate impact, changing the very fabric of our society. These three developments are the creation of writing, the invention of the printing press, and the development of the Internet. Writing began in ancient Mesopotamia, an area which consists of modern-day Iraq, Syria, and Turkey. Mesopotamian writing in pictographs began ca. 4000 B.C., and the Sumerian Cuneiform script developed ca. 3600 B.C.[3] By 3000 B.C., a cuneiform alphabet of 400 signs was in common use.[4]

Although there is no copy in existence, the earliest known code of laws was Urukagina's Code of ca. 2350 B.C. Urukagina's Code "is mentioned in other documents as a consolidation of existing 'ordinances' or laws laid down by Mesopotamian kings. An administrative reform document was discovered which showed that citizens were allowed to know why certain actions were punished."[5]

The most ancient law code that is still in existence is Ur-Nammu's Code from ca. 2050 B.C. "Archaeological evidence shows that it was supported by an advanced legal system which included specialized judges, the giving of testimony under oath, the proper form of judicial decisions and the ability of the judges to order that damages be paid to a victim by the guilty party. The Code allowed for the dismissal of corrupt men, protection for the poor and a punishment system where the punishment is proportionate to the crime. Although it is called 'Ur-Nammu's Code,' historians generally agree that it was written by his son Shugli."[6] Only five articles of the code have been deciphered.[7]

Another code that exists only in fragments is the *Laws of Eshnunna*, from ca. 2000 B.C. Many of the principles that are contained in this code are familiar to us. For example, "If the boatman is negligent and causes the sinking of the boat, he shall pay in full for everything the sinking of which he caused."[8]

The most ancient code that we have in its entirety is the *Code of Hammurabi*, completed ca. 1750-1700 B.C. According to the Prologue, "When Marduk sent me to rule over men, to give the protection of right to the land, I did right and righteousness . . . and brought about the well-being of the oppressed."[9] This was a complete code, containing 282 clauses. The clauses covered "a vast array of obligations, professions and rights including commerce, slavery, marriage, theft and debts."[10] In addition to the *Code of Hammurabi*, "every city had its inheritance of law, founded largely on decisions of the courts and corresponding more or less to our common law, and these were either incorporated by Hammurabi or not superseded by him; thus in deciding a legal case the judges of his time could give as their ruling that 'the law of the citizens of Sippur shall be the law applied to the parties.'"[11]

Hammurabi's code even contained provisions of judicial procedure. For example, "If a judge try a case, reach a decision, and present his judgment in writing; if later error shall appear in his decision, and it be through his own fault, then he shall pay twelve times the fine set by him in the case, and he shall be publicly removed from the judge's bench, and never again shall he sit there to render judgement."[12] From that provision, it appears that decisions were regularly rendered in writing. Although the punishments appear extremely harsh by 21st century standards, we can still celebrate the attempt to provide fair and consistent justice to the people of Babylon.

There are a number of other ancient codes that are significant, including the Code of the Nesilim, written by the Hittites ca. 1650-1500 B.C.E.,[13] and the Laws of Manu, written in India between 1280 and 880 B.C. The Laws of Manu formed the basis of the caste system in India. "The Laws of Manu used punishment sparingly and only as a last resort. . . . The members of the higher castes were punished more severely than those of the lower castes."[14]

The biblical tradition of law began when the Ten Commandments were handed down ca. 1300 B.C. The Old and New Testaments both contain numerous statements of law and justice, as do other Jewish and Christian documents. Justice was a basic principle of the Bible. "Justice, Justice shall you pursue, that you may thrive in the land which the Lord your God gives you."[15] The Talmud also contained a lot of church law. Other sources of church law include St.

Augustine, St. Thomas, and Canon Law. The biblical and Church Law tradition was well known to the Romans and to Justinian.[16]

Greek and Roman Law

Greek law codes started with Draco's Law in 624 B.C. Draco "was called upon to set down his [ordinances and decisions] in writing, and thus to invest them essentially with a character of . . . generality. . . ."[17] Draco took the existing laws and put them in writing "so that they might be 'shown publicly' and known beforehand."[18] These laws were so harsh that we derive the word "draconian" from this code.[19] Between 594 and 592 B.C., during the golden age of Greek democracy, Solon reformulated the laws of Draco. His reforms were substantial, and gave rights to those who were not members of the noble classes. "Rights and freedom to hold office were in proportion to income, but even the poorest had access to the assembly of the people. . . ."[20]

In Rome, one of the most important developments occurred with the creation of the Twelve Tables. In ca. 455-450 B.C.E., a commission of 10 citizens gathered to create a system of laws that would be accepted and binding upon both the privileged class (Patricians) and the unprivileged class (Plebeians). The commission initially wrote 10 tablets, but then added two supplements. (This seems to be the beginning of our fondness for supplementation.) The Twelve Tables consisted of the following: Procedure for courts and trials; Debt; Rights of fathers (paterfamilias) over the family; Legal guardianship and inheritance laws; Acquisition and possession; Land rights; Torts and delicts (Laws of injury); Public law; and Sacred law.[21]

At some time between 110 C.E. and 179 C.E., the Institutes of Gaius were written. This is a complete code of law and procedure, and is very important both in Roman legal history and in the development of modern law. According to Gaius, "All people who are governed by laws and customs use law which is partly theirs alone and partly shared by all mankind. The law which each people makes for itself is special to itself. It is called 'state law,' the law peculiar to that state. But the law which natural reason makes for all mankind is applied in the same way everywhere. It is called 'the law of all peoples' because it is common to every nation. The law of the Roman people is also partly its own and partly common to all mankind."[22]

As mentioned in the section on Civil Law in Chapter 9, *Federalism*, the Emperor Justinian ordered a compilation in A.D. 533. The *Corpus Iuris Civilis*[23] formed the basis of the Civil Law system, and is still influential today in many parts of the world.

After the fall of the Roman Empire, chaos reigned in Europe. In the period known as the Dark Ages, libraries were burned, literacy was practically non-existent, and government consisted mostly of small clans and warlords.[24] The only places where libraries survived were in Ireland, the Byzantine Empire, and the Muslim world.[25] Not until the days of Charlemagne (786-814) did the concept of written law revive.

Gutenberg and the Printing Press

If the beginning of writing was the beginning of our law, the invention of printing was the second most important event in our legal development. The printing press allowed books and documents to be copied easily. It made publication and book ownership inexpensive, and led to mass dissemination of knowledge. Prior to this time, the written law was kept in regional or provincial centers. The small villages did not have access to the written law. With Gutenberg's invention, law codes could be distributed much more widely. "The spread of printing . . . ripped apart the social and structural fabric of . . . Western Europe and reconnected it in ways that gave shape to modern patterns. The availability of printed materials made possible social, cultural, familial, and industrial changes facilitating the Renaissance, the Reformation, and the scientific revolution."[26]

In the days before the invention of printing, books were often written or copied by hand. There were some methods for automating book production, but these methods were not very efficient. For example, wood block carvings were used to reproduce illustrations.[27] However, this was a very labor-intensive process that was not suitable for mass production of the written word.

Around the year 1450, Johannes Gutenberg (d. 1468) improved several existing technologies, and combined them with a new invention. "The four components of the press — moveable type, ink, paper and the actual press — were all familiar tools at that time. The combination of these four elements created a revolution in the printing industry."[28] His revolution was the beginning of the printed book. The *Gutenberg Bible* (the *Bible of Forty-Two Lines*) was published on August 15, 1456.[29] This is the oldest surviving printed book. "In thirty years the printed word spread across Europe and was one of the reasons for the Renaissance period, a period of learning and artistic endeavor. Although most of Europe still remained illiterate, those that could read could now share ideas in a printed format."[30]

Now that the printed word was widely disseminated, legal publishing could begin. This was especially important for the Common Law system used in England and her colonies. The English case reporters actually predate the printing press, but mass production led to mass knowledge.

Meanwhile, the laws of the rest of Europe continued to be based on Roman law. In 1804, Napoleon I provided the first modern update to Justinian's code. Because the *Code Napoleon* was based on modern views, it became very influential throughout Europe. Quebec subsequently adopted the *Napoleonic Code*. During the 19th and early 20th centuries, European colonialism led to the adoption of the *Napoleonic Code* in many other parts of the world, particularly Latin

America, Africa, and the Middle East. This process of cultural dispersion was made possible in large part by the availability of the printing press.

Legal Research and the Online World

The modern American legal publication system was based on West's "National Reporter System" and *Shepard's Citations*. From the 1880s to the 1990s, the system of legal publishing was static. In the 1970s Lexis and Westlaw created new ways to search the law, but did not really change the way that law was recorded. Starting in the 1990s, free Internet-based research and online subscription databases provided a wealth of data for lawyers, librarians, and other researchers. Many courts and legislative bodies began to publish their data electronically. "As Gutenberg's printing press ignited the Renaissance, computers, the Internet and networking are igniting the Digital Renaissance. . . ."[31]

In 1997, the U.S. federal court system considered a proposal to change its accepted citation format. The new format, which was proposed by the American Bar Association, would have allowed lawyers to cite to documents found on the web, as well as documents that are published in the official reporters or the West National Reporter System. The "vendor neutral citation" proposal (called that because it did not refer to the publications of any one particular company) would have allowed attorneys to cite cases by stating the year, a designator of the court, and the sequential number of the decision. Paragraphs would be numbered. Although the U.S. courts did not adopt this proposal, the fact that it was seriously considered points out the enormous change that occurred in just a few short years.[32] Even the major legal style manuals have gotten into the act. Beginning with the 18th edition of the *Bluebook* in 2005 and the 3rd edition of the *ALWD Citation Manual* in 2006, rules have been established for vendor-neutral citation of electronic resources.[33]

As the importance of Internet research continued to grow, many courts posted previously unpublished opinions. These unpublished cases have been accessible for a number of years through microfiche, newsletters, and looseleaf services. However, unpublished cases were not very useful to attorneys because most courts do not allow unpublished cases to be cited.[34]

In August 2000, a panel of the 8th Circuit Court of Appeals declared that the rule forbidding the citation of unpublished cases was unconstitutional. The case was *Anastasoff v. U.S.*[35] The reasoning of the court was that "[i]nherent in every judicial decision is a declaration and interpretation of a general principle or rule of law. This declaration of law is authoritative to the extent necessary for the decision, and must be applied in subsequent cases to similarly situated parties. These principles, which form the doctrine of precedent, were well established and well regarded at the time this nation was founded."[36] The panel concluded that the Constitution did not allow courts to ignore previous decisions; to do so was an abuse of judicial power.

Unfortunately for the proponents of unpublished cases, the case was de-clared moot by the time the entire 8th Circuit heard the case *en banc*. As a result, the complete court never considered the question of citing unpublished cases, and "the constitutionality of that portion of Rule 28A(i) which says that unpub-lished opinions have no precedential effect remains an open question in this Cir-cuit."[37] While some courts have followed the panel decision in *Anastasoff*, the status of unpublished cases is currently undecided.

Vendor-neutral citation and unpublished cases are in many ways the last frontiers in legal research. Both rely in large part on access that has only been possible since the development of the Internet. Vendor-neutral citation formats have been discussed or adopted in several states,[38] and use of unpublished opin-ions is on the rise. It remains to be seen what will happen in the future.

Do we still need books for legal research? (Why books still matter)

Several times every day in the course of my work as a librarian, I hear people express the opinion that books are no longer necessary, since "everything is now online." A second opinion that I sometimes hear is that books are unnecessary, and libraries (and librarians) are no longer needed. Although these statements raise hackles for most librarians and publishers, the myth is something that we need to contend with on a regular basis. So what is the truth—are books still needed for legal research? The answer is an unqualified YES!

In the past 30 years, Computer-Assisted Legal Research (CALR) systems such as Lexis and Westlaw have done wonders for the field of legal research. Starting in 1993, large amounts of information have become available via the internet. Libraries subscribe to subscription databases and e-book collections, while the general public accesses e-books via their Kindle, Nook, iPhone, or BlackBerry. Yet books are still very important. I will talk about three very common myths. These myths are: "Everything is available on the web for free"; "Everything is available on Lexis or Westlaw"; and "Computer-Assisted Legal Research is less expensive!" Yet, as pervasive as these myths have become, they are not an accurate representation of the field of legal research.

Myth #1: "Everything is on the Web!"

Myth number 1, the idea that "everything is on the web," is probably the most pervasive misconception in the world of research. In order to see if that is true, let's take a look at what is available on the free web.

The popularity of the Internet has certainly changed everything, and much information is available online. The advent of the internet has been a godsend for lawyers, librarians, and legal researchers. Statutes and administrative regula-tions are currently available for the federal government and all 50 states, with some material also available for the District of Columbia, Puerto Rico, Guam, and the Virgin Islands.

One task that has been made easier by online research is preparing a Legislative History report. With bills from Congress and state legislatures available at your fingertips, researching legal history becomes merely a matter of time, rather than the Herculean task it had formerly been. And certainly any researcher who has taken the time to curse the index to the *Code of Federal Regulations* knows how wonderful life has been since the CFR became available online.

However, life is not perfect on the internet. Remember that not all years are available, and there are differences between states in the amount of material you can find online. For example, New York has placed all of the opinions from its highest court (the Court of Appeals) online dating back to 1992, but Alabama only has the state Supreme Court opinions since 1998 available on the web. And cases from the U.S. Supreme Court only date back to 1893.[39] Why don't they put everything online? The answer is based on economics.

The biggest factors preventing digitized collections are the costs involved. Items don't just appear on the web; they have to be scanned, the images must be adjusted or copyedited, etc. This is not done by a student worker or a lower-level staff person, but by a professional whose salary costs money. Digitized items take up a lot of space on a server, and that also costs money.

There is also the issue of actually creating the site and organizing it so that the user can find what he or she is looking for. This is the science known as taxonomy. Taxonomy is very much related to cataloging, and is usually done by trained catalogers with library degrees. (The difference is that if you call yourself a cataloger you get paid $35,000; if you call yourself a taxonomist you get paid $65,000. This is one of the reasons that libraries find it so difficult to hire catalogers these days.) Taxonomy also costs a lot of money. Everything that you do to put together an online collection costs money, and in this age of shrinking budgets an online collection is not always the first priority.

Myth #2: "Everything is available on Lexis or Westlaw!"

The release of Lexis and Westlaw in the 1970s revolutionized legal research. With the aid of the computer, many different types of information can be readily available at your fingertips. Unlike the free web, CALR systems tend to give you extensive coverage of legal resources. This is especially true with case law, which is often date-restricted on free websites.

Yet there are significant differences between the ways in which legal research is conducted online and the way in which legal research is conducted in paper. Instead of searching for the rules which underlie our legal system, we instead concentrate on searching for facts. According to Barbara Bintliff, Director and Professor of Law at the University of Colorado Law Library, "Computer-assisted legal research actually starts from the opposite direction of traditional book-based research by looking for factually similar cases first. This leads to a thought process that puts its first and strongest emphasis on the facts; the legal rules become secondary."[40]

Commenting on Bintliff's analysis, Kendall Svengalis stated that "[r]elying solely upon the results of a fact-based computer search, the attorney may not ascertain the underlying rules which provide the conceptual framework to predict the outcome of a case. In light of these observations, such concept-based legal research tools as the traditional key-number digest, legal encyclopedia, law review article, and legal treatise provide a necessary complement to computer-assisted legal research systems."[41]

Another consideration that most people don't think about is that not all search engines are created equal. A recent interaction with a client at my library illustrated this point.[42] A very senior faculty member had used the same database at Western Kentucky University and at another school. With an identical search, he received substantially more hits at the other school, causing the professor to assume that the database at Western Kentucky University was not the same as the database at the other university. It turned out that the other university had purchased the database from a different vendor, and the search algorithms behaved differently from the one at Western Kentucky University.

Search engines vary considerably. For example, what happens if you type two words into a search engine without using quotation marks or connectors? Let's say that you are looking for cases involving real estate. If you type the words REAL ESTATE into the search box without using quotation marks, what do you get?

If you are using *Westlaw*, the search REAL ESTATE is the equivalent of typing REAL *OR* ESTATE. You will find everything with the word REAL or with the word ESTATE. The same search on *LexisNexis* is treated as if you had put it in quotation marks. Meanwhile, this search on *EBSCOhost* brings up the same results you would get if you typed REAL *AND* ESTATE. The *EBSCOhost* search retrieves results that have both words, although they might not necessarily be together as a phrase.

Even the same database can change over time. For example, in 2010 *EBSCOhost* changed its default treatment from phrase searching to *AND* searching. Researchers who were used to the old default got different results after this change was made. The way to reduce the search engine problem is to put all phrases in quotation marks, every time, and in every database. At the same time, put a connector between every word that is not in a phrase.

Although librarians are familiar with the differences between search engines, many users are not. Researchers often run into problems because of issues such as controlled vocabularies, treatment of adjacent search terms, and differences in the truncation marks and wildcard characters. It is very important for librarians to educate users about the limitations and differences of search engines and databases.

For all of these reasons, books still play a role in the legal research process. After all, the print collections in a law library provide access to an overwhelming amount of material that has never been placed online. With a few pages in a legal encyclopedia, researchers can learn the rule and find the major cases and statutes. This method of research is lost when the user goes online. Even online versions of *American Jurisprudence* and *Corpus Juris Secundum* are more difficult to use and take more time than using the print version, and many law librarians believe that statutory research is more efficient in print.[43] For this reason, I usually tell library users to start with the legal encyclopedia in print, and to only go online after they have learned what the search terms are and what the major cases say.

Myth #3: "Computer-Assisted Legal Research is less expensive!"

Some attorneys believe that using CALR is more economical than using books. After all, lawyers tend to think in terms of billable hours. It's only natural, since that is how they are paid. So it is certainly understandable if a lawyer thinks that the cost of her time is worth the cost of using CALR. Understandable, but wrong!

At one time, the only kinds of contracts that were available for Lexis and Westlaw were based on the amount of time you used the system. This transactional pricing was very expensive. It was very difficult to predict what the charges would be from a particular research session. Students and new lawyers who were used to having unlimited passwords in law school would often get into trouble by running up large bills.[44] For example, in early 1994 I was working at the Guam Territorial Law Library in Agana (now known as Hagatna), Guam. After the law clerks at the Guam Superior Court ran up a research bill of $49,000 in one month, I was called in to provide training in the use of Lexis and Westlaw, as well as to discuss print research and the use of the law library.

The pricing structure changed once the Internet became popular and newer companies such as Versuslaw, Lois, and Hein began competing in the legal research market. It is now possible to obtain fixed-rate contracts for both Lexis and Westlaw, although practitioners may still choose to use the transactional pricing instead. Attorneys often think that the new fixed prices mean that CALR systems are more economical. However, they are not necessarily correct, so care needs to be taken when dealing with fixed-price contracts.

As recently as 2002, Kendall Svengalis wrote: "Except in some clearly defined circumstances, legal researchers should resist the use of CALR until less expensive alternatives have been exhausted."[45] However, by 2009, he had changed his tune to recommend purchasing used back issues of the regional reporters. Svengalis wrote:

The steeply rising cost of bound reporter volumes acquired in a serial fashion from the publisher can no longer be justified by the cost-conscious attorney.
The monies spent on one year's worth of bound regional reporter volumes
. . . could be far more effectively spent on a LexisNexis or Westlaw subscription plan providing the full range of primary law for your state. The only bound
volumes you should acquire are . . . used or free for the cost of postage. Once
acquired, these sets should not be supplemented in print. Current decisions
should only be accessed online.[46]

Another option, even less expensive, is to use a local law library for research materials. While some law libraries are part of a university or run by a
county, others are for bar associations or by membership. Whether or not the
local law library requires a membership fee, it is still the most economical alternative for conducting legal research. Remember that the cost of the National
Reporter System is the same for a law library as it is for an individual. County or
bar association law libraries often have online or print subscriptions to the major
reporters, digests, and a citator (*Shepard's* or *KeyCite*), as well as other important resources. Therefore, using the law library whenever possible will save
money.

Lawyers who do not have access to a local law library may still benefit
from the resources of nearby colleges or universities. Many institutions subscribe to products such as LexisNexis Academic, Westlaw Campus, ProQuest
Congressional, or RIA Checkpoint. Depending on the customs of the region,
many libraries will allow local lawyers to visit and to use their database subscriptions on-site.

In 2009, Kelly Devlin surveyed the law-lib discussion list to find resources
that law librarians preferred to use in print rather than online. She also asked
why these items are preferred in print. Several people mentioned that books,
monographs, treatises and legal encyclopedias (such as *American Jurisprudence*) are easier to browse in print than online. It is also easier to compile legislative histories from printed statutes. Several people found the printed versions
of *U.S. Code Congressional and Administrative News* to be easier to use than
the online versions.[47]

The question of whether to subscribe to print or online (and which database)
comes up on a regular basis. In 2010, an attempt to determine which service
provided the better "value" led to the following comments:

> If by "value" you simply mean "price x quantity," then both services are,
> for all practical purposes, equivalent in value: they are both expensive, but they
> also offer a tremendous amount of information. . . . But if by "value" you mean
> "highest return on investment for lowest cost," then you're really talking about
> a research strategy that many of us have advocated for years. This cost-saving
> research strategy starts with understanding research as a process, continues by
> initiating the particular research task in low-cost secondary sources (in print or
> electronic format), then finding as many primary sources as possible at the
> lowest cost (again, sometimes requiring access to print sources), and finally

confirming or updating one's research with the high-cost, high-quality electronic vendor databases such as LexisNexis or Westlaw.

To this end, you may wish to tell your client that a qualified law librarian offers the highest value when undertaking legal research. Without such a librarian to steward the sorts of low-cost resources that research should begin with (or merely to point researchers toward these resources), any business proposition that presents legal research starts out losing value, by throwing critical monetary resources directly into high-cost, high-quality vendor databases without any apparent consideration of lower-cost alternatives to this task.[48]

Conclusion

It is vital that law be published, regardless of format. Without legal publishers, many of our freedoms would disappear. As Sir William Blackstone wrote over two centuries ago, the law "may lastly be notified by writing, printing, or the like; which is the general course taken with all our acts of Parliament. Yet, whatever way is made use of, it is incumbent on the promulgators to do it in the most public and perspicuous manner; not like Caligula, who . . . wrote his laws in a very small character, and hung them up upon high pillars, the more effectually to ensnare the people."[49]

Imagine a world with no written law. A world where what the authorities say is the law. Would our fundamental freedoms survive? The publication of our laws constitutes one of the safeguards of our liberty.

Legal researchers have to contend with three very common myths: "Everything is available on the web for free"; "Everything is available on Lexis or Westlaw"; and "Computer-Assisted Legal Research is less expensive!" Yet these myths are not correct. As important as Internet and subscription databases have become, many items are simply not available at all, or are only available for limited time periods. There are significant issues with the way in which materials are retrieved on the computer. Also, online research is not always more economical than print, particularly if there is a decent-sized law library in close proximity to the law office.

After studying these myths, I conclude that database subscriptions are more economical for small practitioners (even though they are used more at large law firms). Large firms are better served by purchasing used print reporter back issues while accessing up-to-date decisions online. Yet both the large firms and the small firms would be better off to use nearby law libraries instead of online subscriptions.

With a little careful analysis, we can see the truth behind the three myths of legal research. So, do we still need books for legal research? The answer is a resounding YES!

At the same time, it is important to realize that online research is here to stay. Research tools such as *Shepard's Citations*, the *Federal Register*, and the *Digests* are easier to use online. While I still prefer the print versions of *Ameri-*

can Jurisprudence and C.J.S., online versions of specialized encyclopedias and practice materials provide searching capabilities that are simply not available in print.

Many libraries have converted their print subscriptions to online (even at law schools, where *Shepard's Citations* is all but disappearing in print). Rita Reusch theorized that this shift came from the convergence of improvements in online research and financial pressures on libraries.[50]

Throughout the centuries, written law has given society rules to live by, and ideals to strive for. The printing press made reproduction of books feasible, and the Internet made publication easy. With the heritage of the printed law book keeping our liberty intact, we can rest assured that legal publishers and law libraries will play an important part in the world of tomorrow. As the future becomes the present, the written law ensures that we also look at our past. After all, as the noted 20th-century philosopher George Santayana expressed so well, "those who cannot remember the past are condemned to repeat it."[51]

Notes

1. Shakespeare, Henry VI, Part II, Act IV, Scene ii.
2. *id.*
3. Michael H. Harris, History of Libraries in the Western World, 4th ed. (Metuchen, NJ: Scarecrow Press, 1995) at 17.
4. *id.*
5. Lloyd Duhaime, *The Timetable of World Legal History* (Victoria, BC: World Wide Legal Information Association, 2000), *available at* http://www.wwlia.org/hist .htm#2350bc.
6. *id.*
7. *id.*
8. *The Laws of Eshnunna*, Trans. Anet Albrecht Goetz, 161-163, paragraph 5. *In* The Ancient Near East: An Anthology of Texts and Pictures, Ed. James B. Pritchard (Princeton, NJ: Princeton University Press, 1958) at 133.
9. *Code of Hammurabi*, Prologue, Trans. L. W. King, Ed. Richard Hooker. *In* World Civilizations (Pullman, WA: Washington State University, 2000), *available at* http://www.wsu.edu:8080/~dee/MESO/CODE.HTM.
10. Duhaime.
11. Sir Leonard Woolley, The Sumerians (New York: Norton, 1965) at 91-92.
12. *Code of Hammurabi* at § 5.
13. *The Code of the Nesilim*, in Paul Hasall (ed.), Internet Ancient History Sourcebook (Bronx: Fordham University, 1998), *available at* http://www.fordham.edu/halsall/ ancient/1650nesilim.html.
14. Duhaime.
15. Deuteronomy 16:20.
16. For an explanation of Church Law, see the entry on "Law" in 8 The New Catholic Encyclopedia 543 (New York: McGraw-Hill, 1967).
17. G. Grote, History of Greece [Pt. 2, ch. 10, vol. 3], *in* J. N. Larned, 1 History for Ready Reference from the Best Historians, Biographers, and Specialists: Their Own Words in a Complete System of History for All Uses *at* 146 (Springfield, MA: C. A. Nichols, 1892).
18. *id.*
19. Black's Law Dictionary 443 (5th ed. 1979).
20. Larousse Encyclopedia of Ancient and Medieval History (Feltham, UK: Hamlyn Publishing Group, 1972) at 109. *See also*, Oxford International Encyclopedia of Legal History, Ed. Stanley N. Katz (Chapel Hill, NC: Oxford University Press, 2009).
21. The Twelve Tables (451-450 B.C.).
22. *Commentaries*, The Institutes of Gaius, Book 1, §1, Trans. W. M. Gordon & O. F. Robinson (Ithaca, NY: Cornell University Press, 1988).
23. W. M. Gordon & O. F. Robinson, *Introduction*, The Institutes of Gaius at 8.
24. Jerome Blum, Cameron Rondo, & Thomas G. Barnes, The European World: A History (Boston: Little, Brown, 1966) at 15.
25. Harris at 67.
26. Michael C. Emery, Edwin Emery, & Nancy L. Roberts, The Press and America: An Interpretive History of Mass Media [8th ed.] (Boston: Allyn and Bacon, 1996) at 3-4, *quoted in* Jeremy Harris Lipschultz, Free Expression in the Age of the Internet: Social

and Legal Boundaries (Boulder, CO: Westview, 2000) at 41.

27. Annemarie Marino, *The Printing Press* (2000), *available at* http://www
.sunysuffolk.edu/~maria29/printingpress.html.

28. *Johannes Gutenberg: A Biography* (2000), *available at* http://www.lysands.com/
History/People/johannesgutenbu_tpy_ly.htm.

29. Tanya Demjanenko, *Johann Gutenberg* (2000), *available at* http://publish.uwo
.ca/~tdemjane/johann.htm.

30. Marino.

31. Ian Jukes & Ted McCain, *From Gutenberg to Gates: Education in an Online
World*, Keynote Address at the TechEd 2001 Convention, Ontario, California (March 26,
2001), in 15-5 Education at a Distance 5 (April 2001), *available at*
http://citeseerx.ist.psu.edu/
viewdoc/download?doi=10.1.1.100.1896&rep=rep1&type=pdf.

32. *Comment on proposed citation rules*, email from Bryan M. Carson, Hamline
University College of Law Library, to Joan Countryman, United States Judicial Conference (March 4, 1997), *available at* http://www.hyperlaw.com/jccite/054.txt.

33. *See*, Rita Reusch, *By the Book: Thoughts on the Future of Our Print Collections*,
100-3 Law Library Journal 555, 557 (2008). *See also*, Darby Dickerson, ALWD Citation
Manual: A Professional System of Citation, 3d ed. (New York: Aspen, 2006); The Bluebook: A Uniform System of Citation, 19th ed. (Cambridge, MA: Harvard Law Review
Association, 2010).

34. The 8th Circuit Rules of Appellate Procedure reads as follows:

> **Citation of Unpublished Opinion**. Unpublished opinions are not prece-
> dent and parties generally should not cite them. When relevant to establishing
> the doctrines of res judicata, collateral estoppel, or the law of the case, how-
> ever, the parties may cite any unpublished opinion. Parties may also cite an un-
> published opinion of this court if the opinion has persuasive value on a material
> issue and no published opinion of this or another court would serve as well. A
> party who cites an unpublished opinion in a document must attach a copy of the
> unpublished opinion to the document. A party who cites an unpublished opin-
> ion for the first time at oral argument must attach a copy of the unpublished
> opinion to the supplemental authority letter required by FRAP 28(j). When cit-
> ing an unpublished opinion, a party must indicate the opinion's unpublished
> status.

8th Circuit Rule 28A(i) (1998), *available at* http://www.ca8.uscourts.gov/rules/
local1298.pdf.

35. Anastasoff v. U.S., 223 F.3d 898 (8th Cir. 2000).

36. *id.*

37. Anastasoff v. United States, 235 F.3d 1054, 1056 (8th Cir. 2000).

38. Vendor-neutral citation formats have been adopted in North Dakota, Louisiana,
Maine, Mississippi, Montana, New Mexico, Oklahoma, South Dakota, Utah, and Wisconsin, as well as the U.S. Court of Appeals for the Sixth Circuit. *See*, Peter W. Martin,
Introduction to Basic Legal Citation (Cornell, NY: Cornell Legal Information Institute
2003), *available at* http://www.law.cornell.edu/citation.

39. For more information on the availability of cases and codes online, *see* Findlaw,
available at http://www.findlaw.com/casecode.

40. Barbara Bintliff, *From Creativity to Computerese: Thinking Like a Lawyer*, 88

Law Library Journal 338, 345 (Summer 1996).

41. Kendall F. Svengalis, The legal Information Buyer's Guide and Reference Manual 2002 at 115 (Barrington, RI: Rhode Island Law Press, 2002).

42. In the interests of patron confidentiality, I am not identifying the database that was used or the other university that he used it at.

43. Reusch at 557.

44. Svengalis 2002 at 115.

45. Svengalis 2002 at 115.

46. Kendall F. Svengalis, The Legal Information Buyer's Guide and Reference Manual 2009 at 69 (Barrington, RI: Rhode Island Law Press, 2009).

47. Kelly Devlin, *Print (and Other Resources) Which We Prefer to On-Line Versions*, posting to law-lib@ucdavis.edu, September 11, 2009 (used by permission).

48. Dennis Kim-Prieto, *Re: Westlaw v Lexis Value*, posting to law-lib@ucdavis.edu, May 27, 2010 (used by permission).

49. Sir William Blackstone, *Of the Nature of Laws in General*, 1 Commentaries on the Laws of England 1765-69, § II, *available at* http://www.exlaw.com/library/bla -102.shtml.

50. Reusch at 556.

51. George Santayana, 1 *The Life of Reason* (London: Constable & Co., 1905). Santayana (1863-1952) was one of the most acclaimed philosophers of the 20th century.

Bibliography

1789 pay raise amendment returns to haunt Congress. (1992). *Congressional Quarterly Weekly Report, 50,* 1230.

Adams, Anne. (2003). *Basic Administrative Law for Paralegals.* (2nd ed.) New York: Aspen Law & Business.

Administrative Office of the Courts. *Court Locator.* Available at http://www.uscourts .gov/court_locator.aspx.

Administrative Office of the Courts. *United States District Courts.* Available at http://www.uscourts.gov/districtcourts.html.

Alford, Roger P. (2006). "Outsourcing authority?" Citation to foreign court precedent in domestic jurisprudence: Four mistakes in the debate on "outsourcing authority." *Albany Law Review, 69,* 653-681. Available at http://www.albanylawreview.org /articles/Alford.pdf.

Amann, Diane Marie. (2004, October). "Raise the flag and let it talk": On the use of external norms in constitutional decision making. *International Journal of Constitutional Law, 2(4):* 597-607. Available at http://www.aals.org/am2005/fripapers /1030amann.pdf.

Amar, Akhil Reed. (1992, April). The Bill of Rights and the Fourteenth Amendment. *Yale Law Journal, 101,* 1193-1284. Available at http://www.saf.org/LawReviews /Amar1.html.

Ambrogi, Robert J. (2010, February 1). Three's a crowd? Bloomberg Law officially enters the high-end legal research service market, *Law Technology News.* Available at http://www.law.com/jsp/lawtechnologynews/PubArticleLTN.jsp?id=120243954226 7&Threes_a_Crowd.

American Law Institute. (2009). In *Wikipedia.* Available at http://en.wikipedia.org/wiki /Restatement.

Andriani, Lynn. (2008, January 21). New York fights "libel tourism": New bill will protect authors from foreign lawsuits. *Publishers Weekly,* 12. Available at http://www.publishersweekly.com/pw/print/20080121/1651-new-york-fights-e2-80-9clibel-tourism-e2-80-9d-.html.

Apple, James G., & Deyling, Robert P. (1995). A Primer on the Civil-Law System. Washington, DC: Federal Judicial Center. Available at http://www.fjc.gov/public /pdf.nsf/lookup/CivilLaw.pdf/$file/CivilLaw.pdf.

Articles of Confederation. (2003, February 26). *Ben's Guide for Kids to the U.S. Government.* Available at http://bensguide.gpo.gov/9-2/documents/articles.

Articles of Confederation. Available at http://www.yale.edu/lawweb/avalon/artconf.htm.

Association of Legal Writing Directors. West regional reporter coverage [Appendix]. *ALWD Citation Manual* (2nd ed.). Gaithersburg, MD: Aspen, 2000, 1A. Available at http://www.alwd.org/cm/cmAppendices/FirstEditionAppendices/App1A.pdf.

Bailey, R. Kevin. (1997). Note: "Did I miss anything?" Excising the National Security Council from FOIA coverage, *Duke Law Journal, 46(6),* 1475-1517. Available at http://reunion2001.law.duke.edu/shell/cite.pl?46+Duke+L.+J.+1475.

Ballard, Terry. (2010). Library of American Civilization titles available free on the web. Hamden, CT: Quinnipiac University. Available at http://www.quinnipiac.edu /x1849.xml.

Barton, J. L. (1994). Gentilis and the interpretatio duplex, in A.D.E. Lewis & D. J. Ibbetson (Eds.). *The Roman Law Tradition.* Cambridge, UK: Cambridge University Press.

Bassett, Debra Lyn. (2003, Spring). The hidden bias in diversity jurisdiction. *Washington University Law Quarterly, 81*, 119-150. Available at http://lawreview.wustl.edu/inprint/81-1/p119%20Bassett.pdf.

Big Search Engine Index. (2009). *Directory of Law Search Engines.* Available at http://www.search-engine-index.co.uk/Reference/Law_Search.

Bintliff, Barbara. (1996, Summer). From creativity to computerese: Thinking like a lawyer. *Law Library Journal, 88(3)*, 338-351.

Birks, Peter, & McLeod, Grant. (1987). Introduction. *Translation of Justinian's Institutes.* Ithaca, NY: Cornell University Press.

Birnbaum, Robert. (1988). *How Colleges Work: The Cybernetics of Academic Organization and Leadership.* San Francisco: Jossey-Bass.

Black's Law Dictionary. (1979). 5th ed. St. Paul, MN: West.

Blackstone, Sir William. (1765). *Commentaries on the Laws of England* [1st ed.]. Oxford, UK: Clarendon Press. Available at http://www.exlaw.com/library/bla-102.shtml.

————. (1765). Of the nature of laws in general, in *Commentaries on the Laws of England.* Available at http://www.exlaw.com/library/bla-102.shtml.

Blum, Jerome, Rondo, Cameron, & Barnes, Thomas G. (1966). *The European World: A History.* Boston: Little, Brown.

Borlase, Rod. (1995, 1999). Anatomy of a West judicial opinion (with correlations to Westlaw). *Borlase Law Library and Legal Research Guides.* Available at http://www.rodborlase.com/Guides/OpinionAnatomy.html.

Bowen, Catherine Drinker. (1986). *Miracle at Philadelphia: The Story of the Constitutional Convention, May to September.* Boston: Little, Brown.

Boyer, Allen D. (1994). Francis Bacon. *Michigan Law Review, 92*, 1622-1636. Available at http://eel.st.usm.edu/paprzycka/spr97/sci/baconf.html.

Bracton, Henry de. (1999). In *The LAW Museum Hall of Fame.* Available at http://www.wwlia.org/hallfame.htm.

Bradley, Curtis A. (1998). The Charming Betsy canon and separation of powers: Rethinking the interpretive role of international law. *Georgetown Law Journal, 86*, 479-537. Available at http://scholarship.law.duke.edu/cgi/viewcontent.cgi?article=2099&context=faculty_scholarship.

Brant, Irving. (1941). James Madison. Indianapolis: Bobbs-Merrill.

Bratz, David C. (1984, December). Comment, Stare decisis in lower courts: Predicting the demise of Supreme Court precedent. *Washington Law Review, 60(1)*, 87-100.

Bristol, Rodger P. (1970). Supplement. *Charles Evans' American Bibliography.* Charlottesville: University Press of Virginia.

Brownlie, Ian. (1987). *Principles of Public International Law.* 3rd ed. New York: Oxford University Press.

Buergenthal, Thomas, & Maier, Harold G. (1990). *Public International Law in a Nutshell.* 2nd ed. St. Paul, MN: West.

Bureau of National Affairs. *U.S. Law Week Product Structure.* Available at http://www.bna.com/products/lit/uslw.htm.

Burns, Edward McNall. (1968). *James Madison: Philosopher of the Constitution.* New York: Octagon Books.

Burns, James McGregor, & Overby, L. Martin. (1990). *Cobblestone Leadership: Majority Rule, Minority Power.* Norman, OK: University of Oklahoma Press.

Burns, James McGregor. (1978). *Leadership.* New York: Harper & Row.

Calabresi, Steven G., & Lev, Daniel. (2006). The legal significance of presidential signing statements. *The Forum, 4(2)*, 8-26. Available at http://fedsoc.server326.com /pdf/Calabresi,%20Signing%20Statements.pdf.

Cambridge History of English and American Literature: An Encyclopedia in 18 Volumes. (1907–21). New York: Bartleby.com. Available at http://www.bartleby.com/218/ 1313.html.

Carson, Ada Lou, & Carson, Herbert L. *Royall Tyler*. Boston: Twayne Publishers.

Carson, Ada Lou. (1985). *Thomas Pickman Tyler's "Memoirs of Royall Tyler": An annotated edition* (unpublished Ph.D. dissertation, University of Minnesota) (available from ProQuest Dissertations & Theses, Publication No. AAT 8526403).

Carson, Bryan M. (1997, March 4). *Comment on proposed citation rules*. Email from Bryan M. Carson, Hamline University College of Law Library, to Joan Countryman, United States Judicial Conference. Available at http://www.hyperlaw.com/jccite/ 054.txt.

———. (2000, November). Publishing the Law: The Origins of Legal Publishing. *Against the Grain, 12(5)*, 68-72, 76.

———. (2001, December). Written Law from Gutenberg to the Internet: A Historical Perspective. *Against the Grain, 12(6)*, 74-76, 78.

———. (2005, June). How to File a Freedom of Information Act Request. *Against the Grain, 17(3)*, 82-85.

———. (2007). The Law of Libraries and Archives. Lanham, MD: Scarecrow Press.

Citation of unpublished opinion. (1998). *8th Circuit Rules of Appellate Procedure*. Available at http://www.ca8.uscourts.gov/rules/local1298.pdf.

Cohen, Harlan G. (2006). Supremacy and diplomacy: The international law of the U.S. Supreme Court. *Berkeley Journal of International Law, 24*, 101-163. Available at http://www.csb.uncw.edu/people/eversp/classes/BLA361/Intl%20Law/Required%20 Readings/2.Intl%20Law%20of%20US%20Sup%20Ct.ssrn.pdf.

Cohen, Michael D., March, James G. J., & Olsen, Johan P. (1972, March). A garbage can model of organizational choice. *Administrative Science Quarterly, 17(1)*, 1-25.

———. (1986). Leadership in an organized anarchy. In *ASHE Reader on Organization and Governance in Higher Education*. Lexington, MA: Ginn.

Comment, Supreme Court no-clear-majority decisions: A study in stare decisis. (1956). *University of Chicago Law Review, 24(1)*, 99-155.

Congressional Research Service [by Michael John Garcia]. (2006, September). *Interrogation of Detainees: Overview of the McCain Amendment*. Available at http://www.coherentbabble.com/signingstatements/CRS/CRS-L33655.pdf.

Congressional Research Service. (2002-2004). Amendments to the Constitution First Through Tenth Amendments. *U.S. Constitution Annotated*. Washington, DC: Government Printing Office. Available at http://supreme.justia.com/constitution/ 018-bill-ofrights.html.

Continental bank note. (2009). In *HistoryWired*. Available at http://historywired.si.edu/ object.cfm?ID=437.

Cooper, Phillip J. (2005, September). George W. Bush, Edgar Allan Poe, and the use and abuse of presidential signing statements. *Presidential Studies Quarterly, 35(3)*, 515-532. Available at http://www.pegc.us/archive/Articles/cooper_35_PSQ_515.pdf.

Cornell University Law Library. (2010). *Basics of Legal Research*. Available at http://library.lawschool.cornell.edu/WhatWeDo/ResearchGuides/Basics.cfm.

Crook, John R. (2008). Supreme Court overturns presidential directive seeking to implement ICJ decision. *American Journal of International Law, 102(3)*, 635-638.

Cross, Frank B. (1988). The constitutional legitimacy and significance of presidential "signing statements." *Administrative Law Review, 40(2)*, 209-238.

Davis, John F., & Reynolds, William L. (1974, March). Juridical cripples: Plurality opinions in the Supreme Court. *Duke Law Journal, 1974(1)*, 59-86.

Dean, John W. (2009, January 9). The damaged institution of the presidency, how the Obama administration intends to restore it, and what we can expect from new OLC head Dawn Johnsen. *Findlaw's Writ.* Available at http://writ.lp.findlaw.com/dean/20090109.html.

———. (2006, January 13). The problem with presidential signing statements: Their use and misuse by the Bush administration. *Findlaw's Writ.* Available at http://writ.lp.findlaw.com/dean/20060113.html.

Dean, Stewart. (2008). My Politics Page. Available at http://inside.bard.edu/~sdean/personal/pol/index.html.

DeCrew, Judith. (2006). Privacy. In *The Stanford Encyclopedia of Philosophy.* Available at http://plato.stanford.edu/entries/privacy.

Dellinger, Walter. (1993, November 3). *The Legal Significance of Presidential Signing Statements.* Available at http://www.usdoj.gov/olc/signing.htm.

Demjanenko, Tanya. (2000). *Johann Gutenberg.* Available at http://publish.uwo.ca/~tdemjane/johann.htm.

Devlin, Kelly. (2009, September 11). *Print (and other resources) which we prefer to on-line versions.* Posting to law-lib@ucdavis.edu, September 11, 2009.

Dickerson, Darby. (2006). *ALWD Citation Manual: A Professional System of Citation.* 3rd ed. New York: Aspen.

Dorf, Michael C. (2009, January 12). All the president's IMs: Are federal record-keeping laws out of step with modern communications? *Findlaw's Writ.* Available at http://writ.lp.findlaw.com/dorf/20090112.html.

Due Process. (2009). In *Constitution.net.* Available at http://www.usconstitution.net/consttop_duep.html.

Duhaime, Lloyd. (2000). *The Timetable of World Legal History.* Victoria, BC: World Wide Legal Information Association. Available at http://www.wwlia.org/hist.htm #2350bc.

Dunlap, M. (1981). Where the person ends, does the government begin? An explanation of present controversies concerning "the right to privacy." *Lincoln Law Review, 12(2)*, 47-76.

Early American Imprints, 1639-1800 [microform, available on opaque microcard]. (1984). New York: American Antiquarian Society/Readex Microprint.

Eggspuehler, Chad M. (2007-2008). Note, The s-word's mightier than the pen: Signing statements as express advocacy of unlawful action. *Gonzaga Law Review, 43(2)*, 416-512.

Elazar, Daniel J. (1982, Autumn). Confederation and federal liberty. *Publius: The Journal of Federalism, 12(4)*, 1-14.

Emery, Michael C., Emery, Edwin, & Roberts, Nancy L. (1996). *The Press and America: An Interpretive History of Mass Media.* 8th ed. Boston: Allyn and Bacon.

Equity and common law: Bacon and Cowell; Coke. (1907-21). In Cambridge History of English and American Literature: An Encyclopedia in 18 Volumes. Vol. 8, sect. 1313. New York: Bartleby.com. Available at http://www.bartleby.com/218/1313.html.

Evans, Charles. (1941-1959). *American Bibliography: A Chronological Dictionary of All Books, Pamphlets, and Periodical Publications Printed in the United States of*

America from the Genesis of Printing in 1639 Down To and Including the Year 1820. New York: P. Smith.

Fairman, Charles. (1949). Does the Fourteenth Amendment incorporate the Bill of Rights? *Stanford Law Review, 2(1)*, 5-139.

Farber, Daniel A. (2007, Fall). The Supreme Court, the law of nations, and citations of foreign law: The lessons of history. *California Law Review, 95*, 1335-1386. Available at http://www.law.berkeley.edu/mishkin/papers/Mishkinarticle(Farber)10-17.doc.

Federal Agency Index. (2010). Louisiana State University Libraries. Available at http://www.lib.lsu.edu/gov/index.html.

Fein, Bruce. (2006, June 27). *Statement of Bruce Fein Before the Senate Judiciary Committee, Re: Presidential Signing Statements*. Available at http://www.fas.org/irp/congress/2006_hr/062706fein.html.

Fiels, Keith Michael. (2003, July 16). *ALA's Response to the CIPA Decision*. Posting to rusaaccess@ala.org. Available at http://www.rpls.ws/Links/CIPA2.htm.

Fisher, Louis. (2006). Signing statements: What to do? *The Forum: A Journal of Applied Research in Contemporary Politics, 4(2)*, 1-10.

FOIA Website. (2005). U.S. Department of Commerce. Available at http://www.osec.doc.gov/omo/FOIA/FOIAWEBSITE.htm.

Form G-639, Freedom of Information/Privacy Request. (2009, February 4). U.S. Citizenship & Immigration Services. Available at http://www.uscis.gov/files/form/g-639.pdf.

Freedom of Information Act Guide. (2007). U.S. Department of Justice. Available at http://www.usdoj.gov/oip/foia_guide07.htm.

Freedom of Information Act. U.S. Department of Justice. Available at http://www.justice.gov/oip/index.html.

Freeman, Brian A. (2001, Winter). Expiating the sins of Yoder and Smith: Toward a unified theory of First Amendment exemptions from neutral laws of general applicability. *Missouri Law Review, 66(1)*, 9-82.

Frickey, Philip P., & Smith, Steven S. (2002, May). Judicial review, the congressional process, and the federalism cases: An interdisciplinary critique. *Yale Law Journal, 111(7)*, 1707-1756. Available at http://www.yalelawjournal.org/pdf/111-7/FrickeyFINAL.pdf

Furrow, Dwight. (2004, May/June). The privacy paradox. *The Humanist*, 64-70.

Garber, Marc N., & Wimmer, Kurt A. (1987). Presidential signing statements as interpretations of legislative intent: An executive aggrandizement of power. *Harvard Journal on Legislation, 24(2)*, 363-396.

Garvin, Peggy. (2010, April 21). The government domain: New & free regulations trackers. LLRX. Available at http://www.llrx.com/columns/govdomain45.htm.

Georgetown University Law Library. (2010). *Basics: Finding a case (opinion), Cases and Digests Tutorial*. Available at http://www.west.thomson.com/documentation/westlaw/wlawdoc/lawstu/lsdig02.pdf.

————. (2001). *What is an Agency Decision? Administrative Law Tutorial*. Available at http://www.ll.georgetown.edu/tutorials/admin/7a_what.html.

Ginsburg, Ruth Bader. Remarks on writing separately. *Washington Law Review, 65(1)*, 133-150.

Goldsmith, Jack, & Levinson, Daryl. (2009, May). Law for states: International law, constitutional law, public law. *Harvard Law Review, 122(7)*, 1791-1868. Available at http://www.harvardlawreview.org/issues/122/may09/goldsmith_levinson.pdf.

Gordon, W. M., & Robinson, O. F. (1988). Introduction. *Translation of The Institutes of Gaius*. Vol. 8. Ithaca, NY: Cornell University Press.

Gross, Doug. (2010, April 14). Library of Congress to archive your tweets. CNN. Available at http://www.cnn.com/2010/TECH/04/14/library.congress.twitter/index.html.

Grossberg, Michael. (1990). Some queries about privacy and constitutional rights. *Case Western Reserve Law Review, 41(3)*, 857-866.

Grossman, George S. (1994). *Legal Research: Historical Foundations of the Electronic Age*. New York: Oxford University Press.

Grote, G. (1892). History of Greece (Pt. 2, ch. 10, vol. 3). In Larned, J. N. *History for Ready Reference from the Best Historians, Biographers, and Specialists: Their Own Words in a Complete System of History for All Uses*. Springfield, MA: C. A. Nichols.

[Guam] Office of the Attorney General. (2010). About the Guam Code Annotated. Available at http://www.guamattorneygeneral.com/guam_code.php.

Hacker, Lewis M. (1947). *The Shaping of the American Tradition*. New York: Columbia University Press.

Hale, Matthew. (1997). *The History of the Common Law of England: Part I*. New Haven, CT: Avalon Project. Available at http://www.yale.edu/lawweb/avalon/econ/hale01.htm.

Hale, Robert. (1866). Statement of Rep. Robert Hale. *Congressional Globe*, 39th Congress, 1st session, 1064-65.

Halstuk, Martin E. (2005). When is an invasion of privacy unwarranted under the FOIA? An analysis of the Supreme Court's "sufficient reason" and "presumption of legitimacy" standards. *Florida Journal of Law and Public Policy, 16*, 361-400.

Harris, Michael H. (1995). *History of Libraries in the Western World*. 4th ed. Metuchen, NJ: Scarecrow Press.

Hasall, Paul (Ed.). (1998). *Internet Ancient History Sourcebook*. Bronx, NY: Fordham University. Available at http://www.fordham.edu/halsall/ancient/1650nesilim.html.

Henkin, L. (1984). International law as law in the United States. *Michigan Law Review, 82(5/6)*, 1555-1569.

Hilden, Julie. (2005, December 20). Television and the marketplace of ideas: What role will developments like TiVo and a la carte cable play in promoting free speech? *Findlaw's Writ*. Available at http://writ.news.findlaw.com/hilden/20051220.html.

History Research: Library of American Civilization. (2008). San Francisco State University Library. Available at http://www.library.sfsu.edu/research/guides/lac.html.

Hochschild, Adam S. (2000). Note, The modern problem of Supreme Court plurality decisions: Interpretation in historical perspective. *Washington University Journal of Law & Policy, 4*, 261-287. Available at https://www.law.wustl.edu/journal/4/Hochschild.pdf.

Holdsworth, William S. (1994). *The Historians of Anglo-American Law*. New York: Lawbook Exchange.

Holdsworth, William S., et al. (1937). A History of English Law. 2nd ed. London, UK: Methuen.

Houdek, Frank. (2005, Fall). *Using a West Digest to Find Cases by Subject*. Carbondale, IL: Southern Illinois University School of Law Library. Available at http://www.law.siu.edu/lawlib/guides/westdigests.htm.

Hyman, Andrew T. (2005). The little word "due." *Akron Law Review, 38*, 1-58. Available at http://andrewhyman.com/articles/due.pdf.

Jackson Purchase. (1992). University of Tennessee at Martin. Excerpt from Kleber, John E., *The Kentucky Encyclopedia*. Lexington, KY: University Press of Kentucky. Available at http://www.utm.edu/departments/acadpro/library/departments/special_collections/wc_hist/jackpur.htm.

James Madison gets his way as Congress ducks issue: Leaders reluctantly ignore 203-year time period in ratifying 27th amendment on pay raises. (1992). *Congressional Quarterly Weekly Report, 50*, 1323.

Johannes Gutenberg: A Biography. (2000). Available at http://www.lysands.com/History/People/johannesgutenbu_tpy_ly.htm.

John Locke. (1997). In *Routledge Encyclopedia of Philosophy*. New York: Routledge.

Jukes, Ian, & Ted McCain, Ted. (2001). *From Gutenberg to Gates: Education in an Online World*. Keynote Address to the TechEd 2001 Convention, Ontario, California (March 26, 2001). In *Education at a Distance, 5(15)*, 5-22. *Available at* http://citeseerx.ist.psu.edu/viewdoc/download?doi=10.1.1.100.1896&rep=rep1&type=pdf.

Katz, Stanley N. (Ed.). (2009). *Oxford International Encyclopedia of Legal History*. Chapel Hill, NC: Oxford University Press.

Kello, Carolyn Bingham. (2003, Fall). Note: Drawing the curtain on open government? In defense of the federal advisory committee act. *Brooklyn Law Review, 69(1)*, 345-394.

Kennedy, Duncan. (1979, Spring). The structure of Blackstone's commentaries. *Buffalo Law Review, 28(2)*, 205-382.

[Kentucky] Office of the Attorney General. (2010). *Opinions of the Attorney General*. Available at http://ag.ky.gov/civil/opinions.html.

Kentucky Secretary of State. *Frequently Asked Questions*. Available at http://www.sos.ky.gov/land/nonmilitary/coformations/faq.htm.

KeyCite at a Glance. (2010). Available at http://west.thomson.com/documentation/westlaw/wlawdoc/web/kcwlcqr6.pdf.

KeyCite depth of treatment of the cited reference. (2010). *KeyCite at a Glance*. Available at http://west.thomson.com/documentation/westlaw/wlawdoc/web/kcwlcqr6.pdf.

KeyCite Tutorial. (2010). Available at http://lawschool.westlaw.com/help/tourkeycite/menu.htm?Unit=menu.

Killian, Johnny H., Costello, George A., & Thomas, Kenneth R. (1992, amended 1996, 1998, 2000). *The Constitution of the United States of America: Analysis and Interpretation*. Washington, DC: Congressional Research Service. Available at http://caselaw.lp.findlaw.com/data/constitution/article03/09.html#3.

Kim-Prieto, Dennis. (2010, May 27). *Re: Westlaw v Lexis Value*. Posting to law-lib@ucdavis.edu, May 27, 2010.

Kimura, Ken. (1992). A legitimacy model for the interpretation of plurality decisions. *Cornell Law Review, 77(6)*, 1593-1628.

Kingdon, John. (1984). *Agendas, Alternatives, and Public Policies*. Boston: Little, Brown.

Kirk, Russell. (1958, April). The First Amendment and religious belief. *The Catholic World*. Available at http://www.ewtn.com/library/HOMELIBR/1STAMEND.TXT.

Kirman, Igor. (1995). Note, Standing apart to be a part: The precedential value of Supreme Court concurring opinions. *Columbia Law Review, 95(8)*, 2083-2119.

Kirtley, Jane E. (2006). Transparency and accountability in a time of terror: The Bush administration's assault on freedom of information. *Communication Law and Policy, 11(4)*, 479-509.

Kovacs, Diane. (2008). *2008 Core Reference Tools*. Available at http://www.kovacs.com/results08.html.

Ku, Julian G. (2001, Fall). Customary international law in state courts. *Virginia Journal of International Law, 42(1)*, 265-338. Available at http://www.hofstra.edu/pdf/law_ku_customary_international.pdf.

La-Legal.com. (2010). *How the Code Napoleon Makes Louisiana Law Different: Louisiana Law, A Short History Lesson*. Available at http://www.la-legal.com/history_louisiana_law.htm.

Larned, J. N. (1892). *History for Ready Reference from the Best Historians, Biographers, and Specialists: Their Own Words in a Complete System of History for All Uses*. Springfield, MA: C. A. Nichols.

Larousse Encyclopedia of Ancient and Medieval History. (1972). Feltham, UK: Hamlyn Publishing Group.

Law Reports. (1907–21). In *Cambridge History of English and American Literature: An Encyclopedia in 18 Volumes*. Vol. 8, sec. 1312. New York: Bartleby.com. Available at http://www.bartleby.com/218/1312.html.

Lazarus, Edward. (2008, March 27). A recent Supreme Court decision on the Vienna Convention reaffirms that Justice Stevens, at eighty-eight, remains a force to be reckoned with. *Findlaw's Writ*. Available at http://writ.news.findlaw.com/lazarus/20080327.html.

Leavitt, Noah. (2003, May 24). Is Oklahoma a new human rights hot spot? Why the state's judges and governor were right to stop an execution that nearly violated international law. *Findlaw's Writ*. Available at http://writ.lp.findlaw.com/leavitt/20040524.html.

Lee, Malinda. (2008). Reorienting the debate on presidential signing statements: The need for transparency in the president's constitutional objections, reservations, and assertions of power. *UCLA Law Review, 55(3)*, 705-744. Available at http://www.uclalawreview.org/articles/content/55/ext/pdf/3.2-1.pdf.

Lewis, A.D.E., & Ibbetson, D. J. (Eds.). (1994). *The Roman Law Tradition*. Cambridge, UK: Cambridge University Press.

Lilly, Graham C. (1998). Making sense of nonsense: Reforming supplemental jurisdiction. *Indiana Law Journal, 74(1)*, 181-196.

Linder, Douglas O. (2005). *Introduction to the Free Speech Clause, Exploring Constitutional Law*. Kansas City: University of Missouri–Kansas City School of Law. Available at http://www.law.umkc.edu/faculty/projects/ftrials/conlaw/firstaminto.htm.

Lipschultz, Jeremy Harris. (2000). *Free Expression in the Age of the Internet: Social and Legal Boundaries*. Boulder, CO: Westview.

Llopis, Ana Peyro. (2005). *The Place of International Law in Recent Supreme Court Decisions* [Global Law Working Paper 04/05]. New York: New York University School of Law. Available at http://www1.law.nyu.edu/nyulawglobal/workingpapers/GLWP0405Peyro.rtf.

Madison, James. (2005). *The Constitutional Convention: A Narrative History, from the Notes of James Madison*. Larson, Edward J., & Winship, Michael (Eds.). New York: Modern Library.

———. (1947). Views of the political system of the United States. In Hacker, Louis M., & Zahler, H. S. (Eds.), *The Shaping of the American Tradition*. New York: Columbia University Press.

Marchant, Robert. (2003, May). Federal preemption of state law. *Wisconsin Legislative Reference Bureau, 3*. Available at http://www.legis.state.wi.us/lrb/pubs/consthi/03 consthiIII051.htm.

Marino, Annemarie. (2000). *The Printing Press.* Available at http://www.sunysuffolk.edu/~maria29/printingpress.html.

Marshall, Sibyl D. (2007, May 30). *Foreign Case Law - Answers Summary.* Posting to law-lib@ucdavis.edu.

Martin, Peter W. (2000). *Introduction to Basic Legal Citation.* 2000-2001 ed. Cornell, NY: Cornell Legal Information Institute. Available at http://www.law.cornell.edu/citation.

————. (2003). *Introduction to Basic Legal Citation.* 2003 ed. Cornell, NY: Cornell Legal Information Institute. Available at http://www.law.cornell.edu/citation.

Mauldin, Sarah K. C. (2010, May 14). *FOUND Florida Librarians - Citing to Florida Administrative Law Reports.* Posting to law-lib@ucdavis.edu.

Mayer-Schonberger, Viktor. (1990). Substantive due process and equal protection in the fundamental rights realm. *Howard Law Journal, 33(2)*, 287-320.

McKeeve, Kent. (2006). *Researching Public International Law.* New York: Columbia University Law Library. Available at http://library.law.columbia.edu/guides/Researching_Public_International_Law.

McLendon, Michael K. (2007). State governance reform of higher education: Patterns, trends, and theories of the public policy process. *Higher Education: Handbook of Theory and Research, 17*, 57-132.

Meta-Search Engines. (2010). Berkeley: University of California Berkeley Libraries. Available at http://www.lib.berkeley.edu/TeachingLib/Guides/Internet/MetaSearch.html.

Michaelis, Laura. (1992, May 23). Both chambers rush to accept 27th amendment on salaries. *Congressional Quarterly Weekly Report, 50*, 1423.

Mick, Jackson. (2009, October). British copyright org threatens singing store employee then apologizes, *Daily Tech* (October 23, 2009). Available at http://www.dailytech.com/British+Copyright+Org+Threatens+Singing+Store+Empl oyee+Then+Apologizes/article16592.htm.

Microbook Library of American Civilization. (1971/1972). Chicago: Library Resources.

Mount, Steven J. (2008). Constitutional topic: Due process. *The U.S. Constitution Online.* Available at http://www.usconstitution.net/consttop_duep.html.

Murphy, Sean D. (2004). Contemporary practice of the united states relating to international law: Implementation of Avena decision by Oklahoma court. *American Journal of International Law, 98(3)*, 581-583.

National Park Service. (2009). *Vermont Regional History.* National Register of Historic Places. Available at http://www.cr.nps.gov/nr/travel/centralvermont/vhistory1.htm.

Ness, Eric C. (2006). *Deciding Who Earns HOPE, PROMISE, and SUCCESS: Toward a Comprehensive Model of the Merit Aid and Eligibility Policy Process* [unpublished doctoral dissertation, Department of Leadership, Policy, & Organizations, Vanderbilt University].

Neuborne, Burt. (1987). The binding quality of Supreme Court precedent. *Tulane Law Review, 61*, 991-1002.

Novak, Linda. (1980). Note, The precedential value of Supreme Court plurality decisions. *Columbia Law Review, 80(4)*, 756-781.

O'Connor, Sandra Day. (1998, Spring). On federalism: Preserving strong federal and state governments. *Supreme Court Review, 35*, 4.

Olson, Kent. (2010, March 19). *Re: State Constitutions.* Posting to law-lib@ucdavis.edu.

Palmquist, Ruth A. (2009). *Bibliometrics.* Available at http://www.gslis.utexas.edu/ ~palmquis/courses/biblio.html.

Percival, Robert V. (2001, December). Comment, Presidential management of the administrative state: The not-so-unitary executive. *Duke Law Journal, 51(3),* 963-1014.

Peters, B. Guy. (1999). *American Public Policy: Performance and Promise.* 5th ed. New York: Chatham House.

Peterson, William G. (1981, March). Note, Plurality decisions and judicial decision making. *Harvard Law Review, 94(5),* 1127-1147.

———. Splintered decisions, implicit reversal and lower federal courts: Planned Parenthood v. Casey. *Brigham Young University Law Review, 1992(1),* 289-311.

Pritchard, James B. (ed). (1958). *The Ancient Near East: An Anthology of Texts and Pictures.* Princeton, NJ: Princeton University Press, 1958.

Public Papers of the Presidents: About. (2005, July 6). Washington, DC: Government Printing Office. Available at http://www.gpoaccess.gov/pubpapers /about.html.

Rakove, Jack. (1982, Autumn). The legacy of the Articles of Confederation. *Publius: The Journal of Federalism, 12(4),* 45-66.

Ray, Laura Krugman. (1990). The justices write separately: Uses of the concurrence by the Rehnquist court. *U.C. Davis Law Review, 23(4),* 777-832.

Reuben, Paul P. (2010). Royall Tyler. In *PAL: Perspectives in American Literature—A Research and Reference Guide.* Available at http://web.csustan.edu/english/reuben/ pal/chap8/tyler.html.

Reusch, Rita. (2008, Summer). By the book: Thoughts on the future of our print collections. *Law Library Journal, 100(3),* 555-562.

Revesz, Richard L., & Karlan, Pamela S. (1988). Nonmajority rules and the Supreme Court. *University of Pennsylvania Law Review, 136(4),* 1067-1134.

Robak, Michael. (2009, July). The Bloomberg citator: A first look at BLAW's citation function. *AALL Spectrum, 13(9),* 24-29. Available at http://www.aallnet.org/ products/pub_sp0907/pub_sp0907_Bloomberg.pdf.

Robinson, O. F. (1997). *The Sources of Roman Law: Problems and Methods for Ancient Historians.* London, New York: Routledge.

Rosen, Jeffrey. (2000). *The Unwanted Gaze: The Destruction of Privacy in America.* New York: Random House.

Rosenkranz, Nicholas Quinn. (2005, April). Executing the treaty power. *Harvard Law Review, 118(6),* 1867-1939.

Ross, Richard J. (1998). The commoning of the common law: The Renaissance debate over printing English law, 1520-1640. *University of Pennsylvania Law Review, 146(2),* 323-462.

———. (1998). The memorial culture of early modern English lawyers: Memory as keyword, shelter, and identity, 1560-1640, *Yale Journal of Law and the Humanities, 10(2),* 229-326.

Rozell, Mark J. (2002). Executive privilege revived? Secrecy and conflict during the Bush presidency. *Duke Law Journal, 52(2),* 403-422.

Saint Germain, Christopher. (1513). *The Dialogue in English, between a Doctor of Divinity, and a Student in the Laws of England.* Transl. William Muchall. Ann Arbor, MI: University of Michigan Library. Available at http://name.umdl.umich.edu/AGY 1099.0001.001.

Salzmann, Victoria S. (2000). Are public records really public? The collision between the right to privacy and the release of public court records over the Internet. *Baylor Law Review, 52(2),* 355-380.

Sample FOIA Letter. *FOIA Website.* U.S. Department of Commerce. Available at http://www.osec.doc.gov/omo/FOIA/FOIAWEBSITE.htm.

Santayana, George. (1905). *The Life of Reason.* London: Constable & Co.

Schnader, William A. (1967, November). Introductory remarks to the Uniform Commercial Code. In *Martindale-Hubbell Law Digest Uniform Commercial Code.*

Setear, John K. (2005, May). A forest with no trees: The Supreme Court and international law in the 2003 term. *Virginia Law Review, 91(2),* 579-676.

Shakespeare, William. Henry VI.

Shaw, Ralph R., & Shoemaker, Richard H. (1958-1966). *American Bibliography: A Preliminary Checklist for 1801-1819.* Metuchen, NJ: Scarecrow Press.

Sheehan, Catherine F. (1994). Note: Opening the government's electronic mail: Public access to National Security Council records. *Boston College Law Review, 35(5),* 1145-1201. Available at http://lawdigitalcommons.bc.edu/cgi/viewcontent.cgi?article=2005&context=bclr.

Shepard's Citations Tutorial. LexisNexis. Available at http://www.lexisnexis.com/Shepards/printsupport/shepardize_print.pdf.

Shufflin' Sam's Long Step. (1960, April 4). *Time Magazine, 75,* 15-17. Available at http://www.time.com/time/magazine/article/0,9171,869437,00.html.

Shuman, S. I. (1953, April). Constitutional Law: Due Process: Vague and Indefinite Statute. *Michigan Law Review, 51(6),* 922-924.

St. George, Tucker. (1803). *Blackstone's Commentaries: Notes of Reference, to the Constitution and Laws, of the Federal Government of the United States; and of the Commonwealth of Virginia. In five volumes. With an Appendix to Each volume, Containing Short Tracts upon such subjects as appeared necessary to form a connected view of the Laws of Virginia, as a member of the Federal Union.* Philadelphia, PA: William Young Birch and Abraham Small. Reprint ed. by Jon Roland. Austin, TX: Constitution Society, 2003. Available at http://www.constitution.org/tb/tb-0000.htm.

Staggs-Neel, Jo. (2005, April). *The Freedom of Information Act.* Presentation to the Kentucky Library Association Academic Section Conference.

Status flags used in KeyCite for treatment of cases and statutes. (2010). *KeyCite at a Glance.* Available at http://west.thomson.com/documentation/westlaw/wlawdoc/web/kcwlcqr6.pdf.

Steinhardt, Ralph G. (1990). The role of international law as a canon of domestic statutory construction. *Vanderbilt Law Review, 43(4),* 1103-1198.

Strong, Jonathan. (2011, April 15). *Obama Signing Statement: Despite Law, I can do what I Want on Czars.* The Daily Caller. *Available at* http://dailycaller.com/2011/04/15/obama-signing-statement-despite-law-i-can-do-what-i-want-on-czars/#ixzz1KNG1XCmn.

Substantive Due Process. (2006). In *Pennsylvania Legislator's Municipal Deskbook.* 3rd ed. Harrisburg, PA: Local Government Commission, General Assembly of the Commonwealth of Pennsylvania. Available at http://www.lgc.state.pa.us/deskbook06/Issues_Citizens_Rights_04_Substantive_Due_Process.pdf.

Svengalis, Kendall F. (2002). *The Legal Information Buyer's Guide and Reference Manual 2002.* Barrington, RI: Rhode Island Law Press.

————. (2009). *The Legal Information Buyer's Guide and Reference Manual 2009*. Barrington, RI: Rhode Island Law Press.

Tetley, William. (1999). Part I, Mixed jurisdictions: Common law vs. civil law (codified and uncodified). *Uniform Law Review, 4(3)* 591-620. Available at http://www.unidroit.org/english/publications/review/articles/1999-3.htm.

————. (1999). Part II, Mixed jurisdictions: Common law vs. civil law (codified and uncodified). *Uniform Law Review, 4(4)*, 877-907. Available at http://www.unidroit.org/english/publications/review/articles/1999-4a.htm.

The Bluebook: A Uniform System of Citation. (2010). 19th ed. Cambridge, MA: Harvard Law Review Association.

The New Catholic Encyclopedia. (1967). New York: McGraw-Hill.

Thurmon, Mark Alan. (1992). Note, When the Court divides: Reconsidering the precedential value of Supreme Court plurality decisions. *Duke Law Journal, 42(2)*, 419-468.

Tonus, Jill Jarvis, & Lovrics, Catherine. (2010, April 27). *Copyright and Privacy Questions Around Your Public Tweets and the New Library of Congress Archive and Google Replay*. Slaw.ca. Available at http://www.slaw.ca/2010/04/27/copyright -and-privacy-questions-around-your-public-tweets-and-the-new-library-of-congress-archive-and-google-replay.

Turley, Jonathan. (1993). Dualistic values in the age of international legisprudence. *Hastings Law Journal, 44(2)*, 185-272.

————. Presidential papers and popular government: The convergence of constitutional and property theory in claims of ownership and control of presidential records. *Cornell Law Review, 88(3)*, 651-732.

Tushnet, Mark. (2005-2006). When is knowing less better than knowing more: Unpacking the controversy over Supreme Court reference to non-U.S. law. *Minnesota Law Review, 90(5)*, 1275-1302. Available at http://local.law.umn.edu/uploads/images/3277/Tushnet_Final.pdf.

Tyler, Royall. (1790). *The Contrast, A Comedy; In Five Acts*. Philadelphia: Pritchard & Hall. In [Microform] Early American Imprints, First series, no. 22948.

————. (1800-1810). *Reports of Cases Determined and Argued in the Supreme Court of Judicature of the State of Vermont*. 2 vols. New York: I Riley.

Using the Digests. (2010). St. Paul, MN: West. Available at http://www.west.thomson .com/documentation/westlaw/wlawdoc/lawstu/lsdig02.pdf.

Vazquez, Carlos Manuel. (1995, October). The four doctrines of self-executing treaties. *American Journal International Law, 89(4)*, 695-723.

————. (2008). Treaties as law of the land: The supremacy clause and the judicial enforcement of treaties. *Harvard Law Review, 122(2)*, 599-695. Available at http://hlr.rubystudio.com/media/pdf/vazquez.pdf.

Walterscheid, Edward C. (2004). Musings on the copyright power: A critique of Eldred V. Ashcroft. *Albany Law Journal of Science & Technology, 14(2)*, 309-358.

Warren, Samuel D., & Brandeis, Louis D. (1890). The right to privacy. *Harvard Law Review, 4*, 193-220. Available at http://www.ilrg.com/download/4harvlrev193.txt.

Wasserman, Rhonda. (2004). *Procedural Due Process: A Reference Guide to the United States*. Westport, CT: Praeger Greenwood.

Weekly Compilation of Presidential Documents. Washington, DC: Government Printing Office. Available at http://www.gpo.gov/fdsys/browse/collection.action?collection Code=CPD.

West, John B. (1889). A symposium of law publishers. *American Law Review, 23*, 400-407.

West's 11th Decennial Digest. (2004). St. Paul, MN: West.

Whaley, Douglas J. (1968, February). A suggestion for the prevention of no-clear-majority judicial decisions. *Texas Law Review, 46(3)*, 370-378.

What Is a Portal? (2001, November 12). InfoZen, Inc. Available at http://www.infozen.com/portal.html.

What Is a Portal? (2001, November 12). Portal King, Inc. Available at http://www.portalking.com/portal.htm.

What is an agency record? (1980). *FOIA Update, 2(1)*, 3. Available at www.usdoj.gov/oip/foia_updates/Vol_II_1/page3.htm.

Wildman Harrold Allen & Dixon. (2009, December 2). *Court Holds That Metadata Is a Matter of Public Record.* Available at http://www.wildman.com/index.cfm?fa=resourcecenter.briefingroomdetail&oid=6091&rss=1#page=1.

Wilson, James. (1787, June 16). Comments of James Wilson. In *The Debates in the Federal Convention of 1787 (Notes of James Madison).* Available at http://elsinore.cis.yale.edu/lawweb/avalon/debates/616.htm.

Woolley, Sir Leonard. (1965). *The Sumerians.* New York: Norton.

World Civilizations. (2000). Pullman, WA: Washington State University. Available at http://www.wsu.edu:8080/~dee/MESO/CODE.HTM.

Wright, Charles Alan. (1983). *Law of Federal Courts.* St. Paul, MN: West, 1983.

Yeager, John L., et al. (Eds.). (1986). *ASHE Reader on Organization and Governance in Higher Education.* 2nd ed. Lexington, MA: Ginn.

Yeazell, Stephen. (2009, Fall). When and how U.S. Courts should cite foreign law. *Constitutional Commentary, 26(1)*, 59-74.

Your Right to Federal Records: Questions and Answers on the Freedom of Information Act and Privacy Act. (2004). Pueblo, CO: U.S. General Services Administration and U.S. Department of Justice. Available at http://www.pueblo.gsa.gov/cic_text/fed_prog/foia/foia.htm.

Zane, John Maxcy. (1998). *The Story of Law.* 2nd ed. Indianapolis, IN: Liberty Fund.

Index

Table of Cases

Table of Statutes

About the Author

Bryan M. Carson is Professor, Coordinator of Reference & Instructional Services, and Special Assistant to the Dean for Grants & Projects at Western Kentucky University Libraries. He received his B.A. degree in Economics from Adrian College, J.D. (law degree) from the University of Toledo, M.I.L.S. from the University of Michigan, and Ed.D (Higher Education Leadership & Policy) from Vanderbilt University's Peabody College of Education.

Bryan is a member of the Kentucky and Ohio bars. He has written extensively about intellectual property, access to information and legal issues relating to libraries, and has spoken at numerous state and regional conferences. Bryan's book *The Law of Libraries and Archives* (published in 2007 by Scarecrow Press) can be found in over 585 libraries, including the U.S. Supreme Court Law Library. He writes a popular column, "Legally Speaking," for the journal *Against the Grain*. Bryan has taught classes for the Library Media Education (school media) Master's degree program at Western Kentucky University, including "Ethical and Legal Implications in Instructional Design," which was the first online class in the U.S. on intellectual property.

Bryan is a member of the Kentucky Bar Association, the Louisville Bar Association, the Warren County Bar Association, the American Library Association, the Kentucky Library Association, and the American Intellectual Property Association. He was chair of the LAMA Governmental Advocacy Skills Committee (2005-2006); co-chair of the RUSA Access to Information Committee (2005-2006); chair of the Kentucky Library Association Library Instruction Round Table (2003-2004); and chair of the Kentucky SOLINET Users Group (2003-2004).

DATE DUE